UCE PUNCHES

Second Edition

What You Say & Do Next... Matters

CHALLENGING THE WAY YOU COMMUNICATE

Kendall Hunt
publishing company

Kendall Hunt
publishing company
4050 Westmark Drive • P O Box 1840 • Dubuque IA 52004-1840

ISBN 978-0-7575-6481-9

Printed in the United States of America
10 9 8 7 6 5 4 3 2 1

What You Say and Do Next . . . Matters!

Unique Features:

Written with contemporary flare and an eye on popular culture, Bruce Punches' *What You Say and Do Next . . . Matters!* is a new and refreshing introduction to interpersonal communication. Its unique features include:

- The looks and reading style of a modern magazine combined with a focused, organized presentation of information.
- Lively commentary referencing sports, entertainment, music, and current events.
- Focused, cut-to-the-chase units to prevent information overload and reader fatigue.
- Informal, relaxed prose.
- Stimulating content to augment lectures and spark engaging analysis.
- Practical pointers and strategies for improving interpersonal communication.

Dear colleagues and students:

Dear colleagues and students:

The units in this textbook focus on the major concepts and theories relating to interpersonal communication. They allow today's busy student a chance to learn a lot about interpersonal communication by reading a cut-to-the-chase textbook in less time without experiencing "information overload."

Students are introduced to key ideas not just once but repeatedly throughout the textbook. References are made to previous material and concepts reappear often. Students are encouraged to answer the "Your Turn" sections while they are reading which ask them to relate the concept or theory to their personal life, create their own example, or explain an opinion they have. The end of the unit discussion questions, vocabulary review, and skill builders allow for further application and summarization. After reading a section, students are encouraged to pause and quickly summarize what they've read and/or answer the reading comprehension question before moving on to the next section. This book incorporates numerous narratives, current events, humor, a contemporary writing style, and references to popular culture to entice and maintain a high reader interest level.

To get the most out of this text, students are encouraged to highlight and write in this book. This book was written as a textbook and as a workbook. Many students choose to keep this book at the conclusion of the course and refer to it often as future situations arise. They see it as an important part of their reference library.

A portion of the proceeds from this book supports the following charitable organizations: World Vision International, The Arbor Foundation, The Sierra Club, DeVos Children's Hospital, Operation Smile, and Watoto Child Rescue.

Author Bio

Bruce Punches is a licensed psychotherapist, professor, and professional speaker. He earned undergraduate degrees in communication and secondary education. He also earned two graduate degrees in interpersonal communication and counseling psychology. His 2010 textbook, *What You Say and Do Next . . . Matters*! is now available by Kendall/Hunt Publishing. Bruce Punches teaches interpersonal communication and public speaking at Kalamazoo Valley Community College. Bruce Punches is the founder and CEO of *Bruce Punches & Associates*, a professional communication and leadership training firm based in Rockford, Michigan.

Bruce Punches welcomes your feedback and ideas regarding this book. For more information, questions, or correspondence please don't hesitate to contact Bruce Punches by visiting: www.brucepunches.com or emailing bruce@brucepunches.com.

Author Acknowledgments

George Matthew Adams once said, "There is no such thing as a self-made man [woman]. We are made up of thousands of others. Everyone who has ever done a kind deed for us, or spoken one word of encouragement to us, has entered into the make-up of our character, and of our thoughts, as well as our success." I am deeply grateful to the following individuals who played an instrumental role in helping me complete this book and inspiring its content.

- Torrey Tremayne Thomas "**T3**". Thank you for all that you do and for all that you are. I appreciate your help with the selection of pictures, words of encouragement, and the numerous meals and cookies you brought to my computer. *God Bless!*

- To my distinguished colleagues William deDie, Chair of the English Department, and Vikki Dykstra, professor of English at Kalamazoo Valley Community College. Thank you for proofreading and editing the units of the textbook. I also wish to extend my heartfelt thanks to my colleagues Pat Conroy and Sadie Miles for their support, ideas, and willingness to pilot this textbook in their classes.

- To my great friend and dedicated proofreader Anthony Cherette. Thank you for your great insights and feedback. We did eat a lot of pizza!

- To the talented team at Kendall/Hunt Publishing: Senior Acquisitions Editor Chris Trott and Amanda Smith, Senior Project Coordinator. Thank you for your commitment to excellence and help with seeing this project through to completion.

- To my students who shared their ideas about what they wanted in a book and took such an interest in its content!

- To my dancing dynamos and daughters: Kaitlin Analise and Avery Taylor Punches. Yo "sweet P!" *What's up* "Spanky?" You bring a smile to my face and pour sunshine on my soul. You make daddy proud!

- To my biggest teachers: Beverly and James Punches. You taught me what it means to give, without expecting something in return. You instilled the virtues of hard work, commitment, and compassion. You prepared me for life's tests by opening doors of opportunity, running with my passions, and most importantly, demonstrating how to love unconditionally.

- To all my friends who enrich my life with great times and conversations!

Table of Contents

1 importance

© POOL/Reuters/Corbis

Importance Unit 1

Appreciating the importance of effective interpersonal communication is the focus of Unit 1.

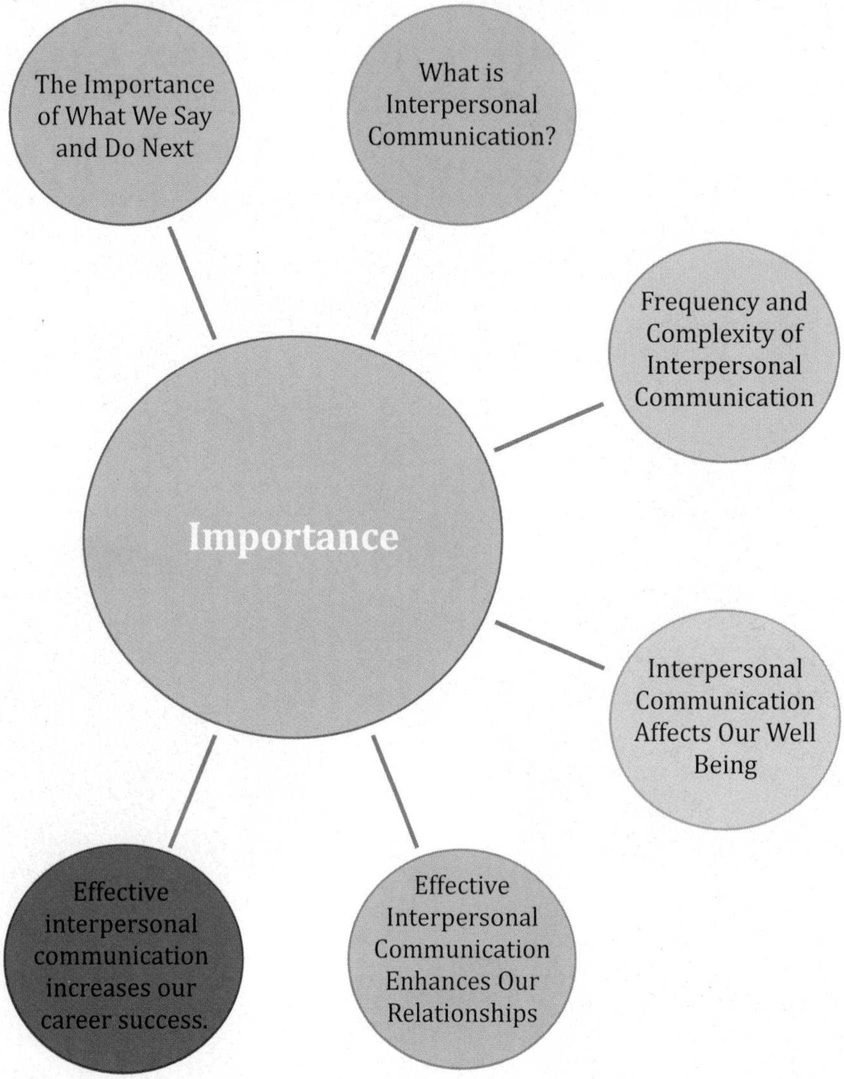

Unit 1 Learning Objectives

As a result of reading and studying Unit 1, you will be able to:

1. Recognize the importance of what you say and do next.
2. Explain the difference between communication and interpersonal communication.
3. Describe the unique nature of interpersonal communication in terms of its frequency and complexity.
4. Appreciate how effective interpersonal communication enhances our well being, relationships, and career success.

A 76-year-old man pays a visit to his doctor for an annual physical. The physician examines the man. Concerned, he sends him immediately to the lab for a battery of tests with strict instructions to return in a week for the results. The next day, while picking up a suit from a downtown dry cleaner, the doctor observes his patient smiling broadly and walking arm-in-arm with a beautiful young woman. After a week, the patient returns to the physician's office for the test results, and says, "Thanks doc! I followed your orders. Like you said, have fun with a hot mama and be cheerful!" The doctor gasps! "I didn't say that. I said you have a heart murmur and be careful!"

Somewhere else in the world, a small plane carrying an instructor and student makes its final descent. The wings teeter awkwardly upon approach. The plane slams the runway hard, bounces roughly, and swerves to a harsh stop. The shocked instructor jumps out of the plane, throws his clipboard on the pavement, and exclaims, "That was an absolutely terrible landing you just made!" "Me?" the shocked student says, "I thought you said you were landing the plane!"[1]

Like the doctor and flight instructor, have you ever found yourself in a difficult or embarrassing situation as a result of miscommunication? Today's headlines circulate a cornucopia of missteps and mishaps resulting from communication snafus: *"Ringo Walks off 'Regis and Kelly' Over Verbal Flap," "Communication Caused Texas Transportation Department's Billion Dollar Error," "Woman's Tap Dance Classes Confused with Lap Dances," "Hulk Hogan Clueless Wife Filed Divorce Papers," and "Bay Oil Spill Caused by Communication between Crew."*

News reports, such as the following, detail a hodgepodge of hazardous, potentially avoidable situations:

- A Massachusetts shift officer was told to assemble his team of firefighters at the corner of Harrison and Cleveland streets. He assumed it was the demolition training location, as opposed to a rendezvous point. Using sledge-hammers and saws, the firefighters smashed windows, knocked down walls, and sliced gaping holes in the roof of an empty Victorian home. The fire department's training was considered a major success—until they learned it was the wrong house.[2]

"Traffic control, please repeat that . . . did you say 'near miss!'"

- In Louisville, Kentucky, a patient was expecting his surgeon to remove a cancerous growth from his penis. The surgeon, Dr. John Patterson, was under the impression he was authorized to do what was "medically necessary" to remove the cancer, so he performed a complete penile amputation. In his lawsuit, the patient claims this wasn't one of the "medically necessary" possibilities he had in mind.[3]
- A verbal gaffe between a postal delivery driver and a cargo representative freaked out workers at a Pets Plus store who were expecting to receive a delivery of "live" exotic fish valued at over $1,000. Instead, they received the body parts of a deceased San Diego man, Jon Kenoyer, who had donated his body to medical science.[4]

- With 30 seconds remaining, Michigan's DeShawn Sims launched a three pointer from the top of the key in a crucial 2009 NCAA game with Wisconsin. The ball ricocheted off the rim allowing Wisconsin to run the clock down. The 60-55 loss, and Sim's move, was not what Wolverine coach John Beilein intended. In a huddle just seconds before, Beilein told Sims what he wanted: "I was saying 'patience' to him in his ear. He thought I was saying 'take it.' So I've got to use a different word other than patience."[5]
- A melee broke out resulting in a triple shooting at the Minxx Gentlemen's Club and Lounge after Tennessee Titans cornerback, Adam Jones, pulled out $81,020 and showered strippers with money "as a visual effect." The strippers, unaware it was intended as a publicity stunt, assumed it was a generous token of appreciation for their choreographed performance and started picking up the money at the end of their performance. Jones tried to stop them and their manager. An altercation erupted. Security rushed in. A man pulled out a semi-automatic and shot three people: one woman in the head and two security guards. At press time, both security guards were in critical condition, one paralyzed for life.[6]

The consequences of miscommunication are potentially far reaching. Miscommunication can trigger a lawsuit, irreparably alter a person's anatomy, wreak emotional havoc, cost a game, or end a life. *What You Say and Do Next* explores the causes of miscommunication and highlights ways to reduce its frequency. It also examines how we can enhance the quality of our life with effective interpersonal communication.

. . . **Catch this!** www.youtube.com Mayday (Radio Operator's Miscommunication)

What You Say and Do Next . . . Matters!

Hitch (Will Smith) is a New York City self-proclaimed love expert and one man version of Matchmaker.com. He lends his expertise to Albert Brennaman (Kevin James), a financial advisor enamored over society heiress Allegra Cole (supermodel Amber Valletta). Hitch preps Albert for his next make-it-or-break-it date with Allegra:

Albert: "It's just one dance."

"When you're wondering what to say, or how you look . . . just remember . . . she is already out with you. That means, she said yes, when she could've said no . . ." Hitch (2005)

Hitch: "No! One dance. One look. One kiss. That's all we get Albert! Just one shot to make a difference between happily ever after and 'oh he's just some guy I went to something with once' . . . 8 out of 10 women believe that the first kiss will tell them everything that they need to know about a relationship. And believe me, she has definitely thought about it."

Albert: "She has?"

Hitch: ". . . wrap your head around this. Tomorrow night Allegra Cole could have her last first kiss."[7]

Like Albert, what we say and do, next, can let us in or show us the door. It can make or break a deal, turn a friend into a foe, or swap happiness with heartbreak. It can mean the difference between momentary lust and something lasting. It can draw out the best and worst in any given situation. Like a game of chess, every communication move we make elicits a response. Each turn fashions a new set of circumstances. Communication moves, like lifting our finger off a game piece, are irretrievable. Where we are at in a conversation or relationship is indicative of all the previous communication moves which have occurred. It is important to consider our options and calculate our moves. Dr. Peter Senge, organizational expert and author of the *Fifth Discipline* lends this perspective:

"No matter how many times the same insult is repeated, our next response can be creative rather than retaliatory. No matter how long parties have not been speaking to each other, the next time they meet, one . . . could speak. No matter how ingrained and toxic the pattern that two groups are caught in, the next move one side makes, can break the chain. No matter how much you feel thrown by what the other person just said and did, if you give yourself time to regroup, what you say can put the relationship back on track. Even when it is very difficult not to strike back, your next comment can heal rather than hurt."[8]

Like a game of chess, can you think of a different metaphor to describe the importance of our communication choices?

Our ability to communicate interpersonally impacts how we live, who we become, and where we go in life, personally and professionally. Our communication is the engine that fuels a successful relationship, a positive work climate, a winning team, and a profitable enterprise. If we chose not to apply successful communication approaches in our interactions, we experience the alternative. This is poignantly articulated by Susan Scott, author of *Fierce Conversations*:

". . . if we lower our standards about how often we talk, what we talk about and . . . what degree of authenticity we bring to our conversations—it's a slow and deadly slide. . . . Our work, our relationships, and in fact, our very lives succeed or fail gradually, then suddenly, one conversation at a time. . . . Perhaps you receive a major wake-up call. You lost your biggest customer . . . your most valued employee, . . . your job . . . the loyalty of your team, your grip on your eighteen-year marriage, or the cohesiveness of your family. Perhaps your company is experiencing turnover, turf wars, rumors, departments

A husband and wife are at a party chatting with some friends when the subject of marriage counseling comes up. "Oh, we'll never need that," the wife explained. "My husband and I have a great relationship. He was a communication major in college, and I studied theater arts. He talks a lot, and I act like I'm listening."

Ahajokes.com

not cooperating with one another, long overdue reports and . . . strategic plans that still aren't off the ground. . . . Once you reflect on the path that led to such a disappointing or difficult point and place in time . . . remember . . . the conversation which set things in motion."[9]

Our communication behaviors, as we'll explore throughout this unit, significantly influence our physical and psychological health. They impact the kind of relationships we have with people and our career success. Before we examine the role communication plays in these crucial areas, let's define it.

. . . How would you summarize this section of the unit? Why is what we say and do next important?

What Is Communication?

Oscar: "Both my parents were born in Mexico, and they moved to the United States a year before I was born, so I grew up in the United States. . . . My parents were Mexican."

Michael: "Wow, that is a great story. That's the American Dream right there, right? Um, let me ask you, is there a term besides 'Mexican' that you prefer? Something less offensive?"[10]

Michael Scott (Steve Carrel), the socially inept manager of the fictitious Dunder Mifflin Company, attempts to communicate with Oscar Martinez (Oscar Nuñez) during a cultural sensitivity training exercise—albeit an unsuccessful one. What exactly is communication? **Communication** is the dynamic process of creating, sending, and attaching meaning to messages. There are different fields of study in communication. This book is a study of interpersonal communication. **Interpersonal Communication** occurs when we interact one-on-one or with others in small group contexts.

If Michael Scott posed his off-base question to Oscar privately, this is one-on-one or **dyadic communication**. Unfortunately, he did so in front of other staff members. When three or more people are communicating with each other in a given context, this is **small group communication**. Interpersonal communication scholars are particularly interested in studying how small groups interact to disseminate information, make decisions, and accomplish tasks. We communicate interpersonally—dyadically and within small groups—a lot. As a process, interpersonal communication is also complex.

© NBC Universal/Photofest.

"I am Michael, and I am part English, Irish, German, and Scottish, sort of a virtual United Nations!" *The Office* (2010)

. . . What is communication? What is interpersonal communication?

The Frequency and Complexity of Interpersonal Communication

A lot of our time is devoted to interpersonal communication and communication in general. According to research, by the time we blow out the candles on our 18th birthday cake, we will have vocalized approximately 60 million words! We speak an average of 30,000 words a day! We're involved in some form of communication seven out of every ten waking hours![11] The late UC Berkeley scholar Walter Loban estimated that we listen an equivalent of a book a day and speak a book a week![12, 13] One study found that business professionals interact with people approximately eighty percent of their business day.[14]

In fact, even if we are not speaking or listening directly to a person, we have the potential to communicate. If a person has the capacity to observe our behavior, he or she can derive meaning from it. As communication scholars Ronald Adler and Neil Towne state: "Whatever you do—whether you speak or remain silent, confront or avoid, act emotional or keep a poker face—you provide information to others about your thoughts and feelings."[15]

People spend a lot of time communicating with others but may not think much about how well they do it. Just as patients tend to overestimate how much skin their hospital gowns cover, people overrate their communication skills. They also rely on ineffective patterns of communication—unless they see their communication for what it is and strive to change it.

Take the men in VH1 reality series *The Pickup Artist.* The show features eight "socially awkward" men struggling to tackle their greatest fear—approaching women. These self-described diehard masters of dating disasters are selected to live together for the purpose of learning how to woo women and "pick up" much needed social sophistication. They compete for the title of "Master Pick-Up Artist" and a cash reward of $50,000. Helping them in this often painful process is "Mystery," a real life "Hitch," who has mastered the art of the "approach." Mystery observes the men and helps them scrap approaches which don't work. Mystery's techniques include the "open set," "the number close," and the "kiss close."

"Any guy can sweep any girl off her feet, he just needs the right broom?"

Fortified with this information, Mystery's protégées venture outside their supportive enclave to practice their methods at clubs, shopping malls, and coffee houses. Hidden cameras catch every faux pas and success.[16]

Research This! What is Mystery's "kiss close?" Go to www.vh1.com/show

If concealed cameras captured our communication with others on any given day, what would the world see? How often would we want to cut to commercial? Is it safe to say we'd all benefit from a "Mystery?" Wouldn't it be great if we had someone who would point things out and help us with our communication? *What You Say and Do Next . . . Matters* is like "Mystery" in a way. It provides practical suggestions grounded in research and communication theory to improve our interpersonal interactions. Questions we'll entertain include: How can we offer sympathy to a friend without "Dr. Philing" her? How do we best respond to an unwanted sexual advance? What do we say when our six-year-old screams "I hate you?" Is there a way to know if our communication at work elicits eye rolls more than respect? How do we avoid the pain of hearing our romantic partner say, "It's too late to apologize. It's too late"—or something similar to *One Republic's* hit song?

The interactive, interdependent nature of interpersonal communication lends itself to both rewards and challenges. Like a disclaimer for a diet advertisement, we can say that individual results will vary depending on what we say, how we say it, when we say it, and who we say it to. As a process, communication is daunting at times. Look at what scholars Velma Walker and Lynn Brokaw say is involved when we communicate:

- What we intend to say.
- What we end up saying.
- What the other person hears.
- What the other person thinks about what we said.
- What the other person then says about what we said.
- What we think about what the other person said about what we said.
- What we then say about what we think about what the other person just said about what we said![17]

"The real art of communication is not only to say the right thing at the right time, but to leave unsaid the wrong thing at the tempting moment."
Dorothy Nevill

In addition to the complex nature of communication, certain people are simply difficult to talk to. These are often the people who matter the most to us. Dr. Paul Swets, author of *The Art of Talking So That People Will Listen: Getting Through to Family, Friends, and Business Associates*, states that people create barriers which make it difficult for us to penetrate. We also erect walls with the wrong communication approach or tactic. He says, "Our words sometimes produce the very opposite effect of what we intend. We hurt another's feelings, provoke anger, and create psychological distance, even when what we really desire are understanding, intimacy, and companionship."[18] Fortunately, research and theory from the interpersonal communication field can help us improve our well-being, relationships, and career success!

. . . How is interpersonal communication complex and challenging at times?

Interpersonal Communication Matters to Our Well-being!

A family celebration erupted the day James J. Pelosi was formally notified of his acceptance at West Point, the oldest (established in 1802 by President Thomas Jefferson) and one of the most distinguished United States military academies. This *carpe diem* dream come true had Pelosi stoked. He was on his way to earning the title of full-fledged lieutenant, sharing this accomplishment with an impressive line-up of famous West Point graduates such as Edwin"Buzz" Aldrin, Ulysses Grant, Dwight Eisenhower, Thomas Stonewall Jackson, Douglas MacArthur, and Norman Schwarzkopf.[19] As a successful third year cadet, he garnered the respect of his peers and was a candidate for the West Point Honor Committee, comprised of distinguished cadets elected by their peers with the mandate to promote and enforce West Point's strict honor code.[20]

Things took a dramatic turn for Pelosi when he was accused of cheating on an engineering exam. He was found guilty by the Honor Committee, despite having his case thrown out by the Academy Superintendent who expressed concerns that the evidence was questionable. Pelosi, under a provision in the Academy Honor Code, was ostracized—sentenced to "silencing" for the remainder of his junior year and all of his senior year.

For eighteen months, he was not allowed to talk to anyone including his best friend, who cried in silence when Pelosi was sentenced. While other cadets socialized and dined around him in the cafeteria, Pelosi ate all his meals by himself *every* day at a table for ten! He was the

Vincent A. Guariglia: Defense Visual Information Center.

target of occasional ice cubes at dinner and had his mail and locker vandalized. His personal belongings were ransacked, and he frequently had to fish his clothes from the latrine. Pelosi had no one he could turn to or talk to regarding these malicious acts. He couldn't use his communication to address his grievances or control what was happening around him. He had to live by himself, separated from his unit, in a three person dorm room. Pelosi battled loneliness, anxiety, and depression. He lost 26 lbs (despite already being in shape) in his first few months of silencing.

Pelosi endured this Quasimodo sentence and made it to graduation (one of a select few in the academy's history). When his name was called, he stood up nervously and walked across the stage to receive his diploma, expecting a resounding chorus of boos. Instead, cadets surrounded him and patted him on the back. They applauded him for his tenacity and determination. Pelosi was completely taken aback. He didn't know what to think. He was shocked and stood there not knowing what to say or do. Fighting back tears, Pelosi states, "It was as if I were a person again . . . . I know what isolation does for animals. No one at the Academy asks how it affects a person. Does that seem strange?"[21, 22]

Have you ever received the "silent treatment?" How did it feel?

Fostering relationships is essential to our emotional and physical well-being. We need meaningful interaction, companionship, and company. Dr. Henry S. Lodge, a renowned doctor of geriatrics and professor at Columbia Medical School, states that "Love, companionship, and community are woven deeply into our DNA. Emotional connection is a biological imperative, and we pay a high price for ignoring it."[23] James Pelosi's communication and relational deprivation resulted in a host of physical (hypertension, weight loss) and emotional (anxiety, low self-esteem, loneliness, and depression) maladies.

Research this! Does West Point still adhere to its "silencing" policy?

Pelosi's experience represents two kinds of isolation: social and relational. A **social isolate** is a person who spends a significant time alone or away from people. A **relational isolate** is a person who lacks close, personal relationships. A person can be one or the other, or both. For example, a person can be around or even work with people quite a bit and still be a relational isolate.

One doesn't have to live under a "silencing" policy like James Pelosi to experience the deleterious effects of social and relational isolation. Some people choose to isolate themselves from others or live without close, meaningful relationships. Their isolation may stem from their inability to create, develop, and maintain relationships. Social anxiety, personality/mood disorders, hyperactivity, shyness, low self-esteem, and/or poor interpersonal skills may exacerbate social or relational isolation.

Our choices often lead us to a place of isolation. The demands of work and school and our entertainment-saturated culture can, like *Pac Man*, gobble up time otherwise spent enhancing the quality of our relationships with friends and family. College students maintain hectic schedules between one or more jobs and college classes. They, along with single parents who juggle the demands of work and parenting, can fall easily into the social and/or relational isolate categories. Columbia Medical School professor, Dr. Henry Lodge, states, "Long commutes, computers and cubicles at work, and entertainment enticements at home have created a world where isolation is the norm rather than the exception."[25] An inordinate devotion to surfing the Internet, watching DVDs, listening to iPods, or playing computer or entertainment (PlayStation, Nintendo, Xbox) games carves away time devoted to initiating and building meaningful relationships. The results of numerous studies appear to substantiate the concerns of many interpersonal communication experts and social scientists. A quarter of Americans say they have no one they can talk to about personal troubles, double the number who were similarly surveyed in 1985. Overall, the number of people Americans have in their closest circle of confidants has dropped from around three to about two. In sharp contrast to a 1985 survey, nearly 50 percent more people in 2004 reported that their spouse is the only person they can confide in.[26]

Sailor and adventurer W. Carl Jackson ventured solo across the Atlantic Ocean on his sailboat for 51 consecutive days. Jackson describes a challenge he didn't anticipate:

"I found the loneliness of the second month almost excruciating. I always thought of myself as extremely self-sufficient, but I found life without people had no meaning. I had a definite urge for somebody to talk to, someone real, alive and breathing."[24]

Dr. Robert Putnam is a Peter and Isabel Malkin Professor of Public Policy at Harvard University. His extensive longitudinal research encompassed 500,000 interviews and a painstaking data collection process on reported activities that create ties and build relationships. The results are detailed in his 2000 book, *Bowling Alone*, a modern classic of great interest within political, educational, and social circles.

Are we becoming a relationship starved society? Why or why not?

Researchers: Internet robs us of time with others.

Researchers at Stanford Institute for the Quantitative Study of Society (SIQSS) purport that 31% of the U.S. population spends an inordinate time on the Internet, which results in seventy minutes less time interacting with family members and twenty-five minutes of sleep per day.[30]

According to Putnam, the average American participated in a club meeting every month during the 1970s. In 1998, that rate dropped 60%. In 1975, American adults entertained friends at home an average of fifteen times a year. A comparative survey in 1998 found the frequency cut in half.[27] This same survey found that Americans engage in 33% fewer family dinners and 45% fewer social visits compared to those surveyed since World War II.[28, 29]

A *Crucial Minutiae* blogger voiced her appreciation for something we may not want to take for granted: "Friends and family. Gotta have em. They're great for eating next to, dancing with, second opinions, inside jokes, bear hugs, reality checks, and inspiration."

Many psychologists theorize that positive relationships, such as the ones we have with

friends, serve as a buffer between us and the stresses of life. Micah Sadigh, associate professor of psychology at Cedar Crest College, states, "You need friends you can talk to . . . knowing you have people to support you keeps you healthy, mentally and physically."[31] One study found that having a vibrant social life and several positive, close relationships are one of the most significant predictors of an individual's overall happiness. [32]

Conversely, researchers have measured increased levels of cortical, a stress hormone, in lonely people. In one study, UCLA psychologist Naomi Eisenberger and a team of researchers utilized MRI technology to measure the brain activity of subjects who were put through a social exclusion simulation. Research participants registered increased brain activity in the anterior cingulated cortex, an area in the brain linked to pain processing and signaling.[33]

Are you feeling lethargic, ill, depressed, bored, and/or tired a lot? You may not be spending enough time interacting with others in a meaningful way or engaging in satisfying conversations. An intimate talk in front of a fire with a date, a lively game of *Taboo* with friends, or a gratifying volley of family stories at the dinner table can induce fun, laughter, and relaxation. A deficiency of close interaction with others, over time, triggers biochemical changes in a person's brain, exacerbating episodes of insomnia and clinical depression.[34] Several studies point to a strong correlation between people who have no or few close friends and elevated levels of anxiety.[35] Rates of colds and infections are four times greater with socially and relationally isolated people.[36] The Journal of the American Medical Association reports that an absence of close social relationships jeopardizes coronary health to an extent surpassing cigarette smoking, high blood pressure, obesity and lack of physical exercise. [37] One study found that women battling metastatic breast cancer double their average survival time if they participate in a support group.[38]

"A good conversation is as stimulating as black coffee."
Anne Morrow Lindbergh

Research suggests on average men die five years sooner than women after the death of their spouse. Why?

When we communicate with people on a personal level, we are apt to smile and laugh more. Recent research supports the theory that prolonged laughing may jettison endorphins into the blood stream.[39] Endorphins are like natural opiates. Other purported health benefits of laughing include reducing a person's pain perception and anxiety, increasing immunity, and reducing certain stress hormones.[40, 41, 42, 43] A study by Vanderbilt University researcher Maciej Buchowski found that ten to fifteen minutes of sustained laughter consumed fifty calories![44]

. . . **Catch This!** For a good laugh go to www.youtube .com ClumsyCatwalkerCausesHilarity

Even if we are not social or relational isolates, disruptions or unresolved conflict within our significant relationships have a deteriorating effect on our health. Our immune system is intricately interconnected to our emotions. Being separated from or the death of a loved one, a break-up, divorce, financial woes, family stress, unresolved anger, and marital strife are examples of interpersonal difficulties that may reduce the immune system's ability to ward off infections and recuperate from illnesses.[45] Studies over the past thirty years consistently show that chronic stress increases a person's risk of immunosuppression and autoimmune disease.[46] In one study, researchers monitored the rate of respiratory infections in sixteen families for a full year. They discovered that illnesses were four times more frequent when the families were under stress.[47] When comparing two groups of pregnant women coping with stressful situations, those who had little or no social support reported three times more medical complications compared with those who did.[48] Another interesting study found that adults who experienced a recent separation or divorce were three times more likely than non-separated or married adults to get in a traffic accident.[49] Teens growing up in families that lack cohesiveness and parental supervision are more likely to drink and drive, and if their parents were recently divorced, are more likely to become sexually active compared to teens growing up in two parent married families.[50, 51]

The evidence is stacked in favor of the following assertion: we need healthy, affirming relationships physically and psychologically. It is through our communication that we create and sustain these relationships.

. . . How would you summarize the link between close, meaningful relationships and physical/psychological health?

What You Say and Do Next Matters to Our Relationships!

One story illustrates a special relationship one famous actress had with a professor in college. Oprah Magazine reported that when two time Golden Globe nominee and actress Maria Bello (*The Mummy: Tomb of the Dragon Emperor 2008, World Trade Center 2006, Flicka 2006, Coyote Ugly 2000)* walked into Father Ray Jackson's classroom her freshman year at Villanova University, she had no idea the 6′2″ 65-year-old ex-marine would influence her in such a profound way. He pulled her aside one day and lauded what she wrote in an essay on the societal contributions of Martin Luther King, Dorothy Day, and Gandhi. He became her mentor. She sought out Father Ray for stimulating conversation and guidance. She spoke to him every day and often had lunch with him. She remembered Father Ray's enthusiastic reaction when she disclosed her plan to pursue a law career and promote peace through social activism.

That plan changed suddenly when, on a whim, Bello enrolled in an acting class. With continued collegiate stage experience, she became hopelessly hooked. She didn't know how to break the news of her career reversal to Father Ray, but was surprised by his response when she told him the news. Father Ray looked her in the eyes and with passion said, "You serve best by doing the thing you love most. Follow your bliss."

Maria Bello did just that. Soon after her graduation from Villanova, Father Ray died. It was then that Maria realized something very profound. Father Ray had taken such an interest in her and knew so much about her, yet she didn't really know him. She pondered questions such as: What made him become a priest? What was his biggest fear? Had his heart ever been broken?

She realized that he offered his time and counsel unconditionally. She took these things from him but was too busy sorting out her own young life to really get to know and appreciate him. At age thirty-eight, she realized that the time and attention you give someone is one of the greatest gifts you can experience.

Bello goes on to write about how in the midst of a crazy schedule, she went to Philadelphia to spend some time with her dad. He had been sick and appeared to have aged significantly since their last visit. They locked arms and walked the tree-lined sidewalks, past the historic shops and along the shaded park. They sat down together and sipped coffee. Nothing earth shattering, just time together. She writes, "Life goes so fast, and there is so much to do. But the moments that have enriched my life the most came when I slowed down and connected with the people I care about." She ends her article abruptly saying that she needed to help her 4-year-old son build a fort with the empty boxes that she piled up for him in the living room. Her son's first name is Jackson, named after the late Father Ray Jackson.[52]

Relationships enable us to create, dream, confide, laugh, cry, feel, grow, inspire, and teach. People we have a relationship with are called significant individuals. In the field of interpersonal communication, **significant individuals** may include people we are connected to romantically, such as a boyfriend or girlfriend, spouse, or life partner. They also include people we know platonically, including friends, coworkers, roommates, grandparents, parents, siblings, cousins, coaches, teachers, or spiritual mentors. Significant individuals have the capacity to influence us. We care about what they think of us.

We also experience various levels of immediacy with those who are significant individuals. **Immediacy** is the degree of closeness or connectedness we feel towards someone. Immediacy can wax and wane for any number of reasons. Just as Ramen noodles are a staple for tight budgeted college students, interpersonal communication is needed to increase immediacy and for relationship initiation, development, and maintenance.

Your Turn: Maria Bello's story exemplifies the potential impact relationships have on us. What are some of the most memorable moments of your life? Most likely, they involved people who you consider significant individuals. Think about a specific event right now. How did the person or people who shared this moment with you contribute to its significance? How would your memory of this event change if any or all of the significant individuals who shared this moment with you were not there? Describe this.

Maria Bello's "aha!" moment gives us pause to think about who matters to us, and what we bring to our relationships. Have we taken some of our relationships for granted? If so, what happens to our friendships? What happens to our families? What happens to our team? What happens to our marriage? Susan Scott, author of *Fierce Conversations* states:

> *"Often we hear people say about their relationships: 'we never addressed the real issue, never came to terms with reality . . . We never stated our needs. We never told each other what we were really thinking and feeling. In the end, there were so many things we needed to talk about . . . the wheels came off the cart.'"*[53]

"Tell your family and friends what you would say for their eulogies now—they won't be able to hear how much you love them from inside their coffin."

~Anonymous

Our communication, or a lack of it, is a major cause of interpersonal conflict. Interpersonal conflict is defined as an expressed or unexpressed tension between people. Usually it involves competing interests or opposing needs. Like a defensive tackle who, in response to a quarterback pass, is flagged for interference, one person perceives the other as a hindrance. Frequently, interpersonal conflict is the result of unmet needs stemming from a breakdown in communication between people. Unfortunately, rather than addressing the conflict in constructive ways, people often use less effective methods or avoid it all together. It is said that conflict is like a rhinoceros in the bedroom closet. Everyone knows it's there, but no one wants to open it.

The results of numerous studies shore up Susan Scott's sentiments. For example, one exhaustive study purports a lack of effective communication as the primary cause of marital breakups, more than any other reason, including money, in-laws, parenting, extramarital relationships and sexual problems![54] In fact, life circumstances can place many demands on a couple, but typically it is a couple's lack of effective communication concerning these demands which ultimately sinks the relationship. This was evident to the avid ten million plus fans of TLC's *Jon and Kate Plus Eight*, a reality show capturing the life of Jon and Kate Gosselin and their eight children, two are eight-year-old twins and six are five-year-old sextuplets. Jon and Kate tried to project an image of a happy couple, including renewing their wedding vows in Hawaii. However, each episode unveiled a systematic shutdown in communication, leading to a very public and painful separation and eventual divorce.

. . . **Catch this!** What's it like to raise eight children under the age of eight? Go to: www.tlc.discovery.com/videos/jon-and-kate-plus-8

On the flip side, married couples who describe themselves as effective communicators also report more positive feelings about their relationship.[55] There are numerous articles and books centering on what adults want from each other in romantic relationships. According to a June 27, 2001 Gallup survey, eighty percent of young adult women responded that a spouse who is able to express his thoughts, needs, and feelings was more desirable than one who had the ability to earn a good living!

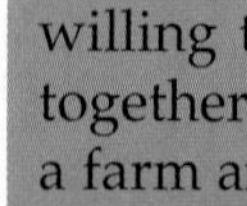

Research this! What do American's think about relationships? Go to www.gallup.com. November 2008: "Relationships, Financial Security Linked to Well-Being.

A husband and wife lock horns in an "I'm right, your wrong" stalemate. Neither are willing to budge or concede. The two drive together in silence. The husband drives past a farm and points to a donkey in the pasture. "Relative of yours?" he asked. "Yes," she replied. "By marriage!"

—Bobbie Mae Cooley, The American Legion Magazine

The quality of interpersonal communication also impacts our work relationships. A 2007 survey of 5,000 households by Conference Board, a market research company that publishes the Consumer Confidence Index, found that 53% of Americans were not satisfied with their jobs.[56] In fact, many Americans complain more about the people they work with or for than any other aspect of their job. Organizational psychologist and CEO of the National Business Research Institute, Ken West PhD., believes that separate from their work tasks and income, there are five main reasons why Americans find their jobs less than ideal:

1) Many workers feel "out of the loop," or excluded from the decision-making process, especially when decisions directly impact them. West quotes Howard Ross, director of a Maryland-based organizational communication consulting firm: "My experience is that people know they can't control everything about their work life, but they do want to feel that they have some legitimate input in order to not feel powerless, de-motivated, and resentful."
2) Employees dislike favoritism and many perceive that their bosses heap unequal praise and opportunities based on who they like more.
3) People find their work unrewarding when they feel like they don't know what is expected of them, and how their work contributes to the organization's mission. There is a lack of feedback on how they are doing.
4) A major cause of employee turnover is a bad relationship with one's direct supervisor. A supervisor's ability to help workers solve problems, listen effectively, give clear instructions and helpful feedback are some of the many factors directly tied to retention and morale.
5) Finally, when people work with each other eight or more hours a day, five days a week, the undesirable behaviors and difficult personalities of coworkers are bound to test people's nerves. A co-worker may interrupt a lot or talk loud. He or she may carry what West calls a built in "bad attitude micro-chip." Every situation is nitpicked. Nothing is quite good enough. The worst is anticipated. He or she complains that no one does anything but is first to criticize those who try.[57]

Based on your work experiences, do you agree with West's statements? Why or why not?

These five challenges to workplace satisfaction are often magnified or mitigated by ineffective or effective interpersonal communication.

The quality of and satisfaction derived from our relationships is tied directly to our communication behaviors. Our ability to communicate may determine whether people want to spend time with us, what they are willing to share with us, and their level of honesty. How we express ourselves, our penchant for storytelling, our listening prowess, the richness of our vocabulary, and our interest in what others have to say puts either a stamp of approval or rejection on our social desirability.

What does it take to initiate, accelerate, and maintain interpersonal relationships? We communicate with people all the time. Most of the time it is impersonal—like when we casually greet customers at work (because we're expected to do so) or ask for a Whopper at Burger King (because we're hungry). **Impersonal communication** is surface level, task-oriented communication between people, often out of necessity or politeness. It serves a needed purpose, but like leftovers from a mediocre dinner, it is uneventful from a relational standpoint. It does not usually forge meaningful, close relationships. It takes, as we'll discover in subsequent units, more to bring a relationship to a deeper level. Our ability to communicate effectively with others matters not only to our well being and relationships, but to our financial and career success.

. . . How is your ability to communicate effectively important in terms of your relationships?

What You Say and Do Next Matters to Your Career Success!

A business journal included an article about a newly hired product design specialist at Texas Instruments. She was invited to join the product improvement team. One day, she left the meeting thinking, "My God, I've ruined my career . . . I just told a guy four levels above me that he was wrong." As it turned out, the man was a high level manager looking for new executive talent. Impressed by her assertiveness and ability to communicate disagreement in a tactful, professional manner, he encouraged her to interview for a high level position, which she did. She was promoted to general manager of one of eight regional divisions for Texas Instruments. The promotion awarded her a bigger office, more perks, and a hefty raise.

What is the secret to career and financial achievement? Is it intelligence? No, a lot of brilliant people are struggling financially.

The 55,000 members of MENSA (I.Q. of 135 mandatory to join) have average annual incomes equal to or less than sixty to eighty thousand dollars. How about talent? Not really, many talented people are unsuccessful. Is it advanced degrees? A degree alone won't guarantee it. The majority of millionaires in the U.S. have an undergraduate degree or less.[58] What about hard work? Many hardworking Americans struggle in dead-end jobs. Success requires varying degrees of intelligence, talent, education and hard work. There are two fundamental pre-requisites to success. Without them, success is improbable. The first is to know what you want to do with your life. Success starts with a vision or a goal that motivates or excites us. The second is the ability to relate to and communicate with the world's greatest asset: people!

Communication skills are synonymous with success in the 21st century.[59] According to the U.S. Department of Labor, formal and informal speaking skills are the trump cards for about eight out ten jobs. Managers, secretaries, and technicians spend thirty-five percent of their time at work in direct face-to-face communication. According to the National Association of Colleges and Employers, a survey of four hundred employers found that communication skills outranked technical competence, work experience, and academic background in importance, relative to advancements and promotions.[60] Out of four thousand human resource professionals, seventy-one percent said that communication skills are, hands down, the key for on-the-job effectiveness.[61] Amazingly, even in the highly technical field of engineering, *Engineering Education* (five hundred engineers surveyed) found that fifteen percent of a typical engineer's upward career mobility was credited to technical know-how and eighty-five percent to communication skills.[62]

The range of jobs you qualify for depends not only on your employment and education history, but your ability to communicate effectively with and lead others. One hundred and seventy companies reported that poor communication skills are the chief reason for rejecting applicants.[63] Seventy-nine percent of New York City corporate executives agreed that the ability to express ideas orally and in writing is a top qualification they look for when hiring. Researchers asked four hundred managers representing a wide range of companies to pick the most critical skills potential employees could bring to the table. The skills they pinpointed as highly desirable are clear articulation, receiving and giving timely feedback, relating positively to others, and functioning effectively in teams.[64] David Peoples, communication expert and author of *Presentations Plus*, states: "Times have changed. Yesterday the most qualified person got the job. Today, among the equally qualified, the best communicator does."[65]

Do you agree or disagree with results of these surveys? Why or why not?

Our ability to communicate interpersonally influences people's notion of our competence, professionalism, product, and company. According to the Society for the Advancement of Education, ninety-percent of firings were based on an employee's poor interpersonal

skills.[66] This is disadvantageous not only for the employee who is fired, but for the company. It generally costs companies more money to hire and train new employees than it does to retain them.

Job posting advertisement for a company:

"This firm requires no physical-fitness program. Everyone gets enough exercise jumping to conclusions, flying off the handle, running to the boss, flogging dead horses, knifing friends in the back, dodging responsibility and pushing their luck."

Financial Times

When it comes to getting hired, keeping our job, moving up, and boosting our earning potential, communication competence matters!

. . . Why are effective interpersonal communication skills important in terms of your career/financial success?

The field of communication includes some of the most exciting careers available. Depending on the college we attend, we can earn an associate's degree (typically a two year process), bachelor's degree (four years) or master's degree (completed in two to three years after a bachelor degree depending on one's academic pace). In addition, a doctorate (two to three years of additional schooling after a master's degree is earned) may be available. How long would it take us to go non-stop, full-time to earn a PhD? On average, it takes eight to ten years. Communication degrees or majors/minors are also a great compliment to other degrees or programs of study. For example, if we want to study law, we may decide to double major in pre-law and public communication for our undergraduate degree. If we want to pursue a career as a limited licensed psychologist, we may major in psychology and minor in interpersonal communication. Heed this caveat and be sure to investigate any school that offers a quick communication degree or one that is strictly on-line. These schools may shortchange us in terms of the training or education we need and may not be recognized as legitimate schools by industry.

Fired For Taking A Slice of Pizza!

A blog from the Internet details what happened to a programmer employed by a mortgage company for 18 months. One day he observed a group finishing a potluck in the break room, and there were a few slices of pizza left. He helped himself to them thinking they were bound for the trash. An employee who planned on taking the food home took offense and told a manager. The manager reported this action to the vice-president. Apparently, the programmer didn't find out the reason for being fired until a month later. There was no warning. No second chance. Given the opportunity, he would have certainly apologized and perhaps offered to pay for the pizza. He left an impression because he found out that his former coworkers now refer to left over pizza as "programmer bait." What went wrong with the communication here? Was this situation handled appropriately?

© Monkey Business Images, 2010. Used under license from Shutterstock, Inc.

One of the best ways we can determine which school or program of study is right for us is to establish a close working relationship with a career placement specialist as well as a college counselor. Our career choice is an important one—one of the most important decisions we'll make in our lifetime. One career placement specialist informed me that he advises students to spend at least two to three hours a week researching and investigating careers throughout their college career because they invest a lot of time, effort, and money in their college education. Your college is likely to offer personality and career interest assessments, job shadowing experiences, and internship opportunities. In addition, we can call and interview someone who is in a career we think we'd like to pursue. Ask lots of questions. This will help us narrow down possibilities. Our aim is to find a career that matches our personality, interests, skills, and financial goals. **Three major academic and career areas exist in the field of communication: interpersonal, public, and mass communication**.

Interpersonal communication explores how people communicate with each other from a relational perspective. Some communication scholars divide this field into two: dyadic and small group. This field of study explores numerous nuances of communication within relationships such as productivity, work climate, relationship satisfaction, openness, and conflict. Specialty areas of study may include group dynamics, listening, gender communication, organizational climate, family dynamics, nonverbal communication, couples, and intercultural communication. Sample job/careers tied to this field:

Counselor
School Principal
Law Enforcement
Management
Human Resources
Administration
Corporate Relations
Social Worker
Sales
Marriage/Family Therapist
Conflict Mediator
Hostage Negotiator
Hospice Director
Diplomat

What do all of these famous Americans have in common?

Joyce Mallick	Opera Star
Tennessee Williams	Playwright
Gary Larson	Cartoonist
David Letterman	Show Host
Spike Lee	Movie Director
John Quincy Adams	U.S. President
Denzel Washington	Actor
Hugh Heffner	Publisher
Brandi Chastain	Soccer Star
David St. Peter	Pres/ Minn Twins
Brian Lamb	CEO, C-SPAN
Richard Gephardt	U.S. Congressman
Connie Chung	News Anchor
Christine Gregoire	Attorney General
Meg Ryan	Actress
Brad Pitt	Actor
Earvin "Magic" Johnson	Pro Sports Owner
Lyndon Johnson	U.S. President
Mark McGrath	Lead singer/ Sugar Ray

They all earned college degrees in communication!

Source: National Communication Association

Public Communication is the study of formal communication between a speaker/performer and an audience. This field focuses on public speaking, persuasion, oral performance, and debate. A partial list of related careers:

State Senator
Announcer
Campaign Manager
Public Relations Officer
Public Affairs
Actor
Business Leader
Public Service
Lawyer
Sales
Spokesperson
Lobbyist
Talk Show Host
Fundraiser
Translator
Health Educator

Mass Communication is the study of communication which relies on technology to reach a large audience. It investigates how media functions and impacts society. Examples include television, telecommunications, advertising, radio, print media, and film. Areas of academic focus include persuasion, advertising, broadcasting, journalism, marketing and public relations. Jobs available for those with degrees and work experience in this field include:

Casting Director
Copywriter Pollster
Media Sales Representative
Film Editor
Copy Writer
Marketing Consultant
Anchor
Newspaper Editor
Script Writer
Photographer
Radio Personality
Media Analyst
Web Designer
Music and Sports Promoter
Documentary Film Maker
Tour Promoter
Talent Agent

Research This! To attend communication conferences, link with professional organizations, or subscribe to industry journals, visit:

National Communication Association
www.natcom.org.
American Communication Association
www.americancomm.org
International Communication Association
www.icahdq.org

Your Turn: What information in this section on interpersonal communication and career/ financial success did you find most interesting? What career or field of study would you like to learn more about? Why?

... What are some of the major fields of study in communication? Can you describe them?

Unit Summary

Our ability to communicate interpersonally influences the quality of our life—our well being, relationships and career success. Numerous studies suggest a correlation between effective interpersonal skills and optimum physical and emotional health. Communication is the building block of every relationship. Relationships add immeasurable meaning and fulfillment to our lives. The quality of our communication directly influences the nature of our relationships. To get a good job, keep it, and get promoted, strong interpersonal skills are indispensable. Scores of careers are tied to communication knowledge and competency. Colleges and universities offer different degrees and their own specialized areas of study. We can also learn from on-the-job experiences and by joining professional organizations such as the National Communication Association.

Key Questions

1. What is communication? What is interpersonal communication?
2. How is interpersonal communication complex?
3. Why are effective interpersonal communication skills essential to our physical and psychological health?
4. How is our ability to communicate interpersonally important in terms of our relationships?
5. How are interpersonal skills tied to career and financial success?
6. What are some of the major fields of communication?

Vocabulary Playback

Communication
Interpersonal Communication
Dyadic Communication
Small Group Communication
Social Isolate
Relational Isolate
Immediacy
Significant Individuals
Interpersonal Conflict
Impersonal Communication
Public Communication
Mass Communication

Focus Group/Class Discussion

- Do you agree that we often repeat patterns of behavior with our communication, even when it doesn't work or is hurtful? Why or why not? What patterns, if any, would you like to break?
- One study found that a miscommunication between patients and their doctors was a major cause of unnecessary hospital admissions. In fact, this occurred two times more often than a physician's treatment skills or judgment. Can you think of other work related situations where clear, effective inter-personal communication is critical? How about in the job that you have now?[67]
- U.S. Senator Joseph Biden was talking about another U.S. Senator, Barack Obama, shortly before the 2008 presidential primary. Biden was widely criticized for a comment he made that some construed as condescending to African Americans, which may have cost him potential votes from Democrats. When asked what he thought of Barack Obama, Biden stated that Barack was the "first mainstream African-American who is articulate, and bright, and clean, and a nice-looking guy." What did he mean by "articulate" and "clean?" Some construed his comments this way: compared to most black males, Barack can speak clearly and intelligently and doesn't have a criminal record. Did Biden unintentionally communicate a racial bias? Biden stated to CNN that he used the word "clean" in reference to something his mother used to say, "Clean as a whistle, sharp as a tack."[68] Biden was either covering up his snafu by throwing his mother into this political skillet or his explanation was sincere. Were people overreacting to Biden's comment? Were their criticisms justified? Why is interpersonal communication challenging at times?

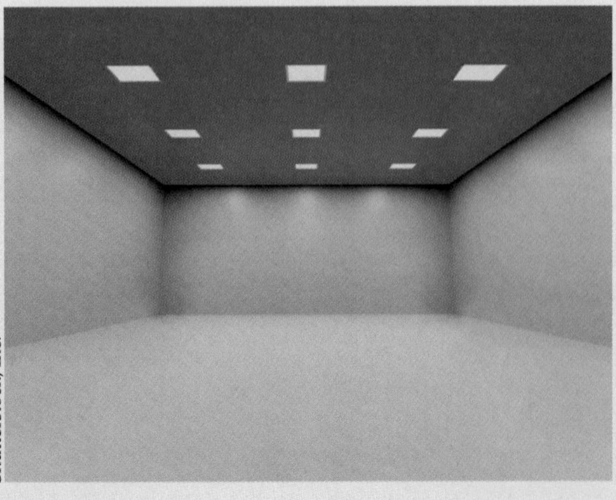

- Tom Hanks plays Chuck Noland, a FedEx executive who is stranded on a remote island for fifteen hundred days, in the movie *Castaway* (2000). To maintain his sanity, he starts talking to a volleyball which washes ashore from the wreckage. As time passes, he needs more than just an object that he talks at. What does he do from a communication standpoint to create a relationship with Wilson?

  . . . **Catch this!** For a humorous look at "Wilson," go to www.youtube.com: Castaway: The sitcom.

- A research team paid subjects money for every hour they could remain alone in a locked room. Of the five subjects, one lasted eight days. Three hung in for two days with one exclaiming "never again." The final subject pounded on the door after just two hours. How long could you last and what conditions would make your isolation more tolerable? [69]
- What other societal factors, such as dual career families, suburban sprawl, and changes in American family structure, contribute to greater social and relational isolation?
- If you were talking to a student who was new to your school and community, what would you suggest he or she do to connect with people and make friends?
- In the movie *As Good As It Gets (1997)*, Jack Nicholson plays Melvin, a misanthropic romance novelist and obsessive-compulsive who is often oblivious to his insensitive remarks. One evening, he takes his love interest, Carol (Helen Hunt), to an upscale restaurant. When he makes an insulting remark about her dress, Carol leans in and glares across the candlelit table at Melvin. In exasperation she says, "Pay me a compliment Melvin. I need one quick." She waits impatiently for his response, poised to walk out on him and the relationship. Melvin realizes his predicament and shifts uneasily in his seat. He knows that what he is about to say and do next matters! After a long pause, he looks deeply into her eyes and says: "You make me want to be a better man." He said the right thing at the right time! Can you think of a time that you said something to someone which had a significant (negative or positive) impact on the relationship? What was it?
- People complain more about their coworkers more than any other aspect of their job. Do you agree with this statement? Why or why not?

Unit 1 Vocabulary Review

___ Communication
___ Interpersonal Communication
___ Dyadic Communication
___ Small Group Communication
___ Social Isolate
___ Relational Isolate
___ Significant Individuals
___ Immediacy
___ Interpersonal Conflict
___ Impersonal Communication
___ Public Communication
___ Mass Communication

A. This is one-on-one or two person communication.

B. A term to describe a person who spends a significant time alone or away from people.

C. This is the process of creating, sending, and attaching meaning to messages.

D. A person who has no or lacks close, personal relationships is considered this.

E. This is a term which refers to the broad field of study which explores how people communicate with each other one-on-one and within small groups.

F. People who are close to us and have the capacity to influence us directly. We care about what they think of us to some extent.

G. This is an expressed or unexpressed tension between people, usually involving competing interests or unmet needs.

H. This is surface level, task-oriented communication between people, often out of necessity or politeness.

I. Communication between three or more individuals.

J. The degree of closeness or connectedness we feel towards someone.

K. The study of communication which relies on technology to reach a large audience.

L. The study of formal communication between a speaker and an audience.

Exercise

There is a story widely circulated on the internet about a professor giving his students a pop quiz. The last question on the quiz read, "Name the woman who cleans this building?" Many students knew of the woman. She wore a smile all the time and was very friendly. She was diligent and took pride in her work. The building was immaculate.

The students thought this question was a joke. One student asked if the question counted on the quiz. "Absolutely," said the professor. "In our careers and pursuits, you will meet many people. Good people. All are significant. They deserve your attention and care, even if all you do is smile, greet them and say their name." (Author unknown)

If you were a professor, and you wanted to impart a lesson to remind your students how important it is to recognize the value of people and our relationships with them, what creative or unconventional approach might you use? Get ready to share your thoughts with the class.

Process 2

Process   Unit 2

Unit 2 introduces the components involved in the process of sending (encoding) and receiving (decoding) messages. Strategies for improving this process are explained.

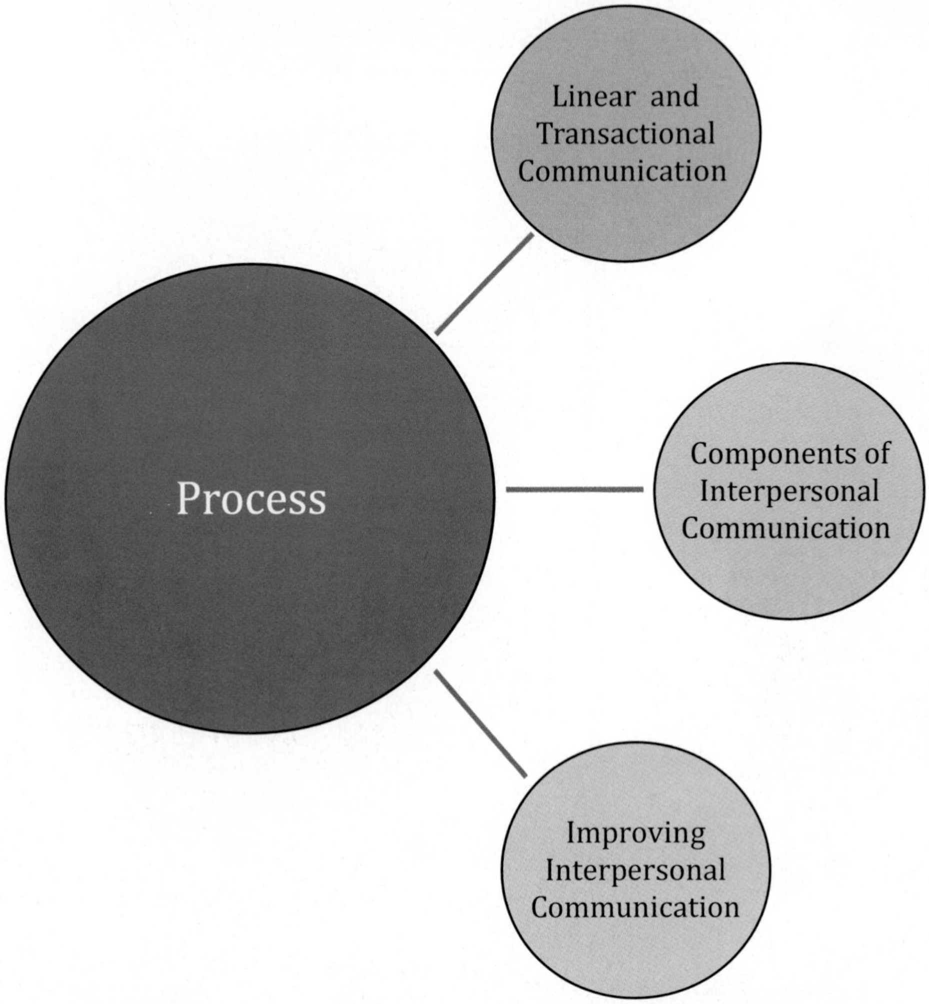

Unit 2 Learning Objectives

As a result of reading and studying Unit 2, you will be able to:

1. Define the components of interpersonal communication.
2. Explain the difference between linear and transactional communication.
3. Appreciate the importance of the following components and their impact on the communication process:
   - Sender/Receiver
   - Message
   - Channel
   - Feedback
   - Context
   - Noise
   - Frame of Reference
4. Understand how to improve the process of interpersonal communication in the following five ways:
   - Know when it is best not to send or receive messages.
   - Reduce and clarify mixed messages.
   - Choose channels strategically.
   - Identify and eliminate sources of noise.
   - Approach people tactically.

Imagine sitting down for a relaxing dinner with family and friends. Suddenly, someone at the table starts choking. You frantically administer the Heimlich maneuver. As you make repeated attempts to dislodge the obstruction, panic sets in. Your attempts to save this person you care so much about are not working. This happened to Dr. Rob Boll, M.D., as he administered the Heimlich Maneuver on Pat Rohrer who had joined Boll and a small group of friends at a dinner hosted by Chicago's St. John's United Church of Christ. As church members watched anxiously, Boll tried to clear Rohrer's air. A nurse standing by did a finger sweep, but snagged only a small portion of a piece of turkey from Rohrer's throat.

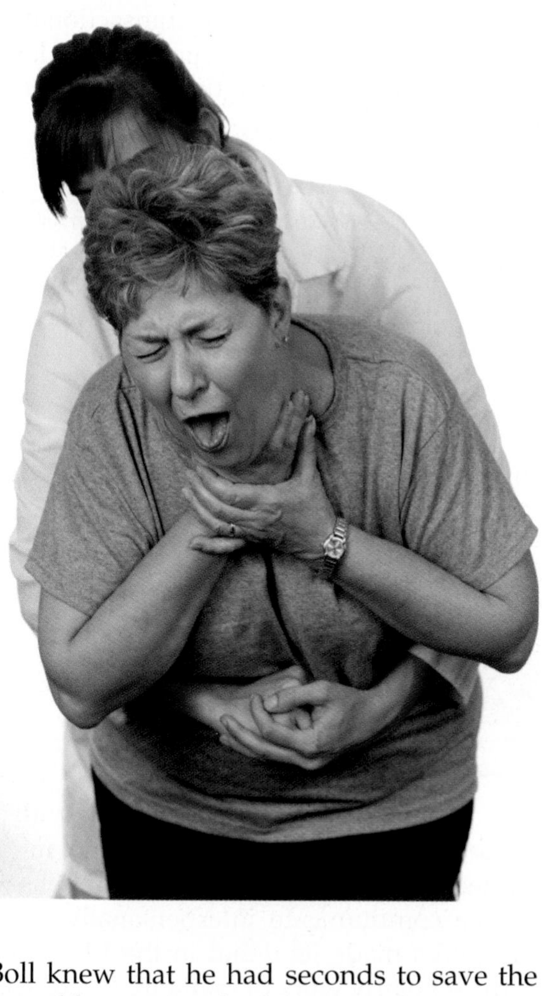

Boll knew that he had seconds to save the 76-year-old woman who lay motionless on the floor. Boll turned to the stunned crowd to summon help and find him a knife. Someone in the room handed Boll a razor-sharp, three-inch switchblade. Boll performed an on-the-spot tracheotomy, something he had observed once during his residency 20 years ago. Boll's mind raced. He listed out loud things he needed to continue. This procedure required things found only in a surgical room with trained surgeons. By sheer coincidence, a boy was there who had a pronounced lung condition requiring a twenty-four-hour-a-day air-way tube. Knowing that her son would survive without it for at least an hour, his mother pulled it out of his chest and handed it to Boll to use as a tracheotomy tube! As if this wasn't already Rohrer's lucky day, an emergency kit was handed to Boll containing a manual resuscitator bag to pump life-giving oxygen into Rohrer's starved lungs.[1]

Everything needed for Pat Rohrer to survive was at hand that exact moment: a doctor, a surgical-like knife, an air tube, and a resuscitator bag. Certain interpersonal communication components were also involved. They played a critical role in the outcome. In this very tense, nerve racking situation, we had a number of senders and receivers exchanging messages using various channels within a certain context. Feedback, the presence of noise, and each person's frame of reference also influenced what happened.

Sender:	transmits a message.
Receiver:	interprets a message.
Message:	what is communicated.
Channel:	how a message is sent.
Feedback:	a response to a message.
Context:	the time, place, and people involved.
Noise:	anything which disrupts or distorts communication.
Frame of Reference:	a person's background or collective life experience.

These components were also present during a highly controversial broadcast between radio commentators Don Imus and Bernard McGuirk, April 4, 2007:

Imus: "That's some rough girls from Rutgers. Man, they got tattoos . . . "

McGuirk: "Some hardcore hoes."

Imus: "That's some nappy-headed hoes there. I'm going to tell you that."[2]

Radio talk-show host Don Imus (L) speaks with Rev. Al Sharpton (R) in New York. Imus apologizes for remarks he made about the Rutgers women's basketball team.

A person's **frame of reference** is his or her collective life experience. This includes his or her upbringing, social affiliations, educational background, and culture. Frame of reference influences how a person perceives a situation. Imus and McGuirk deemed their comments harmless and funny. Many people construed them as stereotypical and racist. Further analysis using linear and transactional communication models will help us appreciate how these components are interrelated.

During their on-air conversation, Imus and McGuirk exchanged messages. A **sender** transmits a message. A **receiver** interprets it. Their inflammatory remarks (messages) regarding the Rutgers women's basketball team led to Imus' firing by CBS. A **message** is what is communicated. Imus and McGuirk communicated to each other and their radio audience using their voices, language, and audio technology as their primary channels. A **channel** is the means by which a message is sent. **Feedback** is a response to a message. The feedback between Imus and McGuirk was immediate because their communication was face-to-face. Feedback also came from radio listeners when they called the show and other media outlets to complain minutes, hours and even days later.

Imus and McGuirk's on-air conversation occurred in a radio studio. All communication takes place in a context or environment. The **context** or environment is the time, place, and people involved when communication occurs. Whenever communication takes place, the presence of noise is likely. **Noise** makes effective communication difficult in some way. Noise may occur within a person, such as Imus' rapid thought process, "Whoa, did I just say that?" or from external sources, such as the hundreds of offended callers who lit up the studio phones lines.

If Imus and McGuirk were both African Americans, would their comments spark the same reaction from the general public? Why or why not? How does frame of reference apply to this?

. . . How would you describe the components of interpersonal communication?

Linear and Transactional Communication

During this century, the study of communication has burgeoned with new research and theories. Scholars have refined models to illustrate what happens when people communicate interpersonally. The linear model made its début in the 1940s, thanks to the scholarly work of mathematicians Claude Shannon and Warren Weaver. The model was explained in an article which later became a book titled, *The Mathematical Theory of Communication.*[3] The **linear model** depicts communication as following a single, straight path. The model starts with a sender who sends a message using a channel to a receiver. The receiver then responds with a message. It occurs in a one-way, back-and-forth manner—like a game of ping-pong. A message is not returned until it is received. If we are by ourselves, and we send a text message to someone or respond to an e-mail, we will not get a response until the person reads our text or e-mail and chooses to respond to us. This form of communication is represented by the linear model.

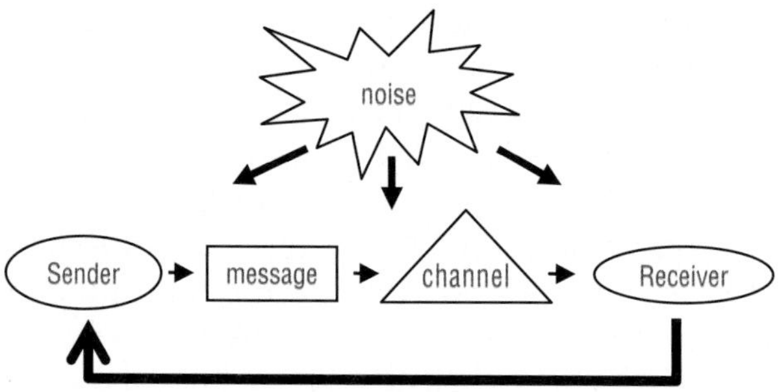

Linear Model

Communication scholars also rely on the **transactional model** to illustrate what happens when people communicate face-to-face or on the phone. In both situations, communication is two-way: people send and receive messages simultaneously.[4,5] When transactional communication takes place, everyone involved has an equal opportunity to create meaning and influence each other's communication behavior.[6,7] For example, let's say you're standing next to a friend at Starbucks waiting to order a white mocha latte. You are talking about an embarrassing moment that happened to you the other day, and your friend starts to smile or nod her head while you're speaking. Both of you are sending and receiving messages at the same time. Even if your friend is completely silent and expressionless, she is still communicating the message: "I am willing to listen to you—or pretend to do so."

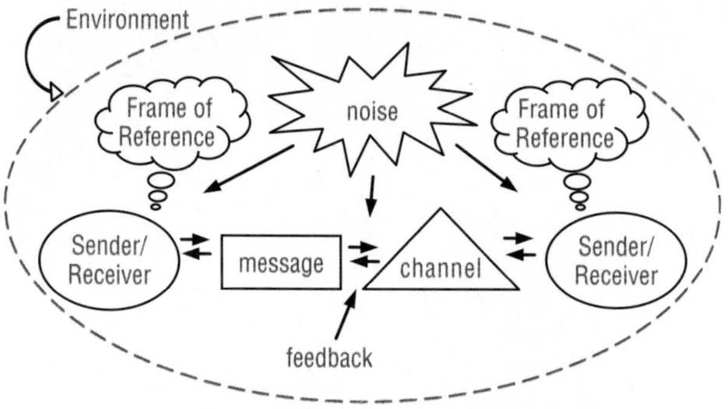

Transactional Model

Let's take a look at a phone conversation to delineate linear and transactional communication. You call a friend, and your call goes to her voice mail. You leave a message. She will listen to it later and call you back with a response. In this case, you'll receive no feedback until she chooses to do so, or you realize she hasn't returned your call in a timely manner. This is linear or one-way communication. Let's say you are on the phone with your dad. As you share your plans to go to a Toni Braxton concert in Chicago, you hear him sigh or the sounds of dishes being washed. You are both sending and receiving messages at the same time. This is transactional or two-way communication.

. . . What is the difference between linear and transactional communication?

Your Turn: Create an example for a linear and transactional communication situation. Explain it.

Whether an exchange is linear or transactional, the components highlighted so far influence the communication process and outcome. Let's examine the significance of each one and a few ways to maximize their application in our daily interactions. We'll start with senders and receivers.

Components of Interpersonal Communication

Sender and Receiver

Bruce Struik did something very sweet for his students. Nearly every day the high school teacher gave someone a cupcake. Four thousand cupcakes later, he was recognized at his retirement as the "Cupcake Man." For the last seven years, he kept an active list of all of his upperclassmen's birthdays. He had a custom cupcake made for each student. He picked the cupcake up on his way to school each morning and often personally delivered it to each student with a smile and a birthday card. He did this for students he didn't even know. For students with a summer birthday, each one received their own personalized cupcake the last day of school. He hoped his gesture sent a message that a student's birthday is a celebration of his or her life. Each student, he believed, needed to feel special, if not always, at least once a year. One boy nearly cried when he received his. Struik learned that the boy's parents forgot his birthday. Another girl, junior Kelly Veenstra, said that the day she received a cupcake, her father was in surgery for cancer in Ann Arbor. She said to Mr. Struik, "You don't know what this means to me." Junior Halieigh Heneveld, upon receiving her cupcake said to a reporter, "It makes you feel . . . blessed."[8]

In interpersonal communication, we send and receive messages. How we send and receive messages can significantly affect others. A sender encodes a message and transmits it. **Encoding** is the mental process of producing a message. The receiver decodes the message. **Decoding** is the mental process of interpreting or attaching meaning to a message.

How a message is encoded or decoded is influenced by the kind of relationship people have with each other—who people are to each other.[9] We call this their relational history. **Relational history** is how long people have known each other. This includes the number of past interactions and what happened when these interactions occurred. For example, we may think twice before saying something to someone we know very little or real well. We may joke a lot more with a certain friend or feel more loose lipped around family members compared to other people we know. Along with our relational history, our interpersonal communication is influence by meta-communication.

Do you alter your communication in any way, depending on who you are speaking to? Why? How does your relational history influence what you say or don't say?

When senders and receivers talk about past communication, how they are communicating now, or how they'd like to communicate in the future, this is called meta-communication. **Meta-communication** is communication about our communication.[10] For example, a couple may establish ground rules for how they are going to talk to each other about a thorny topic. Dante wants to let his girlfriend, Tianna, know he can't stand her best friend, Riesha. He knows he can't expect her to dump her best friend, but he does want to spend less time around Riesha. He says to her, "I want to tell you something, but I don't want you to get upset." Tianna says, "Tell me." Dante says, "Promise you'll hear me out completely before you say anything." Tianna replies "I will. I'll listen with an open mind, like we've talked about before. Let's sit down on the couch." Agreeing on how they will communicate with each other is meta-communication.

The following questions and statements represent or would likely trigger meta-communication:

- "What do you want me to do with this information?"
- "I was just kidding when I e-mailed that message."
- "How can we avoid getting in this kind of argument again?"
- "Let's not tell our parents."
- "It's not what you said; it's how you just said it."
- "I'd like you to not raise your voice at me when speaking."

© Lev Olkha, 2010. Used under license from Shutterstock, Inc.

Sometimes our messages are made clearer by talking about them. Like Tianna and Dante, we can steer our conversation in a more positive direction by clarifying what we are saying to each other and how we can communicate better now and in the future. At the end of this unit, there is an exercise designed to help us meta-communicate in a positive, productive way. Check it out and try this with some of the people you are close to. Next, let's take a look at another key component of interpersonal communication: messages.

. . . How does relational history and meta-communication influence the interaction of senders and receivers?

Message

Grand Rapids Press Columnist Tom Rademacher writes of a high school boy's basketball coach in Oklahoma whose team resoundingly overpowered another team 112 to 2. The coach played his first string exclusively until late in the second half, despite an obvious disparity in talent. Rademacher questions the coach's indifference to the opposing team's players, who had to feel embarrassed and dejected by the devastating loss. Why wait so long to substitute his top talent with his eager to play second or third stringers? Rademacher witnessed the beginning of a similar situation with his son's Rockford, Michigan team. The Rockford coach immediately substituted "vigorously." He rotated players and their positions to balance the talent scale, but at half-time, Rockford's squad amassed 32 points to Freesoil's 0. The Rockford coach then did something Rademacher felt displayed incredible consideration and sensitivity. The coach walked to the opposing team's listless bench and spoke to their coach. The Freesoil coach looked at him incredulously and said "You'd do that?"

Right then, players were traded. "In a flurry, kids started flinging jerseys. . . . Right there on the court. You give me some of your players, and I'll give you some of mine. Let's even this game out." While Freesoil conceded the "official game," sportsmanship and fun factored higher than the final score. Rademacher states: "There was something more important . . . how these kids would feel at the end of the game, at the end of the day . . . maybe even 10 or 20 years from now."[11] Both coaches sent a message to their players: "Winning is not everything."

A **message** is anything that communicates something. A message is verbal and/or nonverbal. **Verbal communication** involves the use of language, spoken or written, to convey meaning to others. When the basketball coaches discussed trading players, this was verbal communication. When the coaches had their teams switch players, this action communicated a nonverbal message. **Nonverbal communication** occurs when people create meaning without the use of language. Nonverbal messages are sent using eye contact, facial expressions, and vocal sounds.

A message is comprised of one or more symbols. A **symbol** is anything that represents something else. A symbol may consist of a letter, word, vocal sound, visual representation (such as a picture, object, article of clothing, or sign), or behavior. According to the late University of Chicago professor Herbert Blumer, we create meaning for certain symbols through our social interaction. Blumer's **symbolic interaction theory** represents the research and reflections of several other scholars, notably sociologist George Herbert Mead and Psychologist John Dewey.[12,13] According to the theory, people need to communicate with each other in order to establish what a symbol means. Once people agree on a symbol's meaning, they create mutual understanding.[14] For example, a scene between rebel leader Morpheus (Laurence Fishburne) and computer programmer by day, hacker at night Neo (Keanu Reeves) from *The Matrix (1999)* illustrates how the two use symbols to create shared meaning. Morpheaus offers Neo one of two pills :

Morpheus: "Take the blue pill and you continue down the rabbit hole. Take the red pill and you wake up at home like nothing happened."

Neo: (Takes the blue pill.)

Morpheus: "I imagine right now, you're feeling a bit like Alice. Hmm? Tumbling down the rabbit hole?"

Neo: "You could say that."

Morpheus: ". . . I know exactly what you mean. Let me tell you why you're here . . . You know something. What you know you can't explain, but you feel it. You've felt it your entire life, that there's something wrong with the world. You don't know what it is, but it's there, like a splinter in your mind, driving you mad . . . Do you know what I'm talking about?"

Neo: "The Matrix."[15]

Your Turn: Think of an example, like the scene from *The Matrix* between Morpheus and Neo, where you learned what a symbol means based on your social interaction with someone. Describe this.(Include the symbolic interaction theory, along with the concepts of message, symbols, and encoding/decoding in your response).

Morpheus' uses words (linguistic symbols) to explain to Neo what the red pill and blue pill mean. The "red pill" represented the status quo. The "blue pill" symbolized a reality check—an opportunity to know what is really happening in the world. By swallowing the blue pill, Neo communicated to Morpheus his willingness to go on a little adventure. As the two men talk, and the blue pill takes effect, Neo soon realizes that with the exception of a small number of renegade humans, the brain of every human on the planet is wired to a "virtual

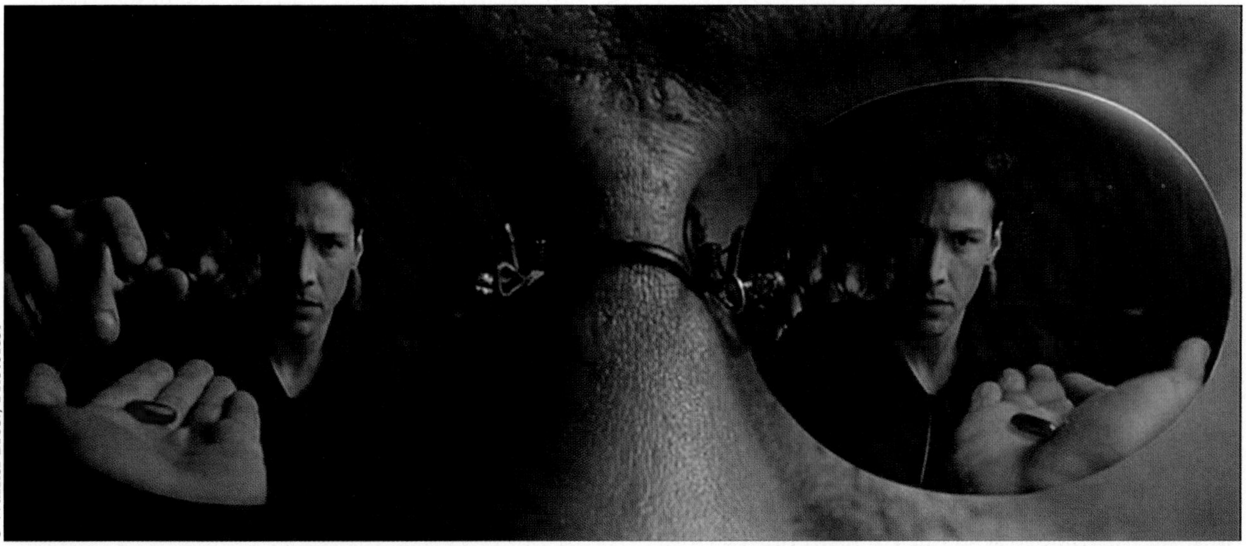

Morpheaus (Laurence Fishburne) and Neo's (Keanu Reeves)interaction helps them establish what meaning they both attach to "The Matrix" (1999).

reality" program called "The Matrix," which is controlled by a race of super computers. As both characters encode and decode this information, the word "Matrix" begins to represent the same thing for both of them. In addition to understanding how we attach meaning to symbols, it is important to understand symbols are influenced by culture.

The "a. o.k." sign we use in America means "everything is good." In France, it stands for "you have zero worth."In parts of Greece and Turkey it is a derogatory sexual gesture or nonverbal equivalent to the middle finger. To be able to smell a person's breath is considered a comfortable personal distance in parts of the Middle East, but in America this is generally a violation of one's personal space. Depending on where you live, the social group or the culture you belong to will attach different meanings to symbols.[16]

Communication scholars and authors Ron Adler and Neil Towne share this example in *Looking Out, Looking In* about pen manufacturer Parker Pen. When the company started selling ball-point pens in Mexico, its ads were intended to read, "It won't leak in your pocket and embarrass you." The company translated the words into Spanish but assumed the word "embarazar" meant to embarrass. When the ads hit billboards and magazines in Mexico, they read, "Our pen won't leak in your pocket and make you pregnant."[17]

Many symbols are bound by race, geographical regions, religion, history, and mass media. Unfortunately, when it comes to cultural differences, we consider them like we do our plumbing—not much, until things go bad. In unit eleven, we'll explore ways to increase our awareness of cultural influences on interpersonal messages. Along with culture, another important consideration when it comes to our messages is the channel we choose.

Think twice about doing this in France or Greece!

. . . How do we attach meaning to messages? How would you describe the symbolic interaction theory and importance of culture?

Channel

Best actress nominee Kate Winslet filed a libel lawsuit which will potentially cost her a lot of money in legal fees. Why? *Grazia* printed an article claiming Winslet was seeing a Chinese diet specialist to lose weight. Winslet has been publically critical of Hollywood's demand for super-skinny models and actresses. She's known for not bending to pressure to lose pounds for roles and is happy with her normal, healthy weight.

Winslet stated emphatically, "I will continue to say what I feel about this issue of women being . . . emaciated. It's out of control. . . . I know I'm a role model to young women. It's a role I take very seriously, and I would never want anyone to think I was a hypocrite in doing something like going to a diet doctor . . . " Her attorney says that Winslet is filing a suit to send a message. Her channel: legal proceedings![18]

Along with Winslet's court action, another recent legal maneuver made international headlines. A court ordered the International Tracing Service to publically reveal archives containing sixteen miles of files in six German buildings. For the first time, millions of documents detailing witness testimonies will now serve as channels describing the atrocities of the Nazis during WWII.

This information exposes the horror of six million Jews killed in death camps in a way never imagined. One file contains the testimony of a twenty-one-year-old Russian prisoner at Auschwitz who stated, "I saw with my own eyes, thousands of Jews gassed daily and thrown into pits . . . I saw how little children were killed with clubs and thrown into the fire . . . blood flowed in gutters . . . and Jews were cast alive in the flames."[19]

Kate Winslet's use of legal proceedings, and the International Tracing Service's newly opened files, are examples of channels. A **channel** is the means or how a message is sent. Channels or conduits can be picked up by the senses: sight, sound, smell, taste, and touch. Examples of channels can include a letter, one's voice, gifts, a sticky note, cologne, computer, or cell phone. An object can serve as a channel. A husband knowing that his wife was "allergic" to household chores, planted a magnet on the refrigerator door with a picture of Martha Stewart, branded with the caption "Martha Stewart doesn't live here." The next day the man came home to discover a magnet next to his, with "Neither does Bob Vila." "Martha Stewart doesn't live here!" is the message. The magnet is the channel.

In 2005, The NBA mandated that players dress professionally off court during league business and banned such things as chains, headbands, t-shirts, sleeveless shirts, and sunglasses indoors.[20] What do you think about this? How is this policy applicable to communication, particularly channels?

When we communicate, we typically use multiple channels. In the movie, *Message In A Bottle* (1999), Robin Wright Penn plays Theresa Osbourne, who, while walking the beach one day, discovers a bottle that has washed

A person's voicemail service is a channel. Here are a few samples of outgoing messages compliments of ahajokes.com:

"Hi, I am probably home. I'm just avoiding someone I don't like. Leave me a message. If I don't call back, it's you."

"Hi, this is John. If you are the phone company, I already sent the money. If you are my parents, please send me money. If you are my financial aid institution, you didn't lend me enough money. If you are one of my friends, you owe me money. If you are a beautiful woman, don't worry, I have plenty of money."

"This machine will gladly take your message; however, the owners do not need siding, windows or a hot tub. Their carpets are clean. They give to charity through the office, and like to mow their own lawn."

ashore. Inside is a beautiful letter with poetry that speaks to her soul. She seeks the author of the letter, and her search takes her to the banks of North Carolina and a sailboat builder Garret Blake, played by Kevin Costner. Blake used his words, the note, bottle, and ocean as his channels.

Compared to a bottle and the ocean's tide, a few taps on a keyboard and an electric current is a faster, more accurate way to get a message out. **Computer-mediated communication** utilizes computer technology (e-mail, instant messaging, and blogging) to transmit messages. In the movie *You've Got Mail (1998),* the main characters played by Tom Hanks and Meg Ryan create a relationship and fall in love by means of e-mail. In fact, e-mail is a primary channel used to develop some romantic relationships.

Research this! What is the difference between an introvert and extrovert? Is there any research suggesting introverts or extroverts use computer mediated communication differently?

Take Katherine Lester, a 4.0 seventeen-year-old at Akron-Fairgrove High School. After glancing at a guy's profile on MySpace.com, she initiated an on-line dating odyssey with twenty-year-old Palestinian Abdullah Jinzawi. They started chatting and were soon talking for two hours a day. Lester made national headlines when her parents discovered she had left the country and flew to the Middle East to meet and possibly marry Jinzawi. Lester lied to her parents about wanting to go on a shopping trip to Canada with friends to get them to help her obtain a passport. The FBI was notified and Lester was apprehended in Amman, Jordan. Lester and Jinzawi appeared on *Good Morning America* together and expressed their desire to marry.[21]

Lester and Jinzawi's story illustrates how many people rely on computer technology as a channel to create and maintain relationships—romantic and platonic. Social networking cites such as MySpace, Facebook, Twitter, Hi5, and LinkedIn are growing rapidly. Facebook, for example, has seen a surge in the number of people creating profiles and connecting with friends and family electronically. The number of people using Facebook has increased 144.9% since last year. As of January 4, 2010, 103,085,520 people used the site. New to Facebook this year, according to *Time Magazine*, is a unique service which allows people to send "real gifts" such as flowers to other users.

Without giving out other member's addresses, the on-line company will send the gift for you using the private address provided by the member when he or she signed up.[22]

How are social networking sites affecting the quality of interpersonal relationships? There is a lot of debate on this. Fans say it is a convenient, quick, and inexpensive way to connect with a lot of different people. Information disseminates quickly. This is certainly a desirable feature. Sometimes information spreads too fast. For example, two sisters in Australia learned that their brother had died in a car accident after reading rest in peace messages people were sending each other on Facebook. Hundreds of people knew about what happened to the family's son and brother before the family did.[23] Dissenters argue that on-line communication cannot replace the meaningful interaction one experiences when interacting with a person face-to-face. They say that it is a very passive activity in which people spend an inordinate amount of time soaking radiation from their monitors rather than going out with people doing fun activities and building memories.

Are social on-line networking sites as good as face-to face communication in terms of creating and building close relationships?

The uses and gratifications theory applies to our discussion regarding computer-mediated communication. It suggests people utilize certain channels such as television, computers, and cell phones to gain immediate and delayed rewards. In addition, this theory asserts that people choose to use certain technology (such as DVDs, iPods, magazines, and software programs) based on the rewards they receive (escapism, entertainment, convenient access to people and information) relative to what it costs them (time, money, and effort).[24] Do you agree with this theory? Why or why not? Fifty years ago, researcher Marshal McLuhan, proposed another theory which posits that there is a symbiotic relationship between humans and electronic media. His **media ecology theory** suggests people create certain technologies and in-turn, these technologies end up recreating who we are. He argued that the media influences every aspect of society, shaping and reorganizing our beliefs, perceptions, and values. Do you agree with this theory? Why or why not?[25,26]

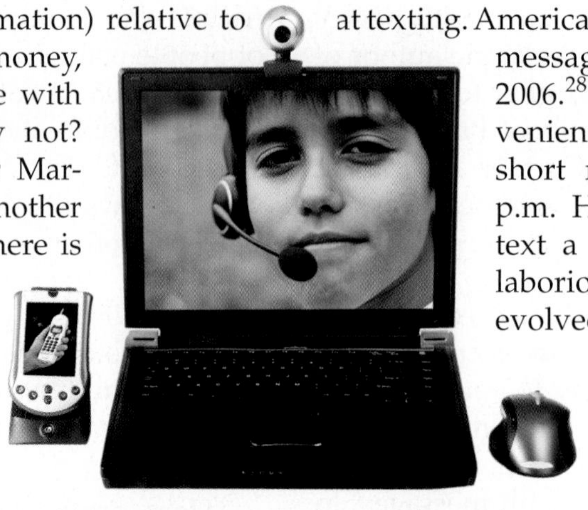

Laptop video conferencing technology enables people to communicate in virtual "real" time just about anywhere, anytime.
© Christopher Meder-Photography, 2010. Used under license from Shutterstock, Inc.

There are certain pros and cons associated with using various channels. Let's take a look at texting. Americans sent sixty-five billion text messages in the first six months of 2006.[28] Texting is a quick and convenient way to shoot a person a short message—"Applebees 5:00 p.m. Happy Hour. Be there." To text a person a long message is laborious. A cybershort-hand has evolved to allow people to send messages quickly. Letters are used to substitute for words. Examples include: SWAK, g2g, lol, btw, 2g2bt, np, nmu?, hbu?, jk!, cyl.

Texting is great especially when we don't feel like taking the time to talk to someone on the phone. Sending someone a text message also allows us to leave people information that they can refer to later on such as directions or reminders.

10 Most frequent uses of the Internet by Americans.

Activity	Number of Users
Use e-mail	58,000,000
Get News	35,000,000
Check Weather	25,000,000
Job Search	24,000,000
Access political info	24,000,000
Learn about a product	19,000,000
Send Instant Message	15,000,000
Search for Schools	14,000,000
Get travel information	10,000,000[27]

"I had this guy leave me a voicemail at work, so I called him at home, and then he e-mailed me to my Blackberry, and so I texted it to his cell, then he e-mailed me to my home account, and the whole thing just got out of control. I miss the days where you have one phone number, and one answering machine, and that one answering machine housed one cassette tape, and that one cassette tape either had a message from the guy or did not. . . . Now you just have to go around checking all these different portals just to get rejected by seven different technologies—it is exhausting."

Mary, (Drew Barrymore) from
He's just Not That Into You
(2009)

© Tyler Olson, 2010. Used under license from Shutterstock, Inc.

Six high school students in Pennsylvania face child porn charges and may be registered as sex offenders for a minimum of ten years after school officials found nude photos of fourteen and fifteen-year-old girls on a student's cell phone. Police investigators found similar pictures on other teen cell phones."Sexting" is sending nude or semi-nude photos via text messaging.[29]

On the flip side, texting is also criticized for several reasons. First, it is often intrusive. Have you ever heard someone say, "Do you really need to be texting right now?" Many special moments and conversations are interrupted by ringing cell phones and text alerts. In addition, texting is the cause of numerous automobile accidents. On July 1, 2008 California joined New York, Washington State, Germany, and Australia in fining drivers who use hand held cell phones and/or text while driving. The laws vary from outright bans to restrictions on certain drivers such as those under the age of eighteen.[30] Along with the channels we use, another important component to interpersonal communication is feedback.

© Elliot Westacott, 2010. Used under license from Shutterstock, Inc.

"I'll admit it. I'm addicted to text messaging. Morning, noon, and night I'm packing away at those buttons and firing off messages at lightning speech. It hasn't always been that way. Just a few years back I never sent a text in my life. Didn't understand the draw. Until now!"

Amber

Your Turn: What are the pros and cons associated with the following channels? Along with your observations, do some research and come back to class with the results of any studies or facts you find.

	Pros	Cons
E-mail		
Instant Messaging		
Chat Groups		
Texting		
Cell Phones		
Letters		
Blogging		

. . . How would you summarize what this section addresses about channels?

Feedback

In Michael Jordon's *Driven From Within*, Fred Whitfield writes of a rift that occurred between Jordan and his long time friend Lance Blanks. The two met at a basketball camp in North Carolina. A friendship flourished between the Pistons and Bulls stars despite the fact that they played against each other at times. In the final game of the 1991 playoffs, Detroit was swept by the Bulls. At the end of the final game, tensions ran high and Isaiah Thomas and some of the Pistons players decided to walk past the Bulls bench without shaking hands or offering their congratulations. Blanks was a rookie on a championship team and didn't know what to do. He followed Thomas' lead and completely ignored Jordan. Several weeks later, the two were about to play a game at a camp they were attending. Without procuring an explanation from Blanks about his behavior, Jordon gave Blanks a verbal lashing: "I thought we were friends. You walk off the court without saying a word. I thought we were bigger than that. I am going to bust your ___ right here in front of everybody. I'm going to embarrass you today." Jordon did just that. He pummeled Blanks. After the game, Blanks didn't talk to Jordan. The two didn't speak to each other for ten years. One day, at a pre-draft conference, Blanks approached Jordan and explained the circumstances and apologized. Jordan shared with Blanks how he felt and accepted his apology. The feedback, albeit ten years late, put the friendship back on track.[31]

Feedback is a verbal and/or nonverbal response to a message. We may choose any number of channels to respond to someone's message. Feedback may come in the form of a letter one writes to express appreciation for a kind act. One woman wrote a letter to the editor of a town's newspaper to thank a person who found her wallet at a Target store. Everything important to her such as her passport, debit and credit cards, cash, checkbook, driver's license, and more was in it. It was returned unopened, with not a dollar missing. She was so moved and appreciative, she wrote a letter to the editor, hoping the person who did this anonymous act would get her message.

We receive feedback when a person responds with a smile, nod, laugh, or a question such as, "What makes you say that?" Something like silence on the phone is a nonverbal form of feedback. Feedback lets us know communication has occurred, how it was received, and whether it was acted upon. A lack of feedback may cause some serious problems. One woman writes to a relationship expert:

"My husband, 'Paul' will not talk about things that worry him. I guess he thinks if he doesn't talk about it, it will be all right. There is no touching in our marriage . . . no romance. He feels that as long as he works hard for his family, nothing is wrong. But I need more. How do I let him know?" [32]

From a communication standpoint, what should Paul's wife say or do? Author Lois Wyse is quoted as saying, "I suppose it was something you said that caused me to tighten and pull away. And when you asked, 'What is it?' I of course said, 'nothing.' When I say 'nothing,' you may be certain there is something." Can you relate to this? Either you couldn't get a person to give you the feedback you needed, or you said something to someone but meant something entirely different. Sometimes the feedback we give and receive is clear, other times it is hard to decipher. [33]

In order to create successful communication, we need to gauge it. We accomplish this with feedback. No feedback, too little feedback, too much feedback, or the wrong kind of feedback can wreak communication and relational havoc. We'll explore ways to improve the quality of our listening and feedback in unit 8.

. . . What is feedback and why is it important?

Context or Environment

Stephen Fried is the author of "Confessions of a Naked Man," an article which takes a revealing look at the things men share with each other while naked in the sauna, a sort of male version of the "Ya-Ya Sisterhood." He coins it the "Yada-Yada Brotherhood." He writes that when he shares some of his "Chest Hair Dialogues" with his wife, she feels he is "cheating on her conversationally." He sympathizes with her jealousy, recognizing that he could open his world to her more, but appears to relish the kind of exchange that men have with other men.

Fried writes of the locker-room one-upmanship, wife bashing, sports play-by-play, trash talk, and political commentary. He observes how the conversations differ when men are in the sauna versus the changing area. Some of the conversations are rich and revealing: "I've heard naked guys say wonderfully moving things about their wives and families, things they'd probably never said to their wives and families." One man, dressed only in his socks, asked him what his plans were for the evening. When Fried said that his wife was gone for the weekend and that he'd be a bachelor, the man said, "Don't do anything stupid while she's away. It's not worth it. Believe me, I know." Fried says that that level of candor is frequent. It is unique to this context or environment.[34] People communicate differently based on who they are speaking to and where they are. Why do people share their most intimate secrets with total strangers? What makes us say what we say to a stranger on a plane, a buddy on the green, a bartender at the pub, or a hairstylist at the salon?

All communication takes place in a context or environment. The context includes the time, place, physical surroundings, and people involved when communication occurs. Physical aspects may include lighting, temperature, seating arrangements, room size, and space between participants.

People bring certain expectations to a given context or environment. Communication is influenced by how much participants know each other, the kind of relationship they have, and the roles and expectations which have emerged based on previous interactions.[35,36] Not only do we expect people to behave a certain way based on previous interactions we've had with them, but on what is considered customary or appropriate for a given context. People are generally expected to behave and interact a certain way at a funeral, comedy club, religious service, or Detroit Red Wings hockey game. The **expectancy violation theory**, originated by University of Arizona communications and family development professor Judee Burgoon, purports that people will react to behavior which is not typical of a person or for a given context. When individuals say or do something uncharacteristic or unusual, people who witness this are emotionally aroused. They will then make cognitive appraisals of the behavior, which they'll interpret as either "good" or "bad."[37,38,39] Certainly, rapper Kanye West caused a stir when he stormed the stage during the Video Music Awards and took the microphone away from 2009 Female Video winner Taylor Swift. West interrupted Swift's live acceptance speech and proceeded to rant about the results saying, "Beyonce had one of the best videos of all time." Swift stood there stunned and members of the audience booed the rapper. The audience reaction illustrates the expectancy violation theory. It is expected that audience members politely listen to an award recipient while he or she accepts the award and gives a brief speech. West violated a significant social norm for an awards ceremony.

People often factor in the environment to accomplish their communication goals. Why is it that a man may take his fiancé to a fancy restaurant to break off the engagement? He is the bearer of bad news. He is betting his filet mignon that the expensive dishware will discourage plate throwing. He hopes his soon-to-be-ex will adhere to the social etiquette people associate with fine dining. No yelling. No cursing. No sobbing. No drama. No tossing him around like her dinner salad. The ambiance is meant to facilitate a graceful bow-out.

Couples may coordinate colors to express their attachment to each other.

Ever go to a comedy club? What did you notice about the lighting and seating? Were small round tables scrunched together? Was the room dimly lit? Was there a stage with a spotlight focused on the comedian? Club after club, you see the same thing: crowded seating, a stage, spotlight, and a darkened room. Why is this so common? Club owners have learned that people laugh more when they feel anonymous. They're more likely to whoop it up, cut loose, and otherwise let their hair down if they don't feel self-conscious. So, club owners pack us like sardines in the dark to draw out a hearty laugh. The stage elevates the performer and the spotlight focuses attention on the comedian to discourage table talk and side conversations. The context is manipulated for a desired effect. Teachers also alter the environment to enhance learning in the classroom. They often seat talkative kids next to more reserved, quiet students to spread out the talkers and reduce chatter.

The size of a room, brightness of lights, opportunities for distractions, room temperature, and arrangements of chairs affect the success of a conversation. People generally feel more apt to express their ideas and converse more when seated in a circle. People associate soft lighting with calmness and bright lights with activity.[40] The color of a room can affect people's moods. Color communicates. Studies suggest people generally perceive that the following colors have an emotional impact on people:

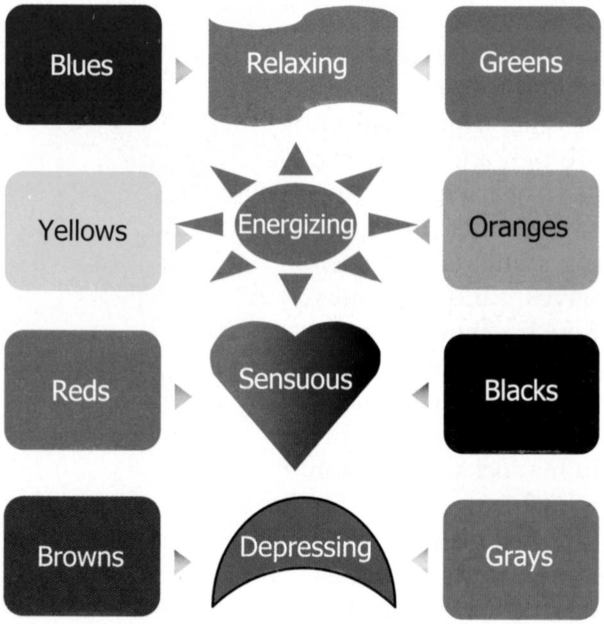

Competent communicators appreciate how the context or environment influences interpersonal communication. They select the best context or alter it to enhance interaction or increase the likelihood of a successful communication outcome. Another important component in interpersonal communication we can exert control over is the presence of noise.

In what ways have you altered the context or environment to improve communication with someone? Has this ever included "not inviting" certain people to a social event? Why did you do this?"

. . . How might a communicator manipulate the environment to enhance communication?

Noise

Lauren Upton, Miss Teen South Carolina, blamed her stage anxiety for her discombobulated response to a live question from a panelist during a Miss Teen USA pageant. When asked the question, "Recent polls have shown that a fifth of Americans can't locate the U.S. on a world map. Why do you think this is?" Upton replied:

> *"I personally believe that U.S. Americans are unable to do so because . . . uh . . . some people there in our nation don't have maps . . . and uh . . . I believe that our education, like such as in South Africa and uh the Iraq, everywhere, like, such as . . . and I believe that they should . . . Our education over here in the U.S. should help the U.S . . . or should help South Africa and should help the Iraq and the Asian countries. So we will be able to build up our future. . . ."*[43]

Like Upton, something interfered with actor Danny Devito's ability to communicate effectively. Devito appeared "live" (sort of) on the November 29, 2007 daytime talk show *The View*. I say "sort of" because he appeared inebriated after drinking eleven shots of Italian liqueur with boy pal George Clooney the night before. During the interview, Devito burped loudly, slurred his words, and was bleeped twice for swearing. He apparently didn't leave a good impression, raising speculation that he was *persona non grata* on the talk show. Sometimes we say and do things we normally wouldn't because alcohol can limit our ability to think clearly and rationally.

Lauren Upton and Danny Devito, experienced noise in the form of anxiety and alcohol. **Noise** is anything that can distort, interfere with, or make communication difficult. It can occur at any point in the communication process. **There are three types of noise: internal, external, and semantic.**

Internal Noise

Internal noise is anything that occurs within a person's mind (psychological) and body (physiological). **Psychological noise** includes day-daydreaming, preoccupation, inattentiveness, rapid thought, stress, and anxiety. **Physiological noise** may include a headache, fatigue, hunger, an itch, indigestion, and pain. Internal noise is often the result of both physiological and psychological causes as both tend to influence the other.

"Once I was pulled over for suspected DUI. The officer standing over me at my window was a source of external noise. While I was not drunk at all, just having some reckless fun, it was still very serious. I got so nervous (internal noise), that I kept interrupting the officer and trying to explain myself before he could even finish a statement. This really irked him and this led to a sobriety test and cumbersome interrogation."

Brandy

External Noise

Have you ever found yourself wanting to cut off a conversation to escape a smoke-filled room or a person's overzealous application of cologne? A person's speech pattern, a high-pitched or nasal voice, yelling, or behaviors such as cracking one's knuckles, chewing with one's mouth open, or gum smacking is equivalent to fingernails scratching a chalkboard for some people.

External noise is anything occurring outside of our mind or body which can make communication difficult. A flickering light in a classroom, poor cell phone reception, or a room's thermostat set too high or low can make one nervy. On the internet, spam and pop-ups are a source of noise. Have you ever tried talking to someone who was transfixed on her computer game or television? Both are typical sources of external noise.

Multi-tasking is an example of external noise.

Semantic Noise

Semantic noise occurs when either the sender or receiver doesn't understand the other's language. If Lance speaks only Spanish and Miguel speaks English exclusively, the communication between them will be difficult. If people use abbreviations or technical jargon such as "DSM 3R", "APA.," or "taxonomy," and there is no shared meaning for these words, semantic noise is present. For example, when John starts talking to Mike about "fly space," "wings" or "scrim," Mike is likely to be confused unless he is familiar with theater and shares the same understanding as John. Surfers, computer enthusiasts, firefighters, and ham radio operators have their own lingo.

Various fields of study and occupations create their own terminology. Patients commonly complain that they struggle to understand their primary care physicians because they use medical jargon that leaves them confused. In addition to understanding how noise may influence communication, we need to also appreciate this last component: frame of reference.

. . . What are the different types of noise? What are some effective strategies for dealing with noise?

Your Turn: Have you encountered either internal, external, or semantic noise in your communication lately? What was it, and how did you handle it?

"I'm a diehard Notre Dame fan. When my girlfriend notices that I'm not paying attention to her she'll say "Notre Dame" in the middle of her sentence to catch my ear. I'll say, "What, what did you say? Did you say Notre Dame?"

Gabe

Frame of Reference

A 19-year-old-girl received an apology from a bus company after she and her boyfriend were kicked off the bus by one of its drivers. The driver ordered them off the bus after exclaiming "We don't let freaks and dogs like you on?" Her offense? Dressed in black, Gothic-style attire, she wore a dog collar around her neck. Her 25-year-old fiancé walked behind her holding the end of a dog leash that was attached to the dog collar, just like a dog owner who is walking his or her dog. She was offended by the bus driver's mean spirited comment and action. She described herself as a human pet. "I am generally animal-like, and I lead a really easy life. I don't cook or clean, and I don't go anywhere without Dan (her fiancé). It might seem strange, but it makes us both happy. It's my lifestyle and my choice. It isn't hurting anyone."[44] The girl's choice to walk leashed to her boyfriend and the bus driver's reaction reflects differences in frame of reference.

On a similar vein, R & B singer Robin Thicke decided to go public with his displeasure over *Vibe* magazine's refusal to place his picture on the cover of the magazine, saying *"I can't be on the cover cause' I'm white."* In an interview with Billboard magazine, Thicke stated that during his interview with Vibe, he expressed how much he loved the magazine and would be thrilled to be on the cover. He asserts he was told that Vibe doesn't put white artists on the cover. The magazine made an exception by putting Eminem on the cover, but it wouldn't do that for Thicke. Thicke refused to state that he considered it reverse discrimination; however, he was quoted as saying "You can't always expect people to be as color blind or open-minded as you want."[45]

How is a gay couple's frame of reference different from a straight couples? Similar?

Thicke's reaction was influenced, to some extent, by his race. His decision to openly question Vibe's artistic tradition and voice discontent to another magazine reflected his frame of reference. Besides his race, Thicke is a talented, successful musician, who has reached international stardom. He loves *Vibe* magazine and reads it religiously. He has wanted to be on the cover for a long time. If any of these factors, which make up his frame of reference, were not present, Thicke may not have even asked to be on the cover or may not have been offended that his request was denied.

Frame of reference is a person's collective experience. This is everything that has happened throughout one's life. This can include one's education, life experiences, talents, gender, sexual orientation, cultural or racial background, exposure to other cultures, and religious upbringing.

A person's frame of reference is an inner filter which colors and shapes one's perception—how he or she sees the world. It is the basis for one's subjective evaluation of what is appropriate or inappropriate, right or wrong, desirable or undesirable, important or unimportant, normal or abnormal.

If you are single and interested in dating, what would be your response be to a friend's offer to line you up with a blind date? If you experienced bad blind dates in the past, what are you likely to say? What if you've had only good experiences? Your frame of reference will influence how you react to this opportunity. Have you ever had dinner at a friend's house when you were a kid? Did you notice how his or her family interacted at the dinner table? How were their interactions different compared to your family? Were they chatty or did they eat in relative silence? If someone didn't like the soup, did the mother act like the Soup Nazi from *The Jerry Seinfeld* show? How were their table manners compared to that of your family? Did they openly discuss topics that in your household were "taboo?" These differences stem from a history of interactions that took place prior to you being there. A difference in terms of frame of reference.

A British schoolteacher in Sudan, Gillian Gibbons, did not intend to insult Islam when she decided it was okay to let her class of seven-year-olds name the class teddy bear Mohammed. When word spread of this, crowds gathered in the streets to protest, with some calling for her execution. Gibbons was arrested for fifteen days until President Omar al-Bashir pardoned her. Something about Gibbon's frame of reference led her to say "ok" to her students' request. It may be that the children came up with the idea to name the teddy bear Mohhamed and were excited about it. Perhaps, Gibbon's simply was not aware of Islam's strict tenets concerning how the prophet Mohammed's name should be used.[46]

. . . Why is it important to factor a person's frame of reference when we communicate interpersonally?

Each person in a given communication context brings his or her own life experiences to the situation. For example, one study suggests that college students who took a debate class prior to the study were more expressive and verbally aggressive compared to those who did not experience a debate class.[47] Since frame of reference has such a significant influence on our interpersonal communication, we'll devote an entire unit to it, unit 11. We now have a better understanding of the components of interpersonal communication: sender, receiver, message, channel, feedback, context, noise, and frame of reference. **Next, let's work on improving our interpersonal communication in the following five ways:**

- **Know when it is best not to send or receive messages.**
- **Reduce and clarify mixed messages.**
- **Choose channels strategically.**
- **Identify and eliminate sources of noise.**
- **Alter the environment to enhance interaction.**

Five Ways to Improve the Interpersonal Communication Process

Sometimes people will ask us to relay a message to someone because they "can't," don't want to, or lack the time. They may think that it's not their place to say anything. They may ask us to speak for them because they predict the message will be received better. On the flip side, **people may, at times,tell us TMI or too much information.** Like a scratched CD, this person's message is unnerving because it's too graphic or personal. Perhaps we've heard this information too many times and need a break from it.

Know When it is Best Not to Send or Receive Messages

An important question to consider often is, "Am I the most appropriate sender or receiver of this message?" We need, at times, to weigh the pros and cons. For example, if we assume the role of a sender or receiver of a message, we may place ourselves in a situation called triangular communication. **Triangular communication involves three people, with one serving as a "go-between" or liaison for the other two.** While this may serve a useful purpose in some situations, what are some reasons why this may not be prudent?

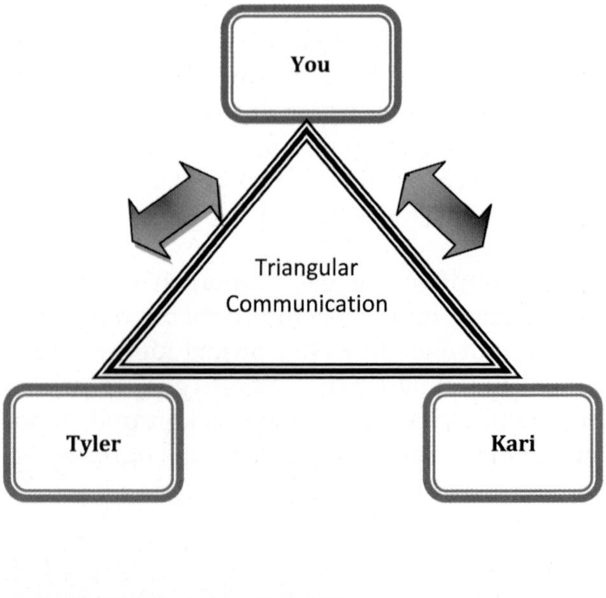

Imagine your friends Tyler and Kari are experiencing significant relationship difficulties. Like the triangular diagram shows, they avoid talking to each other about their issues. They talk to you instead. You begin to speak to each of them on the other's behalf. Before you know it, you are now taking on their problem, trying to help them resolve it. This may get time consuming and emotionally exhausting. You may start giving Tyler and Kari advice. What if you suggest something to Tyler that he tries with Kari and it backfires. Tyler may get mad at you. If you communicate an opinion you have about Kari to Tyler, he may take your comment and use it as ammo against Kari. In a heated argument with Kari, Tyler may say, "Even {insert your name here} thinks you're manic." Now you're in a roller derby with Kari. Kari or Tyler may perceive that you are taking sides. This may, indeed, occur. As you get "pulled in" to their conflict, you may lose your objectivity. Your biases may surface through your communication.

Despite our best intentions, we may want to "pull out" of this Bermuda triangular situation before friendships disappear. If we were friends with Tyler and Kari, we can encourage direct communication by suggesting, "Have you spoken to him/her about this?" We may also encourage both of them to seek the assistance of a trained therapist or trusted mediator. We may also state:

- "This is really awkward for me because I like you both, and I don't want to get caught in the middle."
- "I'm feeling uncomfortable hearing this."
- "I've heard this several times now. I need a break from this topic for a while."

Can you think of situations where triangular communication is appropriate or necessary?

If a person asks us for clarification regarding any of the aforementioned statements, we can lay it out tactfully using an **"I feel . . . because. . . I need"** statement, which research suggests is clear and assertive, and generally not perceived as too harsh or antagonistic:[48]

- **"I feel** uncomfortable telling him this information **because** I don't have all the facts. "**I need** you to discuss this with him."
- "**I feel** uneasy about the jokes you are making **because** I have friends who are gay. **I need** you to respect this."

Your Turn: Create your own "I feel . . . because . . . I need" statement in response to a message you don't want to receive or send.

Reduce and clarify mixed messages

When our verbal message contradicts our non-verbal message, we are sending a mixed message. We may say to someone, "I'll be right there," but take more than an hour to do so. We may say "I don't want to talk right now," but continue talking. We may exclaim, "I'm not angry," just as we're yelling. Each time we run into our friend Hadria, we say, "We've got to get together" or "I'll give you a call," but we never do. This, too, is a mixed message. Research suggests that adults rely on nonverbal messages to determine the true intent of a speaker's message.[49] In other words, they are more likely to believe what isn't being said![50,51] So, if you say you're not embarrassed, but your face is beet red, what's the word?

Mixed Message:"I'm not looking!"

One way to develop greater communication competence is to recognize when we are sending mixed messages. For example, Greg may say, "I know I said I'd like to go; however, I know I said it without much enthusiasm. I'm realizing that I'm not that interested in going." **We can also tactfully clarify when others send us mixed messages.** Research suggests that making an objective observation starting with the pronoun "I" such as "I recall . . . . I sense . . . . I noticed . . . . I heard . . . . I saw . . . . "is less intimidating and confrontational, especially when we express it in a pleasant, calm, soft voice.[52,53]

We may say to a colleague, "Lance, I heard you say yesterday that you support my idea. I also heard today from other staff members that you think otherwise. What do you think of my idea?" We are trying to get clarification on a mixed message. We are doing this in a way that is clear and less provocative. Here are some other examples:

I heard you say you're not mad. I also noticed you are not speaking to me. (observation of mixed message)

What are you feeling? (question for clarification)

I remember you said earlier you were "in the mood."I just kissed your neck and rubbed your ears and you're not responding. (observation of mixed message)

Have your feelings changed? (question for clarification)

Your Turn: Like the examples above, write an "I statement" (I sense . . . . I notice . . . . I heard . . . . I saw . . .) to identify themixed message and ask a question for clarification.

Choose Channels Strategically

Competent communicators use channels which are more likely to produce positive communication outcomes and are best suited for a situation. Kimberly, one of my students, shared how frustrating it can be to get her six-year-old child to follow directions. "It drove me crazy to keep telling him to do things day in and day out. I now have a color chart he looks at daily and checks things off when things are done. It's tied to a reward program. I also find that he reads a lot of the things I say to him because he loves this new channel of communication. I also write notes praising him for his effort."

All channels have strengths and weaknesses. Sometimes, when one channel fails, we need to try something else. For example, a college student shared her struggle to get along with her roommate with a counselor who posts an advice column for students living in the residence halls at Ball State University. "My roommate and I just can't . . . get along. When there is something wrong she acts too afraid to be confronted and rarely says more than one word to me unless I initiate a conversation. She lacks respect for me by having her boyfriend up all the time, making it seem like I need to leave so they can have 'alone time' . . . plus she does loud activities while I'm trying to sleep. I wrote a letter to her once, but she didn't respond and not much changed. I need to confront our issues once again before she drives me mad."[54]

Her use of a letter did not seem to work. There are, however, advantages to expressing our thoughts in writing using a letter or an e-mail as our channel. An advantage is it allows us to think things through. We can type out our thoughts, read them, and rewrite or edit them before they are sent. Some people find it helpful to write something down when their emotions are raw or intense. They come back to it a day or two later and revise their writing to reflect how they feel at a later time.

One disadvantage about using written communication is that it's hard to refute. Once it gets in the hands, computer, or cell phone of another person, it is now a document or record, which can be used against us.

Therefore, as communicators, we need to be careful about what we send in terms of letters, texts, pictures, and e-mails. Written communication may be accessed by other people or shared in ways we don't intend. It may serve as proof in a legal proceeding or employment investigation. This can work in our favor too, depending on the circumstances.

Another disadvantage to sending people written messages is **message overload**. The average American employee receives 50 e-mails a day. A corporate manager typically distributes and reads in excess of 100 documents a day. When we experience message overload, research indicates that we rely on shorthand to respond, which increases the likelihood of errors and mistakes.[55] We also tend to focus our attention on the messages that are simpler or easier to respond to, and put off the messages that are more detailed and time-consuming to respond to.[56] It is, at times, difficult to determine which e-mail messages need immediate attention or when to keep or delete messages.

Another complaint lodged at e-mail communication is the frequency in which people tend to misread them. A manager sends an e-mail message that some employees interpret as critical and condescending. They are upset. This wasn't the manager's intention. She realizes that the information probably needed to be shared face-to-face with all involved. Why would this be the case?

An e-mail or text message is considered **channel lean** because it involves only a few sensory inputs to derive meaning from—words and the use of computer technology. People sometimes have a tough time deciphering the meaning or motive behind a word. Words have various meanings. It is also difficult to convey emotions via e-mails and other forms of written communication. Professors Justin Kruger of New York University and Nicholas Epley of the University of Chicago studied the ability of e-mail senders and receivers to accurately encode and decode emotions. They found that sarcasm for example, was very difficult to convey and decipher.[57] Some e-mail users try to compensate for this channel lean conduit by using emoticons. **Emoticons** are symbols using a keyboard to represent an emotion or an emotional reaction. Symbols, such as :) represents a smile and :D represents a laugh or laughing. The first emoticon to appear online was a smiley. It made its début on September 19, 1982 on a bulletin board posting.[58]

Research this! Who uses emoticons more in their online communication? Men or women? Go to: Wolf, A. (2000). Emotional expression online: Gender differences in emoticon use. *CyberPsychology & Behavior*, **3, 827–833.**

In addition to the difficulties which occur when people apply their own meaning to a word, there is no telling when someone is actually going to read and respond to our e-mail or text message, or if the person even received it, especially with today's sophisticated spam blockers.

Channel rich means that a communication approach provides more immediate and comprehensive sensory information. Research conducted by Columbia University Professor Michael Morris suggests that when negotiators communicate face-to-face, they exchange three times more information as they would via e-mail.[59,60] For example, when you speak face-to-face you are picking up on a lot more than just words, you are also able to take in a person's voice, dress, smell, gestures, facial expressions, posture, and eye movements in real time.

Since face-to-face communication is considered transactional, we can send and receive messages simultaneously. If I begin to say something, and your face flashes a quizzical look, I can instantly respond to your communication by asking a question such as, "Did I say something that was confusing to you?" There's more immediate feedback. We have a quicker way to clarify things and reduce miscommunication.

According to a January 2010 article in the *Journal of Public Relations Research*, researchers Candace White, Antoaneta Vance, and Gena Stafford report workers see on-line communication as an efficient way to send information such as updates, reminders, agendas, and minutes from meetings; however they value the dialogic or face-to-face interaction with managers. While they acknowledged that meetings were time-consuming at times, their perceptions are that this communication context produces better results when it comes to solving problems, building rapport, and making decisions.[61] Communication scholars generally agree on these guidelines when it comes to on-line communication:

- Avoid using on-line sources or text messaging to address problems or controversial topics.
- Conduct communication face-to-face with people privately and with only those who need to be present when the issue is high stakes or personal in nature.
- Avoid using e-mails to issue reprimands or announce dismissals.
- Be sure to get permission from someone before sending out an e-mail about his or her hospitalization, accident, or death in the family. While our intentions may be to inform others so they can join us in offering condolences and support, a person may want this information kept private.[62]

Recognize and Eliminate Noise

Two co-workers carry on a conversation near a work station about a new office policy, and others decide to join the conversation uninvited. Seeing this as a hindrance, the two step into a private office and close the door.

While driving, a couple tries to discuss what to do about their overspending while their two-year-old is screaming infantile obscenities in the backseat. They recognize this high decibel interruption as a significant source of noise and postpone their conversation until later.

We may say to someone, "I'm starting to sweat, which wouldn't be a problem if we were in a sauna. Is this room hot or is it just me?" If the person we are speaking to agrees, we may decide to lower the room's thermostat or open a window to get more comfortable.

These three scenarios illustrate that **it is a sound communication practice to recognize the source of noise and eliminate it if possible.** We also can let people know when we are experiencing noise. Letting a person know what's going on with us reduces the likelihood that he or she will misread anything we say or do. If someone is trying to talk to us about something of significance, and we are ravenously hungry, like one of the walking dead fixed on eating Columbus (Jesse Esenberg) and Tallahasse (Woody Harrelson) in *Zombieland* (2009), we may want to say, "I haven't eaten all day and all I can think of is take-out right now, can we talk about this after I get something to eat?" We may also say, "I'm a little tense about some things that happened at work today, so if I seem short, please don't take it personally." If we seem impatient, spacey, or aloof, people are less likely to assume the worst if we tell them what is influencing our ability to communicate effectively.

Approach People Tactically

When it comes to manipulating the environment to aid communication, another consideration is how we time things. We've heard the adage, "timing is everything." If two coworkers approach an otherwise cool, calm, and collected nursing supervisor about changing the work schedule, the supervisor may blow a gasket, because at that moment, he is hyper-agitated or stressed out.

First thing in the morning or late at night when people are groggy is not ideal to conduct conversations of substantial importance. Conversely, right before or after lunch when people are either hungry or digesting may not be the most opportune time to communicate.

There is an interesting area of thought called circadian or biorhythm theory. This theory suggests that our bodies weave in and out of natural cycles that control appetite, energy, mood, sleep, and libido within a 24-hour period. It suggests people reach their peak energy and productivity levels at different times during the day.[63] For some, it is first thing in the morning, for others the afternoon or evening. Ideally, we'd like to communicate important things during these peak times.

Competent communicators don't assume that the person they wish to speak to is in the best state of mind at that time. So they may ask, "I'd like to talk about our plans for the weekend. Is this a good time for you to talk?" If the person says no, the logical thing to do is to postpone the conversation until a mutually agreed-upon time.

. . . How would you summarize the five strategies for improving the interpersonal communication process?

Unit Summary

Over the years, communication scholars have studied the process of interpersonal communication. They have devised models to explain it. Unit two introduces two of them: linear and transactional. Scholars have also identified the components involved in interpersonal communication. These components include sender/receiver, message, channel, feedback, environment, noise, and frame of reference. We can improve how we communicate by determining when it is best not to be a sender or receiver. We also can avoid and effectively respond to mixed messages. Competent communicators also choose the best channels to increase the clarity of a message and reduce the likelihood of miscommunication. They factor in the context or environment, altering it when feasible in order to enhance an interaction. Finally, effective communicators identify and eliminate noise and consider a person's frame of reference.

Key Questions

1. What are the components of interpersonal communication?How would you describe them?
2. What is the difference between linear and transactional communication?
3. How might we determine if we are an appropriate sender or receiver of a message?
4. When it comes to the messages we send, why is it prudent to consider the frequency and positive value of meta-messages, the influence of culture, and how best to reduce and respond to mixed messages?
5. What should we consider when choosing a channel to relay a message?
6. How might a communicator manipulate the environment to enhance communication?
7. What are the different types of noise? What are some strategies for dealing with noise?
8. Why is it important to factor a person's frame of reference when we communicate interpersonally?
9. What does it mean when we say that a competent communicator knows when not to be a sender or receiver?
10. How would you describe the importance of timing when approaching a person?

Vocabulary Playback

Sender
Receiver
Message
Channel
Context
Feedback
Noise
Physiological Noise
Psychological Noise
External Noise
Semantic Noise
Frame of Reference
Linear Model
Transactional Model
Verbal Messages
Nonverbal Messages
Relational History
Symbols
Meta-communication
Mixed Message
Computer Mediated
Message Overload
Channel Lean
Channel Rich
Emoticons

Theoretically Speaking

- Symbolic Interaction Theory
- Uses & Gratification Theory
- Media Ecology Theory
- Expectancy Violation Theory
- Circadian Rhythm Theory

Focus Group/Class Discussion

- Under what circumstances is it considered rude to text message or use your cell phone? What are some rules for proper phone etiquette?
- Do you think cell phone usage, including text messaging, is addictive? Why or why not?
- Olive Riley was the world's oldest known blogger. The 108-year-old Australian woman used online technology as a channel to chronicle her life, including nearly seventy entries in what she called her "blob" and several "you tube" videos. Her amazing memory and penchant for storytelling captured the hearts of many people. Thousands responded to her from as far as Iceland, India, Iran, and South America. In what ways do you use on-line technologies to connect with the world? How has this technology enhanced your interpersonal relationships?[64]
- A woman is put on short term disability for at least a month by her employer after she presents a note from her physician excusing her from work due to severe depression. After about three weeks, a fellow employee visits her Facebook page and notices pictures of her smiling and having a good time at a concert and on a Caribbean cruise. She reports her to human resources. The woman on short-term disability is immediately fired. The woman claims she was following her doctor's advice to try to have fun and socialize with people to get out of her funk. She threatens to sue her employer for unfair termination. Do you think she has a case? Why or why not? What things should we consider when we create on-line web pages and profileson social networking sites?
- If you were designing the structural layout of your next home or business, what would you do to environmentally enhance the quality of interpersonal communication for those living or working there?
- One student of mine who works with computers and websites shared with me that he often has to explain things to people who lack an understanding of technical terms and acronyms. If he says to a client that the "code has an undefined index error on line 42—check to make sure you have initialized all of your variables and use a print r() statement on your array to check for the missing array element," there is bound to be some confusion. Can you identify a situation where semantic noise occurred between you and someone else? Describe what happened?
- One's lips or kissing can be a channel. It can communicate a desire to be physically intimate or express love. One married man in his late twenties wrote a letter asking for guidance from Jeanne Phillips, a.k.a. "Dear Abby" regarding his wife of three years. Prior to marrying his wife, he enjoyed the act of kissing with past women he dated. His wife, for reasons still not completely known to him, did not like to kiss. Perhaps she had a germ phobia. Maybe her husband had a bad case of halitosis. Another possibility: she lacked confidence in her kissing ability. Her husband's perception was that it had more to do with motivation than skill.[65] If you were in this situation, how would you communicate this to your loved one without causing hurt feelings?
- Numerous websites such as jokesgallery.com list alcohol warnings similar to these:

  Alcohol may make you think you are whispering when you are not.

  Alcohol may make you thay shings like thish.

  Alcohol may cause you to believe that you can dance.

  Alcohol may make you think your ex really wants to hear from you at 4:00 a.m.

  Alcohol is the leading cause of unexplainable rug burns on the forehead.

  Alcohol may make you think that people are laughing with you.

  Alcohol may cause an interruption in your time–space continuum, whereby small or large gaps of time may seem to literally disappear.

  Alcohol may actually cause pregnancy.

  While these examples are meant to be humorous, alcohol use and abuse is a serious problem. As a source of noise, how does alcohol affect our ability to communicate? What are the personal, relational, and social consequences of alcohol impairment.?
- A Grand Rapids, Michigan woman, Ann Marie Linscott, placed an ad on craigslist.org and immediately received three interested responses. There was also a speedy response from the police who came to her home and arrested her. Linscott allegedly posted an ad on the popular cite for a contract killer to take out her husband. She offered $5,000 dollars, the same amount she received just days earlier for a college scholarship. What does this story say about cyberspace? What are our ethical obligations in terms of its use? How might we improve computer mediated communication? Should there be more government regulations? Why or why not?[66]

Unit 2 Vocabulary Review

___ Sender
___ Receiver
___ Message
___ Channel
___ Context
___ Feedback
___ Noise
___ Frame of Reference
___ Mixed Message
___ Internal Noise
___ External Noise
___ Semantic Noise
___ Linear Model
___ Transactional Model
___ Verbal Messages
___ Nonverbal Messages
___ Relational History
___ Meta-communication
___ Computer Mediated Communication
___ Channel Lean
___ Channel Rich
___ Symbols
___ Encoding
___ Decoding Message Overload
___ Message Overload
___ Triangular Communication

A. This occurs when either the sender or receiver doesn't understand the other's use of language.

B. A person who interprets a message.

C. This is the means by which or how a message is sent.

D. The mental process of producing a message.

E. We send or receive this when the verbal message contradicts the non-verbal message.

F. Anything which makes effective communication difficult in some way.

G. A person's collective experience, including such things as his or her upbringing, social affiliations, educational background, and culture.

H. A person who transmits a message.

I. A communication approach which involves only a few sensory inputs to derive meaning from.

J. A model which depicts communication as following a single, straight path.

K. The mental process of interpreting or attaching meaning to a message.

L. This is how long people have known each other, including the number of past interactions and what happened when these interactions occurred.

M. This occurs when senders and receivers talk about past communication, how they are communicating now, or how they'd like to communicate in the future.

N. Anything such as a word, sign, or object that represents something and people attach meaning to it.

O. What is being communicated.

P. Communication which involves the use of language, spoken or written, to convey meaning to others.

Q. This occurs when people create meaning without the use of language.

R. This form of communication utilizes computer technology (e-mail, instant messaging, and blogging) to transmit messages.

S. This is a response to a message.

T. This is anything occurring outside of our mind or body which can make communication difficult.

U. A model which illustrates how communication is two way; people send and receive messages simultaneously.

V. This is a form of interpersonal communication which involves three people, with one serving as a "go-between" or liaison for the other two.

W. We experience this when we receive too many messages or too much information all at once.

X. A communication approach which provides more immediate and comprehensive sensory information.

Y. This is the time, place, and people involved when communication occurs.

Z. This is anything which occurs within a person's mind (psychological) and body (physiological) which may make it difficult to communicate.

Meta-communication and Self-Monitoring Exercise

Meta-communication occurs when people talk about their interaction and/or communication with each other. This can also include talking about the relationship: how it is, and where it needs to be. Any time we talk about our relationship with someone, we invariably end up talking about our communication. Select a person with whom you have a valued relationship. Use the following questions to stimulate meta-communication. In one or two paragraphs, type a brief synopsis of who you spoke to, the general topic of conversation, and how the conversation went based on your responses to the self-monitoring questions below.

Meta-communication Conversation Starters

- Think of a recent conversation you had that did not go well. Remind the person about it. Ask the question: "How could I have communicated better?" How could we avoid this kind of outcome in the future?"
- Are there ways in which I can improve my communication with you? What are they?
- When we have experienced conflict in the past, what is it about my communication which makes the conflict worse? Better?
- What do you like about our relationship? What would you like to see more of? Less of?
- Is there an issue in our relationship which you feel we need to talk about? If so what? What do you need from me?

Self-Monitoring

Self-monitoring is a term used in the interpersonal communication field to describe the process of analyzing our communication with others. Use the questions below to trigger an analysis of your communication immediately after you complete the meta-communication exercise. The benefits of meta-communication are maximized when we apply effective communication approaches during the conversation.

- Did I allow the person to complete his or her thoughts without interruption?
- Did I listen intently without getting defensive or argumentative?
- Did I paraphrase or restate what the person said?
- Did I agree with or validate the person when he or she shared facts, opinions, feelings or needs which were accurate, reasonable, and justified?
- Did I communicate a desire to "be in the know," by expressing appreciation for his or her honesty?
- Did I communicate a willingness to change aspects of myself and my behavior to improve the relationship, without attacking, blaming, or putting down the person I spoke to?

3

Principles

Principles Unit 3

Understanding the eight principles explained in this unit will help guide us in our interpersonal communication.

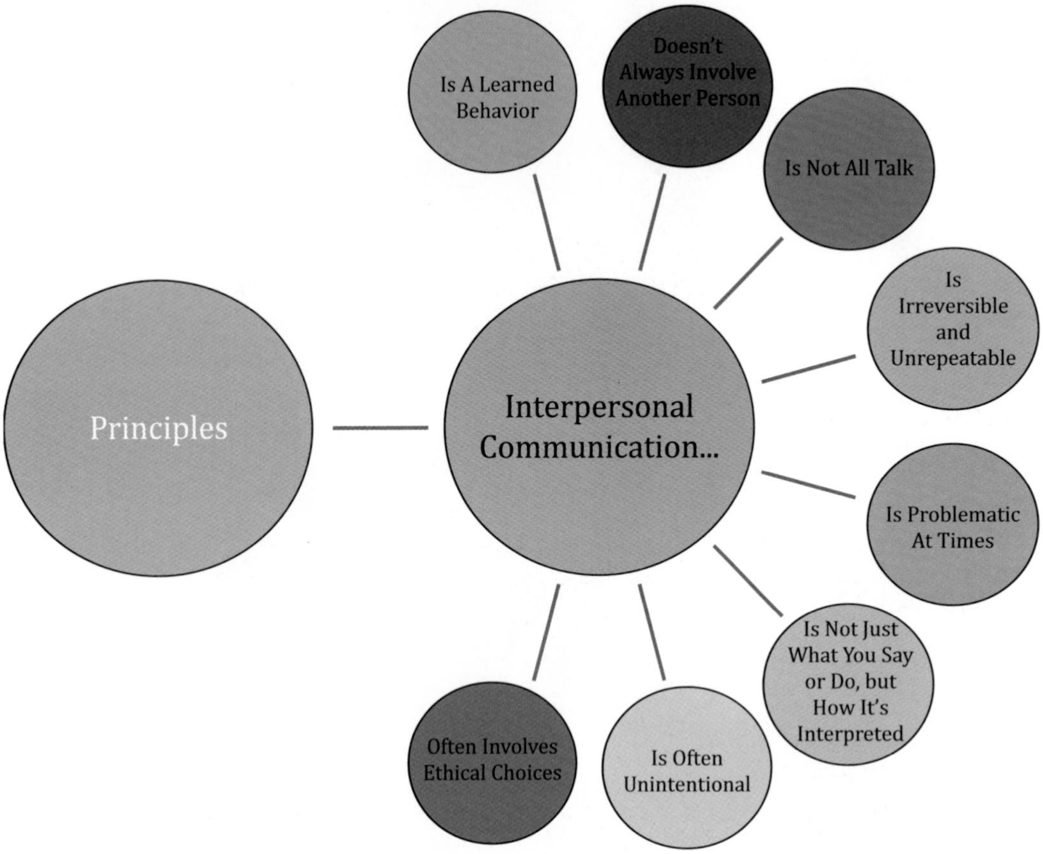

Unit 3 Learning Objectives

As a result of reading and studying Unit 3, you will be able to:

1. Explain how communication is a learned behavior.
2. Describe the four stages of learning a new interpersonal communication skill and the four steps to improving interpersonal communication.
3. Appreciate the importance of intrapersonal communication or self-talk.
4. Understand the role active listening plays in interpersonal communication.
5. Recognize how interpersonal communication is irreversible and unrepeatable.
6. Value how communication is not just what is said but how receivers interpret it.
7. Identify the unintentional aspects of interpersonal communication.
8. Comprehend some of the ethical dilemmas people face in their interpersonal communication and a few widely practiced ethical guidelines.

Gastronomic "Tsunami" Takeru Kobayashi is a 111-lb world-reigning competitive-eating champion who can devour fifty-seven cow brains in fifteen minutes, twenty lbs of rice balls in thirty minutes, and sixty-nine hamburgers in eight minutes. Kobayashi, from Japan, set the 2006 world record at the Johnsonville World Bratwurst Eating Championship in Sheboygan, Wisconsin, by putting away fifty-eight bratwursts in ten minutes. If you can "stomach" watching him, he breaks a hot dog in half, dunks the bun in water, and chews a specific number of times before swallowing. Off-season, he shrinks his stomach by starving and running. He then stretches it with large amounts of water and cabbage. He is purported to eat one Mike Tyson-sized meal a day.[1,2]

Communication is a learned behavior. We can draw parallels between Kobayashi's bratwurst consumption prowess and how we learn to communicate interpersonally.

Communication Is a Learned Behavior

Kobayashi has fine tuned an approach to Olympic-speed binging via watching his competition and personal experimentation. Like Kobayashi, the basis for why we communicate the way we do is observation and trial-and-error. We discover the relationship between cause and effect. We try certain communication approaches and find that they either work or don't. Sometimes, we discover things based on sheer coincidence as we interact with others. We also consciously and unconsciously assimilate the communication behaviors we observe and receive from significant individuals in our lives. For example, when you were a child, did the adult caregivers in your life admit when they communicated poorly? Were they quick or slow to either praise or criticize you? Did you witness individuals relying on manipulation, lying, yelling, or threats to meet their needs? Did you experience calm, open, and rational discussions or were issues and conflicts overblown, sugarcoated, or avoided? Did problems not get addressed until a major "blow up" unleashed a burst of negative emotions, name-calling, and blaming? Were you ignored or given the silent treatment? Were love and affection withheld as a form of punishment? When you made a mistake, were you reminded time and time again what you did wrong or were mistakes addressed once and then forgotten?

. . . **Catch this!** For a good laugh and an example of how we learn certain behaviors via observation go to www.youtube.com Dancing Beyonce' baby!

Throughout our lives, we learn how to communicate as a result of our interactions with others. It was mentioned in unit one that people often adopt and repeat counterproductive patterns of communication. Studies suggest that parents who are highly controlling and rarely express affection may set their children up for a host of social skill deficits later in life.[3] Adults who suffer from various phobias often do so because of communication interactions or events which occurred in their childhood with significant adult caregivers.[4] Adolescents

© ejwhite, 2010. Used under license from Shutterstock, Inc.

who grow up experiencing coercion, violence, or abuse tend to act out in similar ways later in their dating relationships or marriages.[5]

Regardless of how we have been taught to communicate, we have the capacity to change patterns of communication and adopt ones which work better. We say that communication is effective when it helps us achieve certain goals and hopefully enhances the relationship we have with other people.[6]

The four essential ingredients for skilled communication are:

1) A desire to improve, 2) knowledge of effective approaches, 3) practice, and 4) self-monitoring.

> **"The most important thing in communication is to hear what isn't being said."**
>
> **Peter Drucker**

A Desire to Improve

Former NHL Hall of Fame sensation Wayne Gretsky once said, "Skate to where the puck is going, not where it has been." One way we can empower ourselves is to visualize how our lives will improve as a result of our growth as communicators—to appreciate where we can go.

Research posits that some people may have a genetic advantage over others from an interpersonal communication standpoint. There is hereditary link to such things as impulsivity, social composure, wit, attentiveness, assertiveness, extroversion, and language acquisition skills.[7,8,9] However, the major difference between those who communicate well and those who don't is the desire to improve. English composer John Powell said, "Communication works for those who work at it."

Knowledge of Effective Techniques

© sonia.eps, 2010. Used under license from Shutterstock, Inc.

Imagine you and a group of friends are on vacation, basking in the decadent ambience of one of Las Vegas' premier hotels, the Bellagio. You are about to enter the world of high-stakes poker as one of few to ever play in Bobby's Room, a private VIP suite requiring a $20,000 minimum buy-in. Perhaps this is a bit far-fetched. Okay, let's say you are about to risk some of your hard earned money at a game of blackjack, roulette, or craps. If someone approached you with information likely to increase your chances of winning, would you gladly receive it? The goal of *What You Say and Do Next. . . . Matters!* is to stack the deck in your favor from a communication standpoint. Its objective is to boost your odds of creating more successful communication outcomes by expanding your awareness of the techniques interpersonal communication experts and scholars agree are generally effective.

It is important to realize that no single technique or approach is guaranteed to work at all times or with all people. Communication is, and people are, unpredictable and complex. Scholar and author John Stewart says that "No one person can completely control a communication event. No single person or action causes or can be blamed for a communication outcome."[10] Any number of factors may influence the communication between people such as timing, environmental factors, perception, expectations, and emotions.

Practice

There is a difference between knowing about a skill and practicing it. Recently, I started playing lacrosse with my daughter Kaitlin. A freshman in high school, she is trying out for the team for her first time. This sport is completely foreign to both of us. At first, I found it very awkward catching the lacrosse ball with the stick, which has a net attached at the end and a small ledge for the ball to rest on. You have to hold the stick just right and maneuver it while running to keep the ball from falling out! The more I've practiced with Kate, the less "strange" it feels. The same can be said about improving our communication. At first, it may seem shaky when we apply an unfamiliar approach or technique. Personal empowerment coach and author Jack Canfield says, "You have to be willing to look bad sometimes in order to get good." As we prepare to improve our communication competence, let's keep in mind that **research on learning suggests there are four stages we'll experience when we acquire a new skill:**
(AASI) 1) awareness, 2) awkwardness, 3) skillfulness, and 4) integration.[11]

Awareness

This means we are now conscious of a new or better way of doing something. It may also involve looking at a situation differently. Awareness is the initial step in the change process. Harvard social psychologist, Ellen Langer researched and developed a construct she calls mindfulness. She defines it as having a "heightened sense of situational awareness and a conscious control over one's thoughts and behavior relative to the situation." Her research is published in two significant books, *Mindfulness* (1989) and *The Power of Mindful Learning* (1997). In both works, she outlines the advantages of becoming more open to new information and different points of view. Awareness requires receptivity, a willingness to seek out and consider different ideas and possibilities. From a communication standpoint, this may include knowing what kind of communication situation you are in or getting into, the communication options you have, and why some options are better than others.[12,13]

Awkwardness

Our first attempts to incorporate something

new yield a feeling of awkwardness. We may find ourselves thinking, "This is—not me," or "I don't talk like this." As we try out some of the skills and approaches in this textbook, let's resist the urge to stop, simply because it doesn't feel smooth or natural. With time and effort, we will make many of these techniques fit our own style and way of speaking.

Skilled

We are skilled at something when we have practiced it to the point we don't need to think about it much. For example, if you have to confront an employee at work regarding an undesirable behavior, your knowledge of two skills taught in this text, perception checking and "I language," might kick in without a lot of conscious thought or preparation. At this stage, we also know how to segue smoothly from one technique to another. If we are a manager of a computer supply company, we may approach an employee who repeatedly takes longer than allowed breaks with a perception check such as "I noticed that you returned from break fifteen minutes beyond what is allowed. Am I correct?" We may follow our perception check with "I language": "I need you to please adhere to the scheduled break times and return on time." Our message is clear, polite, and assertive. It focuses on the specific behavior we want.

Integration

Integration occurs when we apply a skill on an unconscious level. This is when a skill, such as paraphrasing, is fully assimilated into our daily communication with others. We do it without any thought—kind of like riding a bike. Once we learn how, it stays with us for a lifetime.

Self-Monitoring

Along with a desire to improve, awareness of effective techniques, and practice, the fourth step to improving our interpersonal communication occurs when we take time to analyze it. This is called self-monitoring. Self-monitoring is a process which helps heighten our awareness of how we communicate and relate to others. Research suggests people who are high self-monitors are more cognizant of how they appear to others. They are attuned to how they look, act, and sound. They detect social cues faster and more accurately, as well as anticipate how others will respond to certain messages.[14,15,16] Those who engage in frequent self-monitoring (without getting obsessed with it) tend to possess well developed interpersonal skills.[17,18] People with Interpersonal skills know how to successfully relate to and understand people. To effectively gauge the success of our communication, we look at two things: the process and the outcome. The process is how or the manner in which communication takes place. The outcome is the result or end state of communication.[19]

An ideal time to apply self-monitoring is right after a communication exchange. For example, as soon as we get off the phone with someone, before going on to our next task, we can pause and ask ourselves, "How did I communicate just now? What did I do well? What could I have done better? What was it like for this person to speak with me? Was I listening? If so, what did he or she say?" For this last question, if we don't remember much, this is a wake-up call. There is a distinct difference between passive and active listening. Active listening requires sustained focus and concentration, which we'll explore in-depth in unit 5 on

listening and feedback. Other questions which stimulate self-monitoring may include:

- Did I interrupt?
- Were my directions clear and to the point?
- Did I dominate the conversation or listen intently?
- Did I show an interest in what the other person said?
- Did I show appreciation for the speaker's feedback?
- Did I give unsolicited advice?
- Did I pick the right time and place to communicate my message?
- Did I respond hastily before clarifying what the person said?

We can do this after a couple of conversations every day. With time, we are likely to see a desirable shift in the dynamics of our interpersonal communication.

. . . What are the four steps to improving our interpersonal communication? How would you describe them? What are the four stages (AASI) of acquiring a new communication skill?

When it comes to how we communicate, observation and experience are major teachers, especially during our formative years. This learning continues throughout our lives within various contexts or environments. **We live as a part of many <u>systems</u>. Each has its own <u>culture</u>, from which we learn which <u>roles</u> to perform and <u>rules</u> to follow.**

We Are Part of Many Systems

If we rent a house with three roommates, we operate within a system. If we work part-time at *Ambercrombie & Fitch* or *The Gap*, we work within a system. If we belong to a disk golf club, we participate in a system. In 1968, Hungarian biologist Ludwig von Bertalanffy published his scholarly exploration of what he called **General Systems Theory**. It was applied to numerous scientific fields of study including communication. The theory suggests we all belong to systems and subsystems.

A **system** is comprised of interdependent parts or components which interact or function as a whole. Within a system, there are smaller systems or subsystems. A system may also make up part of a larger system.[20] For example, if you are a member of an interpersonal communication class, it is a subsystem of the campus you attend. If your college or university has more than one campus, your campus is a subsystem of a larger system, which is your college or university. Your college or university is a subsystem of your state government's education department, which funds and regulates your college or university.

According to systems theory, parts which make up a system influence each other. What happens to one part, affects other parts and/or the system as a whole. Also, what happens within one system influences other outside systems. There is an interconnectedness between systems and their subsystems.

What are some systems you belong to?

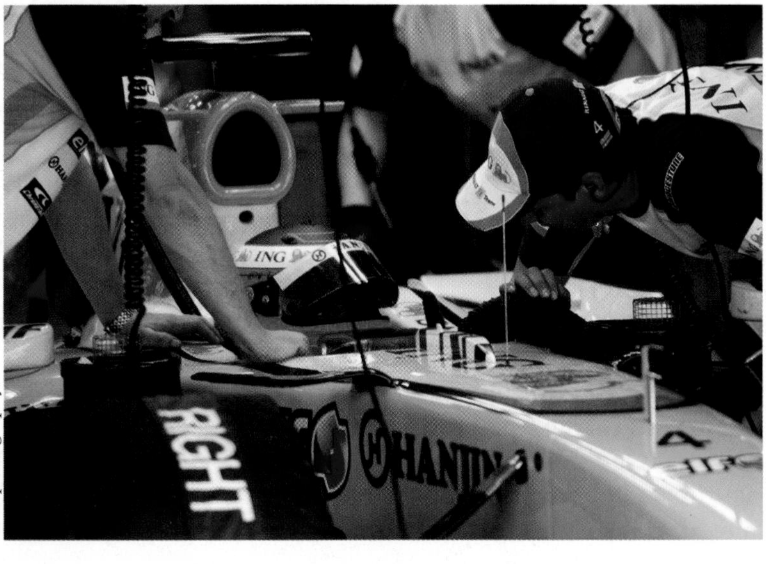

Let's apply the system's theory to a family. Every family in America is a system. One family member's behavior is likely to affect other members. Take a family which consists of a mother, two sons, and a daughter. The two brothers get into a verbal fight and stop talking to each other. Their sister may get involved in their dispute and takes the side of her younger brother, so now her older brother stops talking to her. The mother is tired of the bickering, so instead of taking her three children to the beach, she leaves the house and goes to the mall, alone. If she takes her children to the beach, they may drive in silence. The trip may not be fun for all of them because two or more of them are in a bad mood. The mother feels the strain, and on her way back home with her children is inpatient with a waitress at the restaurant they stop at. In this case, the communication behavior of one or more family members has some impact on the other members, and a waitress, who belongs to another system. Our communication behavior is also influenced by the culture that emerges within any given system.

We Are Part of a Culture

The systems we belong to create their own culture. **Culture is formed by the interactions within members of a system, over time**. It is passed on from one member to another via communication. **Culture** is defined by scholars Larry Samovar and Richard Porter as "the language, values, beliefs, interests, traditions, and customs people share and learn."[21] For example, how members of your family interact with each other will differ from other families because of the unique nature of your family's culture. Your family may celebrate a holiday differently than your neighbors across the street. Your family may develop its own "lingo," set of "taboo topics," and recreational interests. Your family may spend many Saturdays tailgating outside of Spartan Stadium or cheering on the Michigan Wolverines in front of a big screen at home. Other families may not be into sports at all.

If you were an employee for a bank, and you transfer from one branch office to another, you may see distinct differences in how people dress, how they spend their lunch breaks, and the formality of their meetings. These differences are all based on a history of interactions that have occurred prior to your first day at the new branch. In this textbook, unit 11 on frame of reference explores culture in more depth. Within the systems we belong to, not only do we learn how we should communicate and behave, various roles emerge. These roles affect and reflect a system's culture.

Colleges have their own culture as evidenced by how students behave at sporting events.

We Perform Various Roles

Does your group of friends rely on you to organize social outings? At formal events are you the appointed spokesperson for the group? When things get tense, do members of your work team count on you to lighten things up? Through our interactions with others within the various systems we are a part of, people are expected and encouraged to carry out certain roles. Someone may be the "voice of reason," the "disciplinarian," the "negotiator," or the "listening ear." A **role** is defined by communication scholars

Colleges offer classes analyzing its impact on society. Students write term papers and doctoral dissertations dissecting its relevance. Children imitate the characters on playgrounds. Religious leaders condemn it from the pulpit. A lot of the dialogue, like "Respect my authori-tah!" end up as popular catchphrases. The creator's of Comedy Central's *South Park*, Trey Parker and Matt Stone, are lauded and criticized for their satirical lampoons of certain individuals and groups within American culture. Comedy Central's hit cartoon features boy pals Stan Marsh, Kyle Brofloski, Eric Cartman, and Kenny McCormick.

Check out the following spoof on fish sticks and Kanye West in the clip titled "How do you live with yourself?": www.southparkstudios.com/clips/224098.

What do you think makes the show so popular? Are there legitimate concerns regarding how this show may impact society, especially the communication behavior of its viewers? Why or why not?

Rudolph and Kathleen Verderber as "a specific pattern of behavior that a person performs based on the expectations of other members."[22] We see roles emerge between the characters of HBO's *Entourage*. The series centers on Vincent Chase (Adrian Grenier), an actor whose career catapults after he lands a role in a hit movie. Experiencing this with Vince is best friend and manager Eric Murphy (Kevin Connolly), his older brother Johnny Chase (Kevin Dillon) who functions as Vince's personal trainer, chef, and body guard, long time friend "Turtle" (Jerry Ferrara) who is Vince's driver, and Ari Gold (Jeremy Piven), Vince's abrasive but endearing agent. All the guys forge a close relationship. They work hard to advance Vince's career through their various roles, but often disagree on how things should be done.

As a member of a system, is there a role you are expected to perform? Is it a role that you enjoy or dread? Why?

The male version of *Sex In The City?* HBO's *Entourage*

We Learn to Follow Certain Rules

Through the process of observation and trial-and-error, we also learn that our communication is governed by rules both explicit and implicit.[23] A **rule** is a standard which people are expected to follow in a given social context. For example, we are often told what to say in certain situations—referred to as scripted messages. **Scripted messages** are phrases or expressions we say because they are considered socially appropriate. When someone sneezes, we automatically say, "bless you." Expressions that are scripted include, "Excuse me," "I'm sorry," "May I?" "Please" and "Thank you." How you greet customers on the phone or how you initiate a prayer may be scripted. **These scripted messages are encouraged either explicitly or implicitly by significant individuals such as a parent, grandparent, teacher, coach, or boss.**

An **explicit rule** is communicated to us directly in spoken or written form. Our teacher may admonish us for talking during an exam. Our parents may verbally and/or nonverbally reprimand us for speaking with our mouth full or staring at a stranger. Hospitals may restrict cell phone use on certain floors. Social networking sites like Facebook and MySpace may limit the kind of pictures or content one is allowed to post. Companies may have strict written rules prohibiting fraternization with co-workers outside of the work setting. In fact, students who work for companies such as *Hot Topic* and *Hollister* report the companies will fire employees if they catch them sending or receiving personal text messages or making social phone calls with other employees after hours.

. . . **Catch this!** For a good laugh go to www.youtube.com Whose Line Is It Anyway-Change of Letter. See what happens when Drew Carey establishes the explicit rule that cast members must replace all the words that start with the letter "p" with the letter "g" when speaking to each other.

Do you agree with the strict policies some companies have barring dating or social interaction between employees outside of work? Why or why not?

An **implicit rule** is a standard which is not overtly established, yet people adhere to it. Perhaps we follow these rules because of subtle cues or hints we've received. In a social context, we may hesitate to say or do something with someone because someone else did the very same thing to us in the past, which made us feel uncomfortable. We may hesitate to step on an already full elevator. We may not ask very personal questions to someone we hardly know. We tend not to sit next to a stranger in an empty theater. Guys may not talk to or exchange a lot of eye contact with guys they don't know while standing at a urinal in a men's restroom. Yes, this is one of several interesting implicit rules guys follow regarding proper restroom etiquette. Along with learning the explicit and implicit rules we're expected to follow within the various systems we belong to, we also learn that it is often best to adjust our communication depending on who we are talking to, a process called accommodation.

. . . **Catch this!** For a humorous example of the implicit rules for male restroom etiquette go to: www.youtube.com.

We Learn to Accommodate

Our interaction with people teaches us that we become more adept at detecting and understanding the nuances of a person's communication, the more we know a person. **We adjust our communication to accommodate the other person's style of communication**. Howard Giles, Professor of Communication at the University of California, Santa Barbara, worked with other scholars to develop the **Communication Accommodation Theory**. The theory suggests we attempt to alter our communication style to match the style of the person to whom we're speaking. We do this to improve both the communication process and outcome.

This may include adjusting our speech rate, inflection, language, and emotional intensity as we are speaking.[24,25] We may speak differently with our peers than we do with our parents. A teacher will choose words and speak in a manner that her first grade students will best respond to. She will later adapt her communication at home to accommodate the speaking style of her life partner. In social situations, we may also poke fun at ourselves or use self-deprecating humor for the purpose of accommodation.[26]

Researcher William Sharkey found that people put themselves down because generally speaking, people find a little self-flagellation funny. It shows that a person doesn't take him or herself and things too seriously. It can project modesty, shift the focus of embarrassment away from someone else, make conversations more interesting, and ease a tense moment.[27] This appears to work nicely when a person of stature joins a new group or addresses an unfamiliar audience. When Former Vice-President, Al Gore stepped on stage to reveal his much anticipated *An Inconvenient Truth* lecture, he emerged from behind a stage curtain poised to persuade. His enormous global warming slideshow appears on an IMAX-size screen. The applause fades once he is introduced. There is silent, yet eager anticipation in the crowd. Al Gore starts his lecture with: "Hello, my name is Al Gore, and I used to be the next president of the United States." The audience roars with laughter. Al Gore's use of self-deprecating humor worked; however, if he used self-deprecating humor too often or in a different situation, it might not go over as well. Chances are, Al Gore has received some formal training in how to best read and respond to an audience during a speech.

We Learn Formally

Our ability to communicate is learned not only as a result of trial-and-error and observation, but from formal instruction. Classes in communication are shown to help improve a person's skill level.[28] People who take classes are a part of a system which, hopefully, reflects a culture that is supportive and encouraging. Roles and rules are established to allow students opportunities to practice their skills in a nonthreatening environment. Research has found that within this kind of environment students generally gain confidence and feel more comfortable giving speeches and sharing their ideas within small groups the more they do it. Studies have found that people with high communication apprehension (HCA) benefit from formal training.[29] **Communication apprehension** is the fear or anxiety one experiences in a social or communication situation.

Examples of communication situations which tend to produce high communication apprehension include meeting a date's parents, being at a social event surrounded by a lot of strangers, participating in a job interview, or presenting a speech. Along with reducing communication apprehension, researchers have found that after just thirty minutes of formal training, subjects improved their ability to detect deception in interviews.[30] Our interactions with others teach us a lot. Whatever we learn, we can unlearn. This is not necessarily an easy thing to do. It was stated that positive change requires desire, knowledge, practice, and self-monitoring. Do you remember what these mean? We also addressed how our learning takes us through the stages of awareness, awkwardness, skilled, and integration. Can you describe these four stages?

Next, let's look next at a critical aspect of our communication: the communication we have with ourselves.

. . . In what ways do we learn how to communicate interpersonally?

Communication Doesn't Always Involve Another Person

Have you ever carried on a conversation with yourself while showering alone? Ever discussed something while driving—with no one but you in the car? Some of our most engrossing and productive conversations are with ourselves! Oscar Wilde said, "I like hearing myself talk. It is one of my greatest pleasures. I often have long conversations with myself, and I am so clever that sometimes I don't understand a single word I am saying." Talking to ourselves or self-talk is called **intrapersonal communication**. Everyone does it! It is a completely normal form of communication, as long as we are not arguing with ourselves! In other words, if we find ourselves saying, "*Who said that*?" or our conversation sounds similar to Sybil or the *Lord of The Rings* character Smeagol, whose alter personality, Gollum wrestles control of the hapless creature with his signature "*Precious . . . Give me the Precious*," then we may need to speak to someone else—who can help us.

Intrapersonal communication is a potentially healthy form of communication which serves multiple functions. We self-talk silently or out loud, in private or around people. For the sake of avoiding embarrassment, we opt to self-talk silently in the presence of others. We may talk ourselves into approaching an attractive person at a club. While standing in line at the Secretary of State's office, we may ponder how safe we feel upon greeting a disheveled seventy-two-year-old security guard with a limp. We may plan our agenda for the day out loud while sipping a Starbucks coffee during our morning commute. Ever engage in verbal combat with a person who wasn't physically present? Arguing with a person who is not there is a sure fire way to win—usually! In this sense, intrapersonal communication can help us prepare what we will say next time. Interpersonal communication scholar James Honeycutt expounds on the imaginary conversations we have with people in his work titled *Imagined Interactions: Daydreaming about Communication.* In the 2004 *Canadian Journal of Communication*, he states "Imagine a looming inevitable conflict with a loved one. You know it's coming, because there's a very difficult issue that needs discussion. You know your loved one will be defensive and angry when the conversation starts. But if you're lucky, you can have that discussion several times, using your imagination, before the actual encounter. You can experiment with numerous approaches, envision multiple responses you might encounter, and finally choose an informed approach that will hopefully minimize the conflict and maximize the chances of constructive outcome."[31,32]

With our self-talk, we can also say all the things we previously wished we had said to someone, but didn't. In this case, intrapersonal communication is cathartic. **Catharsis** is the feeling of releasing stress or pent-up emotions as a result of talking about something. It is the act of "getting if off your chest."

The productive potential of intrapersonal communication cannot be overstated. We internally process what happens to us and how we interface with the world on a conscious and unconscious level. John Bargh, Professor of Psychology at New York University, calls the part of the processing we do which is unconscious "automatic processing." If you are driving down the street, and looking for an address on a mailbox, you may consciously say to yourself, "Ok, where is 1247 Nelson?" As you are looking, without really thinking about it, you automatically slow your car down so you can see the house numbers better. This is automatic.

Let's say you are on the set of the *Jay Leno Show*. You are backstage waiting for your friend, Jole (Angelina Jolie) to finish her live interview. Consciously, you are focused on the interaction between Jole and Jay, while watching them on the monitor. You suddenly notice someone you find very attractive, looking at you.

Without thinking, you may extend eye contact and smile, or you may look away nervously. At that moment, you respond to this person's overtures automatically, with either confidence or insecurity. Your reaction is greatly influenced by scores of inner conversations you have had with yourself in the past. These conversations reflect how you see yourself in terms of your social desirability, attractiveness, and poise, which are imbedded deep within the recesses of your unconscious mind. [33]

Intrapersonal communication influences our self-concept, attitudes, motivation, and coping skills. What we say to ourselves can reflect what we would hear from a best friend or harshest critic. Many mental health professionals believe the most important primary relationship we have is the one with ourselves. So, in the spirit of self-help guru and host of *Daily Affirmations* Stuart Smalley (Al Franken) of *Saturday Night Live* fame, say to yourself: "I'm good enough. I'm smart enough, and doggone it, people like me!" Stand in front of a mirror, wink twice, smile, and repeat, "If I'm inspired by my own image, just think what I do to other people!"

That may be a little over the top. Seriously, are you faced with something daunting, a dramatic change, or setback? Has life kicked you in the head? Did your boyfriend or girlfriend pull a Beyoncé on you with "to the left to the left, everything you own in a box to the left?" Are multiple demands stretching you like Mel Gibson's character William Wallace in the painfully climatic ending of *Braveheart*? Sometimes we get stuck in our negative emotions. We hyperfocus on what is outside of our control. We make mountains out of molehills or lose sight of the big picture. We brood and waste time mulling over problems versus taking a step-by-step, solution-based approach.

There are six questions designed to stimulate productive, positive, and proactive self-talk. If we find ourselves stuck in the rut, riding an intimidating wave, or stumbling from a setback, we can ask ourselves and answer the following questions:

- Why am I feeling this way? (This is where we get at the root cause of a debilitative emotion).
- What is one positive thing I can do about this? (This question focuses our thoughts on problem solving and productive action).
- What is outside of my control? (This question encourages us to acknowledge the things we don't have a lot of control over and helps us to let some things go).
- What is right about my life? (This encourages us to think about all of the good things in life we can appreciate and puts things into a more positive perspective).
- What has not changed in my life? (This is a great question to ask ourselves when we feel like life is spiraling out of control. Answering this question will help us to see there are many things which are still constant).
- How important is this in the whole scheme of things? (This may give us a reality check when we consider all the other problems, issues, or priorities which can exist in our inner and outer world).

. . . Why is our intrapersonal communication important?

Intrapersonal communication occurs in different ways. Sometimes we may speak to a pet or inanimate object as a form of intrapersonal communication. Do you ever talk to your flat

screen, computer, car, or cat? When we talk to animals or nonliving things, this is called **extrapersonal communication**.[34] Private prayer is also a form of intrapersonal communication. Many people believe they can and do communicate back and forth with supernatural or spiritual entities. Jon Edwards is a self-proclaimed psychic liaison between the living and nonliving. In his show *Crossing Over*, he claims to receive messages from the dearly departed and passes the information on to family and loved ones. Loving pet owners appear on Animal Planet's *Pet Psychic* Sonya Fitzpatrick's show hoping she can read a pet's mind and explain why it's behaving a certain way. Can Edwards and Fitzpatrick really speak to the dead and animals, respectively? Often they appear to be very genuine and accurate. What is their secret?

The communication we have with ourselves is important to us in numerous ways. It affects our interpersonal communication. When it comes to our interpersonal communication, it is wise to understand communication is not all about talking!

. . . **Catch this!** Check these out on www.youtube.com: An example of John Edwards Crossing over with Will Ferrell. Anderson Cooper's dog Molly on AC 360.

Your Turn: When was the last time you talked to yourself? What purpose did it serve?

Communication Is Not All Talk

"Talk to the hand, 'cause the face don't wanna hear it anymore!" is a memorable line from Mike Myer's notorious character, Dr. Evil, in the *Austin Powers* trilogy. The following exchange between Dr. Evil and his son, Scott, humorously depicts the mad scientist's unwillingness to listen:

Scott Evil: "It's no hassle . . . "

Dr. Evil: "Sh!"

Scott Evil: "But . . . "

Dr. Evil: "Sh!"

Scott Evil: "I'm . . . "

Dr. Evil: "Sh!"

Scott Evil: "All I'm say . . . "

Dr. Evil: "Sh!"

Scott Evil: "They're gonna get a . . . "

Dr. Evil: "Sh!"

Scott Evil: "I'm . . . "

Dr. Evil: "Sh!"

Scott Evil: "I'm just . . . "

Dr. Evil: "Sh!"

Scott Evil: "Would . . . "

Dr. Evil: "Sh! . . . Knock knock."

Scott Evil: "Who's there?"

Dr. Evil: "Sh!"

Scott Evil: "But . . . "

Dr. Evil: "Let me tell you a little story about a man named Sh! Sh! even before you start. That was a preemptive "sh!" Now, I have a whole bag of "sh!" with your name on it."[35]

Artist and cartoonist Ashleigh Brilliant quipped, "If you think communication is all talk, you haven't been listening!" Dr. Evil's frequent interruptions and blatant unwillingness to listen characterize a few of the many barriers to effective listening. Preoccupation, information overload, laziness, and stubbornness constitute other obstructions.[36] In addition, listening fatigue increases the longer a speaker uses a monotone voice, goes off on tangents, or communicates a message perceived as idle chatter.

In any given conversation, how often do we interrupt, tune out, or respond prematurely? Research asserts we overrate our listening skills.[37] A lack of listening skills is considered a serious communication deficit of top executives according to a survey of forty Asian and Western CEOs representing an array of multinational corporations.[38] Despite its importance, less than two percent of American adults have formal listening training.[39]

> **"I never learned anything while I was talking."**
> **—Larry King, CNN**

Ineffectual listening is a leading cause of miscommunication. Let's take a look at a tragic outcome of poor listening. A fire doubles every minute. Time is of the essence for people trapped in a residential blaze. Sixty-three-year-old Rich Willemsen burned to death in his apartment building. Dispatchers were told there was a man inside the inferno, yet firefighters made no effort to enter the building. They had enough time. They had the appropriate equipment and training. They didn't race to Willemsen's aid because they didn't know they needed to. They assumed the building was evacuated. It took firefighters eight minutes to respond to the fire, with the fire station just two miles away. The lack of urgency and no order to enter the building had Fire Chief Robert Austin deeply concerned. Something happened. There was a serious communication breakdown with insufficient listening a probable cause. Whose listening was faulty? Was it the dispatchers or the firefighters who responded to the call?[40]

Not only is effective listening critical in a crisis situation, it also matters in relationships and the workplace. The ability to lead, help, learn, and relate is tied to our listening.[41,42,43]

Active Listening is the process of focusing on a message, making sense of it, and responding to it. To focus, we have to block out distractions, direct our attention, and concentrate on the message. We then interpret the message, and while we are doing this, we are responding to it. We may respond by nodding our heads, giving a person eye contact, and/or asking questions. We'll explore the listening process more in-depth and practice techniques such as paraphrasing, repetition, and questions for clarification to improve listening in unit 5 on listening and feedback. It is important for us to keep active listening at the forefront of our efforts to communicate better, considering the irreversibility and unrepeatability of what we say and do next.

. . . Why is active listening important in interpersonal communication? What is involved in the active listening process?

Communication Is Irreversible and Unrepeatable

The irreversibility of communication and its repercussions is dramatically illustrated in the following story. It is by an unknown author who writes about a soldier who, after serving in Vietnam, returned to San Francisco and called his parents. He said he had a favor to ask of them. He wanted to bring home a friend who was seriously injured in the fighting. His friend stepped on a land mine and lost an arm and leg. The soldier said his friend had nowhere else to go, and he wanted to know if his parents could take him in. The parents hesitated. They had converted the extra bedroom into an office. They thought it would be difficult and expensive to rearrange the house to make things handicap accessible. They wanted to relax and enjoy their home without worrying about taking care of someone who might need a lot of help, late in their retirement.

They told their son this. There was a long silence on the line. The son hung up. The parents heard nothing from him. A few days later, they received a phone call from the San Francisco police. Their son died after falling from a 12-story building. The police judged it a suicide. The grief-stricken parents flew to San Francisco and were taken to the city morgue to identify the body. In horror, they recognized their son and his one remaining arm and leg.

Once you say something it's like writing it in freshly laid concrete that quickly hardens. The effect is often permanent. Nothing you say or do will make others forget what you said. It can be years later and suddenly you hear, "This is an example of how you . . . or "This reminds me when you . . . or "You said that last time. . . ." Nowhere is this more obvious than in a court of law. A judge may order a jury to "disregard that last statement the witness made" and admonish the lawyer for asking an objectionable question. The sharp lawyer knows that his question and the witness's answer are stricken from the record by the judge, but the jury will remember what was said.

© Gina Smith, 2010. Used under license from Shutterstock, Inc.

"I was a member of a rock band, and we were performing a benefit concert for patients at a mental health hospital where I worked as a musical therapist. The audience was a little too quiet and unresponsive for my taste. Without thinking I yelled, "Come on, let's get a little crazy!?"

Akio

Our words and actions can never be rewound, nor can the effect they have on people. Prudence Kohl, author of the site, *Hole in the Garden Wall*, writes of a father who decided to help his son manage his anger and understand the consequences of losing his temper. Each time his son said or did something hurtful out of anger, the father told him to go hammer a nail in the fence which encircled their farm. The first day the boy hammered five nails and the next day eight. The first week he hammered a total of twenty-five nails.

This continued daily. As the son learned ways to control his anger, the number of nails that were hammered lessened. Each day, he gradually reduced the number of nails pounded in the fence. One day he did not lose his temper at all.

© Jamie Wilson, 2010. Used under license from Shutterstock, Inc.

Each day that he successfully controlled his anger, he was instructed by his father to pull out one of the nails and was praised. The days passed and eventually the nails were all removed. The father took his son by the hand and took him to the fence. He said, "You've done well son. I am proud of you for removing the nails. However, look at the holes in the fence. Even though you've taken out the nails, the holes remain. The fence will never be the same. When you say things in anger, they leave a scar or a hole. It's like stabbing someone with a knife. You can remove the knife and bandage the wound, but the scar remains.

Your Turn: Describe a time you said something and wish you could reverse its irreversibility.

Not only is communication irreversible, it is unrepeatable. In the movie *Parent Trap* (1998), twins Hallie and Annie, played by media darling Lindsay Lohan, try to get their divorced parents to fall back in love and remarry. During a family trip to London they attempt to recreate with exactness, the romantic night when their parents first met. The evening could not be replicated. Both their parents had changed. Life had moved on. No previous communication act can carry the same meaning once repeated. We cannot duplicate a moment. We cannot reproduce the atmosphere or the sequence of events which led up to the communication act. That is why rumors are so unreliable. When people spread information about other people, they are relying on memory, which is often inaccurate. Also, people's biases and motives often distort things. Pieces of information get deleted, exaggerated, and added.

Similarly, one of my students shared that when she was initially hired as a waitress, she found the regulars very friendly and welcoming. The longer she worked at the restaurant, she discovered that the same customers weren't always pleasant, nor acted the same way each time she saw them. She attributed this to a number of things. On certain days, she felt acutely tired, or her customers were preoccupied with events in their lives. A greeting, an apology, or a look is unique in that moment. People often expect the same results when they use certain communication techniques. A joke, repeated with the same punch line, is different each time. We cannot carbon-copy the comic or her audience. The same goes for flirtation and/or pick-up lines. A guy's best line may charm most women, but it is not guaranteed to work with all women. If the line works for one guy, chances are other guys have discovered the gem, and who's to say the lady hasn't heard it before?

Every communication act is distinctive. It does not occur in a vacuum. We cannot predict with certainty how a person will respond to what we say. A lot of things come in to play such as timing, the person's disposition, personality, sense of humor, gender, or culture.

© ARENA Creative, 2010. Used under license from Shutterstock, Inc.

"While interviewing for a job, I made a few comments that made the interviewer laugh. She seemed impressed with my witty replies and offered me a position. Thinking I had struck gold, I made the same comments in the same way, during an interview that same day, at another company. This particular manager took exception to my sense of humor and informed me that if I wasn't going to take the interview seriously, I needed to leave."

Alivia

© Yuri Arcurs, 2010. Used under license from Shutterstock, Inc.

Sometimes we don't engage someone in a conversation or share what we want to say because we forecast a certain response. We fear an undesirable reaction that may or may not

The best and worst of dating pick up lines:

- "Sorry, but you owe me a drink. [Why?] Because when I looked at you, I dropped mine. "
- "You're so fine you make me stutter, wha-wha-what's your name?"
- "Is it hot in here or is it just you?"
- "You know what? Your eyes are the same color as my Porsche!"
- "Me without you is like a nerd without braces. A shoe without laces. aSentenceWithoutSpaces"
- "My name is Justin. . . . just incredible!"
- "Wish I was cross-eyed so I could see you twice."

materialize. Other times, we speciously assume that because we are happy or enthused about something and want to share it, others are equally pleased or excited to hear it. Along with the irreversibility and unrepeatability of communication, it is wise for us as communicators to understand that communication is the cause of some problems and won't always resolve them.

. . . What do we mean when we say communication is irreversible and unique?

Communication Causes Some and Doesn't Solve All Problems

The probability that a twenty-one-week old fetus can survive outside of the womb is zero. That belief within the medical community was shattered when Miami obstetrician, Guillermo Lievano, delivered Amillia Taylor, who weighed a scant ten ounces. She was the youngest premie ever to survive. Lievano was in no way thinking he'd make medical history as he nervously scrubbed for an emergency C-section. Amillia's mother was in grave danger. She miscommunicated her dates, causing Lievano to believe that Amillia was at least two weeks older. Today's state-of-the-art intensive care nurseries can barely sustain a premature baby at twenty-three to twenty four weeks. Lievano would have focused on saving the mother's life, if he had known that the baby was twenty-one weeks. His medical decisions were based on the communication he received from Amilia's mother. This miscommunication sparked a fiery debate between opponents and supporters of abortion rights regarding the viability of a human fetus and legal protection for second-trimester pregnancies.[44]

Despite our best efforts, we cannot, at times, not miscommunicate. It is said to err is human. Sometimes we are very human. While we can strive to become competent as communicators, we will, at times, fail miserably. Osmo Wioo provides sobering communication maxims, like Murphy's law, in his book *Wiio's Laws—And Some Others*:

- If communication can fail, it will.
- If a message can be understood in different ways, it will be understood in just the way that causes the most problems.
- There is somebody who knows better than you what you meant by your message.
- The more communication there is, the more difficult it is for communication to succeed.[45]

This may paint a bleak picture of human communication, however, there are some universal communication skills or approaches which tend to produce favorable results. As stated earlier, there is no foolproof method or single way to best communicate.[46]

From an intercultural standpoint, what may constitute an ideal way to communicate in one culture may prove disastrous in another.[47] Just the act of confronting a person about a problem may create more conflict and problems. In a study involving college students, researchers discovered that college roommates sometimes created more relational problems by trying to talk them out.[48] Communication Scholars James McCroskey and Lawrence Wheeless report that "more and more negative communication

merely leads to more and more negative results."[49] An example of this is explained by one of my students, Sara, who states: "When my boyfriend and I fight, I tend to want to keep talking and try to fix things, when he just wants to be left alone to cool off. I am the type of person who can't stand the anxiety of a fight and want things fixed right now! So I keep trying to communicate my thoughts and feelings to him, when he doesn't care to talk about it, which only escalates things."

Just as communication is the cause of some problems, we need to accept the reality that it will not solve all problems. Despite our best efforts and skills, we can't always make someone say or do something he or she doesn't want to do. We could be the Kobe Bryant or Serena Williams of communication and still walk away from a conversation feeling very deflated.

Sometimes we erroneously assume communication is like a prescription drug with no side effects. We believe more communication will cure things. That is not always the case. It takes both parties to want to resolve an issue. Further, if parties are not using effective communication techniques, they are apt to draw a line in the sand, or like the soldiers featured in the film *Flags of our Fathers* (2006), dig deeper in their resolve to get what they want without compromising. Some people, as you know, are very stubborn. Others can be self-centered or selfish. They are referred to as **egocentric** communicators. They tend to be fairly self-absorbed. They're fixated on getting what they want. They are never wrong and often refuse to apologize. Developmental psychologist, Jean Piaget, used the term egocentric to describe how children, especially between the ages of two and six, tend to look at the world from one perspective—their own.[50] Like the boy who was asked by his teacher if he was given five chocolate chip cookies and had the opportunity to give one cookie to his sister, how many would he have left. "That's easy," said the boy, "I'd have five cookies." As adults, we can also be very egocentric at times. We make it difficult for others to communicate with us.

We experience limits even with the best communication approaches. However, we don't want to use this as an excuse not to try, or throw up our hands prematurely. People can come around. Sometimes it is a matter of timing or a different approach. Communication can be problematic because it is not just what you say or do but how your communication is interpreted.

. . . How is communication the cause of some and not a remedy for all problems?

© Sean Nel, 2010. Used under license from Shutterstock, Inc.

"This past Christmas, I agreed to accompany my sister to the airport to pick up her fiancé. The flight was scheduled to arrive very late Christmas Day. By the time the festivities of the day came to a close, my energy reserves were completely drained. Struggling to keep my eyes open, I called my sister to ask if she could make the trip alone. I explained, in detail, how, since I had to be at work very early the next morning (work was 2 1/2 hours away), I didn't want to get to bed too late. While inside my head, the justification seemed rationale, many factors would play a role in her negative reaction to my call: her already agitated mood, fear of driving late at night, unfamiliarity with the airport, and her excitement to have me meet her fiancé for the first time."

—Ireal

Communication Is Not Just What We Say or Do, but How It Is Interpreted

After a dismal game on the green, a golfer leaves the clubhouse and walks despondently to his car. A police officer pulls up along side of him, rolls down his window and asks:

Officer: "Did you tee off on the sixteenth hole about twenty minutes ago?"

Golfer: "Yes, how do you know?"

Officer: "Your ball flew out onto the highway and shattered a driver's windshield. The driver lost control and crashed into a second vehicle, causing a ten-car pile-up, which also involved a fire truck en route to a five alarm fire. The fire fighters couldn't make it to the fire, and the building burned down. The highway will be shut down for three hours. So, what do you think you should do about it?"

(Stunned, the golfer thought about it)

Golfer: "I think I better close my stance a little bit, and tighten my grip."[51]

This anecdote illustrates a difference in interpretation. The officer's question implied "What are you going to do about the accident you caused?" The golfer construed it to mean, "What are you going to do to improve your golf swing?" The following example also shows how people often interpret a person's message or actions differently. During the live broadcast of the 2007 Academy Awards, Eddie Murphy left the Kodak Theater with his girlfriend, Tracey Edmonds, immediately after he learned that he did not win the Oscar for Best Supporting Actor in *Dreamgirls.* He was accused by the media and some members of the Academy of being a "sore loser."

Was Murphy communicating his unhappiness with the Academy for being passed over for the honor by leaving abruptly before the show was over? Murphy's media spokesperson stated that it was Murphy's plan to leave right after the award was announced to spend time with his family, like he did at the Golden Globe Awards. The response to his early departure shows how people interpret a person's actions differently. While a few stated it was not a big deal, others felt it made him look like he was only there for his award. They felt it showed insensitivity not stay the entire time to show support to colleagues who were being recognized in other categories.[52]

"I know that you believe you understand what you think I said, but I'm not sure you realize that what you heard is not what I mean."

—Robert McCloskey

While we may have the best intentions, people can interpret our motives or instructions differently. One of my students, John, writes "I was running a machine at work. I told the lady I was working with that the machine had to be turned off when the load reached forty-eight. She nodded like she knew what I was talking about. Before the load reached forty-eight, she turned off the machine. She went by the impeller load instead of the tared load, which are two different things." John encoded a message that his coworker decoded differently.

From unit 2 we learned that encoding is the mental process of creating and sending a message. Decoding is the mental process which involves interpreting and making sense of a message once it is received. Throughout this textbook, we'll explore some of the reasons why people encode and decode messages differently and ways to improve both processes. Just as it is important to understand the complexities of these two processes, it is imperative to realize how pervasive our interpersonal communication is with people, and how often we communicate unintentional messages.

"Last Saturday, my friend Chuck and I were walking through the mall. We went inside a Banana Republic and were looking around. I told him the girls standing next to me at the counter were intense. He looked at them and responded with 'they look a little homely to me.' What I meant was that they smelled badly."

Robert

Your Turn: Identify a time when a person misinterpreted something you said, or you decoded a person's message incorrectly. What happened?

. . . What does it mean when we say that it is not just what you say, but how it is interpreted?

Communication Is Often Unintentional

One college student describes a night of partying at a pub with friends. He was lit. Glassy eyed, he looked his girlfriend in the eyes, smiled, and posed, "Will you marry me?" She screamed, "Yes! Yes! Oh Yes!" She took him seriously, and everyone at the bar made a big deal about it. He didn't really intend to propose. She seemed so excited that he didn't have the guts to fix the mess he made, so he played along for the rest of the night. The next day was not a good one for him.[53]

I heard about a young woman who read an e-mail she received from a coworker. She sent a reply to the coworker and added a personal, "oh, by the way" side bar to the message. She described how sick she felt and identified her symptoms, which included laborious cramps, rank breath, and Linda Blair, Exorcist-like vomiting the night before. Moments later her boss called her to her office to reprimand her. The boss said she should not come to work if she felt that sick and broadcast her personal issues to the entire building. The woman inadvertently responded to an interoffice e-mail.

The two situations just mentioned illustrate how possible it is to communicate unintentional messages. **Unintentional communication** occurs when a person doesn't mean to send a message or does so unknowingly. For example, while parked on the highway in a rush hour traffic jam, we may observe two guys in the car next to us head-bobbing in unison to the dance hit *What is Love?* like the Butabi brothers in *Night at The Roxbury*. If these guys are not aware of our watchful eyes, they are sending unintentional messages. You may have had this happen before where you are talking about someone in a not-so-complimentary way, and unbeknownst to you, he or she is standing right behind you! You obviously didn't intend for him or her to hear what you said. Someone may overhear our phone conversation or catch a glimpse of our text message. If we live in an apartment complex, thin walls or squeaky floors may not provide the sound proofing we need to keep private matters private.

When we accidently call our boyfriend or girlfriend by an ex's name, we have unintentionally committed a "Freudian slip." Psychologist and psychoanalysis founder Sigmund Freud coined this term in his 1901 book *Psychopathology in Every Day Life.*[54] A "Freudian slip" occurs when we say a word that we don't mean to say. An example of this is when a young businessman is having dinner with an important client at an upscale restaurant. The client's daughter is present, and the young businessman is distracted by her beauty. Instead of saying, "Please pass me the salt," he accidentally says, "Please pass me your daughter." George Bush Sr. did this once in a live speech. In referring to former President Ronald Reagan he stated to an audience, "For seven and a half years, I worked alongside him . . . We had some triumphs. We made some mistakes. We had some sex, (quickly correcting himself) some setbacks."

Freud believed that many of these verbal gaffes expose our innermost desires or thoughts which we try to suppress or circumvent. Another cause behind Freudian slips is that as we are saying something, we are thinking about something else. In addition, certain words have similar sounds or meanings, which we can easily cross.

. . . **Catch this!** For some hilarious examples of Freudian slips, go to www.youtube.com Top Ten Live TV Freudian Slip Ups!!

"How lovely you look," gushed a wedding guest to the bride. Then she whispered, "So glad to see you together. I was so afraid he would end up marrying that dizzy, backstabbing, low class blond he used to date."

"Really," replied the bride, "I dyed my hair." www.jokes.com

The pervasive ongoing nature of communication makes it difficult not to communicate unintentionally. Communication is happening everywhere, all the time. What would you do if you saw a baby locked up alone in a car on a hot day? How would you respond if you witnessed an African American woman being racially profiled at a department store? If you met a person for a first date, how would you react once you realized that this person didn't resemble his or her on-line dating profile—at all? This is what makes the ABC series *What Would You Do?* hosted by John Quinones intriguing for many people. Producers set up mock situations, using actors and hidden cameras, to capture people's reactions to different scenarios. In one episode, a female actor portrays a mother who berates her nanny in front of her daughter and within earshot of several patrons at a coffee shop. As her tirade continues, some people appear to ignore the conversation, others appear visibly upset. A few actually step in and try to console the nanny and/or confront the mother about her harsh language. Unbeknownst to everyone, with the exception of the filming crew and actors, they are communicating messages to a world-wide audience.

. . . **Catch this!** What would you do if you witnessed a gay couple being harassed at a sports bar? Go to www.abcnews.go.com/WhatWouldYouDo and click on "Would you help this gay couple?"

Many interpersonal communication scholars believe that it is impossible not to communicate. For example, a student walks into a classroom and sits down next to another student. Neither exchange a glance or a greeting. Has communication occurred? As long as one of them is consciously aware of the other's presence, not acknowledging one another with a nod, eye contact, or a smile communicates the message "I'm not interested in engaging you at this time."

When at home, one of my friends, Joanna, said, "I was lying in bed the other night. I sighed loudly and turned over with my back to my husband. He translated that in a way I never intended. He thought I was mad at him, when in reality, I was exhausted from a long day at the hospital and was uncomfortable lying on my back."

Kare Anderson, a communication expert writes in her article, *"What are You Telling the World?"* that our bodies are a "hologram . . . a three-dimensional movie or full-motion billboard that is constantly showing what is going on inside of us." People are watching us even

when we don't think we are being watched. As long as someone has the capacity to observe us, we have the potential to send messages.[55] A strict poker face during a game of *Texas Holdem*, how we dress, the way we walk, and even what we dangle from our car's rearview mirror (a cross, big pair of pink dice, or a green pine-scented tree) all have the potential to communicate something about us. We may even communicate in our sleep by talking out loud or mumbling something.

For those of us that are parents or plan on being parents someday, we may want to heed this caveat: watch what we say to our toddler. This is humorously brought to light in the hit movie *Meet the Fockers* (2004). Greg Focker (Ben Stiller) tries throughout the movie to win the approval of his in-laws, and fails miserably. In one scene, Greg accidentally uses the word "a—hole" while babysitting little Jack, his in-law's grandson. When Greg's in-laws return from a shopping excursion, Little Jack greets them with his first words, yep, "a_ _ hole!"

Toddlers may not talk much, but they are taking in a lot more than we think. Parents mistakenly assume that because their child doesn't say much, he or she doesn't understand what is being said. According to Dr. Jean Berko Gleason, a professor of psychology at Boston University and author of *The Development of Language*, there is a difference between receptive language and expressive language. Receptive language refers to one's ability to understand and decode a message. Expressive language is the ability to verbalize language orally or in writing. At twelve months of age a child knows an average of fifty words. At eighteen to twenty-one months of age, a child's grasp of the language skyrockets, with an average of nine new words added a day.[56,57]

We have the potential to communicate messages virtually all of the time, knowingly and unknowingly. Since these message can affect others, it is important to pause and think about the ethical ramifications of our communication choices.

. . . What do we mean when we say communication is pervasive and often unintentional?

Research This! What words do one-year-olds tend to pick up first? For answers Go to www.parents.com and type in this search: "What Toddlers Understand When Adults Talk".

A business maverick with his sight set on upper management, invited his boss to his home for a five-course meal. His three-year-old stared at her father's boss. She couldn't keep her eyes off of him. The boss checked his tie, felt his face for food, patted his hair in place, but nothing stopped her from staring at him. Finally, it was too much for him and he asked her, "Why are you staring at me?" Everyone at the table noticed her behavior too and the table went silent. "My daddy said you drink like a fish, and I don't want to miss it!"

ahajokes.com

Communication Involves Ethical Choices

Rosie Costello, of Tacoma Washington, plead guilty to conspiracy to defraud the government. Costello admitted to collecting $280,000 in social security benefits by coaching her two children, Pete and Marie, to act mentally retarded. The woman began training her children when Marie was eight-years-old and Pete was four. She taught them how to look and act the part when the children were interviewed periodically by social security representatives. Her ability to dupe the government continued successfully well into her children's late teenage years, until Social Security officials became suspicious and secured a tape of Pete giving a *Law and Order* performance contesting a traffic fine at a city office.[58]

Costello's behavior raised serious questions about her ethics. Her behavior was unethical because it violated what is considered right or moral by most of society. In this case, she took what didn't belong to her. **Ethics** is the application of moral principles which help guide a person's behavior. Communication scholar Richard Johannesen states that when we explore ethical issues, we are examining what constitutes right and wrong human behavior.[59] **Many communication scholars incorporate the ideals of truthfulness, integrity, fairness, respect and responsibility in their definition of ethical behavior**. Truthfulness is being honest. Integrity means a person's actions reflect his or her principles. Fairness is the effort to operate impartially and give all parties equal access to resources, information, and opportunities. Respect means demonstrating positive regard and consideration for others. Finally, responsibility is holding oneself accountable for his or her actions and communication.[60]

In addition to ethical considerations, there are legal limits to what and how we communicate. For example, threatening to kill a person or soliciting others to kill, especially a government official, will land you in jail or at least net you a visit from the Secret Service. Dan Tilli, age eighty-one, wrote a letter to his town's newspaper expressing his opinion about the execution of Saddam Hussein, stating "they hanged the wrong man." He was visited by Secret Service agents who were concerned that Tilli was referring to President Bush. Tilli stated he could have been referring to anybody, such as Osama bin Laden.[61]

In addition to issuing physical threats, other communication behaviors may get us into legal trouble or jeopardize our employment. If we say or write something about someone which is false or inaccurate (and it can be shown that it had a deleterious effect on the person's reputation, job, business, or product) we can be successfully sued in civil court for either slander or libel. **Slander** is saying things, and **libel** is writing things, which another person finds injurious.[62] Another behavior which is considered unethical is sexual harassment. The Equal Employment Opportunity Commission (EEOC) defines **sexual harassment** as "unsolicited, unwelcomed behavior of a sexual nature." The two major kinds of sexual harassment are known as "quid pro quo" (Latin for "this for that") and "hostile work environment." Quid pro quo occurs when a person of power offers rewards in return for sexual favors or dating opportunities such as getting a drink after work. The other form of sexual harassment, hostile work environment, occurs when a person says or does things of a sexual

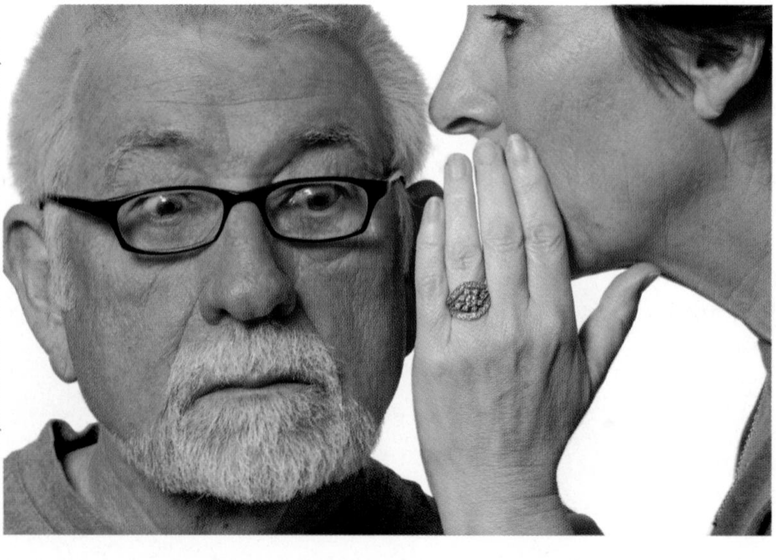

nature which make others feel uncomfortable. Examples may include jokes or gestures, displaying objects, or making comments that are sexually suggestive. [63,64]

Should we say something that's true even if it may hurt a person's feelings? Why or why not?

Along with the legality of what we say and do, our relationships and reputation are influenced by our ethical choices. We all want to be in someone's version of Jack Byrnes' "circle of trust" (*Meet the Fockers,* 2004). We want to trust others, and conversely, we want others to trust us. There is a basic assumption that what people say is true and sincere. Otherwise, people will seriously question everyone's motives. Our believability as communicators rests on the principle that we mean what we say and say what we mean, which is called **authentic communication**.

When our words and actions don't match, when we are caught in a lie, or we make promises we don't keep, we jeopardize our reputation, credibility, and trustworthiness. We may erode the foundation of any relationship: trust.

There appears to be a general consensus within the interpersonal communication field about what constitutes unethical behavior:

- Covering up our behaviors, when they can harm another person, physically, mentally, emotionally, socially, spiritually, or financially.
- Employing messages to coerce someone to do something that is against his or her morals or that is destructive, violent, illegal, or unsafe.
- Spreading rumors that can damage a person's reputation, career, and relationships.
- Name-calling or the use of language to defame, demean, degrade, or negatively stereotype other individuals.
- Using derogatory language like: "injun," "nigger," "wop," "jap," "chink," or "spic" debases people of Native American, African, Italian, Japanese, Chinese, and Hispanic ancestry. "Fag" or "dyke" are derogatory terms for people who are homosexual. Jokes, mannerisms, or sayings that promote stereotypes or poke fun at a person's culture, religious beliefs, sexual orientation, gender, body weight, or physical/mental disability can be offensive and hurtful. We have an ethical obligation to uplift people and defend each person's dignity and self-esteem. We can and should encourage respect and appreciation for diversity.[65]

. . . What is ethics? Why does it matter in terms of our communication choices?

Unit Summary

A keen awareness of the eight principles of interpersonal communication can guide us in our communication choices. These realities are a pervasive part of human communication. These principles include: (1) Communication is learned and can be unlearned. (2) It doesn't need to involve another person. (3) It is just as much about listening as it is talking. (4) Communication is irreversible and unrepeatable. (5) It will cause some and doesn't solve all problems. (6) It is not just what you mean, but how it is interpreted. (7) Communication is often unintentional, and (8) Communication involves ethical considerations.

Key Questions

1. How is the general system's theory applicable to interpersonal communication?
2. How is interpersonal communication a learned behavior?
3. What are the four stages (AASI) of acquiring a new communication skill? How would you describe what each means? What are the four steps to improving our interpersonal communication? How would you describe them?
4. Why is intrapersonal communication important?
5. What is active listening? How is encoding and decoding involved?
6. What do we mean when we say communication is irreversible and unrepeatable?
7. How is communication the cause of some problems and not a remedy for all problems?
8. How is interpersonal communication not just what you say, but how it is interpreted?
9. When we say communication is pervasive and often unintentional, what do we mean?
10. What role does ethics play in our interpersonal communication?

Vocabulary Playback

Self-monitoring
Interpersonal Skills
Process
Outcome
System
Culture
Roles
Rules
Explicit Rules
Implicit Rules
Communication Apprehension
Intrapersonal Communication
Catharsis
Extrapersonal Communication
Active Listening
Egocentric Communicator
Unintentional Communication
Ethics
Sexual harassment
Slander
Libel
Authentic Communication

Theoretically Speaking

- General Systems Theory
- Communication Accommodation Theory

Focus Group/Class Discussion

- Many people argue that the United States K-12 and college education system shortchanges students by not adequately teaching them how to communicate effectively in interpersonal contexts? Do you agree or disagree? Why?
- How are the implicit rules for public restroom etiquette different between males and females?
- When we talk to animals do they understand human language or are they just responding to sounds? Explain your thoughts.
- Is the interpretation of communication more important than its intent? Why or why not?
- Wouldn't it be great if we had access to a kind of "universal remote" that Adam Sandler's character, Michael Newman, stumbled across in the comedy *Click* (2006)! We could pause, fast forward, rewind, control the volume, and mute a person or communication encounter. Like Newman, in a fit of anger, we could slap people while they are in the "pause" mode. They'd experience sudden pain, yet have no clue what just caused it—just kidding! If you were given a remote like this and only two features worked, which two would you choose? Why? How does this hypothetical situation relate to the principles of communication?
- What is the most ethical thing to say when you want to turn down a person's request to go out with you on a second date, (and any other future dates!)?
- When it comes to social or communication situations, which ones do you find most challenging in terms of making ethical decisions?

Unit 3 Vocabulary Review

___ Self-monitoring
___ Interpersonal Skills
___ Process
___ Outcome
___ System
___ Culture
___ Roles
___ Rules
___ Explicit Rules
___ Implicit Rules
___ Communication Apprehension
___ Intrapersonal Communication
___ Catharsis
___ Extrapersonal Communication
___ Active Listening
___ Egocentric Communicator
___ Unintentional Communication
___ Ethics
___ Authentic Communication
___ Slander
___ Libel

A. The ability to successfully relate to and understand people.

B. Communication we have with ourselves silently or out loud; self talk.

C. Saying things which another person finds injurious.

D. The mental process of analyzing our interpersonal communication in order to heighten our awareness of how we communicate with others and pinpoint areas for improvement.

E. What is comprised of interdependent parts or components which interact or function as a whole.

F. A term used to describe the fear or anxiety one experiences in a communication situation.

G. This is how or the manner in which communication takes place.

H. The communication we have with animals or nonliving things.

I. This is the product or end state of communication.

J. A specific pattern of behavior that a person performs ritually to adhere to the expectations of other members.

K. This is a standard which people are expected to adhere to in a given social context.

L. A rule which is not overtly established, yet people adhere to it.

M. The feeling of releasing stress or pent-up emotions as a result of talking about something. It is the act of "getting if off your chest."

N. This is the language, values, beliefs, interests, traditions, and customs people share and learn.

O. The process of focusing on a message, making sense of it, and responding to it.

P. The application of moral principles which help guide a person's behavior

Q. A rule which is communicated to us directly in spoken or written form.

R. Writing things which another person finds injurious.

S. This occurs when a person doesn't mean to send a message or does so unknowingly.

T. A communicator who is self-centered or self-absorbed.

Exercises

Just like the scenes you see on *Saturday Night Live*, your team or cast of characters will create a scene and script (they can be funny or serious) and then act it out showing one or more of the following interpersonal communication principles. Be prepared to discuss how the scene pertains to the principle(s).

Communication is not all talk.
Communication doesn't always involve another person.
It's impossible not to communicate.
You will always mess up.
Communication is not just what you say and do, but how it is interpreted.
Communication is irreversible.
Communication can be intentional and unintentional.
Each communication act is unique.
Communication will not solve all problems.
Communication involves ethical choices

Coffee House Discussion

You may be assigned to or you may choose to form your own "movie club" with friends or classmates. As a group, pick one of the following films (or add your favorite to this list). These are movies with strong communication and relational themes. Your group may choose to watch the film together or separately. Meet at your favorite coffee house and discuss how communication plays a key role in what happens to the characters. Brainstorm and generate a list of how the communication principles apply.

Office Space (1999)
Dinner With Friends (2001)
How To Lose A Guy In Ten Days (2003)
Boys Don't Cry (1999)
The Notebook (2004)
How To Deal (2003)
Sleepless in Seattle (1993)
Notting Hill (1999)
Hitch (2005)
As Good As It Gets (1997)
Goodfellas (1990)
Liar Liar (1997)
What Women Want (2000)
The Firm (1993)
Schindler's List (1993)
Waitress (2007)
Borat (2006)
Here on Earth (2000)
When Harry Met Sally (1989)
How Stella Got Her Groove Back (1998)
Pearl Harbor (2001)
A Walk To Remember (2002)
The Wedding Planner (2001)
Soul Food (1997)
About Schmidt (2002)
Castaway (1986)
Secret To My Success (1987)
What Women Want (2000)
Disclosure (2004)
Enough (2002)
Good Night, and Good Luck (2005)
A Few Good Men (1992)
The Wedding Crashers (2005)
Away From Her (2007)

Six Pack: Six Questions to Stimulate Productive Intrapersonal Communication

Think of a time in which you faced a tough decision or were experiencing negative emotions, stress, or unique challenges. Answer the following questions in as much detail as possible. We can memorize these questions and use them on a regular basis, making them the bedrock of our intrapersonal communication. Be prepared to share your responses to members of the class.

1. What is causing me to feel this way?
2. What can I do about this?
3. What is outside of my control?
4. What do I have to be thankful for?
5. What hasn't changed in my life?
6. How could I look at this differently? How important is this?

Purpose
4

Purpose Unit 4

Our interpersonal communication is driven by various needs. Unit 4 highlights the motives which influence our interpersonal communication.

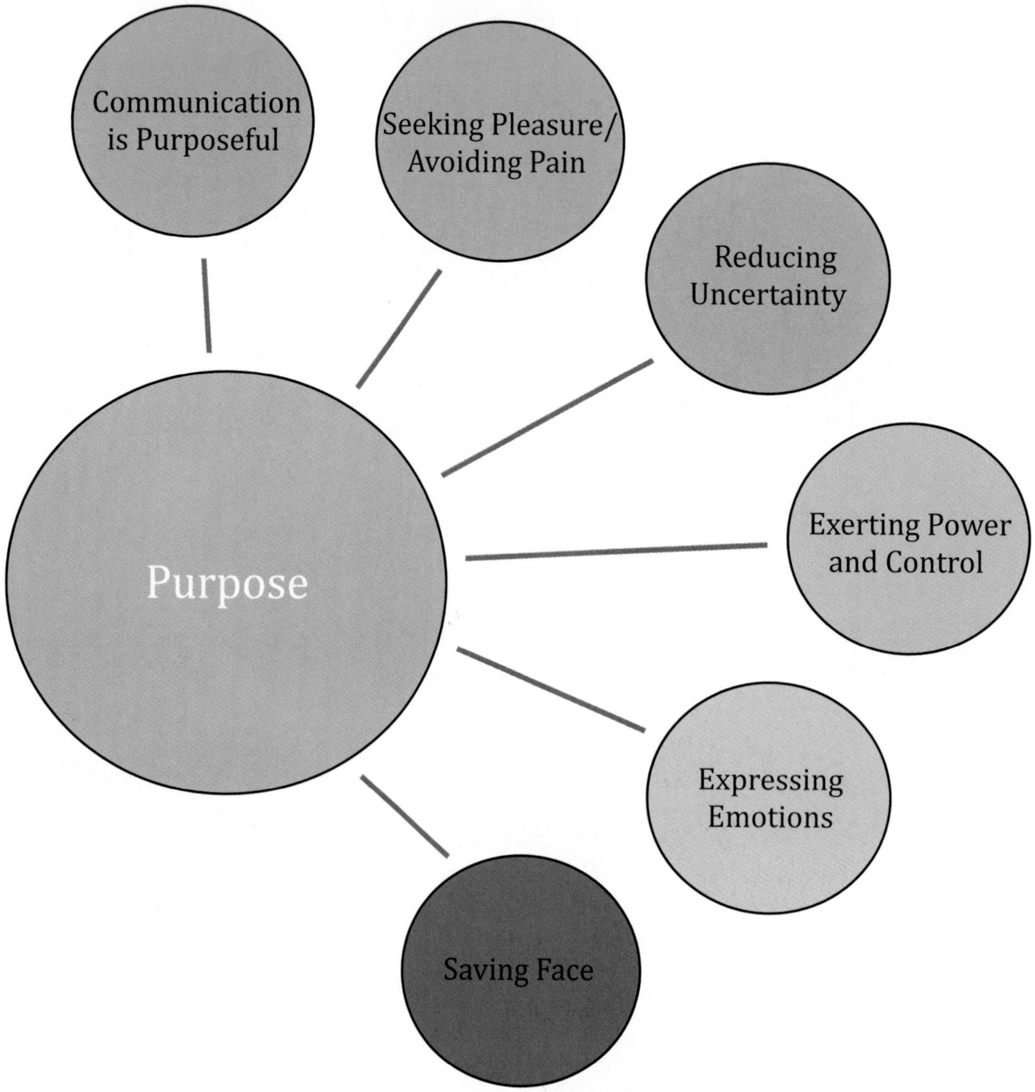

Unit 4 Learning Objectives

As a result of reading and studying Unit 4, you will be able to:

1. Identify the various needs we strive to satisfy with our interpersonal communication.
2. Explain the advantages and disadvantages of direct and indirect communication.
3. Understand how our interpersonal communication is used to seek pleasure and avoid pain.
4. Appreciate why we utilize our interpersonal communication to reduce uncertainty.
5. Describe how we use our interpersonal communication to exert power and control.
6. Learn how and why we rely on communication to express our emotions.
7. Identify what motivates us to employ interpersonal communication strategies to save face.

Cubicle tethered Peter Gibbons (*Office Space*, 1999) is a burned-out software programmer who loathes his job at Initech. His girlfriend has just pulled an MTV's *"Next"* move, kicking him to the curb for another guy. Seeking a meditative escape from his life, Peter decides to visit a hypnotherapist. During the session, the hypnotist suffers a heart attack and dies before pulling Peter out of his altered state of bliss. Oblivious to what has just happened to the hypnotherapist, Peter walks out of the office in a permanent "anything goes," and "I'll tell you what I really think" state-of-mind. In the midst of this, Initech hires consultants to help manage its colossal downsizing, and Peter's job—like a David Blaine illusion—is about to disappear. Ironically, the consultants are impressed with Peter's carefree attitude and blatant honesty, and he is promoted to the ranks of upper management!

One mind-numbing morning, Peter is approached by manager Bill Lumbergh, who speaks in a painfully slow monotone voice, punctuated by an annoying drawl:

Bill: "Hey Peter whaaat's happening." Yaaa. We have sort of a problem here. Yaaaa. You apparently didn't put one of the new cover sheets on your TPS reports."

Peter: "I'm sorry about that. I forgot."

Bill: "Uhmmm. Yaaaa. You see. We're putting cover letters on all TPS reports before they go out. Did you see the memo?"

Peter: "Ya. Ya. I have the memo right here. I just forgot, but it is not shipping out till tomorrow so there's no problem."

Bill: "Yaaaaa. If you could just make sure you go ahead and do that from now on that would be greeaaat. An uhhhhh, I'll be sure that you get another copy of that memo."

A few minutes later another manager, Dom Portwood, drops by Peter's cubicle. Despite Peter's attempt to clearly and succinctly communicate his understanding of the new TPS policy, he's forced to stomach Dom's unnecessary reminder.

Dom: "Hi, Peter. What's happening? We need to talk about your TPS reports."

Peter: "Yeah. The cover sheet. I know. I know. Uh, Bill talked to me about it."

Dom: "Did you get that memo?"

Peter: "Yeah. I got the memo. And I understand the policy. And the problem is that I just forgot this one time. And I've already taken care of it, so it's not even really a problem anymore."

Dom: "Ah! Yeah. It's just we're putting new coversheets on all the TPS reports before they go out now. So if you could go ahead and *try* to remember to do that from now on, that'd be great."[1]

Like Peter, Dom, and Bill, our communication is driven by conscious and unconscious needs. Whether we get our needs met will depend a lot on how we communicate.[2] We want people to listen to us, but sometimes fail to grant others our full attention. We desire to be understood, but frequently overlook how we come across and the clarity of our message. We seek people's cooperation, but commonly rely on the wrong tactics. We sometimes hit singles rather than homeruns with our apologies. At times, we want some kind of action or response from people, but expect them to read our minds.

"I need shoes that look good, provide support, and help me get over my short height complex."

The success of interpersonal communication is similar to choreographed dancing. Dancers who perform do so because they want to look good and impress their audience. In order to do this, they need to be conscious of each other to synchronize their moves. A single misstep by one dancer can affect the combination of movements or an entire routine. Each crew member must be willing to work together and cooperate. Interpersonal communication is similar. There is an interdependence that exists. All parties need to be sensitive and responsive to each other's thoughts, feelings, and needs. What one person says or does influences what the other person says or does next.

Despite his efforts to communicate a clear message to his managers, Peter Gibbon's interaction represents a common interpersonal occurrence: miscommunication. From unit one, we learned that miscommunication occurs anytime a message produces a misunderstanding or unwanted result. **To improve our communication competence and reduce the frequency of miscommunication, it behooves us to understand that human communication is driven by various needs or goals.**

Communication Is Purposeful

Megan McCafferty, a happily married wife and mother of three, "cyberstalked" a guy she fell in love with ten years ago in college. The reason? She needed answers. Her whirlwind romance with "Ben" came to a screeching halt when one day he went AWOL. He stopped calling and coming over. When he saw her at parties, he exited stage—wherever! Despite her attempts to procure an explanation, Ben never disclosed why he was pulling a "dating ding dong ditchin'." He transferred to another college the next semester. Megan just couldn't understand it. She really connected with him and was convinced the feelings were mutual. She needed to know what scared him off. She finally decided to conduct a Google search, with her husband's approval, and found him. Her initial *"Remember me?"* and *"Why did you behave like that?"* inquiry netted a response from Ben about a month later. He provided Megan with this interesting answer: "Love is a scary thing. For a man-child terrified of risk and harm, what could inspire more fear than the possibility of someone shattering his defenses? In some completely . . . backward way, the coldness of my exit was in direct proportion to the desire I felt for you."

He went on to write how his insecurity manifested itself in the classic, "I'll dump you before you have the chance to dump me" dating scenario. For Megan, it closed a much needed chapter in her life. She was relieved to know what he really thought about their relationship. She didn't feel the desire to contact him again—and that was o.k.[3]

Tracking down our ex, an arch enemy, or someone we have wronged in the past, so we can say everything we wanted to say then, but didn't, is not only a popular *Montel Williams*, or *Tyra Banks Talk Show* theme, it is an example of how communication is goal driven. There is a purpose behind our interpersonal communication. We communicate to satisfy certain needs. Renowned Swiss psychiatrist Carl Jung stated, "There is no randomness to our behavior. There is a reason for why we behave the way we do." While this may be true, we may not always have a conscious awareness of our inner drives or their connection to our communication behaviors.

We use our interpersonal communication for a lot of reasons. We may try to outlast competing tribal members on some remote island for a chance at instant fame and money. We may persuade a supervisor to change our work schedule so we can be front and center at next Saturday's *Black Eyed Peas* concert, or return something to Hollister we wore once, but could not afford, like the Iowa woman who told a department store clerk she needed to return the scarf she bought. She claimed it was too tight.

Communication is goal oriented. We communicate to survive, belong, and gain a sense of "self." We rely on our communication to satisfy our emotional, physical, spiritual, and social needs. In 1954, psychologist Abraham Maslow developed a theory to explain human motivation. His **Hierarchy of Human Needs Theory** suggests people strive to satisfy their needs

When it comes to trying to get everyone's needs met, interpersonal communication can get tricky—*It's Complicated (2010)!*

in an upwardly, hierarchical manner. We first focus on our basic needs such as food and shelter. When these needs are satisfied, we devote our time and energy to fulfilling other needs such as stretching our creative capacities or having fun.[4]

Maslow's theoretical exploration led him to author several lauded works such as *Toward a Psychology of Being* and *Theory of Human Motivation*. He describes his theory using a pyramid. The pyramid illustrates how we fulfill our needs in the upper tiers, once lower tier needs are met.[5] Let's compare Maslow's theory to our interpersonal communication. Maslow's theory originated with five tiers. Since then, some psychologists have expanded Maslow's pyramid to include two additional ones, which we'll explore.

Physiological Needs

We'll use our communication to get our survival needs met first. These needs include food, water, sleep, shelter, and clothing. Maslow also included the need for procreation or the expression of sexual feelings here. These needs safeguard our existence and the perpetuation of our species. If we are thirsty, we seek water. If water is not immediately available to us, we are motivated to acquire it—in short order. Maslow coined these needs "pre-potent."

Security Needs

Maslow believed humans have a compelling interest to ensure that everyone's physiological needs are met—not just their own. If they don't, people start getting really mean. Maslow explained that in order to feel safe and protected within a community or society, humans share resources with each other. We need social order and a peaceful existence. We establish this through social pressure, rules, institutions, and laws.

Love and Belonging Needs

Unit one focused a lot on this critical need. It is the need to give and receive affection. We endeavor to create relationships and gain a

The film *I Love You Man!* (2009) depicts the importance of close male friendships. "Slapping the bass! Slappa da bass! Slappa da bass mon!"

sense of connectedness. Someone was inspired to say, "Being with you is like walking on a very clear morning—definitely the sensation of belonging there." The main characters in the hit movie *I Love You Man!* (2009) demonstrate this. The need for love and belonging also resonates in the lyrics of Nickelback's hit song *Gotta Be Somebody.*

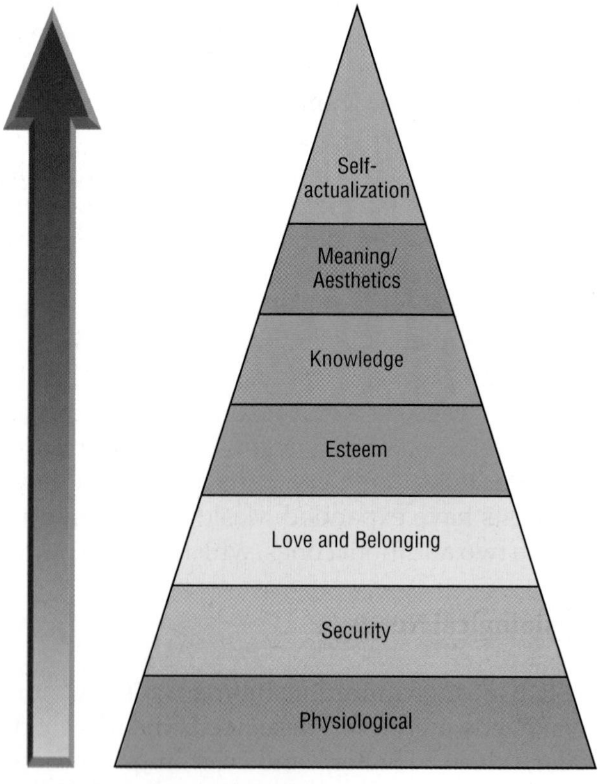

Maslow's Hierarchy of Needs (Revised)

Esteem Needs

We all pursue the admiration, respect, and positive regard of friends, peers, and family members. We need to feel we have value and worth. We will engineer this within ourselves and seek affirmation of it from others. We also desire to dispense appreciation to others because it feels good to make others feel good. Communication behaviors such as smiling at a person, paying someone a compliment, or asking a person his or her opinion regarding something are generally characterized as esteem enhancing. Knowing that we have a positive reputation in certain circles bolsters our self-concept, which is how we see ourselves.

. . . **Catch this!** A catchy theatrical video on the need to give and receive esteem www.youtube.com: validation

Knowledge

When referencing Maslow's Hierarchy of Needs Theory, some scholars and psychologists include this tier to represent our thirst for knowledge. We all have a need to cultivate knowledge and understanding—to know how things work and why things are the way they are. We search for answers to life's questions and mysteries. We satisfy this need through such activities as reading, doing puzzles, taking things apart, attending lectures, visiting museums, joining book clubs, watching the news, and perusing the Internet. University of Southern California neuroscientist, Irving Biederman, theorizes that our brains reward us for new knowledge. His research team conducted a study which found that as we grasp a new concept or comprehend something complex, our brains release natural opium-like substances. He suggests that this may explain our thirst for knowledge and why we have evolved as a species.[6, 7]

Meaning/Aesthetics

Another tier added to Maslow's original theoretical explanation by some contemporary psychologists is our aim for a sense of purpose. We entertain the questions: "What is life all about?" "Why am I here?" "How do I fit into the grand scheme of things?" We look for ways to satisfy our desire to matter and make a difference. This is a major reason why many adults choose to become parents. Some people fulfill this need through volunteer work and community activism, others in religious studies and expression. The exploration and enjoyment of philosophy, nature, and the arts also help us gain a sense of meaning or purpose.

Self-Actualization

Maslow coined **self-actualization** as realizing one's full potential, "To become everything that one is capable of becoming." This is our desire to advance our goals and expand our talents. Maslow saw it as the pinnacle of human needs: "A musician must make music, an artist must paint, a poet must write, if he is to be at peace with himself. What a man can be, he must be. This is the need we may call self-actualization . . . It refers to man's desire for fulfillment, to become actually what he is potentially."[8]

Maslow's hierarchy of needs theory is very applicable to interpersonal communication. For example, we all, at times, fish for praise. We might say to a friend, "I'm not sure this looks good on me (when we know it does). What do you think?" Our question is designed to reel in a compliment. A friend may say to us, "It's going to take a plastic surgeon to shed this weight off." We respond, "Are you kidding, you look great. Your workouts are really paying off." People sometimes put themselves down in our presence, hoping that we'll say something positive in retort. When a person compliments us, it is often a sincere recognition of something they see in us. Sometimes it is done for self-serving reasons. Experience has taught them that when they compliment another person, a compliment is often returned. These tactics are bait to catch a flattering remark or "pat on the back." Which one of Maslow's hierarchy of needs are people trying to meet here with their interpersonal communication?

Let's apply Maslow's hierarchy of human needs theory to another example. In 1980, Candace Lightner's effervescent thirteen-year-old daughter, Cari, was walking down the street near her home when a teenage drunk driver barreled around a corner and slammed into her small frame, killing her instantly. To make sense of her daughter's death, and channel her grief in a positive way, Lightner met with members of her state legislature, one-on-one and in small groups, to persuade them to adopt tougher drunk driving laws. She became a skilled lobbyist and commenced walking the corridors of the U.S. Congress. Her eloquence moved all who heard her. President Ronald Reagan commissioned Lightner to serve on the National Commission on Drunk Driving. She is credited for spearheading the drive to pass the "21" amendment, which denied federal highway funds to states that refused to raise the drinking age to 21. Today, all fifty states have this as the legal drinking age. The legislation is estimated to save the lives of eight hundred people annually.

Lightner is heralded as a catalyst of a major movement in America and was the founder of one of America's most robust political organizations: Mothers Against Drunk Driving.[9] Candace Lightner employed interpersonal and public communication to change people's thinking and alter public policy. Which one of Maslow's hierarchy of needs did Ms. Lightner's actions satisfy?

Do you agree with Maslow's theory? Why or why not?

. . . Using Maslow's Hierarchy of Human Needs Theory, how would you describe the needs we strive to satisfy with our communication?

Communication is the primary tool we use to accomplish our many needs. We'll focus our attention now on five of them in depth. **They include the need to: 1) seek pleasure and avoid pain, 2) reduce uncertainty about people or events, 3) exercise power and control, 4) express our emotions, and 5) save face.**

Seek Pleasure and Avoid Pain

A nine-year-old San Franciscan boy, Semaj Booker, made news headlines when he took his mother's car, drove it to the airport, and without any money or plane tickets, boarded not just one, but two planes before he was caught attempting to get on a third flight. This happened post-9-11 with airport security measures at their peak. Apparently, he was experiencing a lot of problems at home with his mother and was determined to escape to Dallas, Texas to see his grandfather. A spokesperson for Southwest Airlines stated that the company is investigating just how this young man penetrated security, procured passes, and hoodwinked airline crews. This boy's communication was clearly piloted with a purpose![10]

How do you think Booker accomplish this using his verbal and nonverbal communication?

Along with Semaj Booker, U.S. astronaut and mother of three Lisa Nowak's out of the ordinary trip put her in the national spotlight. According to press reports, Nowak unearthed a romantic relationship between Air Force Captain Colleen Shipman and Nowak's lover,

astronaut Bill Oefelein. Nowak intercepted an e-mail message from Shipman to Oefelein on his computer, which detailed their flight plans and rendezvous point. Nowak drove to Orlando, Florida from her home in Houston, Texas to find Shipman. Nowak then trailed Shipman from the airport to her car. Nowak, disguised in a wig and glasses, approached Shipman as she got in her car. She told her that something happened, and she needed a ride. When Shipmen refused, Nowak doused her with pepper spray.

Shipmen called the police with her cell phone. Officers apprehended Nowak and found in Nowak's handbag a new steel mallet, a folding knife, three to four feet of rubber tubing, and several large plastic garbage bags. Officers also seized printed maps to Shipman's home, a half-dozen latex gloves, romantic e-mails from Shipman to Oefelein, and diapers Nowak admitted she wore to reduce stops along the highway.

Nowak claimed that she simply wanted to "talk" with Shipman. Nowak's goals, based on the evidence, suggest that "talk" was not her only mission. This bizarre love triangle between the three gets even more spacey considering Lisa Nowak was married for nineteen years to another man at the time.[11]

Like Semaj Booker and Lisa Nowak, we all need at times to escape from unpleasant circumstances or eliminate a source of distress. The idea that people act in ways to maximize pleasure and minimize physical and psychological pain, was pondered by Aristotle in 300 BC, and later refined by psychoanalysis founder Sigmund Freud. Freud termed his idea the **pleasure principle.**[13]

> The Associated Press reports that 44-year-old Scott Allan Witmer appeared before a Pennsylvania court judge after police arrested him for drinking and driving. Witmer chose to represent himself. He claimed that the police lacked jurisdiction to stop him, because he was his own country. He said that he lives inside himself and not Pennsylvania, and is not legally bound by the state's laws. Witmer's novel approach is a great example of how people use communication to avoid the pain (jail time!) or negative consequences of their actions![12]

Things which may bring us pleasure may include fun activities, relaxation, adventure, closeness, quiet time, or eating something delectable. Stress, boredom, conflict, unpleasant tasks, or some form of punishment may represent pain. Our communication behavior is influenced by what we perceive as desirable or undesirable. We may use our communication to escape from a weekend with the in-laws, milk some sympathy, talk ourselves out of the dog house, or prolong a massage. For example, Jake has Mr. Universe ambitions at the gym one day and comes home with back muscles screaming for a deep tissue massage from his girlfriend, Emily. He is in the throes of her strong hands and his back applauds her attentiveness. He doesn't want her to stop. Emily, meanwhile, has just finished an eight-hour shift serving drinks at the Howlin' Moon Saloon. She wants her pampered boyfriend to give her feet the attention his back is getting. How do they use their communication to get their needs met?

Jake: (Sensing Emily is about to stop) "This feels great. Right there. . . . Up a little. There you go. Wow! Keep it up, baby."

Emily: "You like when I massage your shoulders and back after you've worked out hard."

Jake: "Do I! Knowing that I'm going to get this when I get home from the gym motivates me to work all that much harder."

Emily: "I can just imagine how you feel right now. I feel the same way when you rub my feet after I've worked a long day."

Jake and Emily's interaction typifies how people use communication to capitalize on what may bring them physical and/or emotional pleasure. We may do this directly or indirectly.

Without saying directly to Emily, "I want you, despite being tired, to keep rubbing my back," Jake uses praise, moans, and words of encouragement to indirectly prod Emily to continue. Rather than saying directly, "Jake, I want

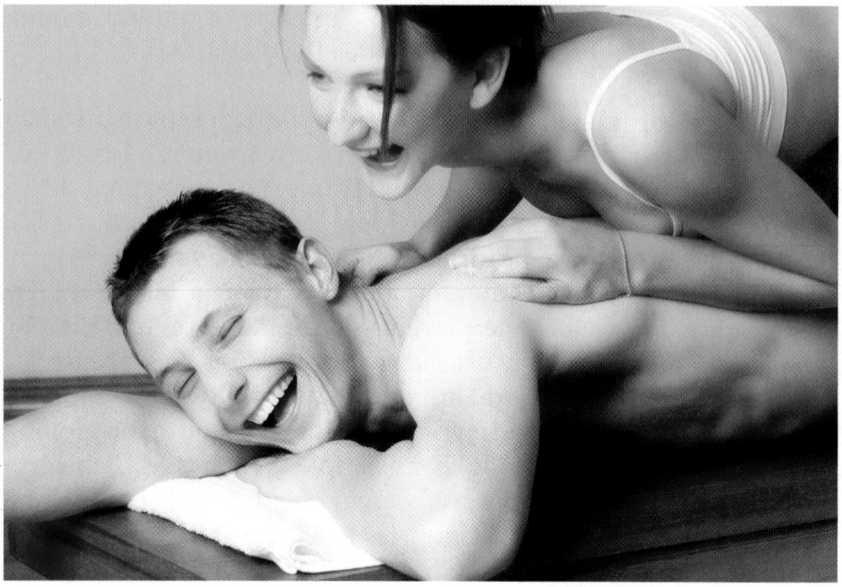

you to rub my feet next," Emily hopes he will get her subtle hint, "I can just imagine how you feel right now. I feel the same way when you rub my feet after I've worked a long day." If Jake's radar doesn't pick up on Emily's indirect message, and he doesn't reciprocate, she may feel disappointed, possibly even mad at him. **Indirect communication** occurs when a message hints at something. It is subtle or suggestive. Its intent is opaque. If Emily says, "Jake, when I'm done rubbing your back, I'd like you to massage my aching feet," she is being more direct in her communication. There is a greater chance Emily will get her needs met with this kind of message. **Direct communication** occurs when a message is sent in a clear and obvious way. Its intent is very apparent.

When we don't communicate directly, we may set ourselves up for disappointment. We often expect people to read our minds. We hint at or allude to things as a "test" to see if a person will meet our needs or expectations. A direct message reduces the likelihood of people misreading or overlooking what we are trying to say. However, there is such a thing as being too direct. What we say may be perceived by the receiver as too blunt or rude. As communicators, we have to walk a fine line here.

Are there times, however, when an indirect message is preferable? For example, Mike shares an idea with his coworker, Dato. Dato thinks Mike's proposal is not only unrealistic, but likely to cause him added stress (pain!) Rather than use a potentially confrontational direct message such as, "I'm concerned that your plan is unrealistic and poorly timed given our deadline is Friday," Dato says something less direct like, "Do you think we can accomplish this and our other projects by Friday?" Mike starts to answer his colleague's question and stops midsentence. He realizes that it is not plausible and says, "Well, I guess this is too much for us to do." Dato is thinking, "Exactly." Dato used a question as an indirect way to get Mike to grasp something.

Sometimes we use indirect messages because we don't want to appear too forward, opinionated, or controlling. We may choose a more subtle message because we are sensitive to another person's feelings or image. Some cultures value a less direct approach in

communication because it is deemed more harmonic and face-saving[14, 15]

Contrast the situations below as they relate to direct and indirect communication and our need to seek pleasure/avoid pain. What do you see as the advantages versus disadvantages of indirect and direct messages?

You want help with the dishes.
(pain avoidance)

Indirect: "Have you seen the sink?"

Direct: "I'd like you to help me do the dishes, please."

You want to hang out with someone.
(pleasure seeking)

Indirect: "What are you up to this weekend?"

Direct: "I'd enjoy spending Saturday evening with you."

You don't want to get off the couch.
(pleasure seeking/pain avoidance)

Indirect: "Is that the phone?"

Direct: "I'm really into this game, would you get that?"

You're embarrassed by your boyfriend's clothing choice. (pain avoidance)

Indirect: "Didn't you wear that a couple of days ago?"

Direct: "You'd look more buff in your green Hollister."

You don't want someone to cook for you.
(pain avoidance)

Indirect: "What do you say we get some take out?"

Direct: "I don't want you to cook tonight—or ever!"

What are the benefits and disadvantages of direct and indirect communication?

Your Turn: In what ways have you communicated directly this week? How about indirectly? What were the results?

We'll learn more about ways to make our messages more clear and non-confrontational in the unit on symbols and actions. For now, it helps us to realize that on a conscious and unconscious level, we have a tendency to communicate in ways which allow us to experience pleasure and avoid discomfort. We also possess another significant need—to reduce uncertainty.

. . . How is our interpersonal communication used to seek pleasure and avoid pain?

We Communicate to Reduce Uncertainty

Greeting students the first day of fall semester, an authoritative, overzealous dean announced, "The female dormitory is strictly off limits for all male students, and the male dormitory to all female students. Anybody found in violation of this rule will be fined $20.00. A second offense will cost you $60.00. A third time will cost you $180.00. Are there any questions?" One student raised his hand and asked, "How much for a semester pass?" (aha.jokes.com)

We are curious. We like to be in the know—to test, and if possible, stretch the limits. We want answers to our questions. We will use our communication to clarify what is ambiguous about a person, situation, or idea. Perhaps that is why shows such as C.S.I. are so popular. People love to solve mysteries.

The need to reduce uncertainty is apparent in every day conversations between people. This is evident frequently in the scripts of television shows and movies. For example, take the conversation between clueless limo driver Lloyd Christmas, who is hopelessly infatuated with the beautiful Mary Swanson (Lauren Holly) in *Dumb and Dumber* (1994):

Lloyd: "What are the chances of a guy like me and a girl like you . . . ending up together?"

Mary: "Well, that's pretty difficult to say."

Lloyd: "Hit me with it! I've come a long way to see you, Mary. The least you can do is level with me. What are my chances?"

Mary: "Not good."

Lloyd: "You mean, not good, like one out of a hundred?"

Mary: "I'd say more like one out of a million."

Lloyd: "So you're telling me there's a chance!"[16]

Communication interactions have some degree of uncertainty or ambiguity. Lloyd's line of questioning is an attempt to reduce uncertainty about his romantic prospects with Mary. He asks questions to probe, clarify, and predict what may happen between them.

The process of using communication to reduce what we don't know is called uncertainty reduction. The ***uncertainty reduction theory*** originated with communication researchers Charles Berger and Richard Calabrese. Their work is explained in a 1975 article which appeared in the journal *Human Communication Research* titled "Some Explorations in Initial Interaction and Beyond: Toward a Developmental Theory of Interpersonal Communication." According to Berger and Calabrese, we ask questions to lessen uncertainty about new situations and people.[17] When we first meet people, we ask questions to find out "Who is this person?" "What do we have in common?" and "What are his or her motives?"

As we reduce our uncertainty about a person, research suggests we tend to feel closer or more connected to him or her—if we like what we are finding out! [18] Besides asking questions, we also share things about ourselves to reduce uncertainty. We do this in hopes that as we disclose things about ourselves, others will reveal things about themselves.[19] One theory suggests the more we share things about ourselves to someone, the greater the chance he or she will reciprocate. The **social penetration theory**, developed by social psychologists Irwin Altman and Dalmas Taylor, posits that as people get to know one another more, they are inclined to talk to each other about a greater range of topics and reveal more personal aspects of themselves in terms of facts, interests, feelings, desires, and opinions.[20]

The dialogue between Lloyd and Mary not only shows a person's inclination to reduce uncertainty, but to make predictions about future interactions. Communication scholar Michael Sunnafrank's **predicted outcome value theory** suggests that in our initial interactions with others, we'll use direct and indirect communication to assess whether it benefits us to have future interactions. If we expect that future interactions will yield relational rewards, we'll continue our efforts to connect and interact.[21, 22]

A **relational reward** is something we want and may get from a relationship. Examples of relational rewards include stimulating conversations, support, good times, and access to information or things we want. If a person is upbeat and positive, we may like being around him or her more often because we value this. We may also share a common passion with someone such as disk golf or trail biking. On the flip side, let's go back to Lloyd and Mary. If what Mary initially finds out about Lloyd does not appeal to her, and she predicts that future interactions will bear this out even more, she will tend to cut off communication and/or utilize avoidance strategies.

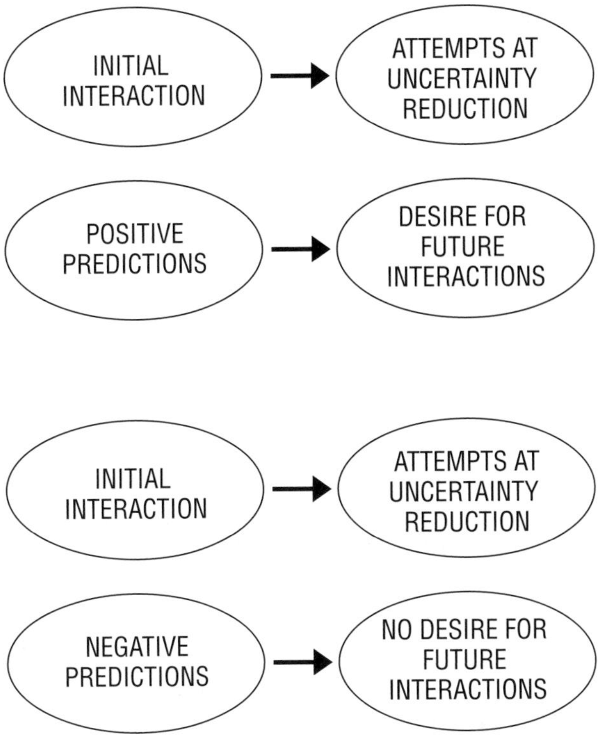

Sunnafrank's Predicted Outcome Value Theory

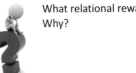

What relational rewards appeal to you the most? Why?

We'll explore in more depth what attracts people to one another and the dynamics of interpersonal relationships in unit 12. Next, we'll look at how communication satisfies our need to have control and exercise power.

. . . How and why do we utilize our interpersonal communication to reduce uncertainty?

We Communicate to Exercise Control and Exert Power

As tears stream down her face, Aliiah turns to her mother, Sandy, and says, "You are my mom, but you haven't been my mom for a long time. If I stopped doing everything for you, in a month you would be dead." Sandy will swallow 60 prescription pills in less than four days. She chases her anti-anxiety, depression, and seizure pills with two pints of vodka a day. She drinks mouthwash when her vodka supply dries up. Sandy is one of millions of Americans who struggle with addiction. Her three daughters, one son, and husband surprised her in her home one day. With the help of a recovering person with long-term sobriety, they confront Sandy in her living room. The air is thick with tension and what happens next is heart wrenching. Sandy's loved ones say things to her that she has never heard or wanted to hear. One at a time, they detail how her alcoholism affects her and them. They then spell out exactly what will happen if she refuses to participate in a recovery program. The consequences include cutting Sandy's money supply, not letting her spend time with her grandchildren, an irreconcilable divorce, and even complete estrangement from her entire family. Their attempts to control and exert power over their mother's addiction are shown on A & E's hard-hitting series *The Intervention.*

. . . **Catch this!** What happens in an intervention? Check one out by going to www.aetv.com/intervention

The Intervention joins a growing line up of reality shows such as *Tool Academy, Big Brother, Megan Wants a Millionaire, Tough Love, Making the Band, College Hill, The Apprentice,* and *America's Next Top Model* which showcase people's efforts to influence their circumstances and other people in self-serving ways. We all feel the need to exert some influence on the people who matter to us. Social scientists have coined the term **compliance-gaining** to describe the strategies people use to get people to think or act a certain way. Researchers have now pinpointed over sixty ways we attempt to gain compliance from others.[23] These strategies include flattery, bribery, logical appeals, bargaining, direct requests, and threats.[24, 25, 26, 27] We learn that we can get people to comply with our wishes as early as the age of one.[28]

To a certain extent, the need to exercise power is normal and healthy. **Power** is defined as the ability to influence other people or events. The perception that we have control of ourselves, the situations we are in, and other people we care about, gives us a sense of responsibility, ownership, and competence. It is a vital part of increasing our confidence, motivation, and self-esteem.

We utilize a variety of different approaches, positive and/or negative to exercise power. For example, a mother was preparing pancakes for her sons one morning. The boys started to argue over who would get the first pancake. The mother saw an opportunity to teach a moral lesson. She turns to her boys and says, "If Buddha were sitting here, he would say, 'Let not my brother wait, I will put him before me and give him the first pancake.' "One of the boys turned to the other and said, "You be Buddha." Her sons missed the point, but the mother certainly tried to sway her sons to value patience and selflessness.

It was reported that when actor Mathew McConaughey was a boy, his mother often made a great breakfast to start the day. Some mornings, Matthew and his siblings weren't always positive and appreciative. On those days, Matthew stated that his mother would clutch them by the arm and march them back to bed. "She'd say don't sit down at the table until you are going to see the roses in the vase instead of the dust on the table."[29]

Our need to exert power and exercise control or to get what we want out of people is also reflected in this exchange between a tight-fisted man who grumbled when a college student delivered his pizza.

Man: "What is the usual tip?"

Student: "This is my first delivery to you. The other delivery guys warned me that if I got a quarter out of you, I'd be doing great."

Man: "That so? In that case, here's five dollars."

Student: "Thanks."

Man: "By the way, what are you studying at the college?"

Student: "Applied psychology." (www.cleanhumor.com)

The student harnessed a little reverse psychology to lasso a bigger tip. We all want to "tip" the odds in our favor at times. From a communication standpoint, we may try to control the behavior of others by politely communicating requests, sharing a personal story, offering encouragement, or expressing our needs or feelings in a nonthreatening way. We may also resort to making demands, issuing threats, acting helpless, feigning ignorance, not involving another person in a decision, concealing our real motives, starting rumors, or lavishing insincere praise. People also find ways to get us to do what they want by setting up rules to discourage the expression of certain thoughts and feelings. Without our knowledge, they form secret alliances with family members or coworkers to vote us off at tribal council, *Survivor*-style. They may use indirect manipulation, overt persuasion, guilt-inducement, deception, and theatrics to influence us.

"Let's stop this before we both say a lot of things we mean."
New York Times cartoon caption.

Our need for power in a given situation, the situation itself, and how we attempt to exercise power, often determines a communication outcome. For example, a statement like "You better do this or I will . . ." is an ultimatum. It is generally considered an ineffective communication tactic, especially between adults.

Typically it is prudent to avoid using this tactic. However, after exhausting all our options, like Sandy's family from *The Intervention*, we may need to rely on issuing an ultimatum to get someone we care about to cease doing something that is harmful to him or her or us. Given the circumstances, an ultimatum may work or backfire. Why would this be the case?

Our own emotional well being, safety, or survival may require us to use deception or theatrics—both techniques are generally considered unethical and unproductive, respectively. However, they worked for an eighty-year-old woman in Hampden, Maine who was alone in her home watching a Super Bowl game. She sensed movement in the shadows of her living room as a man approached her in stealth-like fashion. When she confronted him, he grabbed her and forced her into her bedroom. She thought fast and faked a heart attack. She lied and told the intruder her medication was in her car. She pleaded with him to save her. Not wanting to deal with the drama, the man fled.[30]

Our need to control and exercise power is often prompted by other needs. We may find our job tedious and repetitious, so what might we do to jazz it up? Like one Southwest Airlines flight attendant, we may decide to rap the otherwise uneventful and boring safety instructions

© 2010 by Mark Stout Photography. Used under license from Shutterstock, Inc.

before take-off, as our surprised passengers clapped to the beat! The need for spontaneity and fun may prompt us to use our communication in creative ways to alter what would otherwise be mundane or blah.

. . . **Catch this!** Check out the hip hop flight attendant. Go to www.youtube.com.

According to Maslow's Hierarchy of Human Needs Theory, one of our most significant needs beyond survival is to belong and have close attachments. This is the impetus behind our attempt to control the direction a relationship is heading.[31] Bringing home flowers, planning a weekend getaway, buying a person a present, acknowledging a person's birthday, showing up to someone's housewarming party, and exchanging jewelry are concrete and symbolic gestures designed to rekindle or cement a friendship or romance. To save our marriage, we may even book a trip to an exotic island for an unorthodox couple's retreat as was humorously depicted in the film *Couples Retreat* (2009) starring Vince Vaughn.

We also possess a need to control our conversations. **Conversational control** is the need we have to influence the direction and outcome of a conversation. We may set up rules for how we are going to start a discussion, such as who gets to speak first, how long, and whether or not the listener is allowed to interrupt. We may attempt to control a conversation by steering it in another direction. Sometimes people will talk over each other until someone backs down and listens, or they will raise their voices to drown each other out.

Do people differ in terms of how much control or power they need? Research answers in the affirmative.[32] Psychologist William Schutz's **Fundamental Interpersonal Relations Orientation Theory** states that our need for control can fall somewhere between that of an abdicrat and an autocrat. An **abdicrat** typically relinquishes control, is very submissive, and avoids making decisions. He or she is relieved to let others take charge and is characterized as the happy "follower." An **autocrat** is a power seeker. He or she has a high need to exercise control and make decisions. This is your happy "boss." In between the two ends of the power spectrum is the **democrat**, who fluctuates between both fairly comfortably depending on the situation.[33]

A father may allow his daughter to make choices to encourage her maturational growth and decision making skills. He is abdicratic in this sense. If she is making a decision that he thinks may be dangerous or unhealthy, he may step in and make a decision for her, which is autocratic. In a romantic relationship or business partnership, what is the potential challenge if both individuals are strongly abdicratic? How about autocratic? The following dialogue between Pat and Sadie illustrates what might happen in a relationship between two people who are very abdicratic:

Pat: "Do you want to grab some dinner?"

Sadie: "Sure. Where do you want to go?"

Pat: "I don't care. You can pick?"

Sadie: "I don't care either. We can go wherever."

Pat: "It's like this all the time. We never can make a decision."

Sadie: "I'm sorry. You were the one to ask me where I wanted to go first. I should have offered a place." (Stares at Pat blankly)

Pat: "So, great. Where will it be?"

Sadie: "We could go to Logan's or TGI Fridays. Or how about Olive Garden?

Pat: "Your asking me where I want to go!"

Sadie: "O.k. But when you asked me where I wanted to go, did you have a place in mind?"

Pat: "No. I was hoping you'd just pick a place."

Where do you fall on Schutz's power continuum?

People in close interpersonal relationships find that it takes communication to satisfy the variable needs people have for power. Sometimes we may need to be democratic in order to accommodate one another's need for control and power. We may need to be the opposite of what we are comfortable being. For example, we may need to give over control to someone else, when we really want to be in charge. Along with people's varying need for power, the degree to which people influence us is strongly correlated with the kind of power the person has and how much we value that power.

In 1959, social psychologists John French and Bertram Raven conducted a notable study on power. From this study, they identified and described five sources of social power that people possess. **They labeled them reward, coercive, referent, legitimate, and expert.**[34] The bases of power are described in the shaded box. After reading each, respond to the *Your Turn* question.

French and Raven's Five Bases of Power

Reward Power:
This person can reward us in some way (money, opportunities) for compliance.

Coercive Power:
This person has the ability to punish us (take something away or deny us access to something) for noncompliance.

Referent Power:
This person has the ability to influence us because we like, admire, or are attracted to this person in some way (dynamism, intelligence, success, or fame).

Legitimate Power:
This person is granted power because of his or her formal title, credentials, or position. It originates from the roles people play. It is formally given by an institution, governing body or society. People who posses legitimate power may include police officers, judges, managers, or doctors.

Expert Power:
This person can influence us because he or she possesses knowledge, experience, or skills that we lack.

Your Turn: Look at two of your closest relationships. How do these individuals sway you to do what they want? Which of French and Raven's five bases of power has a bearing on how much these individuals influence you? Based on their theory, which bases of power enable you to influence some of the people you know?

The degree to which we exercise control or allow a person to influence us depends on the context or environment and the nature of the relationship. By context we mean that the situation itself gives a person more power. For example, in a classroom, we may be more inclined to do something our professor asks us to do, even if we don't wish to. According to French and Raven, which bases of power is our professor exercising? If we were at a bar or club, and we ran into our professor, who asks us to do something that we would typically do in a classroom (such as write a brief essay) we may not feel so inclined to do it, especially if the class is over and we've received our grade.

The desire to exercise control over ourselves and the situations we are in is normal and necessary. It may, however, become extreme and manifest itself through compulsion, shaming, blackmailing, surreptitious seduction, physical intimidation, deception, and emotional abuse. Often when people use power in a way that is physically or emotionally abusive, it is done to compensate for low self-worth, insecurity,

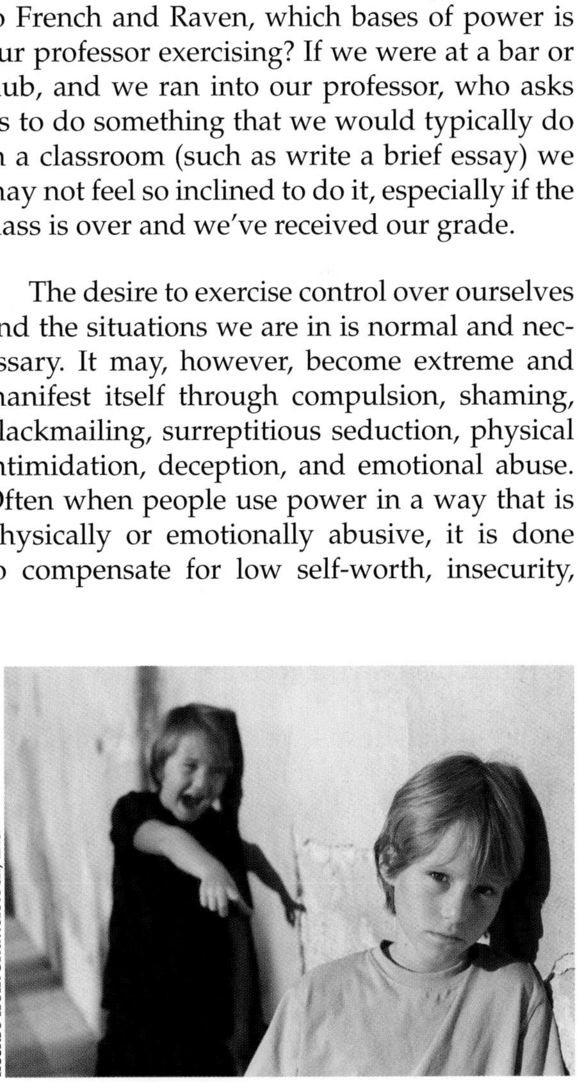

powerlessness, or as a less mature way to cope with secret rage, jealousy, and fear.

The National Crime Prevention Council's *Children and Youth Initiatives* reports that sixty-one percent of children witness some form of bullying every day. A hopeful sign is that fifty-seven percent of the time, bullying stops if someone intervenes or stands up for the victim.[35]

Power and Control in Interpersonal Relationships: A Case Study

In *Emotional Blackmail: When the People in Your Life Use Fear, Obligation, and Guilt to Manipulate You*, psychotherapist Susan Forward breaks down the various ways people control others using direct and indirect means.[36] Let's analyze an example that one may extrapolate from her book. Jay, a construction worker, and Madison, a police officer, have been dating for a long period of time and Jay wants to move in with Madison. He first poses the idea nonchalantly and sees that Madison does not respond enthusiastically. He continues with his hints. They go to another gay couple's wedding, and Jay makes a comment about how happy the couple appear now that they have formalized their relationship and are living together. Madison responds by saying that he is not comfortable with that right now and feels that they have a good arrangement.

Jay begins to use more direct methods to change Madison's mind. While having dinner on Madison's backyard patio, Jay outlines numerous reasons why living together is more sensible. He tells Madison that since most of his belongings are already at Madison's house, the move is easy. Jay shares how things would improve financially since they both could pool their assets and income under one roof. Jay explains how he could help Madison more around the house if he lived there. He says how much he loves Madison and wants to spend more time with him.

Jay's desire to move in with Madison is understandable. It makes a lot of sense to Jay, and Jay has the right to communicate his desire to Madison. In fact, doing so in a direct way is perhaps better since this is very important to him. Madison may agree with Jay's logic and change his mind. However, let's say that Madison rejects Jay's idea. Jay's communication may become more manipulative in a variety of ways. Jay may pose questions that Madison would find difficult to say no to such as, "Don't you want us to spend more time together?" "I only want what's best for us, don't you?"

Jay may employ what is called an obligatory absolute. An obligatory absolute is expressed using the words such as "should," "ought to," or "supposed to." It implies that a person is violating a major norm, value, or principle if he or she doesn't acquiesce. Jay may say to Madison, "People who love each other like we love each other, *should* want to live together." In addition, Jay may imply something that Madison may find threatening, "Perhaps this means we aren't right for each other." He may unveil an indirect threat such as, "If we aren't going to ever make a greater commitment to each other, perhaps we should date other people." He may employ a direct threat or ultimatum, "If you don't want to do this, then I'm out." If Jay repeatedly uses any of these tactics on Madison with success, this is considered a power play.

Power Plays

University of Michigan trained clinical psychologist Claude Steiner wrote extensively on **power plays** and describes them as patterns of communication behavior used repeatedly by one person to get another person to do something.[37] If for example, Jay has worked a lot with Madison to help him complete various graduate projects, he may employ the "guilt tripping" tactic. "Oh, it's great to have me here virtually living with you to help you get through graduate school, but now that you're done, you want your space. How fair is that?" Jay may also apply the "you owe me" tactic. He may say, "I've spent all this time with you helping you do what is important to you, yet you can't do this for me?"

He may try to sway Madison by making promises that are difficult to say no to. "If we live together, we can save money, and I could take you on that African safari you've always wanted to go on." If any of these tactics work, and Jay uses them again and again with success, we would consider them power plays.

If Madison, despite his misgivings, agrees to have Jay move in, he may find that the decision was a good one, or he may regret it. If it is the latter, the resentment is likely to fester unless he communicates this, or he may choose to endure it in silence—although his discontent may reveal itself in other ways later on. Madison can stand his ground and calmly explain to Jay all of the reasons why he is not ready for the move in, trusting that Jay's love for him will enable them to work through this at a different pace. Jay may listen and attempt to understand Madison. He might ask the question, "What would you like to see from me?" or "Where do we need to be in order for you to feel more comfortable with us living together permanently?" Both men will experience different feelings as they discuss this important milestone in their relationship. Hopefully, they can openly share their feelings and needs. They may find some common ground and work out an acceptable compromise.

There are other examples of power plays. People may get us to do what they want by withholding something that is important to us, such as access to someone or something we need. Rather than giving us the attention and interaction we desire, they ignore us or give us the "silent treatment." They retract their affection or exclude us from a social function. In a sense, it is a form of punishment. To avoid being punished, or to shorten the duration of a punishment, we may yield or comply. If we feel that we deserve to be punished in some way, this may feed a person's need to control us. We may feel guilty about a mistake we made and feel obligated to make up for our transgression. The person whom we have hurt knows this, and uses this to get us to do what he or she wants. We allow ourselves to be punished over and over, or we forfeit our own needs repeatedly to make up for what we did.

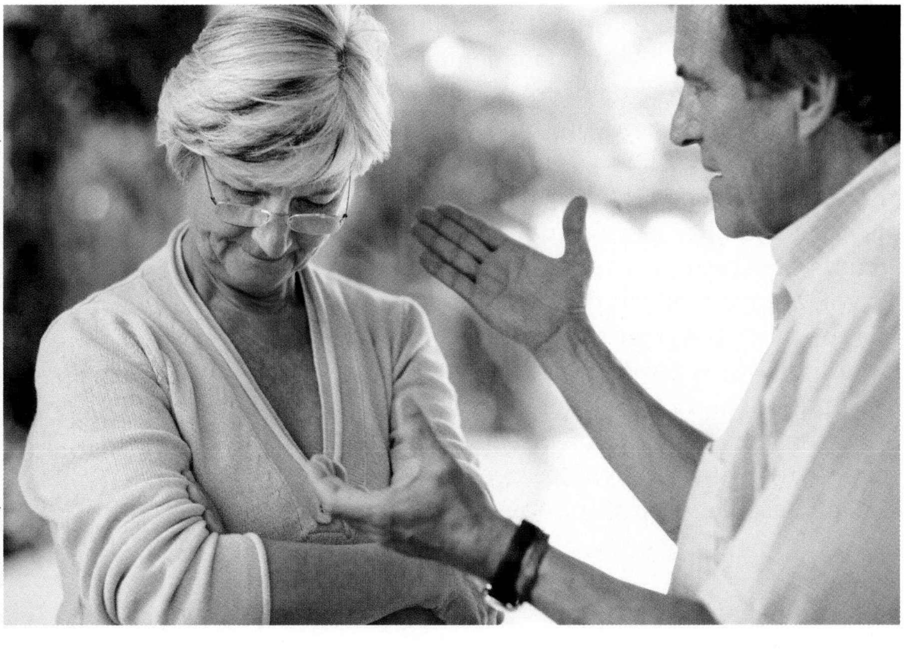

We may also, without fully realizing it, invite those we know or love to use power plays on us. For example, our desire to be needed or important to someone may cloud our ability to discern the difference between love and extreme possessiveness. One of my students shared how a previous girlfriend wanted to spend all of her free time with him. At first, it felt good to Dominic that Kelsey was so into him. It made him feel needed and was a boost to his ego. When he started to express an interest in doing some activities and spending time with friends apart from her, Kelsey became despondent. She asked if he was bored with her and their relationship. She kept inquiring if she was doing something wrong. Kelsey would say, "Why would you want to be with them when you can be with me," or "Why can't I come along." When Dominic did go out with friends after work one day, Kelsey pouted for days. Dominic encouraged Kelsey to pursue some of her own interests and friends, but she seemed disinterested in that. People who are overly dependent or clingy often battle with insecurity and feelings of low self-worth, along with a fear of abandonment or rejection. They feel very threatened by the very person they love so much.

Our propensity to question or discard our own feelings may also make us more susceptible to power plays. Accusations, and what Susan Forward calls pathologizing, are power plays. **Accusations** are statements lobbed at a person to invoke guilt. They imply that a person is being selfish, bad, or unfair about something. The following statements are accusations: "You never really loved me." "You'd rather spend time with your buddies than with your own family," and "You say you're sorry, but you don't mean it." When we try to refute the accusation, the person may respond with a "words are cheap, prove it" statement such as "If you are really sorry, than why don't you do this for me?" It is a strategy that often works. **Pathologizing** is used to make a person question or doubt his or her perceptions or feelings.[38] A person may use one of these statements to suggest that our concerns or needs are out of line, off base, or warped in some way:

- "You're being paranoid."
- "You must be kidding, right? You really think that?"
- "That is so crazy. I can't believe you would be so. . . ."
- "Why would I invite you to go if I was going to secretly hit the casino, after all we've been through, come on now!"

Your Turn: Has someone ever successfully used a power play on you? How? Is there a power play which you rely on to control or influence someone?

We will learn strategies to assertively communicate our needs in non-manipulative ways and to respond effectively to other people's manipulation throughout this textbook, especially Unit 10 on emotions and conflict management. Along with seeking pleasure and avoiding pain, reducing uncertainty, and exercising greater power and control, we use our communication to express our emotions.

Can you identify other types of power plays which you have used before? How about ones that others have used on you?

Research this! To learn how to manage other people's attempts to mislead, trap or hoodwink you, check out these interesting reads:

Emotional Blackmail: When the People in Your Life Use Fear, Obligation and Guilt to Manipulate You by Susan Forward and Donna Frazier

Emotional Vampires: Dealing with People who Drain You Dry by Albert J. Bernstein

In Sheep's Clothing: Understanding and Dealing with Manipulative People by George K. Simon

Saving Beauty From the Beast: How to Protect Your Daughter from an Unhealthy Relationship by Ellen Zelda Kessner

. . . In what ways do we use our interpersonal communication to exert power and control?

We Use Communication to Express Our Emotions

Nine-time Grammy winner and hip-hop sensation Alicia Keys grew up surrounded by pimps, prostitutes, drug dealers, and gangs. She frequently had to step over used needles on the sidewalk while walking to school. Alicia also had dreams for a better life. Her early experience with writing lyrics came from addressing letters to her mom to convey her feelings when things were intense. Writing became therapeutic. At age fourteen, she came home from seeing a movie and wrote her first song called, "I'm All Alone." At the age of sixteen, Keys signed her first record deal.[39] Expressing her thoughts and feelings to her mother and later to her fans was like a pressure release valve. It was cathartic. **Catharsis** is releasing stress or pent-up emotions as a result of talking about something openly. **Opening our inner world to someone we trust is healthy. Talking or writing about our emotions helps us make sense of them.**[40,41] This may be especially true when we fall deeply in love.

We've all heard expressions such as "crazy in love," and "lovestruck." Science writer Kathryn S. Brown once mused, "They say you go a little crazy when you fall in love, but do they really mean clinically mad?" Research suggests that, in a sense, yes! This may have a lot to do with a cocktail of brain chemicals that scientists think sparks romance. A fascinating article written by Lauren Slater in National Geographic highlights a study by Donatella Marazziti, professor of psychiatry at the University of Pisa in Italy.[42] The results of her study suggest that if we are deeply, passionately in love, our brain chemistry is similar to a person diagnosed with obsessive-compulsive disorder. This may

Twilight (2008) "I'm the world's most dangerous predator. Everything about me invites you in. My voice, my face, even my smell. As if I would need any of that. As if you could outrun me. As if you could fight me off."

explain why couples in the throes of passion can't spend enough time together. It may also explain their possessive paranoia, fits of jealousy, all night talking marathons, and generous showering of gifts, flowers, and poems.

Marazziti measured the blood of twenty four subjects who were in the midst of a love affair and compared levels of a brain chemical called serotonin with a control group (the subjects in this group were not in love and had no known mental health problems) and a group with obsessive-compulsive disorder. Serotonin is a brain chemical which helps transmit electrical impulses between nerve cells. Researchers also believe that at the appropriate levels, serotonin induces feelings of well being and serenity. Marazziti found that serotonin levels were significantly lower in the blood of the OCD and "in love" groups compared to the control group.

So, when Blaine Withers hands his girlfriend of six months, Kellen Dewey, a Tweety Bird he wins for her in a successful shooting match at the Ionia County Free Fair in Michigan and speaks softly into her ear with, "I'd do anything for you," his infatuation is not only exacerbated by a lack of serotonin, it is fueled by another chemical called dopamine. Researchers believe that like that of so many cupid struck couples, Blaine and Kellen's feelings for each other will bubble up like a quickly poured glass of Coke on ice. Their feelings will require an outlet. They will communicate their feelings in order to handle them and maintain a level of productivity and functionality needed at work, and when they are apart. They will also express their feelings in order to prolong what human attraction researchers call the "honeymoon" stage—which apparently, for all of us, is on a biological count down. Over time, their dopamine drenched, acute love will wane. A slow, intravenous-like drip of oxytocin will support a more enduring, less euphoric love.[43,44]

Research This! To learn about the latest research on love, read the National Geographic February 2006 article titled Love: The Chemical Reaction or go to nationalgeographic.com.

How can we stay attracted to our guy or girl? Research by Arthur Aron, a psychologist at Stony Brook University in New York and Anthropologist Helen Fisher of Rutgers University suggests the following to kick-start some dopamine secretion: Stare into your romantic partner's eyes for at least two minutes (on a regular basis) while holding hands, sweat together (engage in nonsexual physical activities with each other), start doing novel and spontaneous things together, and take a lot more time with foreplay type activities including massage.[45, 46]

Sometimes we communicate our emotions in ways that are not productive, healthy, or legal. For example, celebrity impersonators in downtown Los Angeles peruse the sidewalks earning a living by posing for pictures with tourists in exchange for tips. When a Hollywood tour guide chastised a forty-four-year-old Chewbacca impersonator for haggling a group of Japanese tourists, the furry Wookiee from Star Wars exclaimed, "Nobody tells this Wookiee what to do," and proceeded to head-butt the guide. The six-foot, five-inch-tall man was charged with misdemeanor battery. Superman and other cartoon impersonators witnessed the incident and complained that such emotional outbursts were bad for business. Chewbacca now joins the likes of Mr. Incredible, Elmo, and the darkhooded figure in the movie "Scream" dubiously reputed for roughing up or threatening tourists.[47]

Rather than strolling the catwalk, British supermodel Naomi Campbell could join Chewbacca sporting a broom for a sidewalk photo opportunity. A judge ordered her on March 19, 2007 to swap her designer fashions for a cleaning suit to complete five days of street cleaning. Campbell, age thirty-six, was accused of altercations with employees involving hitting or throwing her cell phone at them. She attributes her explosiveness to unresolved feelings regarding her father who she claims abandoned her as a child.[48]

How often and how do we let others know when we are angry? How about happy, sad, excited, or frustrated? According to Yale professors Daisy Grewal and Peter Salovey, being

aware of our emotions, accurately identifying them, and expressing them effectively reflects our **emotional intelligence**. People vary in terms of their emotional IQ. A high emotional IQ is positively correlated with physical health, critical decision making, positive relationships, sensitivity to other people's feelings, and appropriate use of humor.[49,50] In the unit on emotions, we'll explore ways to effectively identify, express, and manage our emotions.

Along with our need to seek pleasure and avoid pain, reduce uncertainty, exercise power and control, and express our emotions, we also have a strong need to save face.

> My boyfriend gave me a mood ring the other day. When I'm in a good mood it turns green. When I'm in a bad mood, it leaves a red mark on his forehead."
>
> *www.butlerwebs.com*

. . . How and why do we rely on communication to express our emotions?

We Use Communication to Save Face

At the end of one of his games, Frankie Frisch, manager of the Pittsburgh Pirates, is reported to have approached a spectator who was sitting behind the Pirate dugout yelling criticisms and suggestions at him throughout the seven innings. Frisch asked the man for his name and business address. The fan was flattered. He gave Frisch his business card. Smiling, Frisch replied, "I'll be at your office bright and early tomorrow morning to tell you how to run your business."

When people treat us unjustly, criticize us, or otherwise attack our personhood, we may employ a variety of communication techniques to defend our image or self-concept. **Self-concept** is the view we hold of ourselves. It's our identity. We might not go as far as to threaten to show up at someone's job and tell him how to do it better, but we may confront the person in some other way. We can choose to do this in a direct, respectful, and nonthreatening way, or in an inflammatory, accusatory, and immature manner, similar to what is often seen on shows such as *Jerry Springer*.

Saving face is our desire to protect our image or ego. We use certain communication behaviors such as blaming, making excuses, deception, and rationalization to save face. For example, Mel Gibson felt the heat, not only from the camera lights during an interview with ABC's Diane Sawyer, but on a global scale after spewing a torrent of expletives and anti-Semitic remarks to Malibu police officers during a DUI arrest. When a deputy asked Gibson to step into the squad car, Gibson refused. The deputy then walked Gibson over to the passenger door of the squad car and opened it. The report says Gibson said some unpleasant things, wrestled free, and ran back to his car. The officer chased Gibson, subdued him, and put him inside the patrol car. Gibson reportedly began banging his head against the back of the deputy's seat shouting "F*****g Jews . . . The Jews are responsible for all the wars in the world. Are you a Jew?"

An international outrage erupted on the scale of a Mount Pelée in Martinique. Leaders of various nations and the Jewish community sharply condemned the award-winning director of *Braveheart* and *Passion of the Christ*. Gibson lost deals, endorsements, and friendships after his comments were made public. Gibson agreed to an interview with Sawyer to explain his behavior. He stated, "Alcohol makes people say all sorts of terrible things that they don't mean." Sawyer said, "Many people believe that alcohol just liberates you to say what you really feel" (a truth serum). Gibson replied, "Well, I don't think they know what they are talking about."[51] Some critics argued that Gibson's appearance and comments were damage control, calculated to refocus attention on his bout with alcoholism versus the real question: Is Gibson anti-Semitic? Gibson claimed it was his open bottle of Tequila which was to blame versus any deeply held prejudice. What do you think?

Research suggests that our need to save face is strong because we want others to like and accept us. We want to appear competent and preserve our own autonomy and self-respect.[52] We use our communication to save face in light of incriminating evidence or a moment of weakness. We make excuses for our behavior or explain away a mistake we've made. "I wouldn't have eaten all the chocolate chip cookies if you hadn't made them!" is an excuse for "I didn't have any self-control." "Traffic was so intense, sorry I'm late" is a pretext for "I didn't get up early enough." People who eat more Jay's potato chips (especially the Open Pit Barbeque flavored variety!) than they should use the company's own slogan, "Can't stop eating 'em" for their lack of control. Rather than exercise good old-fashioned self-discipline by having just a few, rolling up the bag, and putting it back in the cupboard, they succumb to the taste. Often people use the word I "can't" as a substitute for I "won't."

We can also use our communication to save face for others. For example, if a friend makes a mistake, we may, in an attempt to preserve his or her image, use humor or minimize the mistake by saying something like, "Hey, you tried," "You did the best you could," or "We all forget things sometimes, don't worry about it." We do this to help someone escape embarrassment or reduce the awkwardness that everyone feels. Korean and Japanese cultures are noted for placing a lot of importance on preserving the image of or saving face for others; however, this is valued in all cultures to some extent.[53] Understanding people's needs or motives, such as to save face, helps us in a variety of ways.

Your Turn: Can you think of a time when you "saved face?" What did you say or do?

Why Understand People's Motives?

Sometimes it may help us make sense of a person's communication behavior by pinpointing his or her possible goals or needs. If we ask ourselves questions such as, "Why is he or she saying or doing this?" "What is driving this person's communication behavior?" or "What needs is she trying to meet?" we may approach this person or the situation differently, perhaps with more patience or understanding. We may not take what the person is doing personally. We also may choose a better response or approach.

We may even quickly cultivate some sympathy. **Sympathy** is the ability to appreciate or have compassion for another person's experience. On a more intense level is empathy. **Empathy** is the ability to deeply understand and relate to another person's situation. To reach the point of empathy, one has to really put him or herself in another person's shoes—to see or experience first–hand what is happening or seriously contemplate (imagine) what an experience must be like for someone. Our ability to sympathize or empathize is an important part of being an other-centered communicator. An **other-centered communicator** is one who is sensitive to and considers the feelings, needs, and beliefs of others.

Your Turn: Besides seeking pleasure/avoiding pain, reducing uncertainty, exercising power/control, expressing our emotions, and saving face, what other needs do we try to meet with our interpersonal communication? Generate five additional examples of how communication is purposeful.

Unit Summary

Being aware of the motives behind people's communication behavior enhances our ability to communicate competently. Unit 4 increases the reader's theoretical and conceptual awareness of how communication is purposeful. Our interpersonal communication is driven by conscious and unconscious needs. It is also the primary means by which we get our needs met. We may rely on direct and indirect messages in order to seek pleasure and avoid pain, reduce uncertainty about people and events, exercise power and control, express and manage our emotions, and save face.

Key Questions

1. What needs do we strive to satisfy with our communication?
2. What are the benefits and disadvantages of direct and indirect communication?
3. How is our interpersonal communication used to seek pleasure and avoid pain?
4. How and why do we utilize our interpersonal communication to reduce uncertainty?
5. In what ways do we use our interpersonal communication to exert power?
6. How and why do we rely on interpersonal communication to express our emotions?
7. What motivates us to employ interpersonal communication strategies to save face?

Vocabulary Playback

Self-Actualization
Pleasure Principle
Indirect Communication
Direct Communication
Relational Rewards
Compliance-Gaining
Power
Conversational Control
Abdicrat
Autocrat
Democrat
Power Plays
Catharsis
Emotional Intelligence
Self-Concept
Saving Face
Sympathy
Empathy
Other-Centered Communicator

Theoretically Speaking

- Hierarchy of Human Needs Theory
- Uncertainty Reduction Theory
- Social Penetration Theory
- Predicted Outcome Theory
- Interpersonal Relations Orientation Theory

Focus Group/Class Discussion

- Many social theorists say that the primary goal of human existence is to communicate. Do you agree or disagree with this? Why or why not?
- Ben Franklin was quoted as saying, "A woman can keep a secret, until she sees another woman." Are women more prone to do this than men? Why or why not? What purpose does gossiping serve? Does this communication behavior relate at all to Maslow's hierarchy of human needs theory? How?
- Compare and contrast uncertainty reduction, social penetration, and predicted outcome theories? How are they similar? Different?
- "He could talk a dog off a meat truck." This saying implies that the person is very persuasive and convincing. We use communication to get people to do what we want. What techniques or approaches work best for you? When does a persuasive tactic become unethical?

Unit 4 Vocabulary Review

___ Self-Actualization
___ Pleasure Principle
___ Indirect Communication
___ Direct Communication
___ Relational Rewards
___ Compliance-Gaining
___ Power
___ Conversational Control
___ Abdicrat
___ Autocrat
___ Democrat
___ Power Plays
___ Catharsis
___ Emotional Intelligence
___ Self-Concept
___ Saving Face
___ Sympathy
___ Empathy
___ Other-Centered Communicator

A. Communication which is suggestive, subtle, or hints at something.

B. The ability to appreciate or have compassion for another person's experience.

C. The ability to influence people or events.

D. The psychoanalytic concept used to describe the need people have to maximize comfort and minimize discomfort.

E. The ability to deeply understand and relate to another person's situation.

F. The need to influence the direction and outcome of a conversation.

G. A person who tends to relinquish power and control to others.

H. A person with a high need for power and control.

I. Patterns of communication behavior used repeatedly by a person successfully to get another person to do something.

J. Releasing stress and pent-up emotions as a result of talking about something openly.

K. The ability to be aware of, identify, and express one's emotions.

L. The need to realize one's full potential.

M. Communication which is obvious, apparent, or clear.

N. A person who fluctuates between or is comfortable being an abdicrat and autocrat.

O. The strategies people use to get people to think or act a certain way.

P. How we see ourselves as individuals or our identity.

Q. The need to protect the positive image we have of ourselves or that others have of us when it is challenged or tarnished in some way.

R. One who is sensitive to and considers the feelings, needs, and beliefs of others.

S. Something we get from a relationship that we want or value.

Exercise

In unit 1, we read about the Vh1 series, *The Pickup Artist*. The show captures life for eight "socially awkward" men struggling to tackle their greatest fear—approaching women. Helping them in this often painful process is "Mystery" a best-selling author and former social oddity who has mastered the art of the "approach." The men venture outside their supportive enclave to practice their approach methods at clubs, shopping malls, and coffee houses with hidden cameras poised to capture every faux pas and unexpected success. Mystery helps the men process their experiences and analyze their efforts to initiate dating relationships.

Your team will identify a goal that everyone will tackle this week. This needs to be challenging but doable. Everyone on the team must feel comfortable with this, too. Like the guys on the "The Pickup Artist" each person will attempt to achieve this goal using a variety of communication strategies. Come back to class ready to describe the situation, the communication approaches used, and the outcome. Each team will be asked to share some of this information and may assume, along with other classmates, the role of "Mystery."

Examples of challenges your team may decide to meet:

- Convince someone to donate money to your favorite charity.
- Persuade someone who lives with you to help you with a dreaded house project or chore and actually do it together.
- Arrange to have coffee and a pleasant conversation with someone at work you don't get along with.
- Assuage someone you don't know very well to loan you some money. Give it right back!
- Get someone you live with to watch a show with you that he or she hates from beginning to end.
- Impress someone enough to go on a date with you.
- Coax someone who doesn't go to a place of worship or is not religious to attend church services with you this week.
- Get a person to engage you in an important conversation that both of you are avoiding.

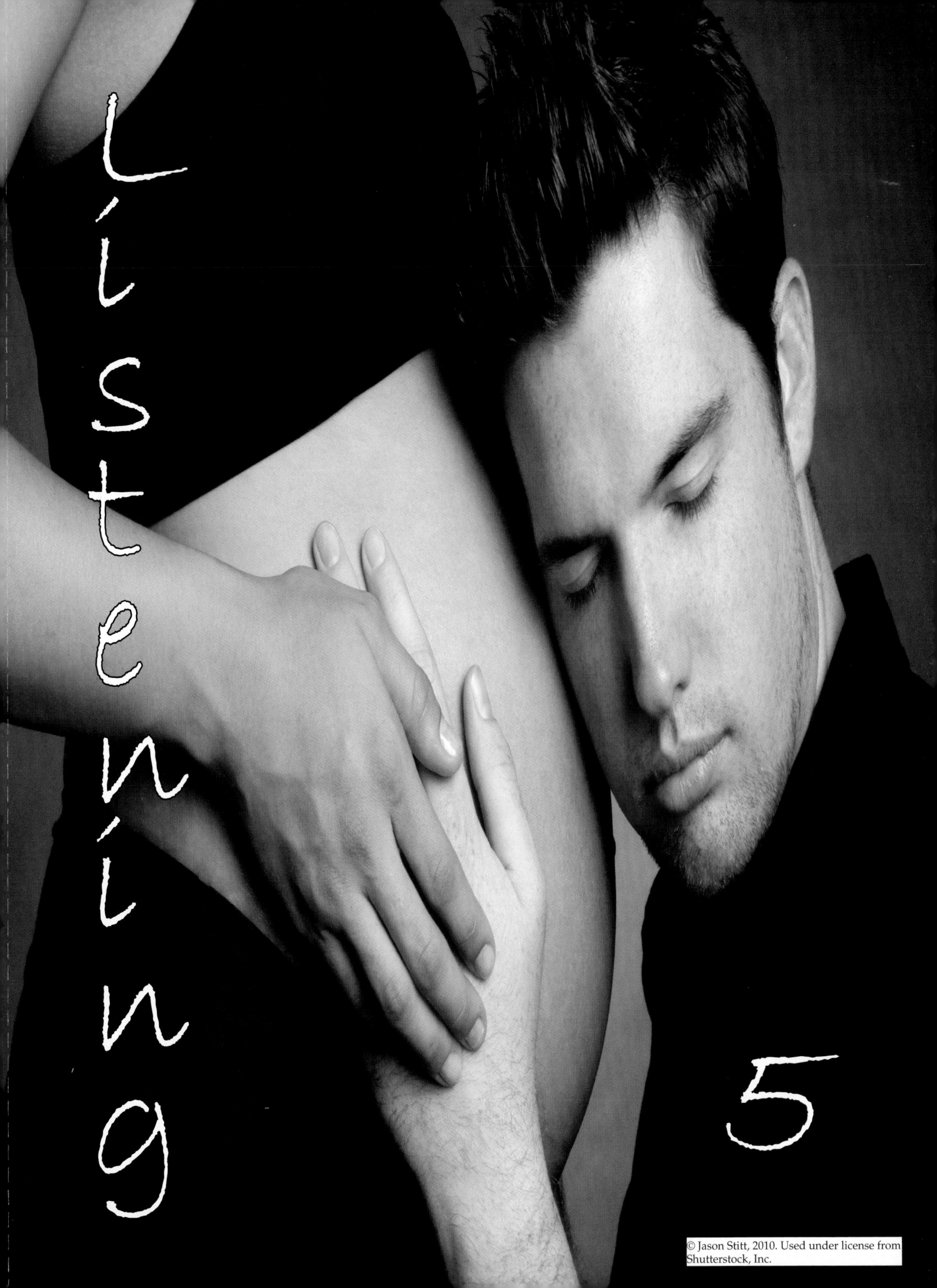

Listening

5

Listening Unit 5

Unit 5 explores the process of active listening and its relationship to feedback. It examines ways to improve listening in our interpersonal communication.

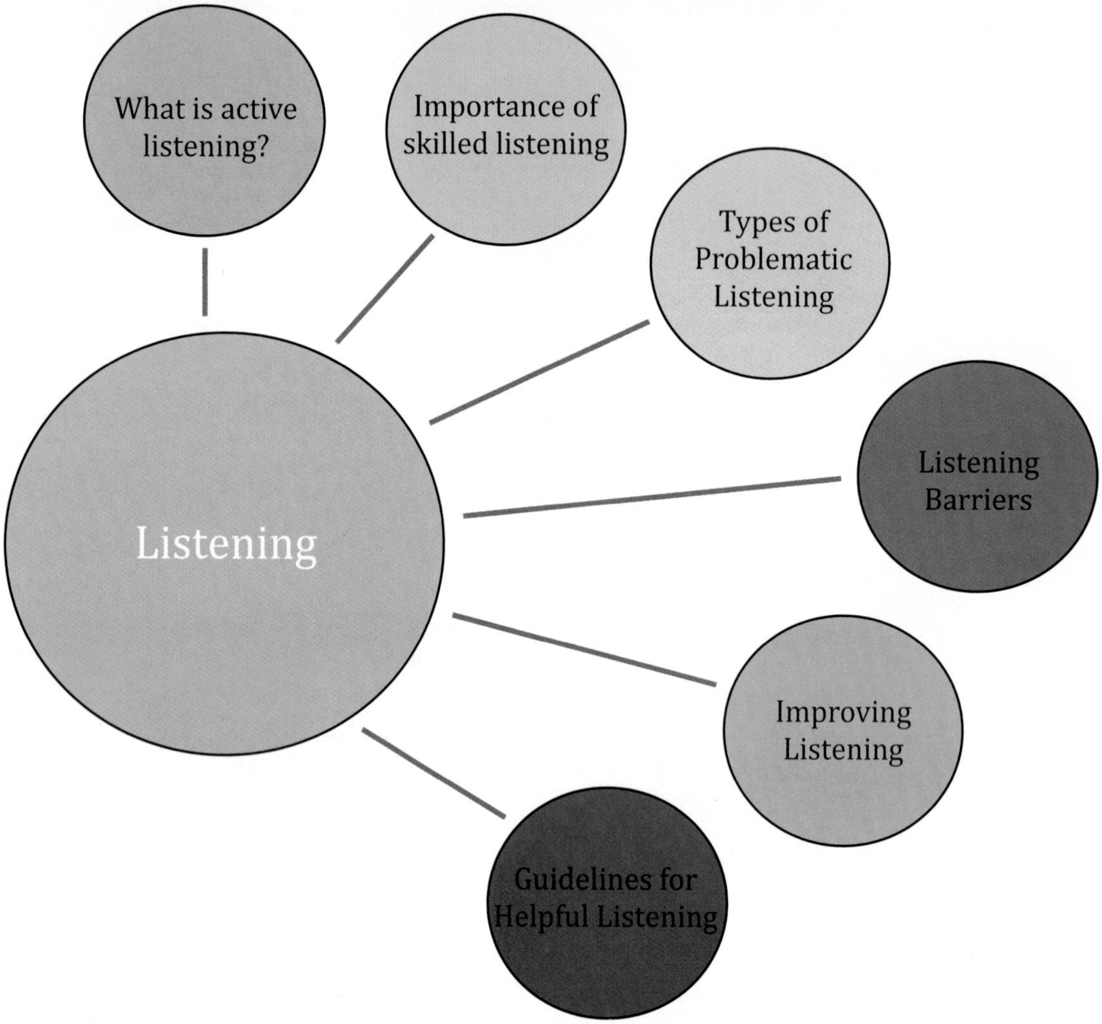

Unit 5 Learning Objectives

As a result of reading and studying Unit 5, you will be able to:

1. Describe the difference between hearing and active listening.
2. Explain the importance of skilled listening.
3. Describe problematic types of listening.
4. Identify barriers to effective listening.
5. Comprehend and practice six techniques for improving listening and feedback:
   - Postponing
   - Rehearsing
   - Paraphrasing
   - Listening Checks
   - Clarifying Questions
   - Mirroring
6. Understand general guidelines for empathetic listening.

Contestants who appear on *Who Wants to Be a Millionaire* are motivated by cash rewards of up to one million dollars for correctly guessing the answer to a variety of questions. It appears they listen very carefully to the questions and multiple choice answers as the stakes are high.

Occasionally, their listening is hampered by something. For example, Chase Samspon, a college junior from Nashville Tennessee, flew in at 3:00 a.m. to make it on the live show, with virtually no sleep the night before. Perhaps sleep deprivation, nervousness, or a combination of both, played a factor in what happened to him. He lasted only a minute and twenty-seven seconds. He is the first person in the show's history to incorrectly guess the very first question. He didn't appear to listen carefully to Meredith Vieira, which you can witness by going to www.youtube.com and typing in *"First question wrong on Who Wants to be a Millionaire."*

Hearing a sound does not mean we are tuned in to it. We may hear someone's voice in the background as we are engrossed in the newspaper we're reading. We may even mumble something like "yeah sure" to the voice. We find out the next day we gave our spouse or life partner the go ahead to buy something very expensive, without realizing it.

What happened? We heard a sound, but our attention was focused on reading. We were asked if it was ok to buy the most expensive children's outdoor play set imaginable for our children. We mumbled "yeah sure," to quiet the sound. We would never knowingly approve such a purchase.

Because we were not actively listening, we come home from work two days later to find our driveway completely blocked off by a Mount Everest-sized pile of lumber, plastic parts, canopies, sand bags, and metal poles for a forty-foot long, four level "train" Donald Trump would likely approve. A tsunami of a credit card purchase now burns a hole in our disposable income from interest charges, as the balance greatly exceeds any foreseeable full payment. We face two laborious weeks, even with the help of a carpenter, to erect the equivalent of a new Disney theme park attraction, which will be the envy of all our neighbors—and their children. Hmmm. This is sounding awfully close to home here.

"You can stop saying 'uh-huh'! I stopped talking to you an hour ago!"

There are certain types of listening which are problematic. There are also barriers to effective listening and strategies for improving our listening skills. We'll explore these later in the unit, but first, let's define active listening and discuss why skilled listening is essential.

What Is Active Listening?

People often confuse hearing with listening. The words are often used interchangeably, however, both are different, albeit interdependent, processes. Hearing is ***a part*** of the process of listening. Without trying to sound too much like Ms. Frizzle from PBS' *The Magic School Bus,* hearing involves sound waves hitting the eardrum which is at the end of the auditory canal. The eardrum vibrates the three smallest bones in the human body (hammer, anvil, and stirrup), which trigger vibrations in the "hearing organ" or cochlea. These vibrations create mini waves in the fluid found inside the cochlea. These waves hit microscopic sized "hair" cells which sway and move to the waves like kelp or algae at the bottom of a lake or ocean. These hair cells send nerve signals to the auditory nerve, which is a bridge between the inner ear and the hearing center of the brain. The brain registers these nerve signals as sound.[1]

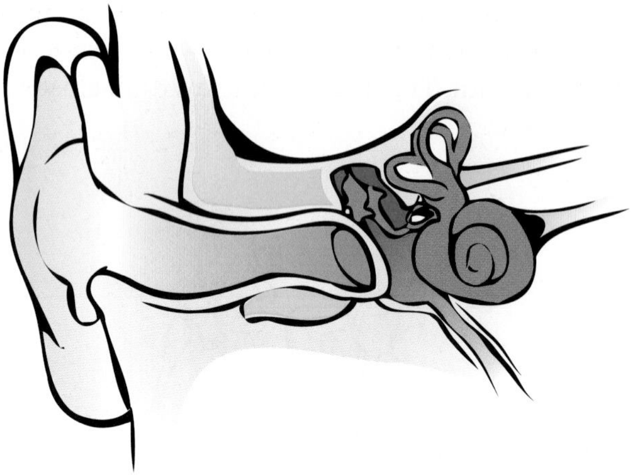

Active listening is more than hearing auditory stimuli. In other words, hearing is a physiological process, whereas active listening is **both** physiological and mental. Unlike hearing, active listening involves concentration and effort.

> Dolphins are purported to possess the best hearing. Their ear holes are about the size of a crayon point. They are able to hear 14 times better than humans.
>
> *Source: San Diego Zoo*

Listening actively and accurately is a four step process. The process involves attending to, interpreting, responding back to, and recalling messages.

Attending occurs when we concentrate or mentally focus on a message. Interpreting a message is **our attempt to make sense of or understand it**. We do this by internalizing a message, or relating it to what we know or have experienced.[2] As we attempt to understand a message we also evaluate it. We begin to form opinions about what we're hearing. **Responding to a message involves some sort of reaction**. Responding may involve stating something or asking a question. We also encourage a speaker to continue speaking by providing nonverbal and verbal **back-channel cues. These behaviors let a speaker know we are following a conversation.[3] They may also aid in our ability to listen effectively.[4, 5]** Here are some examples of back-channel cues:

Nonverbal back-channel cues:

- Leaning in
- Silence
- Focused eye contact and speaking at the same eye level as the other person
- Nodding our head
- Facial reactions such as smiling, or raising an eyebrow
- Placing our hand on the shoulder of the person we are speaking to
- Vocal sounds like "Uh-huh," "hmmmm," and "Ohhhh,"

Verbal back-channel cues:

- Reactions such as "Really." "Wow." "Interesting." "No kidding!"
- Encouragers such as "Go on," "ok." "What happened next?"
- Expressions of understanding "I see." "Yes." "Exactly." "That's interesting."

How is this nurse using nonverbal back-channel cues in her communication?

Recalling is the process of remembering a message. It involves retracing what was said in previous conversations. In fact, people often rate another person's listening skills on how accurately she or he recalls what was said. Just about all scientific measurements of listening incorporate a person's ability to accurately recall information as a measure of listening effectiveness.[6] Now we know the difference between hearing and active listening, let's look at why skilled listening is important.

. . . What is the difference between hearing and active listening?

. . . How is attending, understanding, responding and recalling a part of the active listening process?

Importance of Skilled Listening

Effective listening greatly influences the feedback senders and receivers give each other. I listened to a radio broadcast about a husband and wife who called it quits after twenty-five years of marriage. One of the husband's major complaints was that he was tired of enduring his wife's breakfast. She served the same breakfast every morning of their marriage, and he couldn't stand it. The wife was flabbergasted. She said she made the breakfast because she thought he said he loved it. She hated making it for him every morning because it took such a long time. Here we have a twenty-five year communication breakdown stemming from a lack of feedback!

Let's take a look at a different scenario. Our friend John opens up to us and says,

"My son has a selective memory. He needs frequent reminders to do very important tasks. If I remind him too much, I'm nagging him, and he doesn't like it. If I don't remind him, I'm at fault for neglecting to tell him anything."

In what ways can we relate to this unhappy couple and our friend John? How often do we keep information to ourselves or experience frustration trying to "get through" to someone? Conversely, some people keep information from us or feel the same exasperation for various reasons. One likely possibility is that someone perceives the other as unable or unwilling to listen. People may omit certain pieces of information, tell us things we want to hear rather than what we need to hear, or otherwise shut down if they perceive we are not receptive to certain messages. Chances are we have all heard someone say to us, "I keep telling you . . ." "It doesn't matter what I say," or "You just don't get it." There is wisdom in the words of Dr. Rachel Naomi Remen, who is a Clinical Professor of Family and Community Medicine at the University of California, San Fransico School of Medicine. She writes about the importance of listening:

"The most basic and powerful way to connect to another person is to listen. Just listen. Perhaps the most important thing we ever give each other is our attention. . . . A loving silence often has far more power to heal and to connect than the most well-intentioned words."

Source: www.thinkexist.com

Will and Grace. Paris and Nicole. Abercrombie and Fitch. Venus and Serena, Brooks and Dunn. Beevis and Butthead. All are famous pairs—we can't think of one without the other. Feedback and listening are similar. **Our success at sending and receiving messages hinges on listening.** The feedback we receive reflects the feedback we give. On average, listening to others consumes five or more hours in a typical day.[7] Based on studies of college students, communication researchers Kathryn Dindia and Bonnie Kennedy estimate we spend more time listening than all other communication activities combined. They purport that, on average, people spend 50% of their waking hours listening, 20% speaking, 13% reading, and 12% writing.[8, 9, 10]

Not only does listening dominate our communication, it is tied to our career and relational success. Numerous studies suggest effective listening enhances a person's ability to lead others.[11] Successful salespeople also are noted for their ability to hone in on the subtle and direct verbal messages they receive from their customers or clients.[12] As the shaded box illustrates, an extensive survey of over 1,000 human resource professionals found that listening ranked as the most important skill managers need in the workplace. **In addition to enhancing our careers, effective listening helps us in our interpersonal relationships.**

1,000 Human Resource Professionals Surveyed:

What do you value the most in the managers and supervisors at your company?

1. Listen effectively and guide others.
2. Relate to and work with others one-on-one.
3. Function cooperatively in small groups.
4. Gather information from others to make sound decisions.
5. Write effective business reports.
6. Provide timely, helpful feedback.
7. Knowledge of job.
8. Present a good image for the company.
9. Computer skills and application.
10. Financial knowledge.[13]

Communication scholar and author Steven McCornack states that "When we listen actively, we transcend our own thoughts, ideas, and beliefs, and begin to directly experience the . . . worlds of other people. . . . The result is improved relationships."[14] Research confirms McCornack's statement. In committed relationships, the ability to consider the other person's thoughts, feelings, and needs is a key marker of relational satisfaction.[15] In a survey of marriage counselors, the unwillingness to grasp the other person's perspective when listening was identified as one of the most common communication problems therapists addressed when working with their clients.[16]

People who listen intently and effectively are generally perceived as better conversationalists. People regard them as more genuine, sensitive and helpful.[17] Studies also indicate that people who are aggressive with their listening (interrupting, ambushing, & dominating) may experience less marital satisfaction and more physical violence in their relationships.[18, 19]

Arguments and hurt feelings are preventable with adroit listening. Ineffective listening, on the other hand, may cost us time and money, reduce productivity, and create negative perceptions.

While effective listening is advantageous in several ways, our brains seem to work against us. First, they may tell us we are better listeners than we really are. For example, 94% of corporate managers surveyed rated themselves as good or very good at listening. None of them gave themselves a poor rating. However, a notable percentage of employees who work for these same managers rated them as weak in terms of listening skills.[20] Second, our brains can store a limited amount of information and get easily distracted. Research suggests that if we were to listen to a short talk, most of us would recall about 50% of what we heard.[21] This occurs if we are paying close attention. Furthermore, the average person can comprehend (process) up to six hundred words per minute. The average person speaks (unless he or she has just slammed two cans of Red Bull) in the range of 100 to 150 words per minute. This leaves enough idle time for the brain to head to the beach or barbecue.[22, 23]

© Bagus Insahono - POOL/epa/Corbis

US Secretary of State Hillary Rodham Clinton listens to government representatives and residents in central Jakarta, Indonesia during an Asian tour designed to establish better ties between the United States and Southeast Asia.

© Martin Roe/Retna Ltd./Corbis

Oprah Winfrey is noted for her ability to put her guests at ease during interviews. She listens intently and responds with questions often spontaneously based on the verbal cues of others. Pictured are Mariah Carey, Nick Cannon & Oprah at Rumsey Playfield on September 18, 2009.

In order to improve our interpersonal skills, we need to limit certain types of listening. Listening behaviors which may cause us problems are selective listening, eavesdropping, defensive listening, pseudo-listening, interrupting, and narcissistic listening.

. . . Why is effective listening important to our career and relationships?

Problematic Types of Listening

Ever sit in the middle of a round table with a bunch of people who were all carrying on conversations? Did you find it difficult to hone-in on, or stay with, a single conversation for a sustained period of time? We tend to pay attention to topics which interest us, and tune out those which don't.

This kind of listening is one of several potentially problematic types of listening called selective listening. Let's explore this and five others.

© Alon Brik, 2010. Used under license from Shutterstock, Inc.

Selective Listening

Like surfing channels with our remote, we pay attention to programming which piques our interest. Selective listening **means we find it easier to focus on what we find stimulating, unique, or important.**[24] Conversely, we are guilty of a behavior called insulating when we **tune out someone who is telling us things we find unpleasant.** Sometimes the truth hurts, and we don't want to hear it. We also tune out messages we find repetitious or boring.

Eavesdropping

In the 2005 political thriller, *The Interpreter*, Nicole Kidman plays Silvia Broome, a South African United Nations interpreter. Broome returns to her office after hours to retrieve something. She hears a hushed conversation between two men on the floor of the empty, darkened assembly hall and decides to listen in on the conversation. The two men speak in a rare language which she can interpret. Their words unfold a secret plot to assassinate a foreign head of state. Unfortunately, she is caught in the act of eavesdropping and becomes a target of the killers. Broome tries to enlist the aid of a federal agent, played by Sean Penn, to protect her and foil the conspiracy.

Research This! What exactly does Nicole Kidman's character, Silvia Broome, hear when she eavesdrops on a plot to kill a world leader? See it and hear it on Universal Pictures' *The Interpreter* (2005).

Eavesdropping **occurs when people make an effort to overhear the conversations of others.** Whether motivated by suspicion or curiosity, eavesdropping is listening in on a face-to-face or phone conversation. It may also include reading another person's text or e-mail message. A few caveats regarding this practice:

- People generally don't like others to eavesdrop on them.
- If people are in auditory range of our conversation, they are likely listening to it, even though they may act like they aren't.[25]
- Many people consider eavesdropping unethical because it disrespects those who wish for their conversations to remain private. Other's see it as violation not only of their privacy, but a threat to the trust they've established between them and the eavesdropper.
- In some states, it is illegal to tape record a phone conversation without a person's consent.

Defensive Listening

Have you ever tried telling someone something, and the person responded by cross-examining you like a *Law and Order* prosecuting attorney? You're hit with a slew of questions designed to sidestep the issue or put you on the defensive? Defensive listening is commonly associated with arguments. **Rather than trying to understand what we are saying, people listen mainly to gather information they'll use later in a counter-attack.** As we are speaking, they are formulating a response to deflect or refute the negative information they are hearing. Business professor Steven Golen refers to this as "rebuttal tendency." Golen states that defensive listening is often exacerbated by a person's tendency to jump to conclusions before completely hearing a person out.[26] One behavior characteristic of defensive listening is interrupting. People erroneously believe talking more than listening is a winning strategy.

Interrupting

When we have a conversation, it is easier to understand one another if we take turns. Sometimes, we blurt something in the middle of another person's sentence or finish it because we are feeling excited or impatient. As we learned in unit two, we may also interrupt as a means to get the upper hand in a conversation. This need is called conversational control. Interrupting becomes quite competitive, at times, especially if we feel we "can't get a word in edgewise." Interrupting occurs a lot in an argument. Sometimes it involves two people talking over each other and getting louder and louder until someone backs down. You see this on numerous news shows when guests representing opposing viewpoints debate an issue and on a variety of reality shows such as Oxygen's *Bad Girls Club*, E! television's *Keeping Up With The Kardashians*, and VH1's *Tool Academy 3*.

Most people consider interrupting a person before she or he is finished speaking discourteous, unprofessional, and at times, extremely frustrating. In one study, job applicants who interrupted the interviewer during an interview were viewed less favorably than those who listened intently, allowing the interviewer to finish his or her thoughts and questions.[27]

From a cultural standpoint, surveys of international students studying in America suggest that American students are perceived as less patient with their listening, compared to students from their own country. This perception is shared by students from Africa, Asia, South America, and southern Europe![28, 29]

Research This! Who interrupts more, men or women? Find out what research suggests. Go to reference number 30 or read Sargent, S.L. & Weaver, J.B. (2003). Listening styles: sex differences in perceptions of self and others. *International Journal of Listening*, 17, 15–18.

"We don't see eye to eye. But then, we don't hear ear to ear either."
Busher Keaton, ***The Apprentice***

Psuedo-Listening

Have you ever done this? You are on the phone and the person speaking to you is talking a mile a minute. You are using back channel cues such as "Uh uh . . . really? . . . yeah . . ." but you aren't paying much attention. You're doing something else like paying bills or checking your Facebook. You may even set the phone down while the person is speaking to get dressed or start dinner, and then pick up the phone minutes later as if you had never left the conversation. The person on the other line is oblivious to your brief exit.

We are guilty of **pseudo-listening** whenever **we pretend to listen**. In a face-to-face interaction, we may nod our head as if we are following a person's story, but our mind is far, far away. This is particularly embarrassing when a person asks us a direct question, and we can't answer it.

Is psuedo-listening unethical?

Narcissistic Listening

A person who is a **narcissistic listener** craves to hear one thing in a conversation—his or her own voice. **This person is often long-winded—likes to talk, and talk, and talk.** He or she will listen to others, as long as it serves his or her own interests. A behavior which is characteristic of narcissistic listening is **stage-hogging**.[31] If you are talking about something, before you have a chance to finish your story or thought, a person who stage-hogs will **interrupt you and redirect the conversation back to him or her in some way.** Stage-hogging occurs in the following exchange between Gloria and Kristen:

Gloria: "I had a blast in Chicago last weekend."

Kristen: (interrupting Gloria) "Really? I was there last month. There was this quaint little shop where I found some fabulous art. The dealer's French poodle peed on my new Loeffler Randall boots, that mangy, four–legged, atrocious excuse for a canine. Did you notice the Brenda Burke piece I have above the mantel in my living room, next to my giant book case . . . " blah blah, blah, blah.

What is it like to have a conversation with someone who frequently stage hogs? How often are you guilty of stage-hogging?

. . . How would you describe selective listening, eavesdropping, defensive listening, psuedo-listening, interrupting, and narcissistic listening?

Listening behaviors such as selective listening, eavesdropping, defensive listening, pseudo-listening, interrupting, and narcissistic listening may cause us to inaccurately decode another person's message, respond prematurely, or make it difficult for someone to want to engage us in communication. In addition to these problematic listening behaviors, many factors can exacerbate poor listening. Competent communicators recognize these barriers and strive to reduce, and if possible, eliminate them.

Barriers to Effective Listening

There is a humorous anecdote, compliments of jokesgallery.com, about an elderly man who is driving on the highway. His wife calls him on the cell phone. He picks it up but seems very distracted and hurried.

Wife: "Hess, be careful, I just heard on the radio that there is a madman driving the wrong way on Route 280!"

Hess: "What was that? Ahh. Honey, I can't talk right now. There are a bunch of messed-up drivers driving on the wrong side of the road."

Hess was obviously too distracted by external noise to listen to his wife. In unit 2, we learned that noise is anything which can block or hinder communication. **When we encounter external noise, we usually also experience internal noise.** Hess might experience anxiety (internal noise) as he dodges oncoming traffic (external noise).

A recent news story provides a similar example of how we experience internal and external noise concurrently. A Northwest pilot's plane was boarded by police, not because of an unruly passenger, the pilot lost control of his emotions while passengers boarded the plane. He started yelling at someone he was talking to on his cell phone. He stormed from the cockpit to the on-board lavatory to carry on his tirade, yelling obscenities at the person he was talking to. The 180 passengers were asked to evacuate the plane.[32] Perhaps the person speaking to the pilot on the phone said something (external noise) and continued to say things which triggered an angry reaction within the pilot (internal noise). At that moment, the pilot had several options in terms of handling his emotions in a skilled and professional manner. He apparently chose not to.

Intense emotions such as fear, anger, frustration, or excitement are potential barriers to effective listening. One can appreciate this viewing the nail biter *Hurt Locker* (2008). The film dramatically captures life as a member of an elite Army bomb squad in Iraq. SSgt William James (played by Jeremy Renner) leads a team of soldiers trained to deactivate bombs in the thick of urban combat. Members of the unit live on the edge, their nerves tested daily by the unexpected. Their ability to communicate with and understand each other has life and death repercussions. They are, at times, easy targets. Every civilian is a potential sniper—every trash bag or car a hiding place for lethal bombs. James' unit must rely on information from Iraqis despite the fact that most cannot speak English.

In one scene, James is trying to deactivate a trunk load of bombs in the heart of an Iraqi city. His commander, Sgt. JT Sanborn (Anthony Mackie), and other members of the unit have created a perimeter and are offering cover. Sanborn notices more and more potentially hostile Iraqis popping up on rooftops and appearing out of windows surrounding their location and orders James to abandon the car and leave with them. James is hyper-focused on what he is doing, knowing that at any second the bomb could detonate. Sanborn's repeated warnings cause James to experience what is called **sensory overload**. We experience this when we receive too much sensory stimulation all at once. This also occurs when we attempt to multi-task or juggle multiple demands at the same time. Out of frustration, James throws his ear piece out the car window, cutting of communication with Sanborn. Neither men fully grasp the other's predicament as their fear and stress skyrocket.[33]

© Leah-Anne Thompson, 2010. Used under license from Shutterstock, Inc.

"I have two aunts that are both legally deaf and blind. They have severely poor peripheral vision, but can sort of read lips and hear some sounds. I have grown accustomed to talking to them in such a way that I speak close to their face so they can see my lips as they move and hear my vocal sounds."

—Umar

. . . **Catch This!** To view the very intense first 8 minutes of the *Hurt Locker* go to: www.beyondhollywood.com/watch-8-minutes-of-the-hurt-lockernow

There are numerous other listening barriers in communication. Let's take a look at a few of the common barriers to effective listening. For the following table, match each barrier with its appropriate description.

Hearing impairment ____
Negative expectations ____
Attention Deficit Disorder ____
Closed mindedness ____
Semantic noise ____
Preoccupation ____

A. This is a diagnosed medical condition which affects a person's ability to focus and sustain attention.

B. This occurs when people do not speak the same language or are confused by a person's use of slang, abbreviations, or technical jargon.

C. We say that a person's listening is influenced by this when she or he is unwilling to appreciate or consider another person's message.

D. Rock guitarist Pete Townsend of *The Who* blames years of listening to high level of sounds during concerts and in recording studios for why he struggles today to hear spoken words in a normal conversation.[34] He is one of 5.2 million Americans believed to have this to a significant degree.[35]

E. Statements such as "It doesn't matter what I say," "My idea is better," "This is more than I can handle," or "I've heard it before," reflect this and often cause us to dismiss what a person says, interrupt, or withhold information.

F. This occurs when we have something on our mind. We are thinking about something else other than what the person is saying to us—like what we want to do on our weekend, an argument we had earlier with someone, or which NFL players we're likely to pick for a fantasy football ball tournament.

Research this! Do you think extended use of iPods and MP3 players causes permanent hearing loss? Do we run a greater risk by using earbuds versus muff-type earphones? What does the research suggest? *Start your search by going to* www.livescience.com *and type in "earbuds."*

Your Turn: Can you think of at least three other barriers to effective listening? Which barriers challenge your ability to listen the most? Least? Why?

What's Loud?

Noise	Decibels
Whisper	20
Normal Talking	50–60
Car Traffic	70
Alarm Clock	80
Lawn Mower	95
Rock Concert	100
Jackhammer	115
Jet Engine	130
Gun Shot	140

Source: http://library.thinkquest.org/3750/hear

. . . What are some of the barriers to effective listening? How do they interfere with communication?

So far we've defined what active listening is and its importance as it relates to feedback. We identified some of the types of problematic listening as well as barriers to effective listening. Now, let's explore ways we can improve the quality and accuracy of our listening and feedback. This unit will highlight six strategies for improvement. They are postponing, rehearsing, paraphrasing, parroting, the listening check, and questions for clarification.

Techniques for Improving Listening

Someone invented caller ID What was the primary purpose behind this innovation? Answer: it gives us a heads-up. Before picking up the phone, we can screen our calls. We let some calls go to voicemail when we are not in the mood or prepared to talk at that moment. This is called postponement.

Research This! Who invented caller ID? When was it invented?

Postponing

"Why did I say that?" "What was I thinking?" "I shouldn't have taken that call." Sound familiar? Have you ever regretted something you said? Sometimes it is prudent to take more than a fraction of a second to say something or respond—to slow down the encoding process and allow our brains to fire more synaptic impulses. When we don't we often experience miscommunication. This was seen a lot between Will, Joey, Brittany, and the other cast members from *MTV's The Real World Hollywood 2009*. They showed viewers "What happens when seven strangers live in a house, work together . . ." and don't postpone more of their conversations? Drama!!

Postponement **means delaying communication until another time.** It allows us to think critically about our communication. Communication scholar and author Julia Wood states that "Someone who thinks critically weighs ideas thoughtfully, considers evidence carefully, and evaluates alternative . . . courses of action."[36]

Sometimes we force a conversation when it's not prudent. We feel compelled to answer a question or listen to someone when we shouldn't. Have you ever been in a conversation with someone and noticed she was choosing her words very carefully? Her rate of speech was slow and deliberate, perhaps intermittent, with a long pause or two? At times, it is judicious to give ourselves permission to think before we speak. Taking a few seconds or minutes or days before we speak buys us time to choose our response. We may say to someone:

- "I'd like to hear what you have to say at another time. Right now is not good for me because I am stressed out."
- "I don't know. Let me give it some more thought. I'll call you back in twenty minutes."
- "That's a great question. I need to get back to you this afternoon so I can verify my information and give you a correct answer."

- "Before I commit, I'd like to look at my calendar and check on a few other obligations I have. I'll call you by Friday to let you know. Will that work?"

Sometimes a coworker, roommate, spouse, or friend says or does something which shocks us. We may feel at a loss for words or are so upset that we just don't know what to say. We may know that if we say something, it may likely strike the person the wrong way. An appropriate and strategic response may include the statement, "I'm not sure what to say or how to respond to this. I need to think about this more and get back to you tomorrow." Another statement we can say is, "I'm really uncomfortable with what you just said (did). I need some time to process this."

Your Turn: Think of a time when you should have postponed a conversation but didn't? Describe what happened?

While postponement is generally a very effective strategy, it may not bode well with the person who wants to speak to you. He or she may perceive you are skirting the issue or taking complete control of the conversation. This can lead to further miscommunication or a conflict spiral. To reduce the likelihood of this, consider the following:

- State the reason for postponing.
- Recognize the person's desire to communicate.
- Make a date.
- Follow through.

Let's take a look at a conversation which incorporates these four elements. Mike and his girlfriend Tammy have dated exclusively for three years. The two reside together in a quaint starter home they bought together and in East Grand Rapids, Michigan. Tammy has finished her student teaching and is actively searching for a teaching position. Her exhaustive efforts yield no offers until she receives a call from a school system in Australia. She calls Mike's cell phone to hit him with the news.

Tammy: "I can't believe it. I was just offered a position to teach in Sydney. I think like that's in Australia or something! What do I do? Should I like just take it?"

Mike: "Wow! This is great! Congratulations! Hey, I'm not able to talk about this right now because I'm five minutes late to work, and I have to rush in to meet my supervisor. (**States the reason for postponing**.)

I can tell you're really stoked. You have a lot to tell me. (**Recognizes her need to talk about it.)**

Will it work to talk about this during my break at 10:00 a.m.?" (**Makes a date.)**

State the Reason for Postponing

Mike tells Tammy, "I can't talk right now because I'm five minutes late to work, and I have to rush in to meet my supervisor." It is important to communicate the reason for the delay. It lets the other person know the postponement has nothing to do with him or her or the issue at hand. We want to communicate effectively and something hinders that. A nagging headache, too many listening ears, or being hit with multiple demands on your attention (your screaming child, the burning pot roast, the now-activated smoke detector alarm, and your neighbor at the door) are sound reasons to delay a significant conversation.

Recognize the Person's Need to Communicate

Has this ever happened to you? You say, "This is not a good time," or "I don't want to talk about this now," without a valid reason. The person you are speaking to takes offense and says. "I do. We will." He or she finds a way to engage you by lobbing an accusation you feel compelled to refute, taking your car keys so you can't leave, or following you around the house! To avoid this, Mike might validate Tammy's need to talk, "Wow, how exciting! I know you want to talk about this. It's important." **Validation is any communication act which recognizes or acknowledges another person's thoughts, feelings, or needs**. Mike may then suggest when it would be good time, so that Tammy feels assured that the conversation will happen in a timely manner. We call this making a date.

© Galina Barskaya, 2010. Used under license from Shutterstock, Inc.

Sometimes people are more receptive to our message when we are mutually engaged in a physical activity like walking, or when there is a change of scenery.

Make a Date

Making a date doesn't mean dinner and a movie—although it could! It does mean that a specific time frame is pinpointed by both individuals to return to the conversation. Specific might be "in twenty minutes," "at next Tuesday's staff meeting," "after we put the kids down to sleep," or "as soon as I get out of the shower." Remember, the person may have a real need to address this issue with us now and needs to feel that we recognize and appreciate this need. Also, it is important to involve the person in deciding when the conversation will reconvene. In the above dialogue, Mike asks, "Will it work to have us talk about this during my break at 10:00 a.m.?" This gives Tammy some say in the delay. If Mike arbitrarily decides on the date, she may feel resentful and disrespected.

Follow Through

Here we want to be sure to revisit the conversation like we said we would. If we say "I'd like to talk about this after the game. Is this ok?" and the person agrees to this, not following through may cause the person to perceive this as indifference or avoidance. When Mike calls Tammy during his morning break, he is demonstrating consistency and reliability.

Your Turn: Like Mike and Tammy, create a situation involving a conversation that needs to be postponed. Include all four steps of the postponement method. You may be asked to share your dialogue with your team or the class.

–State the reason for postponing.
–Recognize the person's desire to communicate.
–Make a date.
–Follow through.

Rehearsing

Postponement also gives us time to apply another important technique which is rehearsing. **Rehearsing is preparing and practicing what you are going to say before you say it.** This may involve taking notes, creating an outline of the points you want to make, and practicing it out loud or silently. The benefits of rehearsing include:

- Choosing the right words.
- Anticipating what the other person may say.
- Generating pertinent questions to clarify points.
- Organizing one's thoughts.
- Distinguishing between issues of little and major importance.

"One of the basic causes for all the trouble in the world today is that people talk too much and think too little."
Margaret Chase Smith

Rehearsing is usually an intrapersonal (unit 4) activity; however, you make it interpersonal (unit 1) if you run ideas by someone else or get another person's perspective. Rehearsing may also involve doing some research before you give an answer or commit to something. An important part of the rehearsing process is to consider the other person, to be other-centered (unit 3). We can do a role reversal where we imagine if we were the person receiving our message, how we would want to receive it. This is called perspective taking.[37] **It is putting yourself in the place of another.** We can contemplate the following questions:

- Why is this important to him or her?
- Is there room for me to compromise or negotiate?
- How may I communicate that I understand where he or she is coming from?
- What can I say to show I appreciate this person and the relationship we have?
- Are there points which we both agree on? How might I acknowledge this?
- What questions can I ask which invite dialogue and encourage feedback?
- Does this person deserve an apology? If so, how can I express it?

Have you ever rehearsed what you were going to say before saying it? How did it improve the quality of your communication?

Along with postponing and rehearsing, there are several things we can do to make sure we accurately understand a person's message. We also can clarify the messages we are sending people and encourage more feedback. These techniques include paraphrasing, parroting, and strategic questions. Let's look at each of these techniques starting with paraphrasing.

Paraphrasing

Paraphrasing **is a brief restatement of what a person says in our own words.** Within a sentence or two, we attempt to capture the essence of a person's message. Typically, we start a paraphrase with the following sentence starters "So . . ." "Sounds like . . ." "What I heard you say was . . ." "You . . ." "In other words . . ." "Did I hear you correctly that . . ." Take the conversation between Andie Anderson (Kate Hudson) and two of her colleagues, Michelle (Kathryn Hahn) and Jeannie (Annie Parisse), regarding her next *Composure* feature story in which she is going to conduct an experiment and then write about, *"How to Lose A Guy in 10 Days (2003):"*

Michelle: "Oh, you are never going to pull this off."

Andie: "Watch me. Tonight, I'll hook a guy. Tomorrow, pull the switch. Before the ten days are up, I'm going to have this guy running for his life."

Jeannie: "You're not going to burn his apartment down or bite him, or anything?"

Andie: "No! I'm going to limit myself to doing everything girls do wrong in relationships. Basically, everything we know guys hate. I'll be clingy, needy . . .

Jeannie: "Real touchy-feely." (paraphrases)

Andie: "Yeah."

Jeannie: "Like, call him in the middle of the night and tell him ***everything*** you had to eat that day?" (paraphrases)[38]

Jeannie paraphrases or captures the essence of what Andie is saying in her own words. Let's say our friend Taariq shares how unhappy she is with something her boyfriend is not doing. We paraphrase her: "So you feel that he doesn't show interest in your family like you'd like him to." A paraphrase like this let's Taariq know that we hear and understand what she is saying without necessarily agreeing with her, taking sides, or giving advice. For example, Jason may say to Johnny, "My psych prof is busting us with a lot of work. I don't know how she expects us to do well with a paper and test due the same day." Jason replies, "That's a lot. Should I get someone else for poker tonight?" Here Jason paraphrases what he heard Johnny say and then asks a question to clarify the content of Johnny's message.

What are some of the benefits of paraphrasing? When we paraphrase, we communicate that we are actively listening. This is a very confirming form of communication. It sends the message that we care about what the person is saying. It is a check to make sure we are listening correctly—potentially reducing the likelihood of miscommunication. If we paraphrase incorrectly, the other person will let us know. **Also, if we listen with the intent of paraphrasing accurately, we are less inclined to engage in problematic kinds of listening** such as defensive listening and interrupting.

Stephen Covey, author of *The Seven Habits of Highly Effective People* states "Seek first to understand, before being understood." This maxim deserves some conscious assimilation. If we approach a conversation with the desire to understand a person completely before responding, it may change the direction and outcome of a conversation. Why? Because what we say next is based on a lot more information! **Paraphrasing allows us more time to encode the best response.** A person is more inclined to listen to us in a similar capacity when we actively listen without interrupting and demonstrate our understanding with a paraphrase. This isn't always an easy thing for us to do. We often operate from a "seek first to be understood, before understanding" mode.

Other times it really helps a person to hear what we are hearing. A paraphrase gives a person an opportunity to add to, retract, or clarify his or her message once it is paraphrased back. **When we paraphrase, we communicate: "I heard you, and I understand." People tend to reciprocate with "Now I feel understood, let me understand you."** In addition to paraphrasing, another technique at our disposal is parroting.

Your Turn: Create a brief exchange between two people. Have one character paraphrase the other.

Parroting

When we **parrot** someone, we basically **repeat back word-for-word what the person said**. This is prudent if the information is very important or detailed. It is also good if we want to remember key pieces of information. Below are examples of parroting:

Torrey: "I need you to unlock the studio promptly at 7:00 p.m. for the hip hop aerobics class. Be sure to grab my Janet Jackson CD on your way out."

Markus: "Unlock at 7:00 for the hip hop aerobics and grab J.J. on my way out." (parrot)

Ben: "You're going to turn left at the first light, go to the second light, and turn right."

Emily: "Turn left at the first light. Go to the second light and turn right." (parrot)

While there is a real value to parroting, it is best used selectively. If we try to repeat word-for-word what people said all the time, it would get obnoxious!

The Listening Check

Besides paraphrasing and parroting, another technique which helps us improve listening skills is called the "listening check." Just like muscles need exercise to gain mass and strength, our ability to listen grows in proportion to how much we exercise mental concentration. Every day let's get into the habit of doing the listening check with a few of our conversations. The **listening check** technique **involves asking ourselves a few questions immediately after a conversation to check the accuracy of our listening.**

Right after talking to someone face-to-face or on the phone, we can ask ourselves, "What did he or she just say to me?" It helps to recall the key or main points first. Next, see what we remember in terms of the details. This technique sharpens our concentration. It increases our awareness of the effort that is needed to listen well. This not only trains our "listening ear," it is also a check to help us measure if we successfully eliminated any distractions or listening barriers.

As a part of a listening check, why might it be advantageous to ask ourselves this question immediately after a conversation: "What was not said?"

Using the listening check also helps improve our memory. It's great to recall what people tell us. A first-class memory can save us time, effort, and unnecessary headaches. Sharpening our memory also dresses up our conversational skills. The next time we see a person, we are more likely to remember and follow up on details from the previous conversation. This shows a real interest in, and concern for, people. Take Reggie and Tara. It's been a couple weeks since they've talked last. Tara remembers something from her last conversation with Reggie.

Reggie: "Hi Tara!"

Tara: "What's up, Reggie? How was *Soul Train?* Did you catch lunch with Don Cornelius.

Reggie: (Impressed she remembers this) "Girl you know it. . . ."

Along with paraphrasing, parroting, and listening check, there are several other approaches to improving listening and feedback.

Ask a Question for Clarification

Questions are great for clarifying information and/or extracting additional information from the sender. Sometimes we need further explanation, an example, or a directive. For example, we might say, "I heard you say I wouldn't understand. Why wouldn't I?" The following are also examples of questions for clarification:

Dybbuk: "Why would she do such a thing? I ask you, Velvel, as a rational man: which of us is possessed? *A Serious Man (2009)*

Bruce: "If I forgot to put oil in the brownie mix, is that a problem?"

Roxanne: "What would you like me to do about the situation?"

Ask the Sender to Repeat the Information

A question may serve the purpose of having a person repeat the information or state in a different way. Often what is helpful is to ask for a hypothetical situation or example. This increases our understanding and prevents miscommunication. We shouldn't hesitate to use this technique. Here are some examples:

Collin: "May I have an example of what you're looking for?"

Keagan: "What you're saying is important. I want to make sure I understand. Would you explain that again?"

Repeat Information or Explain It Differently

If we sense the receiver is confused about our message, we can ask the person if he or she wants the message repeated or explained differently. Sometimes we need to state something a different way or provide a concrete example to help a person decode our message accurately. The following quotes illustrate this:

Gloria: "What I mean by 'the best defense is a good offense' is . . . "

Chris: "We can talk about marketing the book nationally as soon as we wrap things up."

Bruce: (looking perplexed)

Chris: "Let me put it another way: no finished book, no marketing campaign."

Ask the Receiver to Paraphrase What We Said

We can also check to see if a listener understands our message by having him or her restate or repeat the information we have given. Here are some examples of this technique:

Dennis: "I'm not sure what I said is clear. Would you please tell me what you heard?"

Kylene: "Just to make sure this makes sense, would you repeat what I just said?"

Kent: "Kate and Avery, so that I know that you heard me, what three things do you need to do before you can sit down and watch *Heroes*?"

If we demand, "Tell me what I just said, now!" The response we'll receive is going to be . . . well . . . not good. Another less effective way to use this is, "Oh yeah, well, if you were listening, tell me what I said!" Be sure this is communicated as a request and not a demand.

Ask Before Telling

Sometimes we assume another person is equally ready or interested to hear what we want to say. Unbeknownst to us, the receiver may have some internal or external noise happening at that moment. If we want to improve a person's receptivity to our message, we can give the person a heads up about the topic and invite the person to converse with us. **Receptivity** refers to **a person's willingness to receive a message or engage in a conversation.** Here are some examples:

Bill: "I wanted to talk to you about the shifts I've been assigned to this month. Is this a good time for you to talk to me about it?"

L.Z.: "Wanted to talk to you about the Serena interview. Do you have five minutes?"

If the person appears to be distracted or says it is not a good time, don't force the conversation. Postpone and mutually decide on a date to reconvene.

The approaches mentioned so far are designed to check our understanding of a sender's message. In addition, when we are senders, they help us to gauge if the receiver is decoding our message in the manner we intend. It also helps us to understand what mirroring is and how it may improve listening and receptivity.

Mirroring

If we overhear two people laughing a couple tables away from us at a café, chances are we will smile even if we don't realize it. This is according to a new study which purports people smile and are prone to laugh when someone else laughs. Laughing is contagious. Sophie Scott, a neuroscientist at London's Global University states, "We've known for some time that when we are talking to someone, we often mirror their behavior, copying the words they use and mimicking their gestures." In her study, subjects who were exposed to different sounds such as a baby's laugh, registered positive responses on MRI scans.[39]

Mirroring is reflecting a person's communication behavior. When someone whispers to you, what do you tend to do? You respond in a hushed tone. If a friend speaks to you, and she is

excited, she may gesture wildly. She may speak fast and loud. You, without thinking, are likely to respond similarly. If I stood in a crowd at a sporting event and stared up in the sky, people will look up, too. They will look to see what I'm "pretending" to see.

Mirroring can enhance the communication exchange, putting sender and receiver in sync. We can also use mirroring to alter or change a person's nonverbal communication. We mirror back the opposite of what we are getting. If someone comes at us incensed, he may talk loud, fast, and aggressively. He may take a step toward us and invade our personal space. Rather than step forward, in response, we can step back. We can lower our voice, speak calmly, slowly, and softly. We can even sit down, which is a less antagonistic posture. The person will likely start to do the same thing. He will begin to calm down, reflecting back what he is seeing and hearing from us. If we want to pump up a lethargic group of our coworkers about a project, we are more likely to accomplish this if we stand up, gesture enthusiastically, and speak with excitement. As we draw this unit to a close, let's talk about one more important aspect of listening: listening to support and help others.

. . . Postponing, rehearsing, paraphrasing, parroting, the listening check, questions for clarification and mirroring are strategies for improving listening and feedback. How would you describe them and use them in your interpersonal communication?

Being There: Empathetic Listening

People often share things with us because they are experiencing personal problems. We engage in **empathetic listening when we attempt to offer support or comfort to someone. Empathy is the state of identifying with or sharing the feelings or situation of another person.** Scholar Jon Hayes states when we demonstrate empathetic listening, we let people "know they have been understood from within their own frame of reference, and that {we} can see their world as they see it while remaining separate from it."[40] When someone shares with us a private struggle, we often feel the need to respond in some way. How do we respond in the most helpful manner? Often, when we try to listen empathetically, we offer advice.[41] Humorist Andy Rooney once said, "I've learned that it is best to give advice in only two circumstances: when it is requested and when it is a life threatening situation." There is a lot of wisdom here. Research suggests that while our advice is well intended, it isn't as welcomed or valuable as we think.[42] Sometimes people are not ready or wanting advice, just someone to talk to who will listen to and validate them. They will likely figure out how to handle things on their own, or they will ask us for help if they need it.

Responses which generally are not well received are:

- Telling a person how he or she should feel or express his or her emotions.
- Telling a person what he or she should do about a problem.
- Minimizing the person's experience. ("You'll get over it." He's better off now." "It could be worse.")
- Claiming we know "exactly how the person feels."
- Offering our analysis of the problem as if we are an authority or know something as fact. ("The reason he's not calling you is . . ." "You're allowing your insecurities to cloud your judgment . . ." "I bet that if you told her . . ."
- Completely ignoring the situation as if it doesn't exist.

Responses which generally are better received include:

- Talk less and listen more. Paraphrase back what the person is saying without adding our analysis. Holding a person's hand in silence may be very comforting to a person.
- Let the person know that we are available to help out or be there. ("I care about you." "I am here for you." "I have you and your family in my thoughts and prayers.").
- Ask the person how we can best help him or her. ("How can I help you through this?" "What do you need from me right now?")
- Let the person know how we feel. Sometimes we feel reluctant to share our feelings because we are guarded about saying the wrong thing. It may be very comforting for a person to hear us state how we feel about a person who is ill or has died. It gives a person a sense that he or she is not alone. ("I am feeling really sad right now. I miss her so much." "I'm feeling anxious about the test results. I can only imagine how you feel.")
- Ask questions which show your concern and interest: "How are you doing?" "When is your next appointment? Would you like me to go with you to it?"
- Ask questions which help a person draw his or her own conclusions or identify coping strategies.

  ("What is helping you get through this?" "What are some of your options?" "Would you like us to brainstorm some ideas together?"[43, 44]
- Rather than avoid the person because you feel awkward about the situation, periodically call or stop by with invitations to go out for a walk, shopping, a game, or some activity which would be enjoyable. Many people who experience bereavement state that after the funeral, many of their friends or family members stop calling or visiting. While it is important to give people their space and privacy, it is also helpful to continue to show our interest and concern without feeling we have to walk on egg shells.

Do you agree with these suggestions for empathetic listening? Why or why not? From a communication standpoint, are there other approaches you think are helpful in these situations?

. . . What are some helpful guidelines for empathetic listening?

Unit Summary

Active listening is more than hearing something. It requires mental concentration and effort. Active listening is a process which involves attending, understanding, responding, and recalling. Listening is tied to the kind of feedback people offer each other. There are certain types of listening which tend to adversely influence our communication. The ones explained in this unit are selective listening, eavesdropping, defensive listening, pseudo-listening, and narcissistic listening. Competent communicators strive to steer clear of these types of listening. They also recognize and limit certain barriers to effective listening such as information overload, negative expectations, closed mindedness and semantic noise. If we are serious about improving our interpersonal skills, we can begin to consciously assimilate certain communication techniques, which are universally considered effective, generally speaking. These include postponing, rehearsing, paraphrasing, parroting, the listening check, questions for clarification, and mirroring. Empathetic listening occurs when we attempt to assist or comfort a person. There are certain guidelines for how to offer support in a helpful manner.

Key Questions

1. What is the difference between hearing and active listening?
2. How is attending, understanding, responding, and recalling a part of the active listening process?
3. Why is effective listening important to our career and relationships?
4. How would you describe the following problematic types of listening: selective, eavesdropping, defensive, psuedo-listening, and narcissistic listening?
5. What are some of the barriers to effecttive listening? How do they interfere with communication?
6. Postponing, rehearsing, paraphrasing, parroting, the listening check, mirroring, and questions for clarification are strategies for improving listening and feedback. How would you describe them and use them in your interpersonal communication?
7. What are some of the helpful guidelines for empathetic listening?

Vocabulary Playback

Active Listening
Attending
Interpreting
Responding
Back-channel cues
Recalling
Selective Listening
Insulating
Eavesdropping
Defensive Listening
Rebuttal Tendency
Conversational Control
Interrupting
Pseudo-Listening
Narcissistic Listener
Stage-hogging
Postponement
Validation
Rehearsing
Perspective Taking
Paraphrasing
Parroting
Listening Check
Mirroring
Empathetic Listening
Empathy

Focus Group/Class Discussion

- Selective listening means we tend to focus more on things that interests us. Which topics pique your interest? Which ones put you to sleep?
- Someone said, *"We were given two ears but only one mouth, because listening is twice as hard as talking."* Do you agree with this statement? Why or why not?
- To practice your listening skills, go to www.esl-lab.com, Randall's ESL Cyber Listening Lab. As a group or class, click on one of the conversation topics under the General Listening Quiz Box. Listen to the conversation and see if you are successful at correctly answering quiz questions which accompany each conversation. What does it take to do well? What do you notice in terms of your level of listening? How is it different compared to casually hearing something? What strategies did you employ to help you listen effectively?
- Recalling information is a part of the listening process. Research suggests people tend to remember information which is unusual versus common. This is referred to as the "bizarreness effect."[45] I tend to remember names better if I associate a person's name with an off-the-wall or unique visualization. For example, if I'm introduced to someone whose name is "Cheryl," I'll visualize her singing *"All I Wanna Do"* on stage with singer-song writer Sheryl Crow. What other strategies are there for improving our ability to recall information? Create some examples.
- Think of a person you confide in a lot. Which qualities does this person possess that make him or her such a trusted sounding board? What kind of feedback do you get from this person?
- How often do you not ask a question to clarify something you don't understand? Why do people do this? How might you avoid this and help others feel less inhibited with their questions?

Unit 5 Vocabulary Review

___ Active Listening
___ Attending
___ Interpreting
___ Responding
___ Back-channel cues
___ Recalling
___ Selective Listening
___ Insulating
___ Eavesdropping
___ Defensive Listening
___ Rebuttal Tendency
___ Conversational Control
___ Interrupting
___ Pseudo-Listening
___ Narcissistic Listener
___ Stage-hogging
___ Postponement
___ Validation
___ Rehearsing
___ Perspective Taking
___ Paraphrasing
___ Parroting
___ Listening Check
___ Mirroring
___ Empathetic Listening
___ Empathy

A. This is the process of attending to, interpreting, responding to, and recalling messages.

B. Communication behaviors which let a speaker know we are paying attention to what he or she is saying. They may also aid our ability to listen effectively.

C. Our tendency to listen more to things we find stimulating, unique, or important.

D. This is when we tune out someone who is telling us things we find unpleasant.

E. This occurs when people make an effort to overhear the conversations of others.

F. This type of listening is less focused on trying to understand what another person is saying and more focused on information one may refute or use as a counter attack.

G. This is a part of defensive listening in which we, as someone is speaking to us, formulate in our minds a response to deflect or refute the negative information we are hearing.

H. This is when we interject a thought before a speaker is finished speaking.

I. This is when we act like we are listening, but we really are not.

J. A behavior in which a person will dominate a conversation by speaking for long periods of time and redirecting a conversation back to him or herself.

K. Delaying a conversation until another time is called this.

L. This occurs when a person recognizes or acknowledges another person's thoughts, feelings, and/or needs.

M. When we practice or plan out what we are going to say to someone in advance.

N. It is the mental process of putting ourselves in the place of another person or considering another person's viewpoint, needs, or frame of reference.

O. It is a brief restatement of what a person is saying in our own words.

P. This is when we repeat back word-for-word what a person says.

Q. This involves asking ourselves a few questions immediately after a conversation to check the accuracy of our listening.

R. This is reflecting a person's communication behavior.

S. This kind of listening involves offering support or comfort to someone.

T. This is a state of deeply understanding or sharing the feelings or condition of another person.

Exercise: Paraphrasing

Paraphrasing is restating a speaker's thoughts. It is an effective technique to improve listening and reduce miscommunication. It also shows that we are interested in and concerned about what the person is saying, which is a form of validation. A paraphrase usually begins with "What I heard you say is . . ." "It sounds like . . ." "Do I understand you correctly . . ." "So . . ." "I sense that . . ." "In other words . . ."

Speaker	**Paraphrase**
"The United Nations is a failed idea and an expensive burden for the United States."	"So you don't think it serves a useful purpose."
"Devon acted so out of character last night. I can't believe he made those derogatory comments about women."	"He didn't impress you with his behavior."
"My parents had another major blowup last night. They were screaming at each other for hours."	"I see this has you really upset."

1. Create your own script between two characters. Show how one could paraphrase the other.

____

____

____

____

____

2. Assume you are having a conversation with a friend or family member and that the following quotes are statements that he or she has just said to you. Write down what you would say to paraphrase this person.

   A. "He just left. Not even a goodbye. I'm thinking everything is going great. One fight and he leaves without a word. He even had the nerve to take that expensive necklace he bought me in Venice."

   ____

   ____

   B. "I'm not sure what I should say to Bobby Sue. She's the sweetest gal I've ever did know. She wants to get hitched right now—a full out, hog wild barnyard wedding! I'm not sure I'm ready for this, but I've never been as happy since I met her, plus were not related!"

   ____

   ____

C. "I'd like you to work this Saturday in the morning because we are short staffed. Next Saturday I could really use more coverage in the afternoon or evening."

____

____

D. "He's hanging out with these guys with bloodshot eyes. He's drawing marijuana leaves on his textbook covers. He has an unusual craving for Cheese Curls. His bedroom is locked a lot and I'm finding towels rolled upon the floor near the bottom of his door. Should I be concerned?

____

____

E. Juno MacGuff from *Juno* (2007): "Yea, you just take Soupy-Sales to prom. I can think of so many cooler things to do that night. Like, you know what Bleek? I might pumice my feet, uh, I might go to Bren's Unitarian Church, maybe get hit by a truck full of hot garbage juice, you know? Cause all those things, would be exponentially cooler than going to prom with you." Source: *The Internet Movie Database*

____

____

Dyadic Exercise: Pair up with someone in class or do this on your own with the people you know. Your professor will give you a list of topics to choose from such as:

Best/Worst Date
Strangest Dream
Proudest Moment
Super Suit (a super power I'd like to have)
Greatest Pet Peeve

In your dyad, each person takes a turn and speaks for one to two minutes. When the speaker finishes, the listener will use one or more of the techniques below to make sure that he or she was listening actively and accurately. The speaker will also use one of the techniques to make sure that the person listening understands what was said.

*Restate what the person said in your own words or **paraphrase**.
*Repeat back word for word what the person said or **parrot**.
*Ask a question for clarification
*Ask the sender to repeat the information.
*Restate what we said or give a concrete example.
*Ask the receiver to paraphrase what was said.

Perception

6

Perception Unit 6

Our perceptions affect how we communicate interpersonally. Unit 6 looks at factors which influence perception and suggests ways to improve perceptual accuracy.

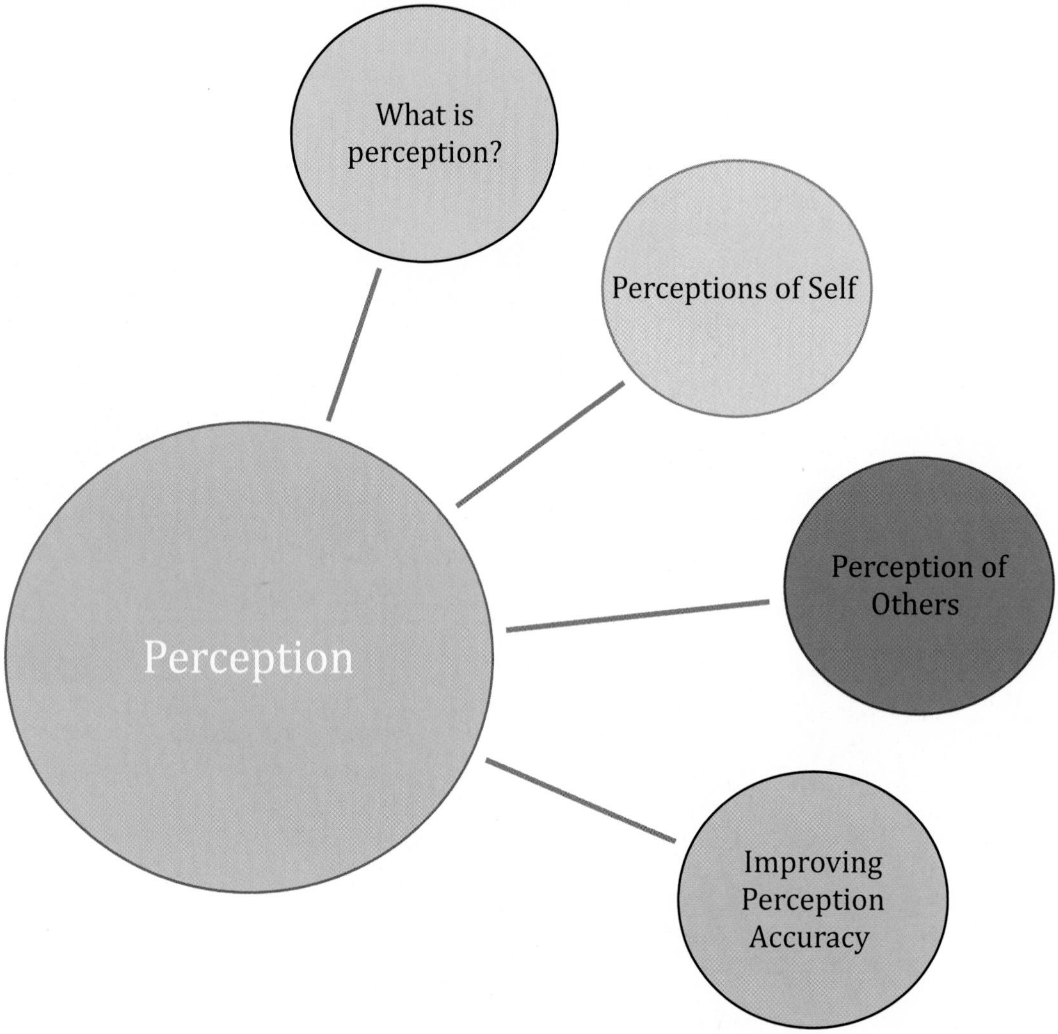

Unit 6 Learning Objectives

As a result of reading and studying Unit 6, you will be able to:

1. Define perception and describe how we select, organize, and interpret sensory information.
2. Understand how perceptions of self and others influence our interpersonal communication.
3. Describe the subjective nature of perception and factors which make perception inaccurate at times.
4. Improve perception accuracy by seeking more information and applying perception checking.

If a particular basketball player missed more than nine thousand shots in his career, lost three hundred games, and missed the winning shot twenty-six times, would you recruit him for your professional team? How about your neighborhood team? Most people wouldn't, but what if I told you this person was Michael Jordan?[1] **Perception** is the process of understanding what we sense. We pick up sensory information from what we taste, touch, smell, hear, and see. We often base our perceptions, such as whether we would want to recruit a certain basketball player, on how information is presented to us. Our perceptions are also influenced by our feelings of self-worth. A documentary called *"Behind The Scenes: The Making of The Sports Illustrated Swim Suit Issue"* gives viewers a rare look into the production of this popular annual photo spread. Interestingly, several models made negative comments about their bodies or looks. One model said she wished she had the body of another model. During a photo shoot on a sailboat, several complained they looked bad in their swimsuits. It looked like they were ready to jump ship! I thought, you must be kidding? *Hello*! These women were selected *because* of their unusual beauty. One of the models is picked for the coveted cover photo of this famous edition. When the magazine's photo editor called the model by phone to share the terrific news, she thought it was a practical joke and hung up on him!

Both the Michael Jordon and *Sports Illustrated* swim suit references illustrate what may influence our perception. We communicate and respond to people based on our perceptions. **Our perceptions influence if we communicate, what we communicate, and how we communicate.** We have perceptions of ourselves and perceptions of others. In this unit we'll explore what perception is, understand aspects of self-perception, identify factors which influence our perception, and learn ways to improve our perception to avoid miscommunication.

Perception Is a Process

It is a part of the human experience to label, categorize, and generalize what we see in ourselves and others. It is how we make sense of our inner and outer world.[2] Scholars of communication and psychology recognize perception as a process which involves selection, organization, and interpretation.[3, 4]

Selection

Selection is the process of focusing on a particular stimulus. In an interesting experiment, the *Washington Post* asked internationally acclaimed virtuoso, Josh Bell, to perform six classical pieces solo for forty-three minutes during the early morning on January 12, 2007 at a busy Washington D.C. subway terminal. Three days prior, people paid around $100.00 a ticket to experience his performance at a sold out concert at Boston Symphony Hall. His violin is valued at an estimated 3.5 million dollars. Amazingly, approximately 1,097 people walked by the musician, without stopping to appreciate his amazing talent. Were they in a hurry to get to work or preoccupied with their plans for the day? Did they ignore Bell because at first glance he looked like one of a number of street musicians seen performing on the sidewalks of the nation's capitol to earn some quick cash. In fact, twenty-seven people dropped a total of $32.00 in Bell's violin case. One woman did stop. She stood a few feet away from Bell for a period of time. When he stopped playing for a moment, the woman said incredulously, "I saw you perform at the Library of Congress. It was fantastic." Astonished that one of the finest classical musicians in the world was performing at this random subway corner, the woman said, "This is one of those things that could only happen in D.C."[5]

. . . **Catch this!** To see how people respond to Bell's unannounced Metro performance, go to www.youtube.com and type in Josh Bell subway experiment. What factors appear to influence whether people stop and appreciate his talent? To see Bell perform in a different context, type in Josh Bell plays Ave Maria.

Since there is a lot of information we can pick up with our senses, we tend to select what we pay attention to based on what stands out, what we find interesting, and what is affecting us the most at a given moment. We may also tune in more to things based on what we have on our minds, where we are at the time, the intensity of a particular stimulus and how familiar we are with the stimulus.[6,7,8] For example, if we are in a hurry to get somewhere in our car, we often focus our attention on the slow drivers, construction, or any other obstacle which impedes our speed. We may not pay much attention to what is on the radio, the stores we zip by, how much we are driving over the speed limit, or the police cruiser which is rapidly approaching us from behind. Our attention is directed at those things which stand out and affect us the most at that moment.

Organization

Once we select what we want to pay attention to, we organize or arrange the information we are selecting. If we see that a highway is congested, we may start to look for other routes or exits. In this way, we are organizing and arranging visual information. We do this with people too. We use words to classify what we can observe about others. We may say someone is Latino, female, and tall after seeing her walk into the same room we are in. We also organize the information we gather about people as a result of our interactions with them. We may say someone is not only Latino, female, and tall, but liberal, outgoing, and a professor after engaging in a twenty minute conversation with her.

Interpretation

After we select and organize sensory information, we then interpret or assign meaning to the sensory information. For example, Jared may see that when he brings up a topic, one of his female friends, Tomika, gets quiet. He interprets her quietness as an indication she is uncomfortable with the subject because she still has feelings for him. He makes what is called an **attribution**, which means he assigns an explanation to her behavior.[9,10] In fact, Fritz Heider writes about this in a book he wrote in 1958 titled *The Psychology of Human Relations*. His **attribution theory** suggests we assign a cause or multiple causes to a person's behavior because we have a need to make sense of what we are sensing. Our attributions may or may not be accurate.[11,12] We may see this occur between a father and daughter. The father starts asking his teenage daughter what her plans are for Friday night. The daughter interprets her father's line of questioning as an interrogation, and attributes his inquiries to his lack of trust in her, which she doesn't like. The father interprets his daughter's behavior (slow to answer his questions and her defensiveness) as resistance and attributes this to her having social plans which may get her into trouble. The attribution each attaches to the other's behavior will influence the communication between them. We may interpret a person's friendliness as fake, conniving, or genuine based on any number of factors. What might they be?

Now that we know what perception is and the process involved, let's take a look at the perceptions we have of ourselves and how they influence our interpersonal communication.

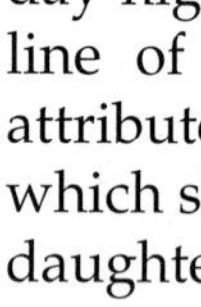

Your Turn: Create an example to show how perception works. Incorporate the process of attending, organizing, and interpreting.

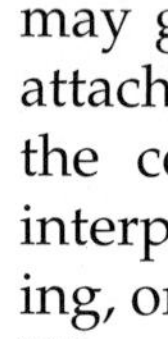

Do you believe people have a sixth sense or ESP? Why or why not?

. . . What is perception? How do we select, organize, and interpret sensory information?

Perceptions of Self

"I had no self-respect. I was depending on others to make me feel good, but they hated themselves too," revealed multi-platinum singer Mary J. Blige. Her album, *The Breakthrough,* garnered eight Grammy nominations. A rare glimpse of her life is shared with *Parade Magazine's* Dotson Rader. Mary's father abandoned her family when she was a little girl and her mother moved them to a public housing project near New York City. She describes hearing women scream and seeing them run frantically down the hallways to escape the fists of violent boyfriends. Every woman she knew there was abused. Her mother was a working woman and left Mary with people she considered trustworthy. Mary was physically hit and verbally abused by them. She was molested at the age of five. As she grew up, she dated boys who were abusive, one of whom put a gun to her head. She saw herself as ugly and hated herself. She states, "You . . . attract people who are like you."

She credits an intervention by a friend, Kendu Isaacs, who challenged her to stop drinking, change friends, and believe in herself. His love and kindness were transforming for her. From there, Mary took life by the horns and started changing how she saw herself. Her healthy decisions fed her growing self-esteem. At first, she was guarded around Isaacs. She had never experienced a man who treated her with such respect. "I never experienced real love before . . . It seemed too good to be true."[13]

A personal account similar to Mary J. Blige is told by "Mia," one of my former students.

> *"Living with my mother was not pleasant. She was married to an abusive man. I was subjected to and witnessed abuse by both my mom and him. She lost custody of us, and we were forced to move to Alabama to live with my dad and step mom. My sister became pregnant at the age of 15. My dad kicked her out of the house. The two of us were extremely close, and I took this really hard. I tried to see her every day after school and would drive my dilapidated love bug which had wire coat hangers to hold the gear shift, bumpers, and muffler in place. At its fastest, it reached 45 mph. My dad attempted to kill himself more than once. After one of his attempts, I walked into his room, and he was lying on his bed not breathing. Later, he blamed me for wanting to end his life. It took me eight years to completely acknowledge that it was not my fault, and I couldn't have prevented his suicidal attempts. I moved out of my dad's house into my boyfriend's apartment. He is the last guy who ever beat me. My dad remarried and practically disowned my sister, brother, and me and claims this woman's son as his own. It has taken me years to try to cope with the pain my dad's choices have caused me."*

Mary K. Blige and Mia's personal accounts illustrate how the verbal and nonverbal messages we receive from significant individuals throughout our lives impact how we see ourselves, and how we end up feeling about ourselves. How we see ourselves as individuals is called self-perception or **self-concept.** Whether we view ourselves in positive or negative ways will impact our self-esteem. **Self-esteem** is how we feel about ourselves or the degree of liking/affinity we have for ourselves. Self-concept is a cognitive appraisal. Self-esteem is an affective or emotional valuation.[14, 15]

Our self-concept is something we construct from our interactions with others.[16] We assimilate the comments people direct at us. We also internalize people's reactions to us, integrating their comments and reactions with our own self-assessments.[17] Ireland-born actor Pierce Brosnan, before he became the face of James Bond, dropped out of high school and joined the circus. In 1991, his wife died in his arms of ovarian cancer, leaving him a single father of three. Asked by *Reader's Digest* reporter Meg Grant how alike he is to the 007 character he portrayed for seven years, Brosnan replied,"I'm perceived as [a]sophisticated, debonair, distant person, this macho guy. And I'm not like that. Following me around for a day would be quite comedic. I'm anything but Bond."[18] Brosnan's description of himself reflects how he sees himself as a person. Comedic actor Jack Black received an ego boost when he was named "Hollywood's Most Unlikely Sex Symbol." Black believes his wit makes him sexy. This may or may not be true. It is quite possible that a number of females may consider Jack Black sexy. Jack Black may think this, too.

In the 2009 Oscar winning film, *Precious*, based on the novel *Push* by Sapphire, it depicts the unfathomable hardships of an illiterate sixteen-year-old girl Claireece "Precious" Jones (Gabourey Sidibe). She lives in the Section 8 tenement in the heart of New York City's Harlem with her unemployed parents. She endures verbal abuse and neglect from her mother, Mary (Mo'Nique). She was raped and impregnated twice by her father, Carl. Inspired by her new teacher Ms. Rain, (Paula Patton), Precious learns how to read and is befriended by a social worker, Mrs. Weiss, (Mariah Carrey), who encourages her to look at herself in a more positive way. The movie dramatically depicts how children internalize the messages they receive from adults, and the tremendous impact this has on them.

. . . **Catch this!** To see the movie trailer for Precious go to www.youtube.com Precious Trailer. What specific messages are directed at Precious by the adults in her life? How would these messages affect her self-concept and self-esteem?

Some women may categorically disagree with the zany actor's self-assessment.

The perceptions we have of ourselves is subjective. How we see ourselves may not be how others see us. This may have a lot to do with our tendency to be overly self-critical. Pop icon Madonna once said during an interview that she might hear a hundred compliments after a concert, and if one comment was negative, she'd focus on that versus the one hundred compliments she received. Comedian and television talk show host Ellen Degeneres writes in her bestselling book, *My Point . . . And I Do Have One*: "We all feel like idiots at one time or another. . . . We think that people are staring at us, sensing our inadequacy, noting our flaws, mocking our clumsiness. But perhaps, sadly, nobody is noticing. Everybody is too busy worrying that they look like idiots to care about you."[19] Many social scientists believe that our sense of reality is not "out there" but created within our minds.[20]

How do we see ourselves? How much does this differ from how others see us? The difference between the perception we have of ourselves and the perceptions others have of us may be small or large. In fact, **incongruence** is a term psychologists use to describe the gap between our own self-perception and reality. Jennifer, for example, may have all of the characteristics and qualities associated with effective leadership. However, if she doesn't perceive that she possesses poise, confidence, and decision making skills, this is an incongruence. Her perceptions, more than her true abilities, are likely to influence her behavior in this area. She may not pursue opportunities to lead. She may think twice before vocalizing her thoughts. She may avoid making decisions or take on a more passive role when conflict arises.[21] For example, former Secretary of State Condoleezza Rice started college at the age of fifteen, holds three degrees including a doctorate in political science, and was Secretary of State in the Bush administration. She would not have reached the highest echelons of power in Washington D.C. had she not seen in herself the ability to comprehend difficult issues, speak intelligently, and broker agreements with various heads of state. Based on her performance in academia and as a government

appointee, it appears there is little incongruence between how she sees herself and what she is capable of doing.[22]

There appeared to be a high degree of incongruence in one of my students who came to class with a letter written about her from a close friend. This was for an assignment where students ask people they know to write about how they perceive them. She had no idea her friend thought so highly of her. She could see that he appeared to think more highly of her than she did of herself. She was surprised and deeply moved by what he had to say:

> *"Jill is an interesting breed, part flower, part cat, a rose with retractable thorns . . . in transition between teen and adult, choosing new responsibilities or choosing—not! Possessing a warm kind heart that seems to enjoy making fun of itself, honest and trustworthy enough to impress any Boy Scout, preferably with a Harley. She is both neatly packed and randomly strewn into a golden box, wrapped up in gilded paper, bound with the finest shiny silk ribbon and duct tape and something resembling a garter belt from Frederick's of Hollywood with a letter attached that reads, 'you can't do much better than this!'"*

While self-concept is how we see ourselves. The beliefs we have about ourselves are called **self-appraisals**. We might believe we are fun to be around at social events. We may consider ourselves very caring and sensitive to other people's feelings. We may believe that we are destined to do something great with our lives. Our beliefs or self-appraisals reflect and reinforce our self-concept. **Our self-concept is comprised of how we see ourselves psychologically, physically, intellectually, socially, and relationally**. Do any of the words in the following categories below describe you?

> **"People do it every day, they talk to themselves . . . they see themselves as they'd like to be. They don't have the courage you have, to just run with it."**
>
> **Tyler Durden in *Fight Club* (1999)**

Psychological/Emotional

happy, enthusiastic, mellow, confident, insecure, suspicious, selfless, cooperative, impatient, spontaneous, organized, hyper, assertive, passive, trusting, optimistic, pessimistic, skeptical

Intellect/Beliefs

mathematical, deep thinker, curious, liberal, poetic, political, conservative, Libertarian, vegetarian, open minded, pro-life, environmentalist, humanist, Wiccan, Taoist, agnostic

Social

clumsy, friendly, outgoing, reserved, loud, quiet, talkative, humorous, partier, team player, loner, gamer, leader, movie buff, family oriented, camper, sports enthusiast, cultured

Roles

father, bartender, son, sister, coach, volunteer, teacher, Marine, police officer, church deacon, accountant, club president, friend, boyfriend, wife, seamstress, rapper, investor

© Andresr, 2010. Used under license from Shutterstock, Inc.

Talents

Musical, athletic, skateboarder, triathlete, dancer, basketball player, card shark, cooking, artistic, acting, writer, contortionist, improvisational comedy, fashion design

Physical/Health/Age

beautiful, stocky, ugly, tall, skinny, healthy, muscular, fat, overweight, well proportioned, even toned, freckled, diabetic, cancer survivor, youthful, old, middle aged

Gender Characteristics/Sexuality

male, metrosexual, female, masculine, feminine, homosexual, heterosexual, bisexual, androgynous, asexual, sexy, transgendered, voyeuristic, traditional, virgin, monogamous, promiscuous

Class/Race/Culture/Ethnicity

American, Muslim, African American, Scottish, Jewish, Hispanic, Asian, Irish, Italian, Greek, Russian, urban, cultured, upper class, educated, blue collar, middle class, French, Cuban, Native American

Your Turn: How would you describe yourself in each of the aforementioned categories? Are there other categories we could use to describe how we see ourselves?

"All my life I said I wanted to be someone . . . I can see now that I should have been more specific."

Jane Wagner

Our self-concept is relatively stable, however, it can fluctuate in short spurts. A promotion at work, a relationship breakup, or a compliment from someone may have a short term impact on our self-concept, causing it to dip or jump suddenly. Our self-concept can also change slowly over time by the messages we receive from significant individuals, by society, and our own self-talk or intrapersonal communication. Our self-concept is also shaped by social comparison. **Social comparison** is evaluating ourselves in relation to others.[23] When I was a teenager, I distinctly remember taking a date to see a movie starring the young Tom Cruise. I looked over at her and noticed that her enlarged eyes were transfixed on Cruise as he mixed his *Cocktails* (1988). I could have sworn that this girl was drooling on my arm the whole movie! I compared myself to Cruise's looks and depiction in the movie and left the theater thinking it was time to hit the gym and get a new life. In other words, the view I had of myself was not very positive, which had an effect on my self-esteem.

We also compare ourselves now, with how we think we should be. Psychologists refer to

this as the **real-ideal comparison**. If our real self-concept differs greatly with our ideal concept, this may adversely affect our feelings of self-worth.[24, 25] Many people won't begin to form an affirming self-concept until they change a fundamental aspect of themselves or achieve their ideal self. Their self-worth is contingent on something such as earning a certain amount of money, successfully overcoming a bad habit, getting a promotion at work, or losing a certain amount of weight. Self-acceptance is the foundation of positive mental health. Self-improvement literature consistently emphasizes the need for us to love and accept ourselves unconditionally. We are encouraged to view ourselves in a very positive, affirming way just as we are now and establish healthy, realistic goals for self-improvement. Self-acceptance entails owning our thoughts, feelings, and behaviors and embracing our strengths and weaknesses.

Along with the real-ideal comparison, we also tend to see ourselves as we believe others see us. The more we accept and like ourselves, the more we assume others accept and like us. Back in the early 1900s, sociologist Charles Cooley created a concept he coined **reflected appraisal**. If we see ourselves a certain way, we presume others do, too. If I see myself as laid back and approachable, I think people look at me similarly. I may see myself as funny or animated, for example. I will likely assume others see me this way as well, especially if people actually tell me I'm a Marlon Wayans or Dane Cook.[26]

The importance we place on the various ways we see ourselves makes a difference in terms of its effect on our self-esteem.[27] If I value being funny and animated in my interactions, and it appears to me that I am, my self-esteem is enhanced by this. If I place a lot of importance on how I look, yet I see myself as out of shape, this is going to have an adverse impact on my self-esteem. While self-concept is how we see ourselves, self-esteem is the feelings or the degree of liking we have for ourselves. Just as we have a certain level of affection for others, we experience these feelings inwardly. A person's self-esteem can be measured by any one of several standardized self-esteem instruments used by mental health professionals. Studies purport a strong correlation between high self-esteem and certain interpersonal characteristics. Research suggests people with high self-esteem typically are more:

- Outgoing and willing to communicate.
- Likely to believe that the love or affection others show them is genuine.
- Positive in their assessment of other people and less apt to put them down.
- Comfortable being watched by others as they attempt a new task.
- Assertive communicating their needs and confident expressing their ideas.
- Able to laugh at and poke fun of themselves.
- Inclined to expect others to accept them.
- Confident defending themselves when they feel they are being criticized unfairly.
- Likely to pursue relationships with people who reinforce their positive self-perceptions.[28, 29, 30]

In addition, people with high self-esteem are also less likely to be critical of their performance, overly concerned about failing or appearing foolish, prejudicial in their views of others, and threatened by people they view as superior or better than them in some way. They are also less likely to compare themselves to others or judge themselves in relation to unrealistic or unreasonable standards.[31, 32, 33] People with high self-esteem tend to expect more of themselves and others. They feel deserving of love, respect, and success. They approach people and situations with a more positive expectancy. One's predictions often result in self-fulfilling prophecies.

Your Turn: From the characteristics and communication behaviors described above, which ones do you see in yourself? Don't see?

"A woman who is nitpicky and critical of you is likely insecure about herself. Her insecurity feeds her jealousy."
—Jennifer Benjamino, Cosmopolitan Magazine

Self-Esteem and Self-Fulfilling Prophecies

A **self-fulfilling prophecy** is the result of what one expects. **Our expectations of an event may influence the outcome.** We tend to live up to our own predictions. We can talk ourselves into and out of failure and success. We can also talk other people into failure and success, too.

The results of a far-reaching 1968 study was published in a work titled *Pygmalion In The Classroom* by researchers Robert Rosenthal and Lenore Jacobson. They teamed up with school administrators to convince unsuspecting teachers at an elementary school that certain students, about 20% of the entire grade, were unusually "gifted." The teachers were given the names of these students and were told to expect the best from these bright youngsters. Unbeknownst to the teachers, these students were actually randomly selected so they represented different academic skill levels from low to high. At the end of the school year, these students had the greatest gains on IQ tests compared to all of the other students. Why did these students emerge as the Harry Potters of their school? Rosenthal and Jacobson speculate that on a conscious and unconscious level, the teachers expected more from these students. They communicated these expectations in various ways. They may have spotlighted the "gifted" students work to a greater extent, called on them more, provided them with more feedback, told them they were bright, and afforded them more opportunities to read or lead. The expectations they had of their students inspired their students to believe they were capable of high achievement, thus creating self-fulfilling prophecies.[34]

In another interesting experiment, dating back to 1890, a new tabulating machine appeared at the U.S. Census Bureau in Washington D.C. The clerks had to adapt to a totally different manual protocol. There was no precedent for how many cards the clerks could punch in a given day, so the inventor made his best guess. He informed the clerks they should shoot for at least 550 cards a day and to exceed that unless they encountered significant fatigue or stress. After a couple weeks the clerks were processing about 550 cards a day. They reported that pushing beyond this number was tiring and stressful. Later, a new group of clerks was hired and assigned to operate the same machines for the first time. No one told them what the daily production goal was. After just three days, the second group cranked out two thousand cards per day with no reported stress.[35]

The first group was told what they were capable of doing. They believed it and achieved it. The second group was not given any expectations about their limitations or potential and produced far more. Our self-fulfilling prophecies reflect and influence our level of self-esteem. For example, researchers have discovered that people who anticipate rejection are more apt to behave in ways that invite it![36] People with higher self-esteem tend to view opportunities and challenges positively. They see the potential versus the obstacle. They anticipate positive outcomes. They are more inclined to take healthy risks because they see themselves as capable and deserving of success and happiness. Research confirms that if we have higher self-esteem, we tend to believe we have a greater sense of control over our lives.[37]

"I see a beautiful young woman. You're naked, she's leaning over you. Oh, wait. She's performing your autopsy! "

We may also limit ourselves based on expectations we have about our skills as communicators. If we doubt our ability to communicate successfully, this may create anxiety. Our anxiety may feed into our doubt causing us to communicate poorly or avoid communication situations all together. According to communication researchers McCroskey and Wheeles, surveys of college students find that ten to twenty percent suffer from "severe debilitating communication apprehension." An additional 20% experience "communication apprehension to a degree substantial enough to interfere with their normal functioning."[38, 39] **Communication apprehension** is the anxiety or nervousness we feel in a given communication context. If we experience frequent anxiety in a lot of communication or social situations such as interviews, social mixers, speaking up in small groups, confronting people, or talking to authority figures, we have **generalized communication apprehension** (GCA). If we feel anxiety in just a few communication situations, we call this **specific communication apprehension** (SCA). **There are four research backed methods to reduce communication apprehension as a source of internal noise: practice, performance visualization, relaxation breathing, and auto suggestions.**[40, 41, 42]

Practice

The more we speak up in class, give speeches, approach and greet people we don't know, volunteer to participate in an activity in front of others, share our opinions at meetings, the less anxious and threatened we'll feel about it. Eleanor Roosevelt once said, "Do what you fear doing and the death of your fear is certain."

Performance Visualization

This involves creating mental images where we see ourselves perform a task with skill and confidence. First, we can picture ourselves in a communicating situation which makes us feel apprehensive. Next, we visualize how we will look as a confident, poised, and relaxed communicator. We can also imagine being spontaneous and having fun. We may envision ourselves behaving a certain way such as smiling appropriately, taking initiative, giving eye contact, demonstrating good posture, listening intently, offering a firm handshake, and introducing people to each other with self-assurance.[43]

Relaxation Deep Breathing

Relaxation breathing involves taking long, slow breaths. We inhale until our lungs are fully expanded. We hold our breath for five seconds and very slowly exhale. While we do this, we attempt to clear our mind of all thoughts and focus on the steady movement and sounds of our lungs expanding and contracting. If we combine performance visualization with deep breathing, this has a very calming effect.

Auto Suggestions

Auto suggestions are statements we make to ourselves silently or out loud regarding our ability to do something. Positive auto suggestions may include: "I can do this." "I have something important to say." "I will do a great job with my presentation." "I will be relaxed and have fun at this party. In fact, as soon as I get there, I will introduce myself to the first person I see." "I have charm, great wit, and sophistication." "I will share my ideas without hesitation or doubt." Positive auto suggestions, stated repeatedly and with conviction, are purported to reduce nervousness and induce more confidence.[44]

How do we influence other people's self-fulfilling prophecies through our interpersonal communication?

> Seen on sign: "Low Self-Esteem Support Group Meets Thursday at 7:00 p.m. Please use rear entrance."
>
> —*National Lampoon's Book of Jokes and RiddlesAhajokes.com*

Part of making sense of our world involves not only figuring out who we are, but how we present ourselves to others. Two interesting concepts relating to self-perception are public image and impression management.

. . . What shapes our self-concept? How does our self-perception influence our interpersonal communication?

Public Image

Florida Republican chairman Jim Stelling sued one of his own state party leaders, Nancy Goettman for libel. He asserts she dashed his chances of becoming the head of the Florida Republican Party. How? Stelling claims she committed character assassination via a letter she wrote to party members. Her letter mentioned that Stelling had not one, not two, not three, but six divorces under his belt. He claims in his suit that the actual number of times he has divorced is five. Stelling is convinced that her misinformation tarnished his reputation amongst Floridians and members of the Republican party! He stated to the judge, "I believe in family values." Stelling's words and actions suggest that he is concerned about his public image. Our **public image** is how we want others to see us.[45]

The contestants on *So You Think You Can Dance?* and *American Idol* see themselves as very good dancers and singers, respectively. This is a part of their self-concept. They hope the judges will assess them similarly and award them cash prizes and instant acclaim. How they want to appear to the judges is their public image. For example, the vocal finalists on *American Idol* are out to wow Kara DioGuardi, Randy Jackson, Ellen DeGeneres, and, if lucky, the hypercritical Simon Cowell. None of them wish to hear

© Fox Broadcasting Co./Photofest

anything remotely similar to Cowell's rejection of one contestant's performance, as quoted on angrysimon.com:

> *"I saw someone the other night who is 28-years-old, and hasn't worked a day since he left college because he's pursuing a dream he'll never, ever realize. He thinks he's a great singer. Actually, he's crap. But nobody has said to him, 'Why have you been wasting your time for eight years?'"*

Our public image may be dissimilar to how we actually see ourselves. We may not see ourselves as a skilled cook, but we may want our date to think we are. We may not self-identify as friendly and assertive, but we may want our supervisor at work, who is about to hand out a promotion, to consider us this way. A plethora of shows such as *Dismissed, Meet My Folks, Temptation Island, Blind Date, The Bachelor, Boy Meet Boy, Paradise Hotel,* and *Joe Millionaire* feature contestants who dive into the reality TV dating pool in hopes someone will pick them in the final round for a chance at money, travel, fame, or at least bragging rights. Bisexual internet celebrity Tila Tequila, in one of MTV's highest Nielsen-rated series *A Shot at Love With Tila Tequila*, must choose one potential long-term love interest between a group of eager men and women. The contestants are obviously concerned about their public face. They want Tila to perceive them as sexy, sensitive, exciting, adventurous, intelligent, and successful, to name a few relational "turn-ons." In fact, they attempt to find out what Tila looks for in a potential mate so that they can "market" themselves accordingly. Their "marketing" attempts are referred to as impression management. **Impression management** is what we say or do to influence people's perception of us.

Impression Management

A humorous site called Comedy-Zone.net posts this anecdote about a businessman who opened the doors of his beautiful new office. He decorated lavishly and furnished it with antiques. He placed his numerous diplomas on a wall for all to see. He caught a glimpse of a potential client standing in the reception area and waved him in. Wanting to appear savvy and successful, he picked up the phone and pretended he had a big deal in the works. He bounced around big figures and made impressive claims. He sealed the deal, Donald Trump style, smiled, and hung up. He then addressed the visitor, "May I help you?" The man said, "Yeah, I think so. I'm with the phone company. I'm here to activate your phone lines."

Filling his office with expensive furnishings, displaying his impressive lineup of diplomas, and his over the top phone performance are examples of impression management. **Impression management involves communicating and behaving in ways to influence people's perceptions of us.** It is our conscious and unconscious attempt to present an image others will approve. Impression management may involve taking credit for something when it's not deserved, embellishing aspects of a story which make us look good, bragging, and disclosing information about ourselves we think will impress others. If a guy wants his female date to see him as a gentleman, he may do things to project that image. He may open the car door for her, pull out her chair at dinner, say "please" and "thank you," and stand up when she leaves for or returns from the ladies room. He may also think twice about belching loudly. When we are on a date, we may say and do things to manage the way our date sees us.

Many newly recruited NBA stars such as Portland Trailblazers 7-foot powerhouse Greg Oden have no problem making thunderous dunks and hitting precision three-pointers on the court. However, in social galas and media events with microphones poised to catch every word and cameras locked on every move, presenting a polished, professional image poses a formidable challenge. Steve Shenbaum, a former actor from *American Pie 2*, *Scorched*, and *Big Fat Liar*, is paid by sports management organizations to train such superstars as Steve Nash, Yao Ming, and Anthony Carmelo on how to improve their poise and social etiquette. He trains them on the art of the "sound bite" and teaches them how to answer questions, share stories, and speak clearly. The idea is to prepare these men for the spotlight. This training and preparation is a form of impression management to enhance each ball player's public image.[46]

"Of course when I first meet a guy, I may let it slip that I have a condo overlooking a lake."
Jamal

Your Turn: How have you used impression management to project a favorable public image?

Impression management is not relegated to individuals only. Couples also project an image. Jennifer Benjamin, author of *Seven Things You Must Know About Other Couples' Love*, writes about the "perfect" couple. "You know, one of those dynamic duos who seem so in sync, so interesting, so crazy in love with each other. We may get the picture that other couples are more infatuated or compatible than we are with our boyfriend or girlfriend. Couples engage in impression management because their relationship is a reflection of themselves. Behaviors such as never talking about their personal problems or arguing in public, being excessively loving, and talking up their dreams, vacations, and life may be an honest reflection of what they are experiencing together or a "top form" presentation to mask the real life at home.[47]

When and how is impression management normal and healthy? If we engage in impression management are we being fake? What are some possible negative consequences of impression management? Can we take impression management to an extreme?

. . . What is the difference between public image and impression management?

Impression Management, Saving Face & Self-Serving Bias

With a head-spinning $19 million dollar contract with the Philedelphia 76ers, NBA star Allen Iverson was compensated handsomely to do his job. Attending practice was, well, a part of the job, at least according to his contract. The enigmatic, outspoken player was criticized a while back for missing a fair share of practices during his stint with Philedelphia drawing criticism from players, sportswriters, and his coach, Larry Brown. During talk of a possible trade, Iverson was questioned during a press conference regarding his no-shows at practice.

Reporter: "Could you clear up the issue of your practice habits since we can't see you practice?"

Iverson: "If I can't practice, I can't practice. It's as simple as that . . . we're sitting here, and I am supposed to be the franchise player, and we're talking about practice. I mean listen, we're sitting here talking about practice, not a game, not a game, not a game, but we're talking about practice. Not the game that I go out there and die for and play every game like it's my last, but we're talking about practice. I know I'm supposed to lead by example and all that, but I'm not shoving that aside like it don't mean anything. I know it's important. I honestly do, but we're talkin' about practice, man. "

(Laughter from the media crowd)

"When you come to the arena, and you see me play, you've seen me play right, you've seen me give everything I've got, but we're talking about practice right now."

(More laughter)

Reporter: "Is it possible that if you practiced more, you would make your teammates better?"

Iverson: "How in the hell can I make my teammates better by practicing?"

The next day, Coach Larry Brown told reporters, "He said 'practice' during his press conference more than he's attended practice."[48] Iverson's reaction is a classic face saving maneuver. **Saving face** is our need to protect our ego or image when we feel personally attacked or criticized. We may feel the need to save face when we make a mistake, fail at an attempt, or when someone implies we are at fault for something. **When we feel the need to save face, we often engage in impression management behaviors.** Specific communication behaviors associated with the need to save face are:

- Blaming others when we are fault.
- Attributing our mistakes to external sources (computer problems, weather, traffic).
- Making excuses, justifying, or minimizing our behavior.
- Refusing to accept responsibility for an error.
- Pretending that we are unaware of a problem or "didn't know something."

The need to save face is readily apparent in the dialogue between the characters Daniel and Susan played by Daniel Travis and Blanchard Ryan in the 2003 nail biter *Open Water*. The film features an American couple who return to the surface after a peaceful dive and discover that their tourist boat left them behind in shark-infested waters off the Great Barrier Reef. Tensions flare and Susan blames Dan because he took her further out from the diving group than she wanted, causing them to return to the surface five minutes late. Not wanting to accept the reality that his choice may have placed them in imminent peril, Dan tries to deflect criticism or blame by accusing Susan of picking the wrong vacation:

Daniel: "The only reason we are out here in the first place is because of your *(expletive)* job!"

Susan: "What?"

Daniel: "If it were not for your job, we would not have thrown our plans out the window, rushed around at the last minute and settled on this *(expletive)* trip! We would be at home, in the middle of our hectic lives, which right now sounds like heaven to me. And in a month's time, seven months ago, we would be where we were supposed to be in the first place, and paying less than we are now to be shark bait!"

Susan: "I can't even believe you'd bring that up right now. You were the one who picked the dates."[49]

In addition to our inclination to want to save face, our interpersonal interactions are influenced by self-serving bias. **Self-serving bias** is our tendency to readily point out other people's flaws or weaknesses while not acknowledging or owning our own. If another person makes a mistake, we are quick to note it.

We attribute it to something inherent or innate to the individual such as a character defect, immaturity, or a lack of common sense. If we make the same kind of mistake, we may point to something outside ourselves as the cause. For example, Jay sees that his friend Ted is having relationship difficulties with his girlfriend. He may say, "Ted has some growing up to do." But when Jay's girlfriend is mad at him about something, he may say, "It's that time of the month again." The alternative to this is Jay taking responsibility for his actions by acknowledging, "I wasn't very sensitive to her feelings yesterday," or "I was late picking her up because I tried to run too many errands." An alcoholic may also demonstrate ownership versus self-serving bias when instead of saying her binge drinking episode was the result of a stressful day at the office, she recognizes, "I'm an alcoholic. I was craving a drink and didn't call my sponsor or get help like I needed to." When people admit their weaknesses, and take responsibility for their actions, they are more likely to actually change them. Many psychologists agree that a mark of maturity is when a client sees his or her negative behavior as something that he or she owns and has control over. People generally respect and admire a person's honest acknowledgement of a mistake made or a lapse in good judgment. Some might even say it is quite refreshing. It is important to know how our perceptions of self influence aspects of our interpersonal communication. In addition, the perception we have of others plays a major factor in how we communicate.

How does taking responsibility for our actions help improve our interpersonal relationships?

. . . What is saving face and self-serving bias? How are both related to impression management?

Your Turn: Think of an example of how you have tried to save face before. Which impression management behaviors did you use to save face? How well did they work? What would you do differently next time? Explain this.

Perception of Others

An anecdote from workjoke.com captures a conversation between two business managers discussing the challenges of running a business. One of them started a practice where she would, out of the blue, surprise her employees by giving them a week off outside of their normal vacation time. The other manager asked, "Why in the world would you do that?" She mused, "It's the best way to really know which ones I can do without." Her motive behind her approach was to gain a more accurate perception of who to retain and who to let go.

Along with having perceptions of ourselves, we have perceptions of others and the world around us. We can raise our communication competency by appreciating the subjective nature of perception.

Subjective Nature of Perception

Why does one person consider a room too cold, the other too warm? Why might two people walk out of a theater at the end of a movie and totally disagree with the movie critics? Perception is subjective and unique to each of us. In one study, a large random sample of men representing a broad spectrum of ages were asked to rank their athletic prowess. Sixty percent ranked themselves in the top 25% or higher and only 6% positioned themselves below average. This is, of course, not statistically possible. In the area of getting along with others, 25% placed themselves in the top 1%! Sixty percent ranked themselves in the top 10%.[50] When fourteen legislators in Michigan were asked to rate themselves on how well they take care of and consider the environment, many rated themselves high despite what they actually did for the environment. One lawmaker gave himself a score of 8 out of 10. Yet, a press investigative study found that he rarely, if ever, recycled, used herbicides on his lawn, and drove a gas-guzzling, ozone-depleting SUV.[51]

In one recently released survey conducted by the Chicago Sun-Times, American men were asked if they would marry the same person if they had it to do all over again. Eighty percent of the men who responded said yes. In a separate *Woman's Day* survey, only half of the women said they would.[52] Our perceptions often do not accurately reflect reality. For example, we may perceive that other people have it made. Our friend may make a lot of money, but unbeknownst to us, has a serious debt problem. By all outward appearances, we may think our buddy is lucky to have such an awesome girlfriend. If we were privy to her private world, we may think differently knowing she has a hard time keeping her hands off other guys. Unlike our parents, our roommate's parents may call him a lot and shower him with gifts, but he may feel, unlike us, tremendous pressure from them to conform to their expectations.

Many things can influence our perceptions. We all hear, smell, and taste things differently. The way our bodies regulate heat varies. We may see things differently based on our age, health, energy level, hunger, and biological cycles. People's self-esteem colors their perception. Research indicates people with low self-esteem are more cynical of and question people's behaviors and motives more.[53, 54] They are more likely to perceive a compliment from someone skeptically. Culture can also play an important factor in influencing our perceptions. Western cultures place a high value on talking. People are encouraged to be talkative or chatty as it is a marker of sociability. However, traditional Japanese and Chinese cultures value silence. Taoist teachings such as "In much talk there is great weariness," and "He who knows, does not speak. He who speaks, does not know" typify Eastern thought and philosophy regarding human interaction.[55] Being present with each other in the moment doesn't require a lot of talking.

Let's look at a few factors which influence perception and a way to perceive and respond to things more accurately using a technique called perception checking.

. . . What do we mean when we say perception is subjective?

We Hold Fast to First Impressions

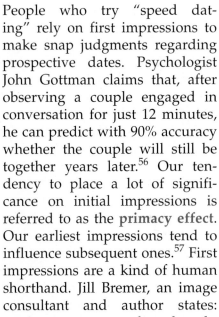

People who try "speed dating" rely on first impressions to make snap judgments regarding prospective dates. Psychologist John Gottman claims that, after observing a couple engaged in conversation for just 12 minutes, he can predict with 90% accuracy whether the couple will still be together years later.[56] Our tendency to place a lot of significance on initial impressions is referred to as the **primacy effect**. Our earliest impressions tend to influence subsequent ones.[57] First impressions are a kind of human shorthand. Jill Bremer, an image consultant and author states: "When you step into a room, people make subconscious decisions about you. Within about thirty seconds, they've judged your economic and educational stature, your social position and your depth of sophistication and success. They're basing those decisions purely upon what they see such as your wardrobe, hairstyle, smile, and posture. After about four minutes . . . you've probably had the opportunity to speak, so they're now taking into account the way your voice sounds, the content of what you say, and how you say it."[58] The problem is many people stick to those initial impressions, when so often they're not very complimentary. While research suggests that our first impressions are significant, they are not permanent and can be changed.[59]

We Assume Others Are Like Us

Sometimes we erroneously assume people think, feel, and need things in the same way and to the same extent as we do. We may think that an issue is not that "big of a deal," and we learn that to someone else, "it is." We may presume, "Oh, she won't mind," because we wouldn't or "He's going to love this," because we would. This gets us into trouble sometimes!

© Junial Enterprises, 2010. Used under license from Shutterstock, Inc.

Our Perceptions are Influenced by Negative and Positive Bias

Sometimes we tend to see the glass as half empty versus half full. If someone says we should date Chad because he's kind, good looking, has a good job, is funny, and has a past gambling addiction, where is our focus? Just one piece of negative information, even if mixed with several positive bits of information, may taint our view of a person. Psychologists refer to this as **negative bias**, which is the tendency to perceive things based more on negative information than positive.[60] Conversely, when two people are in love, they tend to look at each other through "rose colored glasses." They overlook or downplay the other person's negative qualities or characteristics because they are more focused on what they're drawn to about the person or what makes them feel "so in love." This is referred to as **positive bias**.[61]

We Focus On the Obvious

We often put a spotlight on what is immediately perceptible without questioning what lies below the surface. We may step out of a classroom and notice a professor angrily pointing his finger at a student in the hallway and threatening to kick the student out of his classroom. We may question the professor's professionalism or assume she is out of line. However, moments before stepping out into the hallway, we may have missed hearing the student say some highly inappropriate or insulting comments to the professor.

A mother may react hastily in reprimanding her son when she walks in the kitchen and sees him lashing out with a punch to his sister's glasses. The punch did not instigate the fight. His sister was teasing him unmercifully (I have tried to convince my mom of this for years)! Take a look at the following exchange from jokes.com between two different customers and a hotel desk attendant.

Hotel desk attendant: "How was your stay?"

Customer: "Terrible. I got no sleep. Every 15 minutes this loud banging sound woke me up."

Hotel desk attendant: "I apologize for the noise."

(Seconds later, a couple show up to check out.)

Hotel desk attendant: "How was your stay?"

Couple: "Terrible. The guy in the next room was snoring so loudly throughout the night, we had to bang on the wall every 15 minutes to get him to stop."

The first customer focused on what was readily apparent. He assumed the people next door were being rude or obnoxiously loud.

Our Perception Is Influenced by the Relationship We Have With a Person

We view the behavior of people we know differently compared to people who are strangers. If we know we may interact with a person again in some capacity, we may perceive and treat the person differently. In one study, a group of men were asked to rate the public speaking qualities of women who were restaurant owners. The men who were told they would have a private, casual lunch or dinner with the speaker afterwards rated the speaker's performance higher on their anonymous surveys than the men who were not told this, even though the men heard the same speakers.[62] We tend to extend a more generous and forgiving interpretation of a person's behavior if we share a higher level of immediacy with him or her. From unit 1, we learned that **immediacy** is the degree of closeness or connectedness we feel towards a person. Our perceptions are also slanted more positively if we're experiencing a high level of relational satisfaction with someone. On the other hand, if we and someone we are close to are fighting or not getting along, we tend to notice things that get under our skin more. Little things we would otherwise deem as endearing or mildly irritating, now bother us greatly. When we are not "feeling the love," the person's motives are often put on the chopping block with no benefit given to the doubt.[63]

Expectations

When surveyed on whether or not they think life should be easy, a vast majority of people say "No, I can't expect that life is going to be exactly the way I want it." However, do you notice how often people wig out when disappointments or unwelcome challenges pop up? For example, we expect our computer to work 24/7 without a glitch. We tend to overlook the many hours and years of hassle-free usage, and the amazing application of this technology, but when our computer acts up, we veraciously complain to everyone about how terrible it is. Things are fine as long as they work like we want them to. We require the same from people, too. We expect them to respond or handle a situation in a way we would. We often create and maintain expectations which are not fair or realistic and that set the stage for disappointment and conflict.

We can circumvent many of the problems associated with misperception and miscommunication by applying a technique called perception checking.

Your Turn: Think about and write down other factors which may influence how we perceive something.

. . . How is perception subjective?

Improving Communication with Perception Checking

If we want to improve our interpersonal communication skills, we need to accurately assess our perceptions. Considering our perceptions are influenced by many things and are inaccurate at times, it is important to test the validity of what we see, hear, touch, taste, and smell. For example, we are talking to someone and he appears inattentive. We take offense and say, "Forget it. You're too busy with yourself to actually listen to what I am saying." He takes offense because even though it appears he isn't listening, he repeats back verbatim what we said. This is an example of why it is important for us to question the accuracy of our perceptions. This doesn't mean that we should completely discard or ignore them. We may enhance our perceptual accuracy when we:

- talk to rather than avoid people.
- separate facts from people's opinions or interpretations.
- ask questions to clarify what we are perceiving.
- think of alternative reasons for people's behavior other than what we immediately sense.

- take into account people change over time and our perceptions of them may need to change.
- willingly alter our perceptions and consider new information.

Another way to test the accuracy of our perceptions is a technique called **perception checking**. It is a two-step communication strategy used to "check" the accuracy of our perceptions. This is important to use because it allows us to approach a person in a non-threatening way before jumping to conclusions. It gives us a pause and helps us double check what is happening before we react hastily or overreact. There are two steps to this method. The first involves making an observation of what we are sensing using an "I statement." Examples include: I sense . . . I noticed . . . I heard . . . I saw . . . I observed . . . I get the feeling . . . I wonder. . . . The pronoun "I" is less threatening or confrontational. It communicates that the perception comes from you, and may not be 100% accurate. We want to be specific and clear about the behavior we perceive—focus on the behavior without attaching any critical labels or evaluative comments to our observation. The second step is a question or series of questions we can ask for clarification.

The Two-Step Method:

1. State your observation using an:
   "I statement."
2. Ask a question for clarification.

Here is an example. During lunch with a friend, I say something critical about the "expensive" menu prices. My friend smirks, shakes his head, and says under his breath, "Bruce, you are so cheap." Now let's say something about my frame of reference makes me very sensitive to this kind of label. Someone who I loved deeply broke up with me, and this was one of the stated reasons for it. I start to get upset and am about to snap back, but I pause, take a deep breath, and while keeping my composure say:

"I heard you say a minute ago that I am cheap." (Observation)

"How is it that I'm cheap?" (Question for clarification)

My friend tells me that the last three times we've gone out to lunch, he has paid the bill. I stop to think and realize I've let him pay the bill the last three times. Now I can see where he's coming from and that his perception is quite understandable. So rather than react with a mean retort, I am more likely to say something like, "You are right. I could see why you'd think so. Let me be sure to pay for this one and the next two to catch up."

Perception checking places us in what author Stephen Covey says in his book, *Seven Habits of Highly Effective People*, the "seek first to understand before being understood" mode. Perception checks allow us to address a situation with more information. Usually, there is more to the story, and more to what we perceive. The language used such as "I sense . . . I noticed . . . I heard . . . suggests to the receiver that we are basing our perceptions tentatively, and on what we are observing with our senses. The questions are designed to probe and clarify rather than respond in a knee-jerk fashion. Perception checking allows us to broach a topic and initiate a conversation in a relatively nonthreatening way, as opposed to putting a person on the defensive with a premature accusation. An example might be that I come home to find my guitar out of the case, and I immediately get angry that my daughters were playing on it without my permission. Before jumping to conclusions or getting too upset, I state:

"I see that my guitar is not where I left it." (Observation)

"Did you take it out of the case and play it?" (Question for clarification)

My daughter may say, "I opened it up because I needed a pick, but I didn't mess with the guitar." In that case my response will be based on more information, and I will choose a more appropriate response such as, "Good, glad to hear it. Thanks for not playing it like I asked you. Please just remember to close the case and put it back in the closet when you're done grabbing an extra pick."

A humorous quip by Drew Carey is a good example of the two-step perception check. A man is sitting in front of his television with a cold Leinenkugels Big Eddy and a large pepperoni pizza watching his favorite team, the Detroit Lions. The game is intense and the Lions are actually winning. He hears a knock on the door and sees a snail sitting there on the porch. Annoyed, he bends down, picks up the snail, and throws it as far as he could. Six months later there is a knock at his door. He opens it and there sits the same snail.

Snail: "I noticed that you threw me as far as you could six months ago." (**Observation**)

"What was that all about?" (**Clarifying Question**)

The snail may be less upset once it hears why the man rudely pitched him off the porch like Pedro Martinez. The snail can now view what happened, not just from its perspective, but from the man's too. Here are some other examples of perception checks:

"**I heard** you say just now that I am acting just like my father." (Observation)

"What do you mean?" (Clarifying Question)

"**I noticed** that you left in a rush when Emily came into the room."(Observation)

"Were you uncomfortable for some reason?" (Clarifying Question)

"**I see** that the shirt I bought you still has the tag on it, and it's been in the bag for about two weeks." (Observation)

"Would you like to find another shirt that fits your size or style better? Have you forgotten about it?" (Clarifying questions)

During the next two weeks, before responding to what we initially see or hear, let's try a perception check a couple times per day. Remember that our tone of voice is important. If our voice sounds sarcastic, angry, or condescending in any way, this technique will lose its effectiveness. In unit two, we were encouraged to engage in frequent self-monitoring. Self-monitoring is taking a moment to analyze our communication with others. Think about a time recently when you were involved in a misunderstanding or conflict due to a misperception. How could you have reacted with a perception check before you responded? Would the outcome been different had you applied this technique?

Your Take: For each of the following situations, make an observation using "I language." Follow each with a question or two to clarify or confirm your perceptions.

1. After making dinner for you and your roommate, you notice she leaves soon after and returns home with an empty bag from Taco Bell.

Observation:

Question(s) for clarification:

2. Your parents visit you and your family for the weekend. You get the feeling that your spouse or life partner is uncomfortable or tense.

Observation:

Question(s) for clarification:

3. Your mother gives you silence on the phone just as you share with her that you are dating someone you introduced her to three days ago.

Observation:

Question(s) for clarification:

. . . What is perception checking? What steps are involved? What are the merits of this technique?

Unit Summary

We make sense of our world with our perceptions. Perception is the process of understanding sensory information. We have perceptions of ourselves and the world around us. The perception we have of ourselves is called self-concept. How we see ourselves is influenced by the interaction we have with others, our own self-talk, and social comparison. Our self-concept has an impact on how we feel about ourselves, which is our self-esteem. People with high self-esteem typically demonstrate certain communication behaviors which differ from people with low self-esteem. We generally care about how others see us—our public image—and we tend to use impression management to project a positive image to others. Finally, many factors affect our perception, making it highly subjective and prone to error. As communicators, we can ask more questions and apply the technique of perception checking to reduce the problems associated with misperception and miscommunication.

Key Questions

1. What is perception? How do we select, organize, and interpret sensory information?
2. What shapes our self-concept? How does our self-perception influence our interpersonal communication?
3. What is the difference between public image and impression management?
4. What is saving face and self-serving bias? How are both related to impression management?
5. What do we mean when we say perception is subjective?
6. What are some of the factors which influence our perception?
7. What is perception checking? What steps are involved? What are the merits of this technique?

Vocabulary Playback

Perception
Attribution
Self-Concept
Self-Esteem
Incongruence
Self-Appraisals
Social Comparison
Real/Ideal Comparison
Reflected Appraisal
Self-Fulfilling Prophecy
Communication Apprehension
Generalized Communication Apprehension
Specific Communication Apprehension
Public Image
Impression Management
Saving Face
Self-Serving Bias
Primacy Effect
Positive/Negative Bias
Immediacy
Perception Checking

Theoretically Speaking

- Attribution Theory

Focus Group/Class Discussion

- Egocentric is a term Psychologist Jean Piaget refers to as the developmental stage children ages two to six are in. It is characterized by an inability to see another person's perspective. One is considered egocentric when he or she is hyper-focused on his or her feelings and needs. Adults regress to this stage from time to time.[64] How might egocentricism influence our perceptions as adults? Think of an example.
- The impact a compliment or praise has on someone depends on how much the receiver thinks the compliment or praise is sincere and deserved, how specific the compliment is, and if it is delivered immediately versus delayed.[65]

  What other factors influence how a compliment is received?
- Think of a time in which you used communication to "save face." What did you say or do? Would it have been better for you not to have done so? Why or why not?
- How does impression management relate to authentic communication?
- Along with sight, smell, taste, touch, and hearing, do you believe people base their perceptions on a "sixth sense" or ESP? Why or why not?
- Self-esteem is tied a lot to our communication behaviors, what are some ways that we can raise our self-esteem? Is it possible to have too much self-esteem?
- We all may know someone like the girl whose boyfriend cheats on her. He treats her terribly, calls her humiliating names, and may even physically assault her. She keeps going back to him for reasons nobody can figure out. What are possible reasons for this?
- People who have a negative self-image often have a hard time accepting compliments graciously. Do you agree with this statement? Why or why not?
- Because we base our communication on our perceptions, a misperception may birth negative emotions such as jealousy, distrust, and resentment. Think of an example to support this statement.

Unit 6 Vocabulary Review

___ Perception
___ Attribution
___ Self-Concept
___ Self-Esteem
___ Incongruence
___ Self-Appraisals
___ Social Comparison
___ Real/Ideal Comparison
___ Reflected Appraisal
___ Self-Fulfilling Prophecy
___ Communication Apprehension
___ Public Image
___ Impression Management
___ Saving Face
___ Self-Serving Bias
___ Primacy Effect
___ Positive Bias
___ Negative Bias
___ Perception Checking

A. We see ourselves as we believe others see us.

B. What we say or do to influence people's perceptions of us.

C. How we see or interpret things based on our five senses.

D. How we want others to see us.

E. Our tendency to size ourselves up or evaluate ourselves in relation to other people.

F. The degree of liking or affinity we have for ourselves; how we feel about ourselves.

G. A two-step communication approach involving an observation using "I language" followed by a question for clarification to check the accuracy of one's perceptions.

H. The result of what is expected.

I. The difference between how we see ourselves and reality.

J. Our need to protect our ego or image when we feel personally attacked, make a mistake, or when someone implies we are at fault for something.

K. Our tendency to compare ourselves now, with how we think we should be.

L. This is our tendency to readily point out other people's flaws or weaknesses while not acknowledging or owning our own.

M. Our tendency to place a lot of significance on initial impressions.

N. The tendency to perceive things based more on negative information than positive.

O. The tendency to perceive things based more on positive information or characteristics than negative.

P. An explanation or reason we give to another person's behavior.

Q. How we see ourselves as individuals.

R. The beliefs we have about ourselves.

S. The anxiety or nervousness we feel in a given communication context.

Exercise: Perception Checking

For the following scenarios, write a two-step perception check. Focus only on the behavior and address it without making any assumptions or critiques.

1. Observation: "I noticed . . . I sensed . . . I heard . . . I saw . . . I get the feeling . . . "
2. Question(s) for clarification:

Example:	Ever since you were told you could borrow your roommate's shirt, he or she has mentioned three times how expensive it is.
Observation:	**"I've noticed** that ever since you said I could borrow your shirt for the wedding, you have mentioned that it is expensive several times."
Questions for Clarification:	"Are you concerned that I may not return it in the same condition? Are you having second thoughts about letting me borrow it?"

1. Someone is talking to you and says, "You just wouldn't understand."

   Observation:

   Question(s) for clarification:

2. Your roommate just said to you that you don't help out enough around the house.

   Observation:

   Question:

3. Your closest friend has not returned your phone call in over a week. You call her again and this time she picks up.

   Observation:

   Question:

4. Your roommate said that he would leave for the weekend. You were pleased to hear this because you've wanted to have the house to yourself. It is late Saturday and your roommate hasn't left yet.

   Observation:

   Question:

---

5. Just as you say something, your friend rolls his or eyes at you. Before you react or get defensive, you "check" what the eye rolling is all about.

   Observation:

   Question:

---

6. You notice that every time you and a close friend embrace, the embrace and casual kiss is getting longer and stronger.

   Observation:

   Question:

7. Write down a brief scenario and show how you would approach a person with a two-step perception check.

7

Self-disclosure

Self-Disclosure Unit 7

Understanding the importance of self-disclosure in interpersonal communication is the focus of Unit 7.

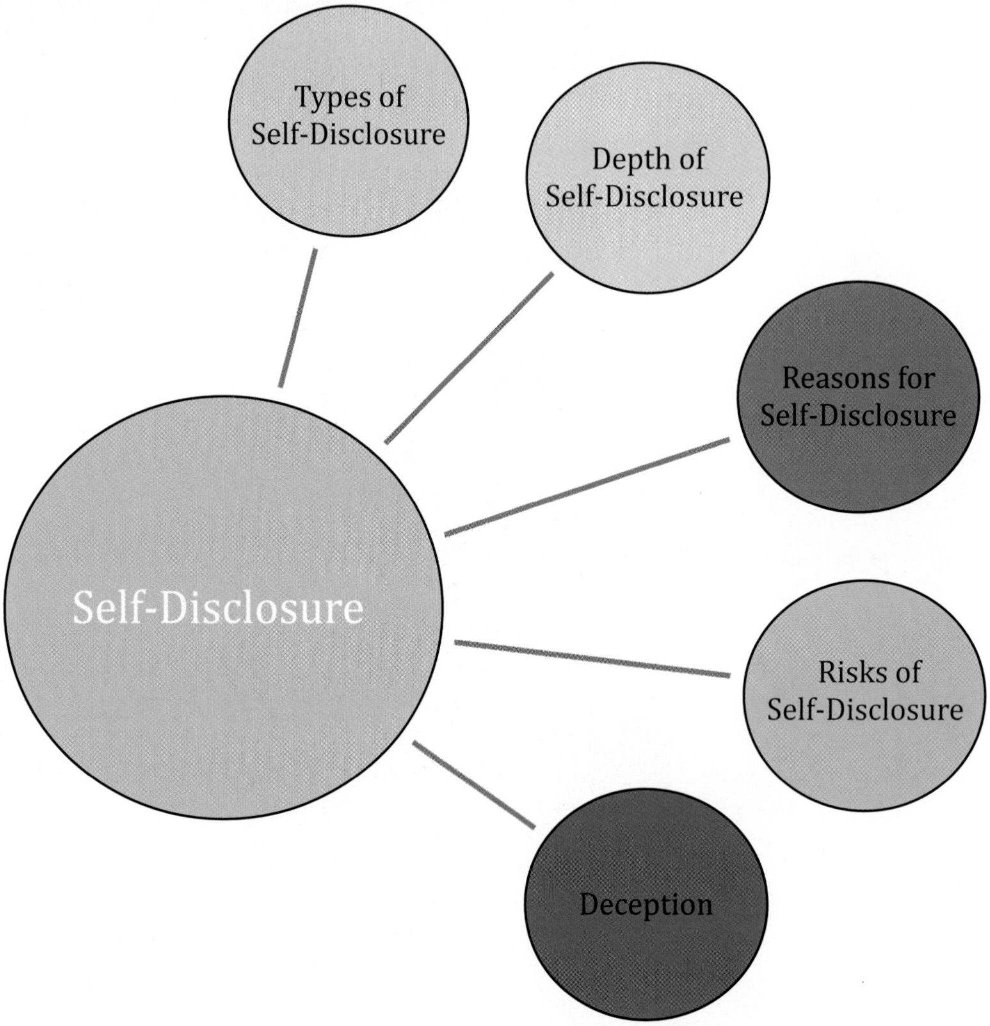

Unit 7 Learning Objectives

As a result of reading and studying Unit 7, you will be able to:

1. Identify the different types of self-disclosure.
2. Appreciate how self-disclosure varies in terms of depth.
3. Explain the reasons why we self-disclose.
4. Describe the risks involved when we self-disclose.
5. Analyze how and why people use deception in their interpersonal communication.

Fans of Grammy award–winning gospel sensation Kirk Franklin did a double take when he unveiled publicly his private struggle with pornography. The dynamic Christian hip hop artist, respected for his impressive musical talent and dedication to charitable missions, voluntarily disclosed his past addiction to pornographic materials with the blessings of his wife, Tammy. The two appeared on national television with Oprah Winfrey. In a candid interview exclusive, *Ebony* magazine later quoted Tammy as saying that when Kirk first told her about his addiction she was hurt, but she said "For him to tell me, to trust me, it brought us closer. We pride ourselves on being friends, and . . . as a woman it taught me that he needed a safe place to fall—on me."

Kirk's early exposure to pornography as a youth later led to an ever-increasing craving for it. His habit was fully entrenched prior to and during his marriage. Kirk confessed to tiptoeing outside in his boxers and rummaging through the trash to retrieve videos he dumped earlier. Kirk shared that his addiction caused difficulties with his emotional and physical intimacy with Tammy. It produced unrealistic expectations and warped his perceptions of a healthy, loving, and spiritual relationship. One day, Tammy states that Kirk approached her and said, "Tammy, I want to share something with you because I want accountability. I want you to know so we can walk through this together. I'm tired of it, and I don't want to hide it anymore."

Self-disclosure is sharing personal information about ourselves with others. **Self-disclosure varies in terms of its type, depth, reasons, risks, and level of honesty. In** their interview with Ebony magazine, Kirk and Tammy Franklin revealed different types of self-disclosure which included personal facts, opinions and feelings. The depth or level of disclosure was significant. They had reasons for their disclosure. Self-disclosure, depending on its depth, may carry with it certain risks. Finally, all self-disclosure varies in terms of it level of honesty.

What is your reaction to the Franklin interview? What do you see as the pros and cons of their self-disclosure?

Types of Self-Disclosure

When we share things about ourselves with others, we do so in the form of **facts, opinions, feelings, and needs.**

Facts

What do bulletproof vests, fire escapes, windshield wipers, and laser printers all have in common? All were invented by women. On average, right-handed people live nine years longer than left-handed people. The first couple shown in bed together on prime time TV was Fred and Wilma Flintstone. These interesting statements come from a website called interestingfacts.org. We can research or conduct a study to confirm the accuracy of these claims. If I say that suicides occur more on Monday than any other day of the week or that motor-vehicles crashes kill more men between the ages of 25 and 44 than any other accidental cause, I am communicating facts. I can back up these statements using mortality data from the National Center for Health Statistics. The

center utilizes reliable scientific methodologies and reports their results to public and governmental agencies. [2]

Facts are provable or measurable pieces of information. We often disclose facts about ourselves. Examples may include: "I have twelve points on my driver's license for speeding (yes some facts are not cool!)," "I'm a Capricorn," or "I received a fat lip playing Wii last night." Former Calvin Klein supermodel and actress Brooke Shields revealed that after delivering her baby Rowan, she was overwhelmed with an unshakable sense of foreboding and despair. She spent days curled up in a fetal position with no desire to get out of bed. She was diagnosed with severe postpartum depression. Shields disclosed personal facts. What she said is verifiable.[3]

Opinions

One of the late Chris Farley's most memorable characters was Matt Foley—motivational speaker of *Saturday Night Live* fame. Here he espouses opinions meant to inspire young people watching his show:

> *"Now you kids are probably saying to yourselves, hey, I'm gonna go out and I'm gonna get the world by the tail and wrap it around and pull it down and put it in my pocket. Well I'm here to tell ya that you're probably gonna find out as you go out there that you are not going to amount to jack squat! You're probably going to end up eating a steady diet of government cheese, and livin' in a van down by the river."*[4]

Foley's comedic antithesis of a pep talk represents an expressed opinion. **Opinions** are beliefs about how things are or should be. Lee Bienstrock, an associate vice president at Trump Mortgage said, "The office is like an aquarium. The weak get eaten by the strong." Bienstrock voiced an opinion. I may say to you, "He lives a life of a lot of almosts," "She could do a lot better, if you ask me," "Chinese food is not as healthy as it is touted," or "Grrrrr baby, very grrrr!" These are opinions. They expose our biases, perceptions, values, and priorities. Mr. T, the 80s pro-wrestling icon known for his tough demeanor and heavy gold jewelry, now vents his opinions on his reality show, *I Pity the Fool*. After learning of British actress Sienna Miller's bitter "Don't you know who I am," reaction to a bouncer's request to see her I.D. outside a nightclub, Mr. T declared: "I pity the fool! She needs to eat a large piece of humble pie." Regarding the party princess Lindsay Lohan, he concluded, "I pity the fool! She's a little prima donna. Right now nobody's put her in check. If they fired her the first time, she would straighten up real quick."[5]

Opinions are not absolute or provable. They are difficult to measure with certainty. There can be a thread of truth to an opinion, for sure. Many times, when people share their opinions, they express them as though they are facts. For example, we are new employees, and a coworker says, "Don't bother the boss with any questions or problems first thing in the morning, she is really mean and impatient." If we decode this opinion as a fact, we may never approach the boss in the morning. This may make our ability to work effectively and efficiently difficult. Rather than accepting what our coworker says hook, line, and sinker, we may take a few mornings to observe our boss to see if she is unapproachable. We may approach her one morning with a question and see how she responds. We may even ask her when it is a good time to approach her with questions or concerns. As receivers, we need to listen critically to what people say and differentiate between fact and opinion. It may be prudent to question people when they state an opinion as though it were a fact. A great question to ask, without sounding confrontational, is "How do you know this?" or "Where did you get this information?"

Feelings

A **feeling** is an electro-biochemical state of being and/or arousal to a stimulus. We use different words to describe our feelings. Examples of feelings we could disclose include: "I'm in love with you," "I'm feeling down about my performance," or "I get jealous and suspicious when he calls, and you grab your cell and leave the room to talk." When 2003 world time-trial record-holder and British cyclist David Miller's apartment was raided by police, empty vials of EPO, a banned substance, were found. Miller confessed to using the substance. He broke a code of silence regarding performance-enhancing drugs within the cycling elite. He expressed his feelings regarding his usage, saying he kept the empty vials as a "testimony to the shame I felt at doping myself. I was not proud of the doping. I was not happy about it."[6] Our feelings, once expressed, reveal a lot.

Needs

A **need** is something we want or desire. From unit 4, we learned about psychologist Abraham Maslow's Hierarchy of Human Needs Theory. The theory suggests that we have different types of needs ranging from survival to self-actualization. We focus our energy on the needs which assure our survival first. Once those needs are met, we use our communication to help us get other needs met such as security, affection, and knowledge. Often we strive to get our needs met using communication approaches which are not generally very clear or well received such as hints, threats, demands, comparisons, and put downs. "I language" is an approach which is more clear and less confrontational or hostile. "I language" focuses on the behavior we wish for. The request starts with "I like . . . ", "I appreciate . . . ", "I need . . . ", "I love it when . . . ", or "I value . . . ". Compare the approaches labeled "A" with the ones labeled "B". Which ones would you prefer to hear someone say to you?

A. "Wouldn't that be nice." (Hint)

B. "**I'd like** to plan a vacation together."

A. "Fine. I won't put in a good word for you when I see her." (threat)

B. "**I appreciate** when you acknowledge my contributions to the department."

A. "You are going to pay me now." (demand)

B. "**I'd like** it if you would pay the cable bill since I paid it in full last time."

A. "I wish you could be as romantic as Karen's girlfriend." (comparison)

B. "**I'd love** it if sometime you'd surprise me with a lunch date."

A. "Do you think you could stop being so pig-headed and selfish all the time?" (put down)

B **"I would really like it** if you would be willing to allow me to make the plans for this evening. From time to time, I'd like to decide what we are going to do."

Your Turn: Think about the communication you've had with people this week. Generate an example of how you self-disclosed a fact about yourself, a personal opinion, a feeling you had, and a need. What did you say? How was it received? Could you have expressed yourself better?

Listening Critically to Self-Disclosure

Often when we self-disclose, we blend facts with opinions. We might say, "I gained two I.Q. points after reading Bruce Punches' book!" Now if, after reading it, we completed an I.Q. test and our score, compared to that of the same I.Q. test taken prior to reading this book, jumped two points, this is a fact. It can be confirmed or proven. Now, if we extrapolate that the book was the cause for our sudden I.Q surge, this is an opinion—even if we believe this unequivocally. Many possible factors could have led to a heightened score. A correlation doesn't always prove causation. California Governor Arnold Schwarzenegger's explanation to *Men's Journal* writer Spencer Reiss regarding his meteoric rise from professional body builder and actor to top executive of the sixth largest economy in the world, is a hybrid of facts, opinions, and feelings. He is quoted as saying

". . . You have a different mind [set] at different stages in your life. [opinion] I was 15 when I started training for Mr. Universe. [fact] Never flown in an airplane, never seen the beach . . . all of a sudden I'm traveling the world." [fact] Schwarzennegger goes on to say how working now as a governor is something entirely different. He says that crafting policies and laws with various "people who are on your side and people who are not—to make all that come together is the most exciting thing I've done . . ." [opinion and feeling][7]

Many communication experts agree that our ability to respond to messages skillfully is enhanced when we listen carefully and critically—distinguishing the difference between a speaker's use of facts, feeling statements, and opinions. People often state opinions as though they are facts. People often hear opinions and accept them as facts. Some opinions are erroneously based on biases or a person's **frame of reference**. Feelings can be irrational or completely illogical. Facts alone don't prove or justify everything. Facts may be derived from rumors, questionable sources, or faulty research.

. . . What are the different types of self-disclosure? What do we mean when we say it is important to listen to self-disclosure critically?

Depth of Self-Disclosure

"I was an equal-opportunity user—I would try anything once." Tara Connor

All self-disclosure varies in terms of what people are willing to share and how personal and revealing it is. The more revealing the disclosure is, the greater the depth of disclosure. Former Miss U.S.A. Tara Connor went on record that she snorted cocaine and admitted herself into a thirty-one-day treatment program to combat alcoholism. She exposed something very personal. Significant self-disclosure is revealing one's innermost thoughts, hopes, fears, dreams, insecurities, and past experiences.

If I share that I had the flu yesterday with a 102° temperature and spent the evening embracing the porcelain bowl, this self-disclosure is not very significant or enlightening. We wouldn't want to go into great depth talking about it nor would we glean profound insight from it. However, if I share with you that my mother dropped me on my head when I was a baby, and that I suffered a serious contusion that swelled to the size of a tennis ball, this is more private and illuminating. It may even explain a few things to you!

The results of what and how often we disclose can be expressed visually. Sociologists Joseph Luft and Harry Ingham originated a concept which is uniquely tied to self-disclosure. They coined it the Johari Window. Like a window, the **Johari Window** incorporates four panes which provide a visual representation of everything which can be known about us. The panes are labeled **open, blind, hidden, and unknown.** What is known to you and others about you represents the open pane. Things about you that are known to others, but not known to you, constitute the blind pane. Things about you that you know, but others don't know, comprise the hidden pane. Finally, things about you which both you and others don't know make up the unknown pane. Each of us display different size panes based on our communication behaviors.[8, 9] Let's take a look at each of these four panes (see figure):

	Known to Self	Not Known to Self
Known to others	Open	Blind
Unknown to others	Hidden	Unknown

Luft and Inham's Johari Window

Open: Known to Self and Others

At the time of this publication, actor Tom Cruise is a member of the Church of Scientology, and identifies himself as a Scientologist, a religion founded by L. Ron Hubbard. He criticized model Brooke Shields publicly, saying that she didn't need to take antidepressant medication after the birth of her daughter, Rowan, on May 15, 2003. One of the tenets of Scientology is that most medicines are not necessary and the human brain and body can heal itself using certain mind over matter "technologies." Cruise's religion, his adherence to its principles, and his opinion regarding Brooke Shield's reliance on a psychotropic medication are things known to Cruise and others.[10] This is open.

Blind: Known to Others, Not Known to Self

One of my students, "Andi," shared her dilemma in class. Her closest male friend "Jeff," was three days shy of getting married. She learned from what she deemed a very reliable source that Jeff's soon-to-be-bride was cheating on Jeff just a week prior with her ex-boyfriend. Several of the wedding guests were also privy to this information. Andi struggled with whether she should say anything to Jeff, and what she should say. Friends and family were flying in from all over the country for the wedding. The wedding costs were exorbitant. The last time she spoke to Jeff he was elated and excited about the wedding and honeymoon plans. People knew things about Jeff's personal life that he didn't. He was blind to it.

What would you suggest Andi do? Why?

Hidden: Known to Self, Not Known to Others

My friend "Renee" was once married to a successful, handsome Italian named "Frank" for three months. Today, she is forty-years-old, and this was her first and only marriage. During her dating and engagement period with Frank, he wined and dined her. He lavished her with gifts and was quick to showcase his family's fortune. He introduced her to his large network of friends. Frank was gregarious, sweet, and exuded a strong, Chuck Norris machismo that rocked Renee's world. She developed a real bond with his friends. Renee and Frank were soon coined the "perfect couple." Renee put her house on the market and was poised to move in with Frank prior to the nuptials, but he balked at this, thinking it was best that she stay in her house until they were married. Renee sensed his reluctance to be physically intimate but chalked it up to his traditional views. She yearned not just for sexual intimacy, but the warmth and tenderness of hugging and kissing. When she moved in with him after a star-like wedding, Renee noticed things which alarmed her. Often, when she tried to touch him he coiled away. At times, he would literally ignore her. They'd go out with his friends, and he'd be the fun-loving, joke-swapping romantic she had fallen in love with. At home, he was a different person: tense, distant, and stone-hearted. She tried to grin and bear it. She suggested they go to counseling, but Frank rebuffed any third-party intervention. When she asked him if he was physically or sexually abused as a boy, he went ballistic. Fearful, she moved out. He came to her several days later and told her that if she told anybody what happened between them or went for his money, he would kill her. Renee kept the painful truth secret for many years. It was something that she knew, but no one else. Frank's friends believed the breakup had to do with her because he told them so. Frank went on to marry a different woman less than a year later. This was a part of Renee's life that she kept hidden from everyone until much later in her life. It was information about herself that was known to her but not known to others.

Your Turn: You may have heard someone grumble, "I just can't get him to talk or say what he is really thinking or feeling," or "There is so much about her that I still don't know." What might cause a person to keep personal facts, feelings, and opinions hidden?

Unknown: Things Not Known to Self or Others

I remember reading about a guy who had a best friend since the early grades. The two were inseparable. They played sports together, roomed together in college, were best men in each other's weddings, and their children played together in the same neighborhood. When his parents passed away, his best friend was right there at his side. One day, the guy received a call from a social worker saying that his birth mom was trying to get in touch with him. It was unknown to him that he was adopted. It was also unknown to him that he had a twin brother. Furthermore, it was unknown to him that his best friend was his twin brother! This was information that was unknown to him and others. Apparently, his adopted parents never shared this information with him. We may have hidden talents, interests, and weaknesses that we have yet to discover. We may be in the early stages of terminal cancer and not know it. This is information about ourselves which we and others do not know.

Our communication behaviors influence the size of our panes. Large, open panes are ideal. Generally speaking, we want to be in the know. We like people to be honest and genuine with us. We desire others to perceive us as approachable. We like to open up to people and deepen our immediacy and trust with them. **Immediacy** is the closeness or connectedness we feel with someone. Certain communication patterns may influence how much we disclose and the extent other people disclose things to us. **Communication patterns** are repeated communication behaviors which have the potential to communicate messages to others. Consider how the following, depending on their frequency, might affect the size of our open, blind, hidden, and unknown panes:

- We get bent out of shape when someone critiques us or gives us suggestions for improvement.
- We make excuses for our actions.
- We fear what we may share will cause others to reject us.
- We lack confidence expressing our ideas.
- We interrupt people a lot or have poor listening skills.
- We encourage, thank, and praise people for their feedback.
- We disclose things about ourselves to others.

- We are interested in what other people have to say.
- We frequently express critical judgments and opinions.
- We spread rumors and love to gossip.
- When we were children, our parents or grandparents encouraged us to talk about our problems.
- As children, when we had legitimate reasons to be upset about something, we were told: "You'll get over it soon," "I know exactly what you're going through," "Don't be so dramatic," "Be a man," or "I don't care what you think, I'm the adult, and you will do what I say."
- Throughout our childhood, we were frequently told to keep our thoughts to ourselves, or not to question adult behavior or authority, even when it was done respectfully.
- We tend to avoid trying new things, taking healthy risks, or starting new relationships.

Your Turn: How might the above communication patterns increase or decrease the size of our open, blind, hidden, or unknown panes? Are there any patterns that you feel significantly affect one of your panes now?

Our growth as human beings and communicators hinges on the honest self-disclosure or feedback we receive from others. How can we encourage people to share more authentic information with us? This is especially important if other people are a part of an issue, problem, or solution which involves and affects us. How do we get people to address an issue and take responsibility for their communication and actions? It is interesting that the most often heard excuses for why people fail to say or do things are: "I didn't know," and "You didn't ask." How many times have we heard or said one of these statements:

- I didn't know you thought that?
- I didn't realize this was a problem.
- How was I supposed to know you didn't like it?
- Nobody said anything.
- I didn't think it would be a big deal.
- I thought you already knew.
- I was afraid you'd get all upset and wig out.

Straight forward and timely disclosure or feedback reduces miscommunication and supports proactive measures. A lot of problems, if not addressed early, balloon into big ones. If we fail to get people to disclose to us their thoughts, feelings and needs, we are left in the dark. Why wait until we are passed over for a promotion at work to ask our supervisor what we can do to secure her endorsement? Why wait until our spouse or life partner says to us that he or she no longer can tolerate being with us before we ask, "How can I be a better spouse or life partner?" Why wait until our children are grown up and distant before we ask, "What can *I* do to draw us closer?" Why wait until our roommate moves out because he or she can't stand living with us before we ask, "How are things going? Is there anything I can do to be a better roommate?" Again, if we don't want to grow, we can choose not to ask. If we want to stick our head in the sand and assume everything is ok, we can avoid asking important questions. If we are content with stagnation, complacency, and mediocrity in our relationships, we simply avoid procuring feedback from others. We need to remember, however, what Ralph Waldo Emerson said, "You find in life (relationships) exactly what you put into it." What may be keeping us from asking for or giving feedback?

- Are we not confident expressing our thoughts and feelings?
- Are we highly uncomfortable with confrontation or conflict?
- Do we fear rejection or abandonment for being honest?
- Do we feel too vulnerable or insecure to receive criticism?
- Or have we, until now, not seen the need for doing it?

"In the absence of feedback, people make up their own version of reality."
C. Leslie Charles

When we receive criticism or evaluative feedback we often need to fight the urge to get defensive and argumentative. Our words and actions may communicate the message, "I don't want to hear it." Based on our understanding of the Johari Window, our behaviors may cause people to think twice before telling us things, leaving us blind to certain realities. When we receive constructive or even critical feedback do we:

- Fail to take action on the feedback that is given?
- Blow it off or act indifferent?
- Get overly sensitive or take it personally?
- Punish or retaliate? (Give the person the silent treatment, withdraw love, withhold something that the person wants)
- Pass the buck (blame others) or make excuses?
- Attack back? "Oh is that so, well you . . . " or "Ya, but at least I don't . . . "

"Better the devil we know, than the devil we don't."
author unknown

Not only do our communication behaviors have the potential to expand our blind pane, they also may enlarge our open pane. If we are bitten by a poisonous snake, the first thing survivalists say to do is suck out the poison. Asking questions allows us to draw out the poison (negative feelings, unspoken needs) another person is harboring and needs to release. We can consider asking the following questions:

- What makes you say that?
- What would you like me to say or do next time?
- Will you tell me what you mean?
- Will you give me an example so I can better understand what you're saying?
- Do you have any ideas or suggestions?
- How would you like me to respond next time?
- Are there some things that you would like to see me work on or improve?
- What can I do to improve our relationship?

If people are going to feel comfortable telling us things, we will want to make sure we consider our paralanguage when asking these questions. Our **paralanguage** is the vocal aspects of a message which include one's tone of voice. Our tone may be calm and sincere or agitated and sarcastic. In addition, we need to listen without interrupting. Sometimes we have to force ourselves to hear a person out completely. We also need to thank the person for sharing his or her information with us and agree with the points which are accurate or justified, graciously. If we respond by telling the other person that he or she is wrong, or why his or her perception is off base, this will likely cause the person to shut down. Remember, when we are asking these questions, our goal is to collect information which will help us grow and improve as individuals. It is about us creating a larger open pane so that we can become more than we are. Now that we have a better appreciation for the depths of self-disclosure and ways to encourage others to self-disclose more with us, let's explore some of the reasons why people self-disclose.

. . . What is the Johari Window? How would you explain the four panes? How does the Johari Window relate to self-disclosure?

Reasons We Disclose

Reichen Lehmkuhl was a *Top Gun*, a strapping United States Air Force pilot and captain driven to serve his country with distinction. John Amaechi turned down a six-year, $17 million dollar contract to play NBA basketball with Shaquille O'Neal and Kobe Bryant. Esera Tuaolo, an imposing Atlanta Falcons nose guard and Super Bowl XXXIII champion, was the first NFL player in American history as a rookie nose guard to start all sixteen games of the season and was invited to sing the National Anthem in uniform before numerous NFL games. What do all three of these distinguished men have in common? They are gay. All three share their experiences coming out in traditionally homophobic entrenched arenas in their autobiographies, which took book stores by storm and triggered a media frenzy.

© Benis Arapovic, 2010. Used under license from Shutterstock, Inc.

Amazing Race winner Lehmkuhl, in *Here's What We'll Say*, exposes how a secret society of gay cadets flourished and held covert meetings in tunnels below the Academy walls to form friendships and avoid possible outings and disciplinary removal from the Academy. Lehmkuhl's account included a heart-wrenching story of a group of cadets who narrowly rescued a gay cadet, the son of a U.S. Senator, from a suicide attempt.

In his book *Man in the Middle*, John Amaechi writes, "The NBA locker room was the most flamboyant place I'd ever seen. Guys flaunted their bodies, bragged about their sexual exploits, and primped in front of the mirror, applying cologne and hair gel by the bucketful. They tried on each other's $10,000 suits, admired each other's rings and necklaces. It was an intense camaraderie that felt completely natural to them. Surveying the room, I couldn't help chuckling to myself: And I'm the gay one."

It would tear him up inside, but Esera Tuaolo insisted that his long-term partner, Mitchell, stay in the car while his fellow player's wives stood outside the deluxe motor busses to greet their boyfriends and husbands upon their return from out of town games. Tuaolo, in *Alone in the Trenches*, describes how he would sneak Mitchell in his hotel room when his team was staying overnight in a nearby city and dated girls prior to meeting Mitchell just to avoid suspicion. The secrecy and lies took their toll on all three men, who decided to start the process of "coming out." Tuaolo came out to Bryant Gumbel on ESPN's *Real Sports* with his husband and two adopted Samoan children. His home was turned upside down by all the cameras and equipment. During the interview, Tuaolo kept excusing himself to go to the bathroom to throw up. Their reasons for self-disclosure were many. When people self-disclose, they do so with a purpose.[11,12,13] **They may share information about themselves for many reasons including catharsis, validation, altruism, implication, manipulation, and relationship enhancement.**

Catharsis

Catharsis is "getting it off your chest," or the process of releasing pent-up emotions and tension as a result of talking about something. When we disclose things that have a lot of depth, we experience a sense of relief. A very memorable, bone-chilling scene in *The Sixth Sense* (1999) depicts a young boy, Cole (Haley Joel) revealing for the first time his anguished secret. With large, tear-filled eyes and an ashen face, he whispers to his therapist, Malcolm (Bruce Willis), "I see dead people." Opening up starts a process of catharsis. For the Franklins, sharing Kirk's private struggle with pornography was cathartic. When Diane Sawyer asked Tuaolo what it felt like to come out, Tuaolo stated: "A huge burden has been lifted off my back. . . . I feel light as a feather, but when I stepped on the scale this morning, I still weighed 330 pounds."

Altruism

We share information in hopes it will benefit others. Altruism is saying or doing something to help others. Altruistic self-disclosure is meant to impart wisdom and offer hope, inspiration, and encouragement. Tammy and Kirk Franklin's revelations were meant to let other couples know that they are not alone. They wanted to model a way for others to cope with spousal porn addiction in a healthy way. Tuaolo wanted to use his book to break down the stereotypes people have of gay men. He shares how many gay men are very masculine, maintain committed relationships, live as sincere Christians, and raise healthy children. Self-disclosure is often used as a catalyst to promote positive social change. Reichen Lehmkuhl shares his personal experiences as a United States Air Force Captain in order to sway public opinion regarding the military's "Don't Ask, Don't Tell" policy, which he believes is discriminatory. He feels the policy is not backed by any sound evidence proving that gay or bisexual men are less skilled or capable of performing their duties during peace or wartime. He uses his book to drive home a message that gay and bisexual men have served, and will continue to serve, their country with honor and distinction and are bound by the same rules pertaining to sexual fraternization as heterosexual military personnel.

Validation

Sometimes we seek validation through our self-disclosure. **Validation** is recognizing another person's thoughts, feelings, or needs. You may share with your roommate how your boss treated you unfairly. When your friend responds, "Your boss did that? What a bonehead," she is affirming that what you are saying is legitimate or understandable. When someone validates us, we feel affirmed. If someone says to you, "Wow, you handled that well," or "That had to be really awkward," the person is acknowledging something we hope he or she will notice or appreciate in terms of our performance or feelings. It's like a stamp of social approval. **When someone validates us, it reaffirms that we have a right to think and feel a certain way.**

Validation is also a way to express sympathy and/or empathy. We may share a personal dream or goal with someone,

Why is it cathartic for gay and bisexual men and women to "come out?" Are there things heterosexuals can do to encourage gay, lesbian, bisexual, and transgender people to feel safe, comfortable, and free to be themselves publically?

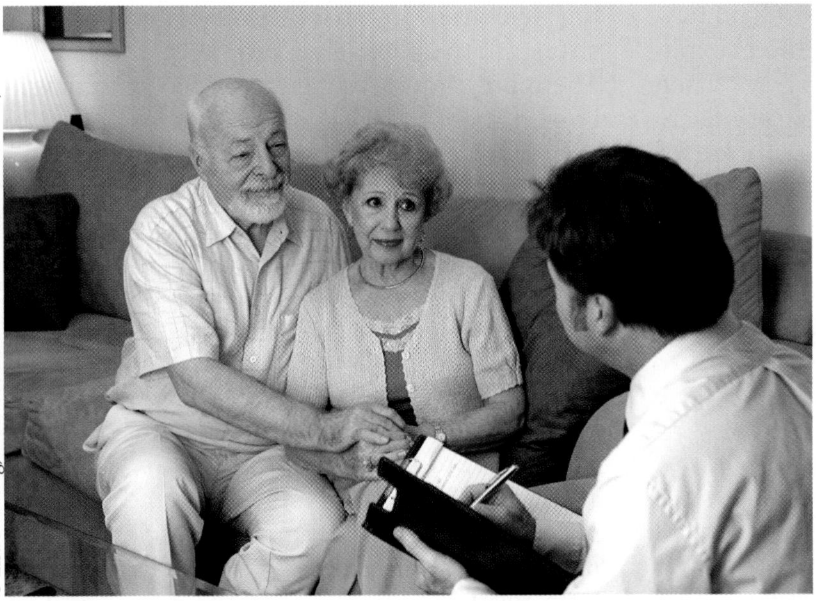

hoping he or she will encourage us and share in our excitement. In 1981, Chris Gardner decided to give up his attempts to sell medical bone density scanners to pursue a more lucrative job as a stockbroker through a full-time internship opportunity. Gardner clings to his dream and shares it repeatedly with his son. The two find themselves alone after Gardner's wife abandons them. To Gardner's dismay, he learns that his internship opportunity doesn't pay him a salary. Together, father and son face homelessness, tax seizure, and despair, yet their frequent conversations about their mutual dreams for a better life sustain them during hard times. Gardner's tribulations and eventual success as a savvy stockbroker are portrayed in the movie *The Pursuit of Happiness* (2006), starring Will Smith and his son Jaden.

Implication—Saying Things Indirectly

When I was a boy, I participated in a rock fight with some buddies, and sure to form, accidentally hurled a rock through a neighbor's car window, shattering it. I was not quick to claim responsibility. My dad shared how after school one day he took an ice cream sandwich out of a cooler at school without paying for it. He didn't feel right about it. He felt bad all these years because he never admitted to doing it. He described the nagging guilt as similar to an infected tooth that throbs until you go to the dentist to get it drilled. The longer one waited, the bigger the drill. I winced at his analogy. Without accusing me or telling me what I should do, he shared his experience to insinuate that it's best to confess. One of my students, Tony, writes:

> *"My sister was having money issues and was slowly beginning to skip payments on stuff. So I disclosed that once or twice I mismanaged my funds and missed a car payment and needed to ask my parents for a quick loan. This happened years ago but by sharing it, I think it helped her realize that it was ok for her to look at this as an option. Stuff happens and parents can sometimes be there for us."*

We might disclose to a boss that another company is expressing interest in us as an indirect way to intimate it's time for a raise. Sometimes disclosing something about ourselves is an indirect, gentle way to nudge or persuade others. Rather than offer unsolicited advice in a direct manner such as, "This is what you should do," we may impart a personal example or story. Instead of coming right out and saying to a date, "I'm a damn good catch," we may use a more subtle approach. We may refer casually to our successes. It is a form of self-marketing.

Manipulation (Getting What We Want)

Why do people disclose the things they do about their spouses when filing divorce papers? Actress Heather Mills filed divorce papers four years after her $3.2 million dollar wedding with former Beatle's star Paul McCartney detailing her husband's alleged domestic violence, alcohol and drug abuse. The actress, who lost her leg in a road accident, claimed that McCartney forbid her from breast feeding because her breasts belonged to him. She stated he choked her once, came at her with a broken wine glass, and shoved her into the bath when she was four months pregnant. Those close to Paul have stated publicly and privately that she is explosive, manipulative, and a gold digger.[14] There certainly is a dark side to people's self-disclosure. All of us have a bag of dirty tricks. We reveal facts, feelings, and opinions as a means to manipulate and control people and events. In *Emotional Blackmail: When the People in Your Life Use Fear, Obligation, and Guilt to Manipulate You* psychotherapist Dr. Susan Forward writes:

> *"Emotional blackmailers know how much we value our relationship with them. They know our vulnerabilities and deepest secrets. They can be our parents or partners, bosses or coworkers, friends or lovers. And no matter how much they care about us, they use this intimate knowledge to win the payoff they want: our compliance."*[15]

She highlights ways people fake helplessness, issue ultimatums, lay on the guilt, apply pressure tactics, and dredge up the past using self-disclosure to get others to bend to their desires. The following are examples of how self-disclosure is used for this purpose. Have you heard anything like this before?

- "I need to look at my other options, then." (fear)
- "I would hope you would, considering all that I've done for you." (obligation)
- "How could my feelings mean so little to you?" (guilt)

Initiate and Grow Relationships

The 23 million people hooked on ABC's hit television series *Grey's Anatomy* love it for its conflict and controversy on and off the set. Actor Isaiah Washington allegedly choked Patrick Dempsey in a skirmish. The two were forcibly separated by shocked cast members. Washington was also rumored to have "outed" or at least called gay cast member T. J. Knight a "faggot." Actors Justin Chambers, Patrick Dempsey, and Kate Walsh took grave offense, as did other cast members. This, combined with working on the set sixteen hours a day, five to six days a week, fueled tensions. Yet, strong friendships emerged from the smoke. There are cliques. Others have become neighbors. Knight throws lavish cast parties. The adhesive between those who are like "brothers and sisters" is the time spent together off the set and conversations involving significant self-disclosure.[16]

We are inclined to disclose more to people based on the support they give us. We'll likely share more with people we like and trust.[17, 18] Affinity toward, and faith in, a person are byproducts of self-disclosure. When we disclose things to others, people tend to reciprocate. They respond to our self-disclosure with their own self-disclosure.[19, 20] **Reciprocity** is a term used in interpersonal communication to describe how people tend to give back what they are getting in terms of communication behavior. Through self-disclosure, we identify commonalities or discover our common ground. **Common ground** is defined as the beliefs, values, interests, and experiences people share. We learn what makes people unique and different from us. We also disclose to reduce uncertainty.

As mentioned earlier in the book, uncertainty reduction theory suggests that we ask questions and disclose things in order to reduce what we don't know about people. We also do this to discover what we share in common and to identify the qualities we find attractive in a person such as his or her beliefs, personality, interests, aptitudes, and experiences. We also disclose personal information to develop trust and deepen emotional bonds.[21] Research suggests a substantial amount of quality self-disclosure between married couples is strongly correlated with high relationship satisfaction.[22] Another study found that the bonds between grandparents and grandchildren deepen with abundant self-disclosure.[23] Overall, self-disclosure is a positive communication behavior which we rely on for a variety of reasons, however, there are some inherent risks involved.

. . . What are some other reasons why we disclose things to people?

Your Turn: Why have you shared some of the things you have with others in the past, other than for the reasons mentioned so far?

Risks of Self-Disclosure

For Kirk and Tammy Franklin, the outcome of their disclosure was both positive and negative. While many praised the Franklins and found help and inspiration, some people were critical of Kirk. They formed negative opinions and judgments. Let's return to the example mentioned earlier about one of my students, Andi. Her best friend Jeff was about to get married and was unaware that the bride-to-be was suspected of a sexual liaison with her ex-beau. If Andi disclosed to Jeff what she found out, what are the risks? Would she ruin one of the most important days of Jeff's life? What if his fiancé found out Andi was talking to Jeff about this? Could she find ways to cut Andi off from Jeff? What if Jeff is in denial and doesn't want to face this? Could this jeopardize Andi's friendship with Jeff? What if Andi approached Jeff's fiancé first? Would Jeff's fiancé deny it and then have time to cover things up with a good story? **Every act of self-disclosure has its inherent risks and benefits.** We may disclose something with the best intentions and have it backfire.

Not everything we share with someone stays private. Some people can be trusted to keep information private, others cannot. Someone we love may pull a "below the belt" punch and use something we shared in confidence to get back at us or hurt us. "Well, at least I don't . . . ," "You should talk, you are the one that . . . " or "Don't turn this into one of your . . . " are all examples of what a person can use as ammo. Based on what we say, people form opinions of us. Our reputation and people's respect for us can turn on a dime, positively or negatively. Sometimes our ignorance shines through what we say when we express our opinions. For example, take a few of the quotes from professional athletes taken from the *Russakoff Rules Sport Forum*:

- "We're not attempting to circumcise the rules."

  —Bill Cowher

- "Nobody in football should be called a genius. A genius is a guy like Norman Einstein."

  —Joe Theismann

- "My sister's expecting a baby, and I don't know if I'm going to be an uncle or an aunt."

  —Chuck Nevitt

- "The Bible never says anything about dinosaurs. You can't say there were dinosaurs when you never saw them. Somebody actually saw Adam and Eve. No one ever saw a Tyrannosaurus Rex."

  —Carl Everett

- "I'm traveling to all of the fifty-one states to see who can stop #85."

  —Chad Johnson

In addition to our public image, our self-disclosure can dramatically change a relationship. That is why it is so important for us to ask ourselves some important questions before disclosing:

- Can I trust this person with this information? Can he or she keep a secret?
- Why am I asking this person to keep it a secret? Did I clearly communicate that I

want the information I share kept private or secret?

- How could this information be used against me? Misconstrued?
- Is this the right time and place to disclose?
- What are my motives for disclosing? Are they questionable from an ethical standpoint?
- Am I sharing things about myself incrementally and slowly or too much, too soon?
- How has the person received private information in the past? How is he taking it now?

"Confiding a secret to an unworthy person is like carrying grain in a bag with a hole."
—Ethopian Proverb

These are important questions to think about on a regular basis. They can guide us in determining what to disclose and whom to disclose to. Another important consideration is how honest we should be with our disclosure. It is important for us to realize that when people share with us their inner thoughts, feelings, and needs, the information they reveal varies in terms of its truthfulness.

Can you identify times when you experienced a negative outcome as a result of disclosing information to someone? How about a positive one? Describe it.

. . . According to the text, what are some of the risks associated with self-disclosure? What are some important questions to consider?

Deception

What is David Hempleman-Adams supposed to do next? He was the first human to pilot a hot air balloon across the North Pole, the first to solo hike to both the geomagnetic north and south poles, and has ascended the highest peaks on every continent! When he took off to complete a solo, three hundred–mile hike pulling a 150-lb sled in minus 50° wind chill, he told his wife and family that he was going on a ski trip with some buddies. The reason for the lie? Hempleman-Adams replied in *Parade* magazine, "What's the point of worrying them?" In fact, his wife, Claire, was completely unaware about his treks to the poles until she picked up a copy of *Britain's Daily Telegraph*. The magazine featured her husband's most recent escapade in which he plunged twenty feet down a frozen waterfall. Despite injuries that included severely torn ligaments in his left ankle, he managed to limp the remaining sixty miles before seeking medical attention. His passion and Claire's concern for his safety clash. Claire, an attorney who manages the home full time, said, "Nothing surprises me anymore."[24] What are the reasons for his deception? Would you tolerate deception like this in a relationship? While we'd like to believe that we are completely honest individuals, the truth is that we all rely on deception from time to time. **There are reasons for deception, potential benefits, ways to recognize potential deception in others, and strategies for addressing deception.**

Reasons for Deception

All self-disclosure, in fact all forms of communication, varies on some level in its honesty. **Deception** is any communication act that is not completely honest. We may pretend we didn't know something happened. We may deceive by feigning a feeling, embellishing a story, withholding information, or outright lying. We may alter our language using doublespeak to present a different reality, usually more positive than it is. **Doublespeak** involves manipulating our words to mislead or alter a person's perception. A presidential candidate may endorse "revenue enhancement" as opposed to "increasing taxes." A city commissioner may refer to "pavement deficiencies" rather than the numerous potholes popping out all over the city. We may give a janitor a more sophisticated title such as "environmental engineer." The Air Force doesn't bomb a television station where people are inside, it "services the target."[25]

> The opposite of total deception is brutal honesty! A first grader was caught making a face at another student. Ms. Jones, the teacher, said to the guilty student, "When I was your age, I was told that if I made that ugly face, it would stay like that." The student replied, "Ms. Jones, you can't say you weren't warned."
>
> *www.goofballhome.com*

We may rely on deception to get things we want, avoid consequences, escape conflict, save face, or exercise power and control. One of my former students, "Erin" shared how she was interested in a guy named "Mitchell." Her girlfriend said, "Watch out with that one, he's a player, trust me." Because of her friend's warning, Erin kept him at a distance because she didn't want to get hurt. Coincidentally, Mitchell started liking her friend because, of course, Erin stopped showing him interest. Her friend started dating him shortly after. It turned out she liked him all along, and lied about him being a player.

© David Huntley, 2010. Used under license from Shutterstock, Inc.

Actions can be deceptive. One girl wanted to get her boyfriend to start giving her flowers. She started sending herself flowers at work and told her inquisitive beau that male clients were buying them for her. It got to his ego because he immediately commenced showing up to work to take her out for lunch. What did he bring each time? Flowers. To get her Rambo, movie–loving boyfriend to escort her to a new romantic indie flick, one girl lied to him and told him the movie had a racy sex scene. He agreed to go and didn't discover he had been duped until the credits rolled. Another woman wanted her new boyfriend to like her female best friend, even though the two clashed. When they were around each other they were cold and distant. At times they'd get rude or even brazenly sarcastic with one another. She started lying to him about all of the nice things her best friend was saying about him to cool the hot coals. The two apparently started to get along better. [26]

These examples are all gleaned from an article in *Cosmopolitan* magazine titled: "Girls Uncensored: How Sneaky Women Get Their Way With Men." The reasons for deception vary and are not, as these examples suggest, relegated only to females. To what extent do we rely on deception? To what length will people go to deceive others? According to ABC News reporters Dean Reynolds and Melissa Sowry, a business called the Alibi Network, a Web-based company, will help you cover up an affair. If you tell your wife you are going fishing for the weekend, when you really are not, you can pay this service to take your fishing gear out, and they'll actually go fishing with it. They'll make sure there is algae weed on your fishing net, mud on your boots, and catch a fish for you to take home. If the date you are on is not working out well, you can arrange to have them call you "from the office" with an "emergency" so you can politely excuse yourself. If you want to impress your date by appearing successful, the Alibi Network will call you several times during a specified period of time with "important business calls" and "big deals." Mike DeMarco the owner of this controversial enterprise, says that 50% of his clients are women. "The funny thing is . . . when men come to us typically they say, 'you know, I made a mistake. I'm in a little bit of trouble. What can you do for me?' When women call us it's . . . 'This is what I want: Boom. Boom. Boom. Boom. Boom.'" So in essence this company is paid to help people deceive others. To his critics DeMarco states, "The thing about lying and morality, it is a very subjective and malleable sort of thing."[27]

What are your reactions to Mike DeMarco's comments? Would you be a critic or supporter of this service? Why or why not?

"I try to be as authentic as possible in my communication with people. I respect myself for this and believe my friends and family value this. Trust is sacred. It is a gift. I can make a mistake and admit it. I can be very honest in my opinions. When people ask me what I think, I tell them my honest thoughts and feelings even if the truth hurts. I want people to be honest with me, no matter what. That's called being real."

—*Jedidiah*

Is Deception Always Unethical?

Shannen Ross-Miller, a single mother of three from a small ranching community in north-central Montana, will never forget the day she witnessed the carnage and destruction of September 11, 2001. After spending hours transfixed as the events unfolded, she pulled herself away to soak in a hot bath. As she stepped out of the tub, she slipped and broke her pelvis. Ordered by her doctor to remain in bed for the next six weeks, Ross-Miller watched the images caught live on television cameras repeated over and over. She saw planes flying like missiles directly into the World Trade Center towers, bodies falling from the sky; the collapse of the twin towers with thousands of men, women, and children trapped inside. She listened to the reports on the attack on the Pentagon and Flight 93, whose passengers fought valiantly to take over the plane which crashed in Pennsylvania. Her anger and sense of helplessness led her to make some sense out of the attacks. Ross-Miller started researching information on the internet about Arab culture and terrorist organizations. She learned to write and understand Arabic. During the day, she performed her duties as a municipal court judge. At night, when her children were in bed, she went on a "cybersleuth" hunt. She made contact with an Al Qaeda Web site. Within the next several months, she made contacts and promised money in exchange for weapons. She convinced a Pakistani arms dealer to engage her in business and then turned vital information over to the FBI, which alerted Pakistani officials. She later discovered that a National Guardsman stationed at Fort Lewis, Washington, was on his way to Iraq to sell secrets of weapon vulnerabilities to Al Qaeda. She became the central witness in the court case that ensued. The man was immediately discharged from the Guard and imprisoned for life.[28]

Like Ross-Miller, two teens, Mitch and Ein, decided that their use of deception was justified. When their friend Max found out his girlfriend had broke up with him, Mitch and Ein orchestrated an attempt to cheer up their depressed buddy by creating a fictitious profile on MySpace.com. They found a beautiful picture of a brunette model that looked the same age as Max. "Stacey" started sending flattering e-mails to Max. Max's disposition flipped, and he was excited about this new potential love interest. Along with Max, Stacey's profile was accessible to 67 million other registered users, 22% of them under the age of 18.

One man, Michael Ramos, started contacting "Stacey." At first, things seemed innocent enough. As Mitch and Ein wrote back and forth with Ramos, it occurred to them that he seemed particularly interested in other girls between the ages of 15 and 17. When "Stacey" wrote she was only a sophomore in high school, Ramos

wrote, "Age doesn't matter as long as it's OK with you." Tired of Ramos, Mitch and Ein blocked him. Later, they created a different girl named Jessica. Ramos contacted her, too, asking her to meet him. Mitch and Ein decided to "punk" him, so they set up a meeting date at the park. They laughed when they saw him waiting for someone who was not real, and then it hit them that he was pursuing underage girls. They called the cops. Their deceptive ploy netted the bust of Ramos right there in the park.[29]

Everybody lies, but no one likes to be lied to. So, if we don't like to be lied to, why do we do it? Law enforcement and everyday citizens may use deception to ferret out and capture criminals and terrorists. We may deceive in order to get to the truth. Some lies are innocent and often done without any harm intended. If someone asks us how we are doing, and we say "fine," we may say this even though we don't feel "fine." Why? It may be that we don't want to go into the details of our day or lack the time or energy to do so. Perhaps the person has given us sound reason not to trust him or her with personal information.

> "This one girl I really had the hots for said she only dates a guy long term if her cats liked him. Before going to her apartment, I rubbed catnip on my jeans!"
>
> *-Ben*

Does a lie potentially benefit the person being lied to? Some say yes, others say it rarely does. Is there justification for deception? For example, does protecting a person's feelings constitute a legitimate reason to lie? Can deception actually help a relationship? Some interpersonal communication experts and scholars believe that one should strive at all costs to be honest. Others say that honesty is a good goal, but there are times when honesty is not the best policy. This author believes people can be extremely honest and communicate in a way that is sensitive to the feelings of others. For example, let's say that Trevor's girlfriend, Jessica, just surprised him with a dish she slaved over in the kitchen for three hours. They sit down for a romantic dinner and Jessica poses the question: "How do you like it?" Trevor knows she cooked this dinner for him and spent a lot of time on it. He also knows that he doesn't want her to ever cook it for him again. What can he say that is honest, yet sensitive to her feelings?

Jessica: "So, what do you think?"

Trevor: "Baby, I love that you spent three hours of your busy day to make this for me. You are awesome. Thank you for doing this. To answer your question, the meal is too spicy for me and I'm not a fan of black olives. What I really like is that you put your love into it, and that's the best ingredient."

Jessica may feel disappointed; however, she'll know that it was probably not easy for Trevor to tell her the truth. She will not go to the length that she did to cook him this particular meal again. She may inquire more into what Trevor likes to eat or how to make the dish more palatable. By being honest now, Trevor will never have to endure this meal again. As Jessica and Trevor's relationship continues, Jessica will sense that Trevor is honest, even when it is tempting to be otherwise. Her level of trust will deepen with each act of honesty and reach a level not found in many romantic relationships. Now that we've explored the reasons for deception and the ethical considerations involved, is it possible to detect deception in others?

Getting to the Truth

How can we get at the truth? Dr. David Lieberman, a psychologist and author of the best seller *Never Be Lied To Again*, shares how we can be a "human lie detector." He states that there are signs that can tip us off that we are likely being lied to. A person's conscious or unconscious verbal and nonverbal behavior can "leak" when a person is about to lie or in the process of lying. We also call this **leakage**. While these signs or signals are consistent with deception, they are not always completely indicative of it. Here are some examples:

- At the moment of deception, the person avoids making eye contact, his or her hands

- The person asks, "Do you believe me?" or accuses you of being "paranoid" in an effort to cause you to question your intuition.
- She or he prefaces his or her response with, "To be perfectly honest," or "To tell you the truth." Someone who is telling the truth may go to the face or throat, he or she has a nervous smile or laugh, mumbles, has a flushed face, or rate of speech picks up.
- The person adds unnecessary details and is not comfortable with silence or pauses.
- When the uncomfortable part of the conversation is over, the person seems relieved, more relaxed, and the mood changes swiftly.
- A liar often avoids touch at the moment he or she lies.
- The person uses an inanimate object like a pillow to form a barrier between you and him or her.
- His or her response is out of proportion to the question being asked. He or she gets very defensive or goes on a long-winded tirade with his or her response.
- The person makes accusations back at you or tries to steer the conversation in a different direction.

A couple gets pulled over by a cop.

Cop: "License and registration please."

Man: "I'm sorry officer, what seems to be the problem?"

Cop: "I clocked you on radar going 80 miles an hour."

Man: "There must be some kind of mistake. I was only going 65."

Wife: "Oh Harold, you were going at least 75."

Cop: "I'm also going to have to cite you for your broken tail light."

Man: "But officer, I didn't know it was out."

Wife: "Oh Harold, you've known it was broken two months ago."

Cop: "You don't have your seatbelt on so I'm going to have to ticket you for that."

Man: "I just took it off as you were approaching my car."

Wife: "No Harold, both you and I know you never wear your seat belt."

Man: (to his wife) "What the (expletive!) You imbecile. Keep your big trap shut."

Cop: "Ma'am, does he always talk to you this way?"

Wife: "Only when he is drunk."

Source: www.goofballhome.com

doesn't need to qualify it. Granted, some people just say this out of habit, but if this is spoken out of the blue, make a mental note of it.

- The answer seems rehearsed or too polished, like the person had time to practice or anticipate a question. Or, the person may pause when the answer should be very obvious or easy to answer.

In order to more accurately gauge whether a person is being deceptive, we need to compare the cue or leak to how the person typically communicates. For example, a person may pause frequently before answering a question because she likes to think before speaking. Some people avoid eye contact a lot because they are shy, or because it's a cultural norm.

These signs are also harder to detect with a chronic or compulsive liar. People can become skilled at lying. Bottom line: a direct question warrants a direct response. If the person uses sarcasm, has no explanation ("I don't know"), tries to make you appear foolish, questions your intentions, or refuses to answer, this is a possible sign of deception.

There are other signs of deception too. "Takes one to know one." This saying rings true, to some extent when it comes to deception. People often accuse others of things that they are guilty of themselves. The psychological term for this is projection. It's a guilty man or woman's complex. **Projection** is assuming others are like us or are doing what we are doing. We may project negative feelings towards someone with a fervor matching the disdain we have for our own behavior. We are often critical of others in direct proportion to the aspects of ourselves which we don't like.

Another sign of deception is when a person answers but dodges a question. In Dr. David Lieberman's book, *Never Be Lied To Again*, he provides an example of an exchange which occurred several years ago between White House Reporter Helen Thomas and President Nixon's Press Secretary Ronald Ziegler.

Thomas: "Has the President asked for any resignations so far?"

Ziegler: "I have repeatedly stated, Helen, that there is no change in the status of the White House Staff."

Thomas: "But that was not the question. Has *he* asked for any resignations?"

Ziegler: (showing impatience) "I understand the question. I heard it the first time. Let me go through my answer. As I have said, there is no change in the status of the White House staff. There have been no resignations submitted."[29]

Did Ziegler answer the question? No. The question was: "Has the President ***asked*** for any of his staff to submit a letter of resignation?" Other examples of question evasion include:

Question: "Did you have sex with him last night?"

Evasion: "I am shocked you would even suspect me of such a thing."

Question: "Did you take money out of my wallet?"

Evasion: "I have enough of my own money."

Question: "How long have you known?"

Evasion: "That is not important. What matters is . . ."

Question: "Did you call my mother yet?"

Evasion: "I've had so much to do today." (an excuse versus, "No, I've been deliberately putting it off.")

People who are about to be deceptive not only tend to avoid answering the question, but often answer a question with a question. It is often a stalling tactic. They are buying time to **encode** a deceptive message. Examples might be: "Do you think I would make up something this far-fetched?" "What's your point?" "Where is this coming from?" "Don't you know?" "Why are you bringing this up again?"

Here are some examples:

Question: "Are you telling me the truth?"
Response: "Why wouldn't I?"

Question: "Why are you three hours late?"
Response: "Am I that late?"

Question: "Did you?"
Response: "Why is it that every time we talk about this you ask me that?"

These are just some of many examples of how people try to mask deception or avoid being honest. What are some other ways we avoid being truthful or straightforward? There is no surefire way to know when a person is being deceptive unless there is solid evidence of it. We also cannot make other people be honest if they don't want to. From an interpersonal communication standpoint, what is the best way to approach people when we suspect they are being deceptive?

Addressing Deception

Police detectives are trained to interrogate suspects to get to the truth. What are some ways we can respond to a person we suspect is pulling one over on us without sounding like an interrogation scene from *NYPD Blue*? Here are five different approaches: **direct, perception checking, probing, indirect, and covert**. With all of these approaches, it is best if we try to maintain an even, calm, and non-confrontational voice as we do this.

Direct Approach

With the direct approach you come right out point blank and ask a question or make a statement: "Did you just lie to me?" "I don't think you are telling me the truth." "I want you to tell me what really happened."

Perception Check

With a perception check, we identify the behavior which makes us suspect deception using an "I statement" followed by a question for clarification. This is an effective technique because rather than jumping to a conclusion and accusing a person of deception, we are "checking" to see if our perception is accurate:

"**I sense** that because you shifted nervously in your seat, you may feel uncomfortable telling me the truth. Am I right? What happened?"

"**I noticed** just now that you looked away from me and pulled your hand away from mine. Is this because you felt the need to say something which is not true? Why?"

"**I heard** you just add a bunch of details and unnecessary information in your answer. Is this because you are having a hard time being honest with me?"

Probing for the Truth

When people are not giving us the entire truth or are giving us limited feedback, we can ask certain questions to extract more information. Examples might be:

- "You said you liked it. What would make you love the idea?"
- "In what other ways do I make you feel this way?"
- "Are there aspects of what I said that you're o.k. with?"
- "Can you identify one reason why you . . .?"
- "I know you think this is good, how could we make it even better?"
- "I'm glad to hear you say things are fine. Tell me what would make you say 'great'?" (This statement recognizes that it is alright that things are not perfect.)

Indirect Approach

We can also try the indirect approach by asking questions or sharing an opinion that hints at or alludes to something. Instead of inquiring, "Did you take money out of the till?" we may say, "We came up short again last night." We can then wait in silence and observe the person's reaction. We may present a scenario and ask what the person thinks.

Supervisor: "Curtis, someone from the office is taking extra copies of our spring swimsuit issue."

Curtis: "Man. That is not cool. I can't believe someone would do that. I have no idea but someone is asking to get canned. I mean, I've seen them and all, but . . ."

If Curtis appears nervous, adds a lot of unnecessary details in his response, overreacts or avoids eye contact when responding back to you, it may be that he is not being honest. Let's say we think our coworker is bad-mouthing us to other staff.

You: "I can't believe that people assume that they can talk about other people behind their backs and expect that those they're talking about are not going to find out."

After saying this, we pause and let the person we suspect of backstabbing fill in the uncomfortable pause. Sometimes we have to wait and not confront a person on a lie so that we can catch him or her in a much bigger and convincing one later. We can also be covert in our attempts. Again, Dr. Lieberman writes that people may need to be dishonest and coy to get at the truth. He says people use deception to get at deception. Consider his example of an employer who has reason to believe that an employee has lied on his resume:

Supervisor: "Your resume looks great. I want you on the job, but corporate is really busting resumes that aren't completely accurate and honest. We haven't been able to hire some really great candidates because their resumes were not completely accurate. What do you say you and I go through your resume together to clean up any parts before I send this to corporate?"[30]

If the employee accepts the help—busted! Another technique people use is to pretend that they already know the truth. People can also pretend to know the truth:

Josh: "Jeremiah, we need to talk about your taking my car out for secret joy rides. I know you did it so don't even pretend that you didn't."

If Jeremiah doesn't jump to his own defense or declare his innocence, we have a pretty good indication of deception. When I was a freshman basketball player, my team had an end-of the-season party at my coach's house. He wasn't four days older than 21. The coach had a lapse of judgment and allowed a few of his friends to bring in a keg. Before you know it, we had a full-out beer fest. Inexperienced drinkers, almost the entire team, got wasted. One threw up on the coach's furniture. Another player's father picked his son, "Chris," up and Chris threw up in the back seat of his dad's BMW. The school launched an investigation. Each individual player was called down to the office to speak to the principal. The principal was clever in getting the truth out of the players. He said that they already knew who drank, but were trying to firm up who didn't drink. Rather than asking us, "Who drank at the party?" He asked us, "Who wasn't drinking at the party?" Players didn't think they were ratting on someone by pointing out the nondrinkers, yet, by doing so they were also identifying the ones who did.

Was the principal's approach ethical? When is one justified to use deception to get to the truth?

No matter what approach we take—direct, perception checking, probing, indirect, or covert—there are no guarantees that a person is going to be completely honest with us. However, each approach has its merits and can get us closer to the truth. Even if the person doesn't speak the truth to us after using these approaches, we can still communicate our concerns using a nonthreatening "I statement." We can use the "I statement" to communicate what bothers us, and what we want from the person.

- "I am concerned that I'm not getting the truth from you. I need you to be honest with me about this."
- "I'm feeling uncomfortable about some of the things you've shared with me. They don't seem to match information you gave me before. I really value honesty in a relationship. I need to trust you."

If we really want to cultivate honesty in a relationship, we will want to reward a person who takes a risk and tells us the truth. There are different ways to reward a person. This may include not overreacting, praising the person and thanking him for his or her honesty, doing something that he or she would appreciate, or opening up and sharing our honest feelings, too. Can you think of other ways we can, through our interpersonal communication, develop an openness which feels safe and is encouraged?

Your Turn: What are the pros and cons of each of these approaches? Which approach are you likely to use more? Share your thoughts.

James Humes, author of *More Podium Humor* shares a joke about an Episcopal priest who was asked to give a speech about sex to a prep school in Massachusetts. He didn't want to upset his very traditional and old fashioned wife, so he told her he would be speaking about sailing to the student body. A school parent ran across the minister's wife and said that her husband gave a very timely and informative speech to the students. The wife replied, "I'm amazed. He's done it only three times. Each time he gets terribly sick."[31]

. . . Why is deception common in interpersonal communication? What are some of the ways we can recognize deception in others and confront them about it?

Unit Summary

Self-disclosure is sharing personal information about ourselves with others. We reveal who we are by vocalizing facts, opinions, feelings, and needs. Our self-disclosure varies in terms of its depth, reasons, risks, and level of honesty. Deception occurs whenever our communication is not completely honest or accurate. While it is generally assumed that authentic communication is our ideal goal, there may be times when deception is warranted. There are certain cues one can look for to assess the honesty of a message. Ways to confront someone who is not being honest include the direct approach, perception checking, probing, and indirect methods. There are some things we can do from an interpersonal communication standpoint to encourage others to be more honest and authentic.

Key Questions

1. What are the different types of self-disclosure? What do we mean when we say that it is important to listen to self-disclosure critically?
2. What is the Johari Window? How would you explain the four panes? How does the Johari Window relate to self-disclosure?
3. What are some other reasons why we disclose things about ourselves to people?
4. According to the text, what are the risks associated with self-disclosure? What are some important questions to consider when it comes to disclosure?
5. Why is deception common in interpersonal communication? What are some of the ways we can recognize deception in others and confront them about it?

Vocabulary Playback

Self-Disclosure
Facts, Opinions, Feelings, and Needs
Johari Window
Open, Blind, Hidden, and Unknown
Immediacy
Communication Patterns
Paralanguage
Catharsis
Altruism
Validation
Reciprocity
Common Ground
Deception
Doublespeak
Leakage
Projection

Focus Group/Class Discussion

- Have you ever had someone give you too much information (TMI)? How did this make you feel and what was your reaction? What is an assertive and polite way to let a person know when he or she is giving you TMI?
- Do you think people disclose more about themselves on-line compared to face-to-face? Why or why not?
- Would you allow yourself to stay in a marriage to someone like David Hempleman-Adams who frequently goes on high risk adventure trips without his wife's knowledge or consent? Why or why not?
- According to a study conducted by Jeffrey Hancock, assistant professor of communication at Cornell University, over half of men and women lied about their actual height and weight on online dating profiles. Women lied more about their weight. Men lied more about their height. What would you theorize is the reason for these differences? [32]
- The suicide attempt of actor Owen Wilson on August 26, 2007, and the accidental overdose death of actor Heath Ledger January 23, 2008 stirred discussions throughout the country regarding men and their ability to cope with emotional difficulties. Generally speaking, do you think men and women differ in terms of their self-disclosure? Do women have an easier time talking about their problems compared to men? Why or why not?
- Did the principal who questioned Bruce Punches' basketball team about an underage party use an ethical approach to getting to the truth?

Unit 7 Vocabulary Review

___ Self-Disclosure
___ Facts
___ Opinions
___ Feelings
___ Needs
___ Johari Window
___ Open
___ Blind
___ Hidden
___ Unknown
___ Immediacy
___ Communication Patterns
___ Paralanguage
___ Catharsis
___ Validation
___ Altruism
___ Common Ground
___ Reciprocity
___ Deception
___ Doublespeak
___ Leakage
___ Projection

A. Repeated communication behaviors which have the potential to communicate messages to others.

B. Recognizing or acknowledging another person's thoughts, feelings, or needs.

C. The beliefs, values, interests, and experiences people share with one another.

D. This incorporates four panes which provide a visual representation of everything which can be known about us.

E. Using language to evade, mislead, or alter people's perception of something.

F. Assuming others are like us in some way or do what we do.

G. Any communication act that is not completely honest.

H. Revealing personal information about ourselves to others in the form of facts, opinions, feelings, and needs.

I. Our sudden, often unconscious verbal or nonverbal reactions which often expose our true feelings or attempts at deception.

J. The idea that the communication behaviors we direct at others are often returned.

K. Provable or measurable pieces of information.

L. Beliefs about how things are or should be.

M. An electro, bio-chemical state of being and/or arousal to a stimulus.

N. Something we want or desire.

O. Information about ourselves which is known to us and others.

P. Information about ourselves which is not known to us but known to others.

Q. Information about ourselves which is known to us but not known to others.

R. The closeness or connectedness we feel with someone.

S. The vocal qualities of a message including tone, rate, volume, enunciation, and pronunciation.

T. The process of releasing pent-up emotions and tension as a result of talking about something.

U. Sharing personal information with someone with the intent to help a person in some way.

V. Information about ourselves which is not known to us or others.

Exercises

Articles with such titles as "The Lies Dudes Tell to Avoid Relationship Drama" appear frequently in popular magazines targeted at both men and women. Assume you are an editorial team for a popular advice column. Take this scenario and make a mutually agreed-upon recommendation regarding how the reader should handle the situation. Base your recommendations on the material presented in this unit. Be prepared to present your recommendations to the class.

> *"I've started dating this girl, and we really hit it off. We are both feeling it. She wants to date exclusively. I'm up to it. My concern is that she wants to know more about my romantic past. She is curious about what I find attractive. She's asked me if I've been sexual with someone that we know mutually and about my experiences, such as the number of partners I've had and the length of these relationships. What should I say? How should I handle this?"*

Signed, Desperate in Detroit

Exercise: Addressing Deception Using Perception Checking and "I Language"

Perception Checking

Step One: Make an observation of the behavior using "I language." Stick to the behavior you are noticing without saying anything mean or critical. Also, make sure your tone of voice is soft, even, and matter of fact:

"I sense . . . I notice . . . I heard . . . I see . . . I observed . . ."

Step Two: Ask a question or questions for clarification.

"**I see** that you are talking fast and raising your voice. (observation)
Is this because you see the need to cover something up?" (question for clarification)

Using one or more of the deception "cues" or "leaks" described in this unit, write a two-step perception check like the example above.

1. ____
____
____

"I Language"

Use an "I statement" to encourage others to open up and speak honestly. Focus on the specific behavior or outcome you want. Create two examples like the examples below.

- "I really like that you told me what you want, even though you were worried about my reaction."
- "I like to hear you tell me more about the details of your day."
- "I appreciate it when you tell me what is going on with your friendship with Jake. It makes me feel more secure."

1. ____
____

2. ____
____

8 Verbal Communication

Verbal Communication Unit 8

Unit 8 explores how to improve our interpersonal communication using language.

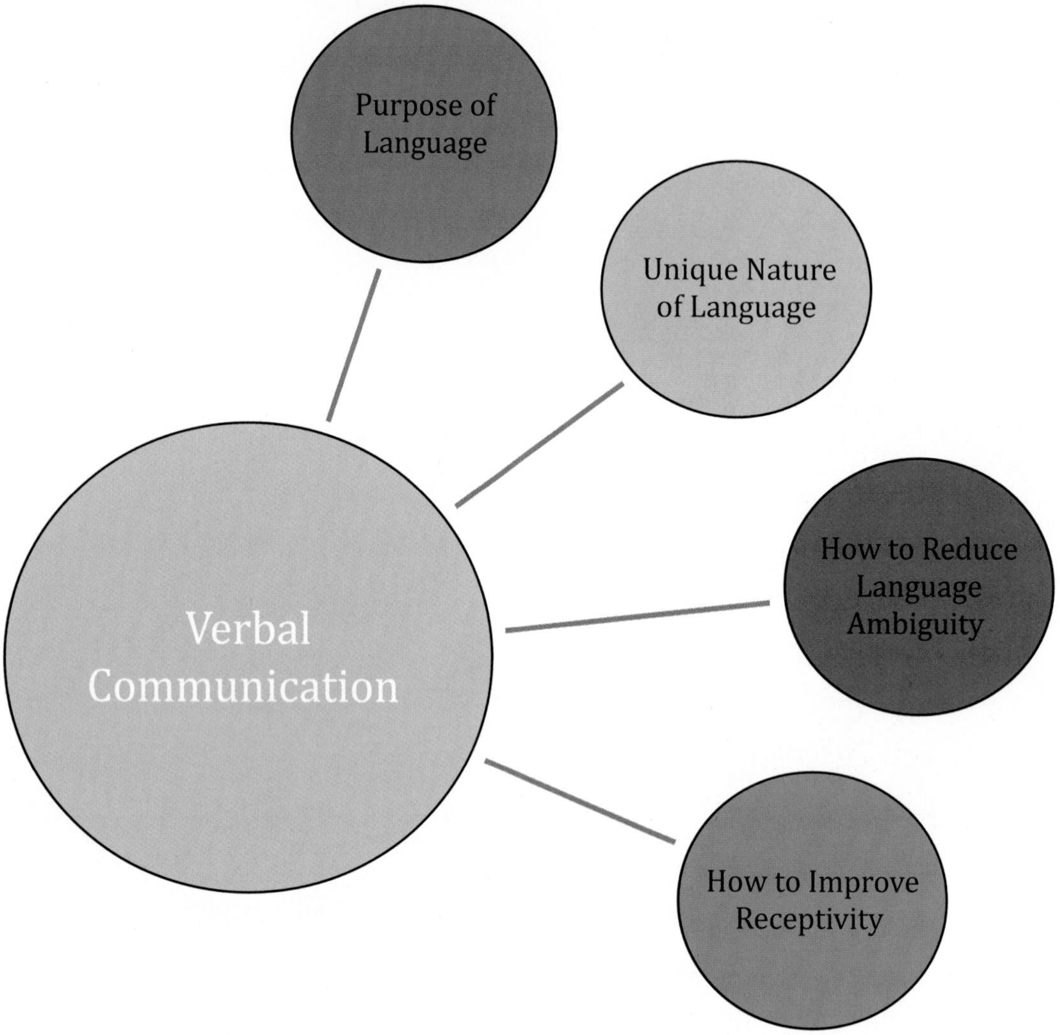

Unit 8 Learning Objectives

As a result of reading and studying Unit 8, you will be able to:

1. Describe the purpose of language.
2. Explain how language is arbitrary, governed by rules, and perpetually changing.
3. Understand how to clarify our language using descriptive and concrete words.
4. Identify ways to address the ambiguous language created by individuals, groups, and cultures.
5. Appreciate the importance of monitoring our use of evaluative, loaded, and trigger words.
6. Understand the significance of the pronoun "we" and conjunction "but," in our verbal messages.
7. Understand and practice effective use of the pronouns "I" and "You" in our verbal communication.

GodSmack. Destiny's Child. Hootie and The Blowfish. Third Eye Blind. ZZ Top. Every aspiring rock band creates a name. Their name often represents something important to the group or its members. One famous rock group chose their name to convey a message to someone from their past. When members of this group launched their fledgling band in high school, their physical education teacher purportedly scoffed at their rock-and-roll ambitions. He gave them detentions for their long hair and derided them for wasting their time with "that music." They named their group with a slightly modified version of the teacher's name to make a point. The group is best known for their hit song, *Sweet Home Alabama*. Their name? Lynyrd Skynyrd.[1, 2]

In the music industry, a group or artist's name is potentially very lucrative. One hip hop performer and producer is apparently doing so well he threw himself a three million dollar birthday bash and recently purchased a $360,000 car—a Maybach 57 saloon—with a chauffeur to boot for his son's sixteenth birthday. After working as an executive with Uptown Records, this Howard University business graduate started his own record label working feverishly from his apartment. His first platinum record was a remix of his "Flava in Ya Ear" single featuring *LL Cool J, Busta Rhymes, Rampage,* and the *Notorious B.I.G* His name is synonymous with monetary success in the music industry, with his own men's clothing line, reality television shows on VH1 and MTV, and an upscale restaurant chain called *Justins*, named after one of his sons. His name—Puff Daddy, P. Diddy, Diddy, and Sean Combs—has evolved over the years to reflect the changes in himself and his public persona.[3, 4]

What's in a name? A lot. A name imparts status and power. It differentiates us from others. It makes us feel human. This is one of the reasons why the Nazis during WWII stripped Jews and other prisoners of their names and replaced them with numbers.

One study found that political candidates with easy to pronounce and/or rhythmic last names faired more favorably in elections compared to candidates with more difficult to pronounce names.[5]

Imagine going through life without a name. What would that be like? Names make up an important part of our language. In unit 2, we defined verbal communication as the exchange of meaning using language, spoken or written. **Language** is the collection of word symbols whose meaning is shared by a group of people. Symbols are defined as anything which represents something. We say language is symbolic because words "symbolize" or represent an idea or object.[6]

Singers Nelly (L) and Diddy converse at an NBA All-Star game in Houston, Texas.

. . . **Catch this!** In response to a neighboring school's use of a Native American mascot, students at the University of Northern Colorado, formed their own intramural basketball team, calling themselves the "Fighting Whites" with a picture of a Caucasian man dressed in a suit as their logo and the slogan "Every thang's going to be all white." They commissioned a company to sell athletic apparel and sales skyrocketed. Do an on-line search of "fighting whites." Also, listen to the "fighting whites" debate between Keith Olbermann, Anderson Cooper and Paula Zahn on www.youtube. What are your thoughts about the team's rationale and word choice for a team name?

The study of all aspects of language is called **linguistics**. Someone who studies language is a linguist. A specialized field of linguistics which focuses on the meaning of words and phrases is called **semantics**. Another is called **Etymology**, which is the study of the origins of words and how they change over time. Most linguists believe humans first started using language somewhere near East Africa approximately 150,000 years ago.[7] Our primitive, upright walking ancestors existed long before this—scientists estimate over 3.3 million years ago.[8] This is a long time to go without language! What took so long? Today, 5,000 to 6,000 languages exist throughout the world.[9]

It is estimated that the human population speaks 10,000 different dialects.[10] A **dialect** is a variation in the way a language is spoken. The English language, for example, is spoken differently in terms of the pronunciation and use of certain words.[11, 12]

What will language look like in 1,000 years? Will our letters change? What will the words we use today mean? Will we even have books?

Pronunciation is defined as the way a word is vocalized. English "sounds" different if you visit Great Britain, Australia, South Africa, or various geographical areas of the United States. For example, in the Northeastern region of the United States, speakers often omit the "r" in certain words like Harvard, car, or park. Along with a word's pronunciation, a person's dialect is identified by the words spoken. In Great Britain, people often refer to a man as a "bloke." The word "mate" is popular in Australia. In the United States, the words for a soft drink differ depending on where you live. People in the Midwest tend to use the word "pop." Those living in the Northeastern area of New England call it "tonic." Southerners often use the brand name Coke to describe all soft drinks. People living in parts of West Virginia and Kentucky generally call it "soda pop."[13, 14]

One interesting study, conducted by communication scholar Jesse Delia, suggests people may perceive others who speak in the same dialect more favorably compared to those who don't. Subjects in Delia's study listened to voice recordings of speakers with various dialects. They were then asked to respond to various questions and statements. Results suggest people not only tend to form more positive impressions of others who speak the same dialect, but they are also apt to stereotypically

What word do you use for a soft drink?

perceive others based on their dialect. Subjects who were not from the Northeastern part of the United States perceived that those who spoke with a Northeastern dialect were "from the city." Subjects who were not from the Southern United States were more likely to perceive a person who spoke in a southern dialect as "less educated."[15]

People often confuse the word accent with dialect. We may hear a person say, "She speaks with a thick southern accent." Actually, she is speaking in a distinct southern dialect. The word **accent** describes how people sound when they attempt to pronounce words in the language which is not their native tongue. For example, some Asian speakers find it challenging to pronounce the "r" and "v" sounds of English words.[16]

The study of language is a fascinating one. To better appreciate language and its role in our interpersonal communication, let's discuss its purpose. What does language do for us?

Research this! What is the Hebrew Bible's explanation for the reason why humans speak so many languages? What do you think about this explanation? What other explanations exist to explain the origin of language?

Purpose of Language

Why do people say a person is a "hot mess," an idea is "radical," or a dessert is "killer?" We use language to label our world. Labels are a verbal shorthand to quickly exchange meaning. Language influences people's perceptions, so we use language strategically to influence and persuade others.[17] Language helps us to share meaning, connect with people, and satisfy our physical, emotional, intellectual, social, and spiritual needs. We use language for other reasons too. These reasons may include, but are not limited to, the following:

1. Make decisions.
2. Convey emotions.
3. Express individuality.
4. Share information.
5. Develop culture.
6. Solve problems.
7. Share memories.
8. Laugh and have fun.
9. Establish credibility.
10. Record history.
11. Share affection.
12. Deepen relationships.
13. Provide comfort and healing.
14. Exercise power and control.
15. Teach important skills.[18]

In addition to helping us accomplish a variety of things, **language is very significant in terms of its impact on our life experiences.** Imagine what our life would be like if no one knew or could speak a language. How would this change the way we experience and think about our world? In the 2009 hit comedy, *The Invention of Lying*, viewers witness what life would be like if humans did not have the capacity to lie. Every person on the planet spoke the truth—at times blatantly. The lead character, Mark Bellison, (Ricky Gervais) is a down-on-his-luck writer who mysteriously discovers that he can lie while trying to withdraw some much needed money at the bank. This results in a string of good fortune for him. In one scene, he tries to describe his uncanny ability to two of his friends and realizes how difficult it is. Since no one lies, there is no word for it. This scene illustrates a statement made by American linguist Benjamin Lee Whorf: "Language shapes the way we think, and determines what we think about." Whorf and anthropologist Edwin Sapir advanced a theoretical perspective called the **Sapir-Whorf hypothesis**. The theory posits that language allows us to think about things a certain way and influences how we see the world. Sapir and Whorf suggested we cannot conceive of something if we lack a word to describe it.[19, 20]

Do you agree or disagree with the Sapir-Whorf hypothesis? Why or why not?

© Kirk Peart Profession Imaging, 2010. Used under license from Shutterstock, Inc.

Unique Nature of Language

Nincompoop. People rarely say this word in America. In Great Britain, it was the most popular word expressed in 2007.[21] Why? That's a great question. Come to think of it, why is there no ham in hamburger or egg in eggplant? Why do we say a person's nose runs and feet smell? Why do fighters box in a ring instead of a square? Why is abbreviation such a long word? Dr. Sondra Thiederman, author of *Making Diversity Work: Seven Steps for Defeating Bias in the Workplace,* makes this illuminating and humorous observation about the English language:

> *"English is a strange language. Did you ever notice that a 'slim' and 'fat chance' are the same thing and that you park your car in a 'driveway,' drive on the 'parkway,' and sit bumper to bumper during 'rush hour?' Why is it that we duck our heads when someone cries 'heads up!' and bring a contract to life when we 'execute' it? How is it possible that to be 'bad' is to be good?. . . What about the fact that 'rough' is pronounced 'ruff,' . . . and that you can buy a 'whole' bag of seeds one 'week,' but be too 'weak' to plant them in the 'hole' by the time you get home?"*[22]

Surfers, for example, may look at ocean waves differently than those of us who are non-surfers. They use more words to describe the types of waves they encounter. Their expanded language allows them to fully capture the essence of their unique interaction with the ocean. Surfers share a language with each other so that they can share their common experiences—allowing them to "live it" together. Language serves many important purposes. Next, let's look at the unique nature of language.

. . . What is the purpose of language?

Why is the English language so full of contradictions and interesting twists? Who determines how language is used? Who makes the rules? People do. People are unique, and so are their experiences. **Inventive minds produce language.** In fact, there is a unique history behind every word. For example, take the phrase "red zone." According to communication scholar Steve McCornack, University of Colorado assistant athletic director Dave Plati was charting game statistics inside the opponents 20 for both Colorado and the Denver Broncos. He coined these plays "inside the 20." Other offensive coordinators and coaches picked up on this and starting using it. Later, Washington Redskins coach Joe Gibbs referred to this area as "the red zone." In 1989, Sports Illustrated used the term in an article, which caught fire with football fans. Now it is widely used and understood as an American football phrase.[23] This is an example of four unique characteristics of language:

- Language is arbitrary.
- Language has connotative and denotative meaning.
- Language is governed by rules.
- Language evolves.

Language is Arbitrary

During one of the episodes of MTV's hit reality show *Jersey Shore*, one of the cast members, 27-year-old Mike Sorrentino, referred to his six-pack abs as "The Situation." When he wanted to say he "had it going on" or "everything was under control" he'd say "The Situation" and point to his chiseled midsection. Members of the cast thought it was cool and started using his expression in a similar fashion. Throughout the season, Sorrentino took every opportunity to lift up his shirt and sport his work of art at his job, for magazine spreads, and on dance floors. This became such a fan favorite, the shameless self-promoter incorporated it as his name: Mike "The Situation" Sorrentino. In fact, "I love 'The Situation'" has popped up on various merchandise including lingerie, dog clothes, and coffee mugs. At press time, Sorrentino was trying to acquire a trademark for his nickname.[24, 25]

Sorrentino arbitrarily decided to name his abs "The Situation" and attach his own meaning to these words. In his communication with others, this meaning became a common understanding. Many others adopted this language in their communication.

Mike "The Situation" Sorrentino, Mel B and Kendra Wilksinson host The Sugar Factory Grand Opening at Planet Hollywood Miracle Mile Shops in Las Vegas.

We say language is arbitrary because words mean what people decide they mean—collectively and individually. Because of the arbitrary nature of language, a misunderstanding can easily occur when we assume people attach the same meaning to a word as we do.

Words Have Connotative and Denotative Meaning

Students in my class shared how a fight broke out at a predominately Caucasian fraternity party near campus. A group of African American males from another college knocked at the front door of a frat house. The risk manager, an upperclassman assigned to protect the property during parties, did not want to allow a bunch of people in that he didn't know. He said that the guys couldn't enter. He suggested that they go to the "ghetto" to look for some parties. Now, what he meant was the "student ghetto," a student rental community near campus known for their weekend parties. The group of African Americans were not from Kalamazoo and attached their own meaning to the word "ghetto." They thought he meant the "black ghetto." They were rightfully offended. A push turned into a punch, and a fight erupted. This example illustrates how important it is to know that words have connotative and denotative meaning.

Denotative is the literal or dictionary meaning people share for a word. **Connotative** is the individual or emotion-laden meaning people attach to a word. For example, the denotative meaning of the word "home" according to the *Merriam-Webster Dictionary,* is "a place where a person resides or lives." The connotative meaning of "home" may be different. It could be a place of "comfort, love, and tranquility," or "discord, stress, and emotional pain." It may mean "the love shack" or "an arbitrary location to hang one's hat for a while." The difference is in the connotative meaning people associate with the word "home."

Here's another example. "What part of 'No' don't you understand?" We've all heard this before. The denotative meaning for "No," according to several online dictionaries, is "an expression of denial or refusal." If my daughter Kaitlin asks me to give her extra allowance money, and I say "no," the denotative meaning for me is "*it ain't happening*." For her, this should mean the same thing. However, if I say no and then frequently give in to her persuasive charm, the connotative meaning of "no" for her is "time to wheel and deal or wear dad down." Connotatively, "no" can mean no, maybe, or even yes.

Language is arbitrary and words have connotative and denotative meaning. **No matter what our intent, people will attach their own meaning to our words.** So, it is important as communicators to know our language is governed by rules.

"I suppose it was something you said that caused me to tighten and pull away. And when you asked, "What is it?" I of course said, "Nothing." When I say "nothing," you may be certain there is something . . ."

Lois Wyse

Language is Governed by Rules

Language is regulated by four kind of rules established by a society or culture: phonological, syntactic, semantic, and pragmatic. **Phonological rules** establish how a word sounds or is pronounced. For example, some English speakers may be corrected if they mispronounce a word such as saying *"axe"* for ask, *"fustrated"* for frustrated, *"liberry"* for library, or *"seketary"* for secretary. When we are uncertain about how a word is supposed to sound, we look up phonetic clues in a dictionary.

Syntactic rules govern the order in which words appear in a sentence. "Did you the iPod bring?" is not the correct order in proper English, however, it is in German.[26] If we were to ask someone, "What is your name?" using sign language, we would sign, "your-name-what?"[27] One of the endearing qualities of the Star Wars character, Yoda, was how he reversed the word order of his sentences. Compared to all of the other characters in the galactic series, Yoda followed a different syntactically rule.

Semantic rules establish what a word means, which we confirm by referring to a standard dictionary. When we translate words from one language to another, we sometimes cause miscommunication because the words may mean something different in another language. Communication scholars Saundra Hybels and Richard Weaver share examples of several famous product marketing blunders. Pepsi's "Come Alive With The Pepsi Generation" commercial in China raised a stir when the company learned that their ad translated into "Pepsi, the drink that will awaken your ancestors from the dead." General Motor's marketing of the Nova hit a sales slump in Central and South America. "No va" means in Spanish, "It doesn't go." The famous "Got Milk" campaign was halted in South America when it was discovered that the slogan in Spanish meant "Are you lactating?"[28, 29]

Pragmatic rules relate to the meaning people apply to a word based on their frame of reference and the context in which the word is used. For example, if a male supervisor says "that looks great on you," we may attach a different meaning to it based on a number of factors or variables: what the supervisor is referring to (piece of jewelry versus our skirt or pants), where we were at the time (at a bar versus at work), how the supervisor said it (matter of fact-like versus seductively), the kind of relationship we have (close versus strictly professional), the frequency of such comments (often versus rarely), our own sex (male versus female) and our sexual orientation. Certain communication acts might also be considered more or less appropriate based on the corporate culture of the company we work for and the formal and informal rules that exist regarding appropriate "social" talk.

A theory called the **coordinated management of meaning** relates a lot to our discussion about pragmatic rules. The theory states that when a person starts an interaction with another person, he or she will suggest how the conversation will proceed and what it means. For example, Kalani sees Gish in the lobby at work. She motions to Gish to follow her to a quiet corner near the elevators. Gish walks over to Kalani, and in hushed tones Kalani shares some information. Gish responds with a whisper. Both have agreed to speak to each other in this manner. They also coordinated a shared understanding that what they are saying to each other is intended for their ears only.

We may overhear a couple at the airport exchanging some harsh words with each other and assume they are having a nasty argument. To the couple, it is mild sparring or playful banter. Why? Coordinated Management of Meaning Theory suggests the two of them have determined as a result of previous conversations that when they talk to each other like this, what they say is not to be taken personally or literally. They may talk like this so often that this exchange is uneventful.[30]

To understand the pragmatic rules that exist in interpersonal communication, **we also need to pay close attention to cultural differences.** Linguistic studies show, for example, that people who are bilingual and multilingual, will interact differently or alter the way they communicate depending on which language they are speaking and with whom. Language is tied greatly to the norms, beliefs, and values of a given culture.[31] For example, one American student shares that when she was teaching English to adults in Mexico as part of a mission trip, she noticed that when she spoke in English, the male students treated her with more respect and seriousness. When she spoke in Spanish, she noticed a change in the interaction. They were more likely to joke around with her and seemed flirtatious. This change in behavior may have something to do with how Mexican men and women interact with each other within their own culture. Along with understanding the arbitrary nature of language, its connotative and denotative meanings, and the rules governing it, let's look at how language changes over time.

Research this! When it comes to using language, who talks more, women or men? Search "Are women really more talkative than men?" Check out: Mehl, M.R., Vazire, S., Ramirez-Esparza, N., Slatcher, R.B., Pennebaker, J.W. (2007, July). Are women really more talkative than men? Science 6, 317, p. 82. from www.sciencemag.org.

Language Evolves

Many words change in meaning over time. This process can occur slowly or suddenly. Up until about 300 years ago, the word "awful" meant "full of awe" or amazing. Today, it means "bad" or "terrible."[32] The word "nice" was an insult in the 13th century. It meant "foolish" or "stupid." Linguist Peter Trudgill states that "meanings can and do change as they are modified and negotiated in millions of every day exchanges over the years between one speaker and another."[33] Changes in culture, technology, the internet, new discoveries, and advertising campaigns are often catalysts for new words. For example, you may have heard someone say, "this is a Kodak moment" or "give me your best Kodak." Kodak is a brand name for camera film. Over the years, the Eastman Kodak Company has produced international ad campaigns depicting the product as ideal for capturing life's beautiful moments. People started using the company's name to imply that "this is a great time to take a picture," or "give me your best smile." Before the invention of the internet, the word "Spam" referred to a can of lunch meat. Now it is widely used to describe unsolicited and often unwanted bulk e-mail.

The remainder of this unit focuses on ways we can improve our use of language in order to communicate clearly and effectively. Ultimately, our goal is to reduce miscommunication and enhance our relationships. The dynamic process involved in sending (encoding) and receiving (decoding) messages is improved when we apply techniques to reduce ambiguity in our language.

. . . What do we mean when we say language is arbitrary, has denotative and connotative meaning, is governed by rules, and always evolving?

Reduce Language Ambiguity

It's been said "meanings are not in words, meanings are in people." Two individuals may agree with what was said, but walk away from a conversation with totally different meanings.[34] Jose' may order a tostada with beans at the Beltline Bar. When he says, "I'll have a beef tostada with beans," does he mean a tostada with beans on the side or a beef tostada with beans inside the tostada? His message is ambiguous and leaves Raul, the waiter, room to decode what Jose is encoding differently. If I say, "I saw a woman club a man with the umbrella," am I saying she wacked him over the head with the umbrella, or that he was carrying an umbrella? A sign above a toilet in an office bathroom read, "Toilet out of order, please use floor below." Is the message suggesting we use the floor the toilet rests on or the bathroom on the lower level? The message is not entirely clear.

What makes language ambiguous is that a lot of words lack concreteness. These words are considered abstract. **Abstract words** are not tangible or easily identified by the senses. They can mean different things to different people. Examples of abstract words include "freedom" "heavy," "daring," or "prosperity." In one interesting study published in

When we don't clarify what we mean we create ambiguity or multiple meanings. Here is a humorous sample of poorly worded signs, advertisements, and marketing slogans:

Restaurant: "All food must pass through the cashier before entering the dining room."

On a display of "I love you only" valentine cards: "Now available in multi-packs."

Los Angeles dance hall: "Good clean dancing every night but Sunday."

Ad: "For sale—antique desk suitable for lady with thick legs and large drawers."

Ad: "Dinner Special—Turkey $2.35; Chicken or Beef $2.25; Children $2.00."

Ad: "Tired of cleaning yourself? Let me do it for you."

Ad: "Dog for sale: eats anything and is fond of children."

Compliments of Jeff Gray at: www.grayarea.org/Research/Ambig/#ADS

the Journal of Experimental Psychology, subjects varied considerably in the meaning they attached to the same set of words. Subjects placed a number next to the same list of words to indicate the probability of something happening. The points they assigned to "doubtful, toss-up, likely, probable, good chance, and unlikely" were quite variable.[35] Not only do people attach their own meanings to words, words themselves have multiple meanings. If we were to look up 500 of the most commonly used English words in The Oxford English Dictionary, each word would have on average 23 meanings.[36]

"What you think I mean is not what I want you to hear. I think." Author unknown.

Semantiscist Samuel Hayakawa created a concept called the abstraction ladder to illustrate how a word has varying levels or shades of concreteness. The messages we send to people are more or less ambiguous based on the words we choose.[37] Let's take the word "chair." If I say "I need a chair." What exactly do I mean? Do I mean something people sit on or someone to lead a team or committee? If I am talking about a chair for my new condo, there are many different types of chairs. Hayakawa's abstraction ladder shows how a word becomes less abstract when we add more descriptive language. If I say, "I want a lime green La-Z-Boy chair," we get a clearer picture. We are starting to encode and decode more of the same thing. If I say "I want a lime-green, La-Z-Boy, leather rocker-recliner which swivels and massages my back," this is more explicit. The definitive details I include enable you to visualize and comprehend what I am saying.

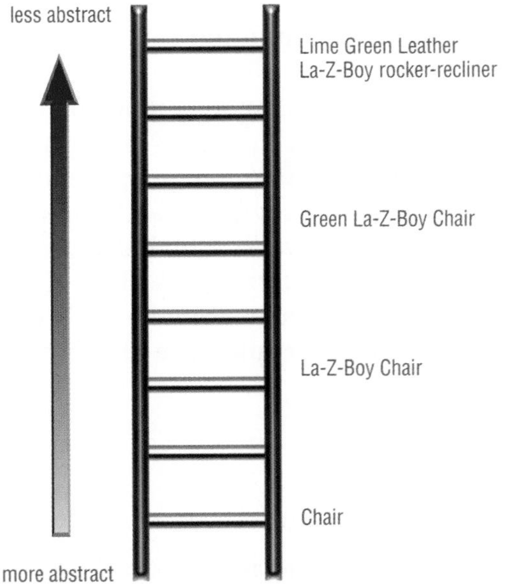

Hayakawa's abstraction ladder.

Use Descriptive and Concrete Language

Being less abstract with our language is important if we want a certain behavior out of someone. If a manager says, "I want you to use your down time more productively," this may mean different things. If she tells an employee, "When there are no customers in the store, I would like you to line up the stock on the shelves and clean the displays like I showed you last week," this is more specific and clearly communicates the behavior she would like to see.

Let's look at a scenario involving the ambiguous nature of words and practice being more clear and specific in our language. Derrik goes to the hair salon and finds out his usual stylist is not in. He agrees to let someone else, Jessica, cut his hair:

Jessica: "How short do you want me to go on top?"

Derrik: "You can take a little off."

Jessica: "Sounds great. "

Jessica goes to town with her shears. She swings Derrik's chair around to face the mirror and his mouth drops to the floor. Jessica's "a little" is Derrik's equivalent of "too much!" A "little off" is ambiguous. However, if Derrik says "I would like you to take off an inch," this message is less abstract. Jessica can visualize what an "inch" looks like. Jessica is also responsible for making sure she understands Derrik's communication.

She may say, "What do you mean by 'a little off?'" She might also stretch out his hair with her fingers to indicate where she would make her cut to see if her idea of "a little off" matches Derrik's. In other words, she can clarify what the two are encoding and decoding. **The use**

For the following table, take the sentence on the left and make it more clear and concrete.	
Ambiguous	**Concrete**
He's an artist.	He is an acrylic painter specializing in south western United States landscapes.
My flight is delayed.	
Is that your car parked outside?	
I'm impressed.	

We can reduce the ambiguity in language by using more descriptive and concrete language, and by monitoring our own and clarifying other peoples' use of ambiguous language. This next section focuses on the ambiguous language created by individuals, subcultures, and cultures.

. . . How can we make our language more clear and concrete?

of questions for clarification is of paramount importance in communication.

From unit 2, we learned that encoding is the mental process of producing a message. Decoding is the mental process of making sense or interpreting a message. Another way we can reduce the likelihood of miscommunication is to express ourselves with clear, descriptive language. The table on this page is an opportunity to practice clarifying ambiguous words.

Your Turn: Create three examples of ambiguous words or sentences. Replace them with concrete language.

Clarify Ambiguous Language

It is important to note that sometimes **people purposely "beat around the bush" or are strategically ambiguous in their language because they are uncomfortable saying what they really think.**[38, 39] They use several different types of language to accomplish this. This section of the unit explores why **we may want to curb our own and clarify other people's use of (EECIS):**

- **Euphemisms**
- **Equivocation**
- **Convoluted language**
- **Idioms: interpersonal and cultural**
- **Slang**

Euphemisms

Did you ever say something that was not meant to be offensive, but was taken that way? **Perhaps not wanting to offend people is one of the reasons we often put a positive spin on the things we say**. In referring to a buddy who is short and wide, Garrison Keillor, host of the radio show *Prairie Home Companion*, describes him as "anatomically compact." Instead of saying his other friend has a huge beer belly, Keillor refers to it as a "generous liquid grain-storage container."[40] Rather than say a person is old, we may use the words "senior citizen" or "chronologically gifted." When we swap less socially desirable words with ones that are more positive and acceptable, we call them **euphemisms** or "kind speech."

Euphemisms allow us to communicate messages which are less emotionally provocative. A real estate agent who is eager to sell a listing may say to a client, "All this house needs is a little TLC," instead of "This is a money pit." In the episode, "Whatever It Takes" from the television show *House*, a euphemism is evident in the dialogue between Dr. House and Dr. Terzi:

Dr. House: "Who were you going to kill in Bolivia? My old housekeeper?"

Dr. Terzi: "We don't kill anyone."

Dr. House: "I'm sorry—who were you going to *marginalize*?"

> **"Euphemisms are unpleasant truths wearing diplomatic cologne."**
>
> **Quentin Crisp author of** *Manners From Heaven*

Euphemisms may be appropriate for several other reasons. We may temper our words to avoid hurting a person's feelings. We may also feel the need to lighten up a potentially heavy conversation. However, euphemisms can be somewhat deceptive and confusing at times. People may perceive a speaker's euphemism as crafty, facetious, or even insulting. Why would this be the case?

Doublespeak is a kind of euphemism often used in political rhetoric. Former Rutgers professor and linguist William Lutz, author of *Doublespeak. From Revenue Enhancement to Terminal Living: How Government, Business, Advertisers and Others Use Language to Deceive You,"* describes how military officials may refer to bombing targets as "aerial ordinance," and "collateral damage" to describe the death of bystanders, destruction of property, and environmental damage resulting from war. **The goal with doublespeak, and euphemisms in general, is to present ideas in more neutral or positive terms.**[41, 42]

Can you think of other reasons why euphemisms are appropriate or inappropriate in our interpersonal communication?

Equivocation

In the example mentioned earlier, when Jessica asks Derrik how he likes his haircut, Derrik wants to say, "I absolutely hate it. You cut my hair way too short." However, he may not want to hurt Jessica's feelings or create an uncomfortable interaction so he simply says, "Not bad" or "What size clipper did you use? Maybe I should go with a #4 next time on the sides." If a friend cooks us something and after the meal asks us our opinion, rather than say it was offensive to our pallet, we may say something nebulous like "It's different," "I'm not sure," or "If only I could handle cayenne pepper better."

When people are deliberately ambiguous or strategically vague with their words, we call this **equivocation**. Often, we use equivocation or evasiveness with good intentions, such as to save face for someone else or protect someone's feelings, however, we may lose some of our credibility in the process. For example, your friend Gia has asked you to serve as a reference for a job she is pursuing. You have agreed to do this, reluctantly. In the past, you have found that she is not always good at following through on things. Your friend's employer calls you for a reference. You are asked the question, "Is Gia reliable and dependable?" You don't

continue a dating relationship. Rather than say, "No" very assertively and communicate why, women may respond to a man's sexual advances with words like, "We better stop," "Hey that tickles," "Slow down tiger," or "I'm not sure we should do this." Some men perceive this less as a clear message to stop and perhaps more as an invitation to keep going or as a challenge.[44] There is, to some extent, a double standard in American society where woman are expected to exercise restraint and be "lady" like, so men may see their resistance more as an attempt to be "good." Some men are known to say things like, "You know you want it" or "don't fight it." It is important to note that in the eyes of the law, "no" means cease or stop. To ignore this has serious legal repercussions.

feel comfortable lying and saying "yes, absolutely," so you may say, "There are times that I recall where she was very reliable." Or you may say "Yes, she can be." In both responses, you are saying that she has, at times, been reliable without saying that most of the time she hasn't. When we do equivocate, we run the risk of appearing like we are evading a question with our words, which may tarnish our credibility and believability. This may cause others to question a lot of other things we say.[43]

Equivocation also occurs when we chose our words to mask or couch our true intentions or feelings. So as to not appear too aggressive or promiscuous, a woman who wants to "sleep" (this is a euphemism for "have sex") with a man at the conclusion of a date may suggest "Would you like to come up for a drink?"

If we are tired of waiting for someone to get off a weight machine at the gym, rather than say, "Your taking too long, move it," we may say "How many sets do you have left?" or "How long are you going to be?" These questions are examples of how we cloak our messages.

Equivocal language is of special concern in the area of sexual assault and date rape. Communication scholars Michael Motley and Heidi Reeder gathered data from college students. They note that women sometimes equivocate when they don't want to pursue physical intimacy, but they really like a guy and want to

Convoluted Words

In addition to equivocation, some speakers create semantic noise when they use complex or **convoluted language**. These words are abstract and rarely used. Often they are polysyllabic (more than three syllables) and difficult to pronounce. They are used in place of simple, easy to understand words, to purposely impress or present information in a favorable way. I saw this written somewhere: "Your conscious proclivity to extinguish the illumination upon exiting warrants hearty approbation," could be easily stated this way: "Please remember to turn off the lights when you leave the room." Umbro designer David Blanch appeared to employ convoluted language to show off the uniform he designed for England's national football team before their game against Slovakia at Wembley. He boasted that the shirt has "intelligent ventilation points," and has "tailored shoulder darts specifically designed to accommodate the biodynamics of the shoulder." It would have been more understandable (albeit less impressive) if he simply had referred to the larger than normal arm holes and a unique shoulder seam when describing his design.[45] The same could be said about a consumer label I read on a bottle of fluoride rinse. It states: "Hold the solution in the mouth for one minute and then expectorate." Expectorate? I hope this meant spit out!

Avoiding convoluted words when they are not necessary is a sound communication practice. Otherwise, it may appear we are trying to impress others. People may perceive us as arrogant or ostentatious. These words may cause others confusion. At times, we may also need to limit our use of a nonstandard expression called idioms if we want to communicate clearly.

"It is often confusing when you read the product labels of body building supplements. It's like the manufacturers want you to think there is something revolutionary about their "milk protein." They use words like: "upregulates multiple genetic signaling pathways. . . ." "Using microsorb amino technology to enhance anabolism."

Erica

Idioms: Interpersonal and Cultural

In the hit comedy *Meet The Fockers (2004),* Jack Byrne's (Robert De Niro) wife, Dina (Blythe Danner), would say "muskrat Jack" under her breath. No one knew what she meant, except for Jack. Jack and Dina decided it meant, "watch what you say, be nice." Since Jack had a tendency to speak condescendingly to their soon-to-be-son-in-law Greg Focker (Ben Stiller), they created this meaning to help Jack monitor his communication behavior while the two planned their daughter's wedding with Greg's parents Rozalin and Bernie Focker, played by Barbra Streisand and Dustin Hoffman.

People in relationships, like Jack and Dina, create what are called **interpersonal idioms**. They attach a different meaning to existing words like "muskrat Jack." Families also create their own idioms. When I was around ten-years-old, I was fighting with my sister. We were yelling and driving my mom crazy. Out of sheer frustration, my mother chucked a bottle of "Magic Shell—the liquid chocolate that hardens on ice cream—at us and it broke open, splattering chocolate all over the hallway. From that point on, whenever one of us got upset, someone would say don't get all "Magic Shell," which meant "bent out of shape," or "flip out emotionally." No one outside our family understood what we meant.

A large community or an entire society may also create what are called **cultural idioms** or colloquialisms. The English language is chock-full of idioms, which are often confusing to international students. Research by communication scholar Wen Shu Lee suggests that the use of cultural idioms is one of the biggest barriers for students whose native language is not English.[46] One of my American students said one day, "It's up in the air." A student from Saudi Arabia took it literally and looked up expecting to "see" something. Other examples of idioms are "it's raining cats and dogs," which means it is raining hard and "feeling under the weather," which means "I'm not feeling well."

Let's take a look at how certain groups or subcultures create ambiguity through slang and jargon.

Cyclists may say the word "bonking" to describe when they have run out of energy.

Slang

Skateboarders may say "slaughter" to describe executing something perfectly. Cyclists may say, "All show and no go," to label someone who isn't fit to compete but has the most expensive bike and accessories. **Slang** is associated with the vernacular of a specific group or subculture. The youth culture is known for creating a lot of slang. There is a segment of the African American community noted for their unique spin on words, referred to as **Ebonics** or Black English. Words which are slang are new to the "language scene" and are not widely known to or used by the general population. Slang is also different from idioms in that the words are altered in some way or completely made up, including abbreviations. Surfers may say "hodad" to refer to someone who hangs with surfers, but doesn't surf. Another form of slang is jargon.

Often referred to as "shop talk," **Jargon** is defined as nonstandard words used by certain members of a profession, trade, or academic community. For example, funeral directors often use the words "Hygienic treatment" to refer to the process of temporarily preserving a corpse.[47] Police officers may use the words "urban camping" to refer to someone who is loitering a long time at a park or is homeless.[48] Jargon, like slang and idioms, is often helpful in that it is a verbal short hand. In emergency rooms, medical personnel will use abbreviations to reduce the time needed to explain what they mean. For example, a nurse may say to a doctor, "we have a GSW arriving in ten minutes by medi." GSW is an abbreviation for someone with a gunshot wound. Medi is short for medivac which is a medical helicopter.[49]

"Pull a **W.O.S. last night**?" W.O.S. stands for "walk of shame." It means to arrive home or at work the next day disheveled and wearing what you wore the other day because of excessive partying into the early morning hours—often having slept somewhere other than your own bed.

In addition to serving as a verbal shorthand, slang and jargon allow segments of the population to create their own identity, culture, and solidarity. It allows them to create a sense of separateness from the dominant culture.[50] In some cases, it gives subgroups status, legitimacy, and power. When members of a trade or profession create their own language or jargon, the general population has to turn to them for understanding. A great example of this is the law profession. People need lawyers to break down complex "legalese" and explain legal language in a comprehensible way.

When we experience semantic noise which is caused by a person's equivocation, or use of a nonstandard word or expression, it is important for us as communicators to seek clarification to prevent miscommunication. We can pose questions such as "What did you mean by 'fly space'?" Sometimes we don't want to appear stupid, so we pretend to understand someone when we don't. However, this can lead to problems. The same can be said when people speak to us in a dialect or with an accent which is hard for us to decipher. We may also need to curb or limit our use of these forms of language to make ourselves more clearly understood.

Your Turn: Create your own example for each of the following types of ambiguous language: euphemism, equivocation, idiom, convoluted word, slang, and jargon.

. . . How would you describe euphemisms, equivocal, convoluted, and nonstandard language? What are some helpful guidelines regarding their use?

Another thing about language we may want to be mindful of is the tendency people have to use what is called in interpersonal communication literature powerless language.

Consider the Pros and Cons of Powerless Language

According to communication research, some of our messages are less clear and direct because our choice of words detract from or soften the tone of our message too much. We call these words **powerless language**. Powerless language may cause a receiver to dismiss or underrate what we are saying. For example, if we were trying to get some sleep in our dorm room and our neighbors are blasting their stereo, we could knock on their door and say we'd like them to turn it down in one of two ways:

A. "Hi, um, sorry to bother you, uh. . . . Would you mind turning down your music just a little. I'm uh kinda having a hard time getting to sleep. Would that be umm a problem?"

B. "Hi. I'm trying hard to sleep so I can do my best on an exam tomorrow morning. The music you are playing is very loud. I need you to please turn it way down."

Which one of the statements above is considered powerless? A is the correct answer. **Speakers who use hedges, vocal utterances, hesitations, disclaimers and tag lines sound less assertive, confident, and authoritative.** This is especially true in North American and European cultures.[51,52] Similar research has also found that speakers who use a lot of powerless language are seen as having less status. They are also viewed as less attractive, competent, and poised.[53, 54] Let's take a look at each of these separately.

Can you think of other instances where powerless language is an appropriate choice?

Hedges

Hedges are words such as "kind of," "sort of," "maybe," "perhaps" "a little," "I suppose," and "I guess." These words suggest uncertainty, passivity, and non-resoluteness on the sender's part. Compare the following statements. The "A" statements are considered hedges. The "B" statements are more clear and direct.

A. "I'm kinda disappointed."
B. "I am disappointed."

A. "Maybe it would be better if . . ."
B. "I want to talk about something else."

A. "Sure, I guess."
B. "I need time to think about it."

Vocal Utterances and Hesitations

Vocal utterances or vocal fillers such as "um," and "uh" are often vocalized during the silent pauses between thoughts. People have the tendency to feel uncomfortable with silence so they fill the voids with a sound. In addition, certain words become vocal utterances when they are used way too much such as "like" and "you know." This is evident in the following two sentences:

- "I wish you would, um, uh, not do that . . ."
- "I can help you with that, uhh let's see, um . . ."

Disclaimers

Received in a similar way as a hedge, a disclaimer tends to draw attention away from or deemphasize the important parts of a message. Disclaimers are found in the following statements:

- "This is probably a dumb question but . . ."
- "It's not my place to say this but . . ."

Tag Questions

With tag questions, sentences start off assertive, but end with a question. The question is often posed in a timid or apprehensive way. Like partly deflating a balloon, a question at the end of the sentence causes it to lose its forcefulness.

- "We should send them a confirmation, don't you think?"
- "Give it another try, what do you say?"

Research by communication scholars Pam Kalbfleisch and Anita Herold suggests that generally speaking, men use more powerful language and less powerless language than woman. Why do you think this is the case?[55]

Sometimes a tag question, disclaimer, or hedge is a better approach than a very direct statement. Sometimes a message is received better when it does come across as less direct or assertive. We may use powerless language to show respect to someone in authority, or to take the harshness out of a message others might feel sensitive about.[56] It really depends on who we are speaking to, the kind of relationship we have with the person, and our culture.

In certain cultures language is used less directly. Korean, Japanese, and Mexican cultures, generally speaking, encourage a less direct use of language to avoid sounding confrontational and impolite. Hedges and tag questions, along with very polite forms of communication, are common and highly valued.[57] If what we are saying is very important, the subject matter affects us significantly, and/or we want to be taken seriously, assertive and direct communication may provide the clarity necessary for others to better understand what we are saying. In addition to reducing ambiguity, our choice of words influences whether people are more likely to tune us in or tune us out.

How often do you use powerless language? What circumstances lead you to use it more or less often?

Increasing Receptivity

In addition to speaking clearly and with less abstraction, another way we improve our verbal communication is to increase receiver receptivity. What we say in a given moment is referred to as a **speech act**.[58] Sometimes we choose words which cause others to respond to us in an uncooperative, defensive, or even hostile manner. **Receptivity** is defined as a person's willingness to consider and respond positively to a message. Whether we're seeking understanding, sympathy, an answer, a commitment, an apology, or a changed behavior, a receiver's receptivity to our message hinges on what we say next. Let's take a look at several things we can do to increase receiver receptivity:

- Use the pronoun "we" and the conjunction "but" strategically.
- Avoid evaluative language.
- Use alternative language in place of trigger and loaded words when appropriate.
- Replace critical "you language" with "I language."

Watch the "We" and Take Out the "But"

The pronoun "we" is an inclusive expression which implies "everyone." Many online communities create a sense of inclusion by using the same language and referring to members at large as "we."[59] "We" language conjures a sense of unity and togetherness.[60] "We can do this." "We are #1!" If we say, "We did a great job," it is a compliment to everyone who receives this message. If we belong to a group and there is a problem or challenge requiring everyone's effort or participation, it is appropriate to say, "We have an opportunity to work together on a new payroll process."

On the flip side, sometimes we speak on other people's behalf when what we say doesn't reflect what they think or feel. We may speak for all members of a group when they haven't given us permission to do so. Rather than say, "We are concerned about the payroll process," it may be more accurate for us to say, "I am concerned about the payroll process." Others will agree with us if they do. We can also ask, "Is anyone else concerned about the payroll process?" Those who agree now have the invitation to speak up.

If we follow the word "we" with a criticism, some people may feel offended because they don't believe they deserve it. If I say to members

of my department, "We can do better with our sales," someone who is trying his or her best, or is having a lot of personal success, may feel unappreciated. If I say, "We need to work on starting our shifts on time," those who are early or punctual may think "Hey, there's no "me" in "we." We may inadvertently cause people to feel undervalued or defensive. If we are in a managerial position and sense that a couple individuals are not performing to our expectations, it may be better for us to address our concerns privately with each individual, rather than with the whole group. Now let's talk about the conjunction "but."

"You're right, I could have said it better, but . . ." I thought you did well, but . . ." "I like you but . . .". When we hear someone use the conjunction "but" between two thoughts, what do we usually do? We tend to focus more on what is said after the "but." Usually what comes after "but" is a statement or question which negates or cancels out the preceding statement. For example, "I'm sorry . . . but I was drunk." When we follow an apology with the conjunction "but" and an excuse, it draws attention away from the apology, making it sound less sincere. It also appears as though we aren't taking a whole lot of responsibility for what happened. To avoid this, we can try to deliver our central ideas without "but":

- "You're right, I could have said it better, **and** I need to think before I speak."
- "I thought you did well, and I'd like to see you add some more interview questions."
- "I like you. I'd like to pursue a friendship with you rather than date."
- "I'm sorry. I drank too much. I said things I shouldn't. I need to curb my drinking."

In all four previous examples, we replaced the word "but" with "and" or put a period at the end of the first sentence. **We also took responsibility for what happened and focused our communication on what we want, or what we need to do in terms of specific behaviors.**

Evaluative Language

Evaluative language consists of words which have very negative or critical meanings. The words suggest that a person is wrong, inferior, or flawed in some way.

Livid that her love interest breaks his promise to immediately cut off his mob ties and escape with her to Las Vegas, *The Mexican's* (2001) Samantha Barzel (Julia Roberts) catapults Jerry Welbach's (Brad Pitt) personal belongings off the second story balcony of the motel they are staying at and launches into this evaluative loaded tirade:

Samantha: "All right. Jerry, I want you to acknowledge that my needs means nothing to you, and you're a selfish prick and a liar."

Jerry: "I . . . Ok. I will acknowledge that I promised to go to Vegas with you. But now we're just slightly delayed. If you want to construe my wanting to stay alive as being selfish, well, then okay. But I have every intention of going with you because your needs are very important to me, sweetheart. Come on. Look at all my stuff here, all over the pavement. Come on, baby? Huh? What do you say? Ok? "

Samantha: "I'm going with or without you, Jerry. What's it gonna be?

(Jerry hesitates).

A [jerk]"

Jerry: "What happened to, uh, 'sweetheart' and 'big love' and all those things you called me in the bedroom last night?"

Samantha: "The only thing I'm interested in calling you, Jerry, is a cab!"[61]

Samantha's use of the words "selfish," "liar," and "jerk" are disparaging. A line from the movie classic *12 Angry Men* (1957) illustrates evaluative language. A fiery argument between two exhausted members of an all white male jury deliberating the fate a young African American man accused of murder erupts when one says to the other: "Ever since you walked into this room, you've been acting like a self-appointed avenger! You want to see this boy die because you personally want it, not because of the facts. You're a sadist."

"Self-appointed avenger" and "sadist" are words with strong, evaluative connotations. Words like "lazy," "dense," "peculiar," and "immature," are also evaluative. Statements like "Whoa, slow down motor mouth," "You're such a slob," and "That's absurd," incorporate descriptors which attack the thoughts, feelings, or personhood of another human being.

People attach strong positive and negative connotations to certain words. These words are called **loaded words.** We could describe a friend who is an avid weightlifter by saying "he's chiseled," or "He's on roids." (using steroids.). We may say that another friend is being "a little adventurous," or "promiscuous." Depending on our word choice, people may perceive what we're saying more or less positively. Actress Barbara Streisand once stated that loaded words are sometimes used in American society to describe women who demonstrate characteristics associated positively with men. A man may be called commanding. A woman is "pushy." A man is assertive. A woman is "aggressive." A man sticks to his guns. A woman is "stubborn." [62]

Along with certain words, statements, taken as a whole, can be belittling. What do the following evaluative comments suggest?

Statement	Meaning?
There you go again.	
You just don't get it.	
You should know.	
How many times do I have to tell you?	

Within the past forty-eight hours, what evaluative words have you heard from others? What have you spoken?

Avoid Trigger Words

In addition to evaluative language, certain words are likely to arouse a defensive reaction from the receiver of a message. Words like "never," and "always," tend to over generalize a person's behavior. For example, when we say, "You *always* say that," or "You *never* apologize," the receiver will likely think of an exception and feel compelled to refute this. Chances are rare that a person "always" or "never" does anything! There are other words which tend not to go over too well with people. Examples include "You have *issues*," "What's *your problem*," and "*You people*." You don't *ever* want to talk about this." "Do you understand *anything* I'm saying." Nothing is more frustrating than when we are trying to say something we feel strongly about and the receiver responds with a callous and cruel "*whatever*." When expressed, it basically means "what you said means nothing to me and it's completely ridiculous, insignificant, and stupid."

Let's now take a look at the difference between the use of the pronouns "you" and "I."

"You" and "I" Language

When the pronoun you is followed by a compliment, the message is generally received very positively. Examples include:

A. "You have put together a comprehensive and detailed proposal."

B. "You are so thoughtful and considerate."

When "you" is followed by an accusation, negative generalization, uncomplimentary comparison or criticism, it generally triggers a defensive response or an attack-counter-attack volley. [63] Like the interactive arcade game *Dance Dance Revolution*, where a person tries to keep up with prompts on a monitor while stomping on circles to the beat of fast-paced music, defensiveness tends to stamp out opportunities to problem solve and resolve conflict.

Accusations

"You forgot my birthday" is an accusation. An **accusation** implies that a person did something bad or failed to do something important. It is often based on an inaccurate assumption.

- "You left me hanging."
- "You're ignoring my calls."
- "You did that on purpose."

Generalizations

"You don't value our relationship" is a generalization. A **generalization** insinuates that something about a person's beliefs, feelings or behavior is representative of something broader and less than ideal. A friend may do something to make us think he doesn't value the relationship, such as forgetting to acknowledge our birthday. This doesn't mean he values the relationship less than us or has always forgotten to acknowledge our birthday.

- "You don't love me as much as I love you."
- "You always forget to fill up the gas tank."
- "You're such a man."

Uncomplimentary Comparisons

"Your sister gets good grades, why can't you is a pejorative or **uncomplimentary comparison**. This statement presents an ideal and then suggests that the receiver is not up to par. "Why can't you remember something as important as my birthday. I remember yours?"

- "You are so much like your Uncle Stewart."
- "Back when I was your age . . ."
- "What do we need to do to get your projections as accurate as Taji's?

Criticisms

A **criticism** suggests that there is something inherently wrong with a person. Do any of these sound familiar?

Making it worse: When a person criticizes you—while talking to someone else on the phone!

- "You did this completely wrong."
- "It's not in your nature to be nice."
- "You're looking sloppy."

Your Turn: Create an example of a "you statement" for each of these four problem areas—an accusation, generalization, negative comparison, and criticism.

According to research, when we need to confront someone about something, statements that start with the pronoun "I" are generally a better approach because they are less likely to cause the receiver to feel personally attacked. "I statements" are usually expressed as "I like," "I appreciate," "I need," "I value," and "I want." What comes next is a clear, short statement which focuses on what the sender wants in terms of a behavior or outcome.[64] Receivers are more apt to listen and consider these messages, especially if the speaker's tone of voice is sincere and calm versus sarcastic and angry.[65]

Let's contrast the following two exchanges between a couple, Cheryl and Rod. In the first dialogue, notice how Cheryl uses "You statements followed by an overgeneralization and a criticism. Note how Rod reacts. Contrast the first dialogue with the second, which shows Cheryl using "I language," which focuses on the behavior desired expressed as a polite request.

Cheryl: "You take me for granted. You expect me to do all this work to prepare for *your* party while you lay there sprawled on the couch playing Super Mario Galaxy and eating Funyuns. I wish I could be so lazy."

Rod: "Hey, you try putting in a twelve hour shift at the dealership. We were short staffed all day. It would be nice to have a few minutes to unwind without you nagging me like Atilla the Hun."

(Rewind)

Cheryl: "I have a lot to do to get ready for your party. I'm also very tired. I would really appreciate your help with getting the house picked up. Would you please give me a hand?

Rod: "I know. "You're right. I had a crazy day at work. I will finish this in five and start with the bathroom." Is that cool?"

In the second dialogue, Cheryl's "language" is clear and assertive, yet free of evaluative language or negative labels. Compare the following "you" statements with "I" statements. How do they sound to you?

A. "You are ignoring my calls."

B. "I appreciate it when you return my calls."

A. "You did that on purpose."

B. "I hope that was not done on purpose."

A. "You always forget to fill up the gas tank."

B. "I really like it when I see the gas tank full after you use the car."

A. "You did this completely wrong."

B. "I need this done a different way."

A. "You were very rude at dinner."

B. "I felt uncomfortable with a few things at dinner."

Study the statements labeled "B." Notice how they are free of accusations, generalizations, and criticisms. They are also void of evaluative language. Again, let's re-emphasize **that the "I statements" which go the greatest distance with people are ones which focus on the behavior or the outcome that is desired.**

From unit 4 we learned that all of us have the need to save face or protect our ego when it is attacked or threatened. Rather than attack the person we are speaking to, it is better instead to focus on the behavior that we'd like to see in the present or future. Contrast the statements labeled "A" with the statements from "B" which focus on the behavior desired. Which would you prefer to hear?

A. "You don't love me like I love you."

B. "I need to know what I mean to you."

A. "You are oblivious to what is going on."

B. "I need you to be more curious about my new job."

A. "You never make any plans for us."

B. "I'd like you to plan something for us Saturday."

A. "You always get your way."
B. "I'd like you to let me decide this."

A. "You are late again."
B. "I like it when you arrive on time."

Your Turn: Think of five situations where you would need to approach a person about a need or concern. Create five "I Statements" (I like . . . I appreciate . . . I value . . . I need.) similar to the examples mentioned so far in this unit. Be sure to avoid evaluative language and focus on the behavior desired.

Unit Summary

We use language for a variety of reasons including sharing meaning, meeting our needs, and building relationships. Language has been around for approximately 50,000 years and has several unique characteristics. Those characteristics include: language is arbitrary, has denotative and connotative meaning, is governed by rules, and evolves over time. We can improve our use of language by making our messages more clear and increasing receptivity. Our messages are more clear when we incorporate concrete and descriptive language. We also improve the clarity of our messages by monitoring our use and clarifying other people's use of equivocal, convoluted, and nonstandard language. Receptivity refers to a person's willingness to listen to and consider our message. Receptivity is enhanced when we carefully choose our words, avoid evaluative language, and use "I language," which focuses on the behavior we desire from someone.

Key Questions

1. What is the purpose of language?
2. What do we mean when we say language is arbitrary, has denotative and connotative meaning, is governed by rules, and always evolving?
3. How can we make our language more clear and concrete?
4. Describe euphemisms, equivocal, convoluted, and nonstandard language? What are some helpful guidelines regarding their use?
5. What does receptivity mean?
6. How would you summarize the unit's suggestions regarding the following:
   - Pronoun "we" and conjunction "but"
   - Evaluative language
   - Trigger words
   - Use of "You" and "I" language?

Vocabulary Playback

Language
Linguistics
Semantics
Etymology
Dialect
Pronunciation
Accent
Denotative
Connotative
Phonological Rules
Syntactic Rules
Semantic Rules
Pragmatic Rules
Abstract Words
Euphemisms
Doublespeak
Equivocation
Convoluted Words
Interpersonal Idioms
Slang
Jargon
Speech Act
Receptivity
Evaluative Language
Loaded Words
Trigger Words
Accusations
Generalizations
Comparisons
Criticism

Theoretically Speaking

- Sapir-Whorf Hypothesis
- Coordinated Management of Meaning

"I feel great when I'm with you."

"I can't wait till I see you later."

"I love that about you."

- Family studies scholar Ted Huston and a team of researchers conducted a longitudinal study involving in-depth interviews with 168 couples at key intervals during the first two years of marriage. Couples were observed in the interviews and their answers and recollections recorded. Researchers then contacted all of the couples thirteen years later to see if they were still married. They discovered that the more verbal affection couples exchange during their first two years of marriage, the greater the chance they'll still be married 13 years later. What do you think about the results of their study? How much do you think a couple's language contributed to their marital longevity? How would you apply the results of this study to your own life?[66]
- Research by psychologist James Pennebaker suggests that when people write about their struggles and personal difficulties, they experience a reduction in stress hormones. In repeated sessions with Pennebaker, clients have reported improvements in their mood after writing about what is troubling them. Putting our feelings into language and writing about them appear to reduce the stress hormone Cortisol.[67] In one interesting communication study, participants were given difficult tasks such as solving difficult math problems with added time constraints or watch videos of couples fighting. One group was asked to affectionately write to someone they loved. Another group was asked to just think about a loved one. The third group did nothing. All three groups gave pre and post study blood samples. The first group experienced a quicker decrease in the stress hormone Cortisol compared to the second and third group.[68] Why would expressing our thoughts in writing make such a difference in terms of lowering our stress? Are there other explanations for the results?
- When stating our feelings and opinions, it is generally better received if we use "I" language versus "you" language. For example, rather than say "You are aggravating me," I may say "I am feeling aggravated right now." Effective communicators own their own feelings and opinions. They realize that in any given moment, they have choices in terms of how they act, what they think, or how they feel about something. No one makes us aggravated, we are choosing to allow something that the person is doing or not doing to affect us. We could always choose to ignore it, laugh at it, forget about it, or look at it in a completely different way. Two more examples are given below. In the following table, take the "You statements" and shift the ownership of your feelings to yourself by replacing them with "I language," which shows ownership. After doing this, discuss how these statements sound to you.

  A. "You don't know what you are talking about."

  B. "I want you to hear some information which I think is more up to date."

  A. "You left me hanging."

  B. "I felt like I was forgotten."

You don't value this relationship.	
You didn't bother to ask.	
You can't take anything seriously.	

- Do you think if the world spoke just one language, it would help the human race communicate better? Why or why not? What would we gain or lose as a result? For in interesting perspective on this, read a synopsis of Andrew Dalby's (2003) book, *Languages in Danger: The Loss of Linguistic Diversity and the Thread To Our Future* online.
- Because they are separate processes, encoding and decoding can yield very different results. During the on-air broadcast at the Mercedes-Benz Championships, *Golf Channel's* first female anchor, Kelly Tilghman, was suspended for two weeks after she said that in order for Tiger Wood's competitors to beat him, they'd have to "lynch him in a back alley." Her comment was in response to analyst Nick Faldo's remark "to take on Tiger, maybe they should just gang up on him for a while." Tilghman's comment was meant only as a compliment. She said it in the spur of the moment

to accentuate Tiger's dominance in the PGA. Others decoded her comments differently.

Some prominent figures, including civil rights activist Rev. Al Sharpton, called for Tilghman's firing. The word "lynch" has strong racist undertones. During the late 1700s up until the mid 1900's, thousands of African Americans throughout the southern United States were brutally tortured, hung from trees, and burned to death by white mobs for perceived "offenses." Hundreds of whites, who supported civil rights, experienced the same fate. Tilghman's strongest supporter was Tiger Woods! Apparently, the two are friends and have known each other for twelve years. Mark Steinberg, a spokes-person for Tiger Woods stated, "Tiger has a great deal of respect for Kelly. Regardless of the choice of words used, we know unequivocally that there was no ill-intent in her comments."[69] How would you relate this example to what you've learned in this unit?

Unit 8 Vocabulary Review

___ Language
___ Semantics
___ Dialect
___ Accent
___ Connotative Meaning
___ Euphemisms
___ Equivocation
___ Idioms
___ Jargon
___ Receptivity
___ Loaded Words
___ A Generalization
___ A Criticism
___ Linguistics
___ Etymology
___ Pronunciation
___ Denotative Meaning
___ Abstract Words
___ Doublespeak
___ Convoluted Words
___ Slang
___ Speech Act
___ Evaluative Language
___ An Accusation
___ A Comparison

A. Words which are created and used by a specific group or subculture.

B. This language includes words which are judgmental in nature and have a negative connotation. They imply that there is something inherently wrong or bad about a person.

C. The literal or dictionary meaning people share for a word.

D. The collection of word symbols whose meaning is shared by a group of people.

E. Words which have very strong positive or negative meanings.

F. This presents an ideal and then suggests that the receiver is not living up to it.

G. A specialized field of linguistics which focuses on the meaning of words and phrases.

H. The study of the origins of words and how they change over time.

I. The way a word is vocalized.

J. People speak with this when they attempt to pronounce words in a language which is not their native tongue.

K. The personal or emotion-laden meaning people attach to a word.

L. The study of all aspects of written and spoken language.

M. Words which are not tangible or easily identified by the senses.

N. Less socially desirable words are replaced with words which are more positive and acceptable.

0. A kind of euphemism often used in political or institutional rhetoric.

P. This occurs when people are deliberately ambiguous, indirect, or vague with their words.

Q. When people create and attach a new meaning to an existing word or words.

R. What we say in a given moment.

S. A variation in the way a particular language is spoken. People who speak English do so differently throughout the world. We say that they speak in various. . . .

T. Rarely used, polysyllabic, and/or difficult to pronounce words.

U. A person's willingness to consider and respond positively to a message.

V. This is a remark which is evaluative or condescending.

W. This implies that a person did something bad or failed to do something important.

X. Nonstandard words used by certain members of a certain profession or trade.

Y. This insinuates that something about a person's beliefs, feelings, or behavior is representative of something broader and less than ideal.

Exercise: Reducing Defensiveness

One of the ways we can communicate our needs to someone without causing him or her to feel defensive is to use "I language," which focuses specifically on the behavior we'd like to see versus the behavior we are getting. Let's take a look at two examples. Compare the statement on the left with the one on the right. Which would you rather hear from someone?

"You are late again."	"I really like it when you are on time."
"Why can't you start acting like I'm as important as your mother?"	"I need you to please check with me before making plans with your mom."
"You can't make up your mind."	"I'd like you to decide what we are doing tonight."

Replace the following statements which are likely to trigger a defensive reaction with an "I statement" such as "I like . . ." "I appreciate . . ." "I enjoy . . ." "I value . . . ". Be sure to focus your statement on the behavior you would like to see.

1. "Who made you my boss?"

2. "You always forget to fill up the gas tank when it is empty."

3. "At dinner you dominated the conversation."

4. "Stop being so sensitive."

5. "You left this morning without saying goodbye."

6. "How many times do I need to remind you to pick up your shoes?"

9 Nonverbal Communication

Nonverbal Communication Unit 9

Unit 9 takes an in-depth look at the nonverbal aspects of interpersonal communication. Strategies for improving nonverbal communication are explained.

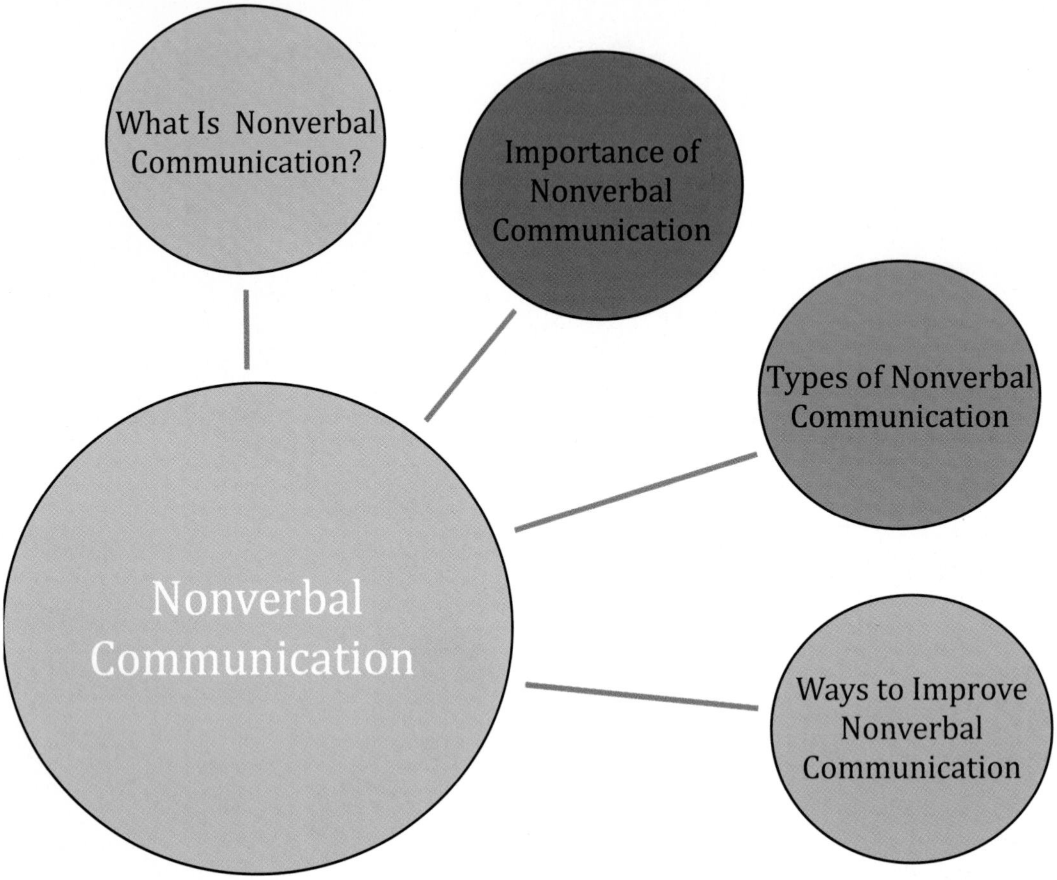

Unit 9 Learning Objectives

As a result of reading and studying Unit 9, you will be able to:

1. Describe nonverbal communication.
2. Explain why nonverbal communication is important in interpersonal communication.
3. Appreciate the importance of the following types of nonverbal communication:
   - Physical Attractiveness
   - Body Language
   - Facial Expressions
   - Eyes
   - Touch
   - Smell
   - Paralanguage and Silence
   - Territoriality and Space
   - Environment and Artifacts
   - Time
   - Actions
4. Identify ways to improve nonverbal aspects of interpersonal communication such as:
   - Increase Awareness of Cultural and Gender Differences
   - Improve Paralanguage
   - Clarify Nonverbal Messages
   - Pay Attention To Nonverbal Messages
   - Increase Expressiveness

Former pole vault champion Bob Richards shares a story of a dedicated football player who put his all into every practice, but remained on the sidelines his entire high school career. Despite this, the young man's father came to all his son's games. In college, this young man saw an opportunity to try out as a walk on. His friends told him he was crazy and would get himself killed. His father said, "Son, don't listen to those who doubt you. They won't live with your regrets. This is an opportunity that is too good to pass up!"

At tryouts, the coaches immediately noticed this player—for his lack of skills and size—but were impressed with his intensity. He eagerly took hit after hit. He frequently stopped to help other players get up off the turf and encouraged his teammates. He was one of the few who stayed after practice to help other players sharpen their play execution. With great excitement, this player called his father to let him know he accomplished something many assumed impossible . . . he made the team! Like high school, the player witnessed the gridiron action from the bench, yet his father was there at every college game to cheer him and the team on. His son counted on his father to be there, and looked for him in the stands. After the games, father and son were often seen walking around the sprawling campus together, the father's arm resting on his son's broad shoulders.

Late in the season, the coach was asked to share the news that earlier in the day, the player's father passed away unexpectedly. In his office, the coach consoled the player as best he could and told him that the team would dedicate Saturday's game to his father. Saturday's contest pitted two arch rivals, both vying for the conference championship. No one expected the player to show up for the game, but at halftime he strode into the locker room and in front of his teammates approached the coach saying, "Coach put me in. I really need to play today. You said we were dedicating this game to my dad. If that is the case, we have no option but to win!" The coach did not want to put a third stringer into such a strategic and tight game, but could not dismiss such an impassioned plea. He said, "O.k. I will send you in, but I may need to pull you out right away."

During the third quarter, this player was given his chance. As soon as he hit the field, he started running, blocking, and tackling like a Heisman nominee. His presence on the field galvanized the team. The opposing team was caught off guard by this unknown player who didn't appear anywhere on their stats. The score was soon tied. In the closing seconds, this player intercepted a pass and made a wild dash to the end zone, delivering the winning touchdown.

Spectators jumped to their feet and danced in the aisles. A celebration exploded onto the field and continued to the locker room.

When things quieted down, the coach found the player standing near his locker. He said, "Son you were fantastic, I never knew you had it in you to play like this." The player said, "Thanks coach. A lot of people in this room know that my father passed away this week. But I don't think anyone was aware that my dad was legally blind. He could not see. Yet, he still came to every one of my football games. Today, I knew he could see me play for the first time from heaven, and I wanted to show him what his son could do."

What this man's father did—his steadfast presence in the stands at every game communicated a powerful nonverbal message: "Son, I am here. I value what you are doing. You are important to me." While the young man was not the captain, quarterback, or a first string player, many would argue he was one of the most influential players on the team. His level of commitment, expressed nonverbally in various ways, also sent a profound message: "Everyone on this team counts! I will contribute to something greater than myself."[1]

What Is Nonverbal Communication?

Bob Richard's story of the football player reminds us that **every action communicates a potential message.** Messages convey the meaning we wish to share with others. Messages are comprised of verbal and nonverbal symbols. This unit focuses on the nonverbal aspects of interpersonal communication such as silence.

A person's silence communicates something. Mia Wallace (Uma Thurmon) and Vincent Vega (John Travolta) allude to this in *Pulp Fiction* (1994):

Mia: "Don't you hate that?"

Vincent: "What?"

Mia: "Uncomfortable silences. Why do we feel it's necessary to yak about {crap} in order to be comfortable? "

Vincent: "That's a good question."

Mia: "That's when you know you've found somebody special. When you can just . . . comfortably enjoy the silence."

Along with certain actions, such as a person's physical presence at a son's game, or the comfortable or uncomfortable silence between friends, a piece of art like Leonardo da Vinci's famous masterpiece, Mona Lisa, may evoke different meanings for people. Art, music, signs, facial expressions, posture, and behaviors are nonlinguistic symbols which convey meaning. Tattoos which do not involve language are nonverbal forms of communication. 36% of American ages 18 to 29 sport one or more tattoos, according to a survey by the Journal of American Academy of Dermatology.[2] A person's tattoo is a symbol that usually stands for something. So can a body piercing. Results from

a Pew survey of 2,020 adults ages 18–24 found that one in four has a body piercing somewhere on their body other than an earlobe.[3] In American culture, an engagement ring is a symbol of commitment, a dove represents peace, and a hand up in the air communicates "be quiet" or "I don't want to hear it."

Nonverbal communication includes any aspect of a message which does not involve spoken or written language. Communication scholars and authors Ron Adler and Neil Towne say that nonverbal communication is all about:

> "Smiling, frowning, laughing,
> crying, sighing . . .
> Standing close to others, being
> standoffish . . .
>
> The way you look:
> Your hair, your clothing, your face,
> your body
>
> Your handshake . . . your posture,
> Your gestures, your mannerisms
> Your voice:
> Soft-loud, fast-slow,
> smooth-jerky
> The environment you create:
> Your home, your room
> Your office, your desk
> Your kitchen, your car."[4]

What does body perspiration potentially communicate?

When we roll our eyes, blush, sweat, stammer, pace, fidget, glance away, walk briskly, bite our lip, cry, attach an emoticon to the end of an e-mail message or play with our hair, we communicate nonverbal messages, intentionally or unintentionally.

Intentional messages are ones we want to send, like reaching out to shake a person's hand as a friendly gesture. Unintentional messages are those we send unknowingly or without intent. We may greet a person at a party and say, "It's so great to see you." If we keep looking over her shoulder at other people in the room while talking to her, we may inadvertently communicate the opposite. Sometimes we reveal what we are really thinking or feeling through nonverbal leakage. **Leakage** is our unconscious, automatic nonverbal expressions. An example of this is when we start to smirk or laugh at something when it is not appropriate. We may catch ourselves doing this and attempt to quickly cover up our mouths with our hands to hide it. A friend may suddenly start to stammer or his eyes twitch involuntarily when he gets nervous. **Microexpressions** are a form of leakage. They involve facial expressions which, like a camera, flash an instant look such as surprise or disgust. We typically have little control over microexpressions, yet they are often very revealing. Certain behaviors like eyelid flutters may communicate something. According to John Stern, Ph.D., Professor Emeritus of Psychology at Washington University in St. Louis, and pioneer of blinking research, a person's eyes blink more often when a person is put on the spot or feels uncomfortable and apprehensive.[5]

Other physiological factors may contribute to sudden and/or excessive eye blinking, so we wouldn't want to jump to any quick conclusions. One has to pay very close attention to eye flutters to derive any meaning from this behavior. Eye flutters are hard to notice unless we have access to new computer technology which is capable of capturing nearly imperceptible eyelid flutters or twitches. It was developed by Dr. Terrance Sejinowski of the Salk Institute for Biological Studies in La Jolla, California. It can detect in real time what the naked eye can't.[6]

Now that we have a solid understanding of what nonverbal communication is, let's discuss its importance. This next section will address how our ability to communicate nonverbally is important to us personally and professionally, how people derive a lot of meaning from nonverbal behaviors, and how nonverbal communication serves various functions.

Research this! There is a lot of interesting information about eye blinking. Go to the Washington University in St. Louis website for the article "The eyes have it: Candidates' eyes could be revealing," at www.news.wustl.edu/news/Pages/4018.aspx

. . . What is nonverbal communication?

Importance of Nonverbal Communication

Knowing how to effectively express ourselves nonverbally is very beneficial to us in several ways. A lot of the meaning in communication is derived from nonverbal behaviors. Nonverbal communication also serves various functions to aid our attempts to communicate.

Benefits of Effective Nonverbal Communication

What we're about to learn in this unit is important because **research suggests being more conscious of our own and other people's nonverbal behavior benefits us personally and professionally.** Numerous research studies have shown that people who apply effective nonverbal approaches in their communication are more likely to experience greater academic and career success. They tend to enjoy more relational satisfaction, cooperation from others, and social popularity. They are also less likely to suffer from hypertension, anxiety, depression, and stress.[7] Skilled nonverbal communication is associated with persuasiveness, attractiveness, and high self-esteem. Communicators who are savvy with their nonverbal communication also experience greater success at garnering cooperation and support from others.[8, 9, 10]

. . . Why is it important to improve our nonverbal communication?

We Derive a Lot of Meaning from Nonverbal Communication

Nonverbal communication carries a lot of weight. Communication scholars estimate that 60 to 70% of the meaning we generate with our messages comes from nonverbal behaviors.[11] Research suggests people place more emphasis on our nonverbal cues over our verbal messages when trying to interpret the meaning of a message. This is because nonverbal behaviors are usually spontaneous expressions of our conscious and unconscious thoughts, feelings and needs.[12]

If our nonverbal messages contradict our verbal messages, research suggests adults tend to believe in the nonverbal message more. In addition, when we communicate nonverbally, we are often using visual, auditory, and tactile channels simultaneously, providing receivers with more messages to extract meaning from. We've all heard the adage that first impressions are usually important. People's initial impressions and perceptions are based largely on our nonverbal behaviors. Also, people's initial assessment of our attractiveness is based on the nonverbal signals we send.[13] In preparation for trial, attorneys often coach their clients on how to dress and groom themselves to influence how a judge or jury will view them.

Nonverbal Communication Serves Various Functions

The effect our words have on people is influenced a lot by our nonverbal behavior. We use our nonverbal behavior to express a lot of our emotions. People also gain better understanding of the emotional aspects of our messages when we express ourselves with our voice, eyes, facial expressions, and gestures.[14] Communication researchers have identified five important functions of nonverbal communication. **Nonverbal communication complements, contradicts, accents, regulates, and substitutes for our words.**

Complements

Nonverbal behavior complements our verbal messages. If we are listening to a friend who is talking, we may say the word "yes" and nod our heads up and down at the same time. If we want to convey confidence and professional poise in a job interview, we will use words that are more powerful, direct, and descriptive. Our nonverbal behavior, such as our posture, eye contact, gestures, and style of dress is used to complement our verbal messages.

Contradicts

To communicate sarcasm, we may say something in a way using our voice to suggest just the opposite, such as "Isn't that just great."[15] In this case, our nonverbal communication helps us to contradict our verbal message. We may also use our nonverbal communication to subtly imply something. When we really want someone to do something for us, but don't want to come out and just say it, we may say something like, "Don't worry, I know you are too busy to help me with my rehearsal tonight," but as we say it, we give the person we're speaking to our best sad, puppy dog face.

© Monkey Business Images, 2010. Used under license from Shutterstock, Inc.

Accents

When we tell a joke, we may make a face or smile just as we deliver the punch line to punctuate its humorous effect. Great comedians, like Wayne Brady, have a knack for drawing out laughs by accentuating their language with bursts of nonverbal expressiveness. We may make whimpering sounds or whistle while we are speaking for effect.

. . . **Catch this!** Wayne Brady does BSB (Backstreet Boys) on www.youtube.com

Regulates

We also regulate our conversations with our nonverbal behavior. **Turn-taking behaviors** are applied in our conversations when we want to let each other know when we are going to take turns speaking and listening. While talking to someone, when we want him to know that we are done speaking and ready to hear a response, we will likely pause and slightly nod our heads. Communication scholars Laura Guerrero, Joseph DeVito, and Michael Hecht describe how we use such behaviors as sitting down, opening our mouths, shutting on or off the t.v. with the remote, extending our hands out, facial expressions, and even touch to signal when we will "begin a conversation, whose turn it is to speak. . . , how to signal others to talk more, and how to end a conversation."[16]

Substitutes

Finally, we rely on nonverbal communication as a substitute for our words. This may happen in a social setting with a group. Someone starts to say something that he or she shouldn't, because someone in the group is not supposed to hear it. If we were standing behind this person we might try to signal the speaker to stop talking or change the subject by making your eyes big, shaking your head no really fast, or drawing a quick line across our neck to communicate "stop, don't go there." Now that we have discussed what nonverbal communication is, and why it is important, let's explore the various types of nonverbal communication in more depth.

. . . Why is nonverbal communication important in relation to interpersonal communication?

Types of Nonverbal Communication

A budding trend, especially in the American hip/hop rap culture is "grills" or mouth jewelry. Aspiring artists and fans are spending upwards of $3,000 to $4,500 or more for removable custom cast "retainers" made with various stones and gold. A $4,500 promotion grill sporting 5-carat white gold and princess-cut diamonds is available from various outlets.[17] People alter their appearance by wearing grills to project an image to the public, or to help a loved one cope with a life threatening illness. After enduring radiation therapy on the heel of two surgeries in her battle against breast cancer, 34-year-old Michelle Zettle of Idaho lost all of her hair. Knowing how much she loved her hair and to help her feel less sickly and self-conscious, her husband, father, sons, brother-in-law, mother-in-law's boyfriend and several colleagues at her place of employment shaved their heads. Altering their appearances sent a tender nonverbal message of unity and support.[18] Both of these illustrations represent how altering our physical appearance can communicate certain messages. It is one of several different types of nonverbal forms of communication.

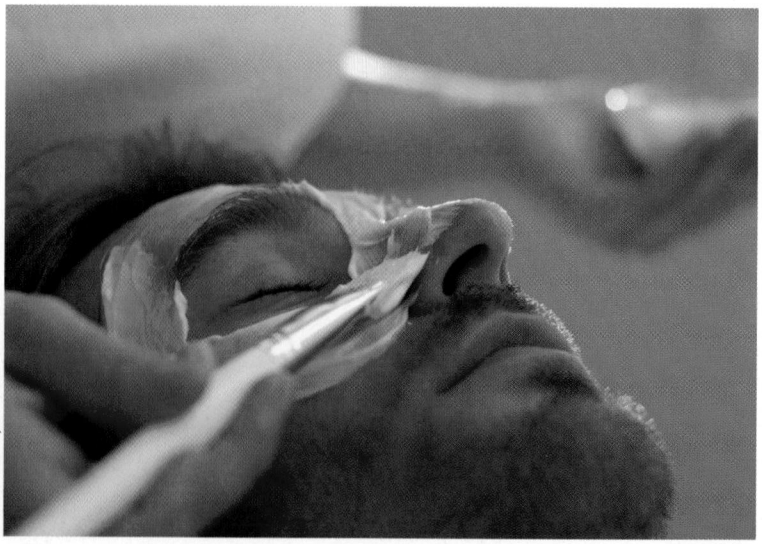

Physical Appearance

Our appearance can transmit potential nonverbal messages. The importance people in America place on physical appearance may have a lot to do with why shows like ABC's *Extreme Makeover* was a ratings powerhouse. The show aired between 2003 and 2007 and depicted what a team of plastic surgeons, cosmetic dentists, hair stylists, personal trainers, dieticians, and fashion experts could do to alter the appearance of people who were unhappy with their body and looks.[19]

Each year, billions of dollars are spent in America on plastic surgery, designer labels, haircuts, and makeup. Why is appearance so important to many people? Are physically attractive people at an advantage over less attractive people from an interpersonal standpoint? Research suggests that a good-looking woman or man has an easier time getting a date.[20] He or she is more likely to have fewer speeding tickets and reduced court sentences.[21] Research has shown that attractive men and woman are seen as more successful, sexy, and sociable. They are also perceived as more interesting and kind compared to unattractive people.[22, 23, 24, 25] In job interviews, attractive people are three to four times more likely to get hired.[26]

Psychologists refer to people's tendency to assign positive attributions to attractive people as the "halo effect". Physical attractiveness is not the only aspect of physical appearance that people show a bias towards. Research suggests that taller people have an advantage. One interesting study found that men 6 feet two inches or taller earned starting salaries 12.4 % higher than their shorter male colleagues under six feet.[27] Does this seem fair? Like it or not, attractiveness and height are aspects of physical appearance which are a part of nonverbal communication. So is it worth our time and money to do what we can to maximize our attractiveness without becoming obsessed with it? What do you think? Where do we draw the line?

. . . **Catch this!** See an extreme makeover conducted by New York Plastic Surgeon Dr. Dan Morello by going to www.youtube .com http://www.youtube.com/watch?v=qZaLi-Wwffo

One aspect of physical appearance which we have a lot of control over is clothing. Clothing is often strategically chosen to establish status and power (suits and uniforms). It can enhance popularity (by wearing trend setting clothes and conforming to newest styles) and help us project a certain image (such as professionalism or adhering to certain dress codes).[28, 29, 30] Clothing influences how people perceive us in terms of our profession, education background, socioeconomic status, personality, and values [31] Clothing artifacts are those things we add to our clothing such as watches, jewelry, purses, glasses, carry bags, brief cases, and shoes. These accentuate the image we wish to project to others.

Research This! Veils are an article of clothing. For an interesting look into the history and purpose of Muslim veils read Eli Sander's article, Interpreting Veils: Meanings Have Changed with Politics, History in The Seattle Times at www.seattletimes .nwsource.com/news/nation-world/infocus/mideast/islam/interpreting_veils.html

Body Language

When it comes to sending messages, our bodies are a major channel. They can communicate a message 5,000 to 6,000 years from now. Archaeologists discovered two skeletons just south of the city of Verona, the setting for Shakespeare's story of Romeo and Juliet. The two, a male and female, are locked in a tender embrace. Archaeologists believe the two were young because they both had a good set of teeth. It is unusual to find a double burial like this from the Neolithic period, so it is theorized the hugging pair may have met a sudden and tragic death.[32]

Our bodies may communicate messages in the present too. New York Jets running back Leon Washington created quite a stir from football card collectors. Washington's waist-up pose appeared obscene. Topps, the company that produces the card, immediately condemned it, offering to replace it for their customers. The controversy hit the fan when the card first came out. Washington said he was making a three fingered "E" salute to his home community on the east side of Jacksonville, Florida. Because of the card's background color and Jackson's uniform color, two of his three fingers, which had white tape on them, were not easily visible, while his middle finger was. The "obscenity" card has increased in popularity, fetching nearly $100.00 on eBay. His body was the channel and his message was unintentional! [33]

Kinesics is the study of how people communicate messages through body movement. Body movements which may send nonverbal messages include posture and gestures. **Posture** refers to how we stand or sit. This can include how we turn our bodies, whether we lean forward or backward, or if we sit with our back straight or slouch. Body movements may also include such things as tapping our foot, crossing our legs, rocking on the balls of our feet, and swaying our hips. Gestures include the specific movements of our arms and hands. **Gesticulation** is the use of one's arms and hands to communicate. **There are four types of gestures according to communication scholars: emblems, illustrators, regulators, and adaptors.**

Emblems

An emblem is a gesture which has its own distinct meaning. Waving at a person signifies "hello." If someone points a finger at something it means "look at it." When a person wants us to "come here," he will take his index finger and motion it in his direction. Flipping a person "the bird" by raising the middle finger is an emblem. [34]

Illustrators

Illustrators are those gestures which help the speaker describe something. If you are in a hurry, you may tell someone who wants to talk to you at length, "I've got to be going." At the same time, you may glance at your watch. As we are sitting at a campfire, we may dramatize a scary story by making a claw with our hand as we describe a creature who is about to attack an unsuspecting victim like Jim Carrey did in the movie *Liar, Liar.*

Regulators

Regulators allow us to signal when we will take turns speaking and listening during our conversations. We may motion with our hand to let a person know to go ahead and speak. We may also use our hands to encourage a speaker to continue speaking, to get to the point, or stop talking, such as putting a hand up.[35] In on-line communication, we may use the abbreviation BRB for "be right back," to serve as a regulator in an electronic context.[36]

Adaptors

Adaptors are gestures which serve a psychological or physical purpose. We may wring our hands or squeeze an object when we are nervous to help calm ourselves down. We may fan ourselves when we feel hot. We may also run our fingers through our hair to improve our appearance, or bite our nails when nervous. Often we are not conscious of these behaviors.[37]

American soldiers in Afghanistan and Iraq are receiving training from a video game the Pentagon hopes will help them communicate with non-English speaking civilians. When language cannot be used, gestures provide a lot of information. Soldiers are taught to get down on one knee and remove their sunglasses when talking to children so that the children will feel more comfortable talking to them. Placing the hand on the heart as you approach someone conveys the message you have only good intentions and are not a threat. The program also demonstrates what not to do. Male soldiers learn not to walk up quickly to a single woman.[38]

Touch

Touch is a potent form of nonverbal communication. It is the primary means by which we demonstrate connectedness, love and affection. An interesting study by scholars April Crusco of the University of Mississippi and Christopher G. Wetzel of Rhodes College found that restaurant servers who lightly and briefly touched the hand or shoulder of a customer when returning change received larger tips compared to a no-touch control group.[39] Touch may potentially create more immediacy if both the sender and receiver are receptive to it. Immediacy is the closeness or connectedness two people feel with each other (Unit 1). It is a strong human need to touch and be touched. In one study, premature babies were found to increase weight and grow faster when touched often or massaged. [40]

We use touch to indicate what a person means to us by the way we embrace or hug a person. The kind of kiss we exchange is an indicator, too, of the kind of relationship we have and the level of intimacy we wish to exchange. We use touch to get a person's attention, or to offer encouragement such as a pat on the back. Touch is also the vehicle for us to engage in other forms of healthy and playful jostling, tickling, and wrestling.

We also use touch to demonstrate status.[41] Research suggests that people of high status are more likely to touch people of low status in most contexts. They are more inclined to tap a person on the top or side of the shoulder or initiate a handshake. Those who are lower in status are not likely to initiate touch with a person of high status. For example, a principle or teacher at a school would be more likely to gently grab a student by the arm to pull him aside in the hallway or tap a child on the head. If a student did this, it would likely be considered inappropriate.

The study of touch and how it communicates messages is called **haptics**. **Nonverbal communication scholars have identified various kinds of touch: affectionate, caregiving, power, and aggressive.**

Affectionate Touch

Affectionate touch occurs between people who care about and love each other. This may involve hand-holding hugging, and kissing.

Care-giving Touch

Care-giving touch is the kind of touch where someone you know or don't know well is assisting you in some way such as a personal trainer spotting us at the gym, a doctor examining us, elderly residents getting help out of a bed, or going to a dentist and having our teeth cleaned.

Power Touch

Power touch may occur when we try to cover someone's mouth so she can't say something embarrassing about us, pushing a person out of the way, grappling with someone on a wrestling mat, or steering someone out of a room.

Aggressive Touch

Aggressive touch inflicts physical harm. Did you know that threatening to hit someone, or putting your fists up like you are going to hit a person is considered "assault" in some states in America?[42] An interesting look into this is found in the discussion section at the end of the unit.

Smell

Dr. Leslie Vosshall, Molecular Biologist at Rockefeller University, conducted a fascinating study regarding how attractive a man is to a woman based on his scent. Men produce a steroid in the body called androstenone, a product of the hormone testosterone. Depending on a woman's "odor gene" or OR7D4 receptor, a man will have either a vanilla or "woodsy" urine scent. When a man perspires, a woman may be attracted or repulsed by his natural scent.[43] For those guys interested in attracting a woman, what can we glean from this study? Buy an upscale bottle of cologne—and use it sparingly—just in case!

Olfactics is the study of smell. Smells play a strong role in affecting our memory and mood. When we make an association between a scent and a memory we call that **olfactic association.** We may associate the smell of vanilla with the baking our mother or father did when we were a child. Cultures throughout the world vary in terms of how comfortable they are with natural body odors. Americans invest a lot more money on soaps, oils, lotions, cologne, and perfumes than people in many other cultures. Some cultures value bathing or showering more often than others do. There isn't a right or wrong here, simply differences. In terms of enhancing our interpersonal communication, it is important to note that room or body orders which people find offensive will detract from communication. Those which are pleasing will likely enhance interaction.[44]

To what extent does the smell of smoke or bad breath influence your ability to interact interpersonally with others?

Facial Expressions

The human face can create over 1,000 different expressions.[45] **Many communication scholars believe that a person's face is the first thing people use in forming initial impressions.**[46]

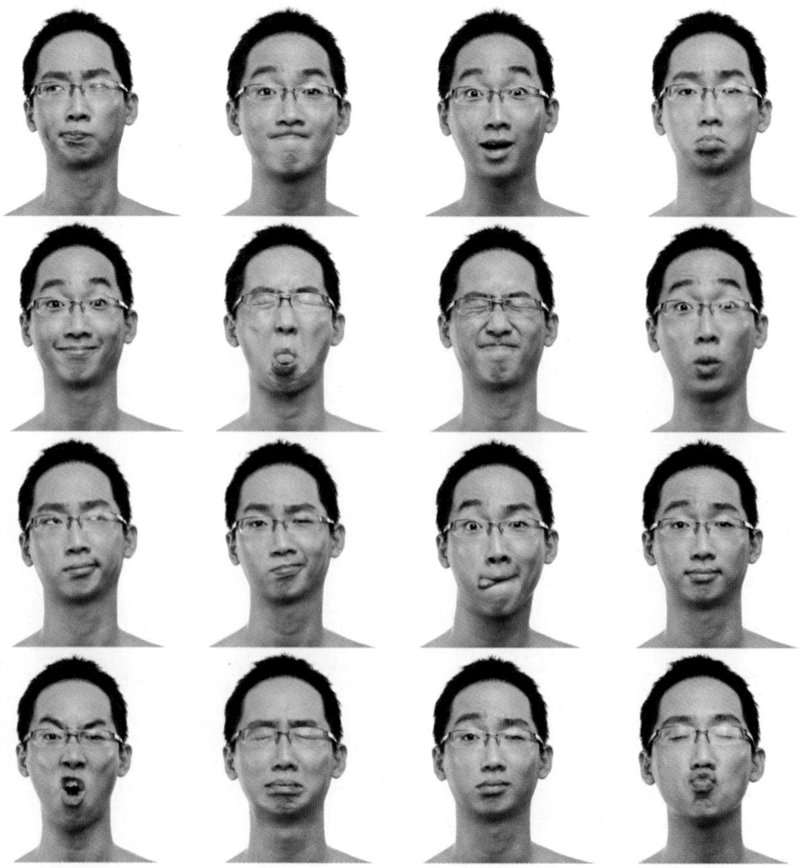

These expressions, when done for a desired effect, are called **facial management techniques**. These techniques are motivated by our desire to communicate our thoughts and feelings, mask them, or influence other's thoughts and feelings.

As we are talking to our colleagues at work, if we are enthusiastic about an idea we have, we may enlarge our eyes, raise our eyebrows, give lots of eye contact, and smile to express and intensify our excitement. We use facial expressions to mask our real thoughts and feelings when we hold back tears while watching a touching movie to escape social embarrassment, or give a friend a fake smile when she describes the perfect vacation she just had—the one we wanted to go on but couldn't. We may also use our facial expressions to influence the emotions or behavior of others. Emergency medical technicians will often appear expressionless or show little emotion to help the injured remain calm.

How many muscles does it take to frown? 64 Smile? 13[47]

Eye Contact

What is one of the first things we do to communicate our attraction to someone? We lock eyes. There is that slightly prolonged glance accompanied by a subtle smile. We may look away nervously. Then our eyes find each other again. In fact, a person's pupils will dilate (increase in size) when he or she sees someone attractive. Dr. Eckhard Hess, professor of psychology at the University of Chicago, found that pupil size increases when a person sees a picture of something that is arousing or pleasant, and decreases when the picture is unpleasant.[48] If we are not interested in a person who is interested in us, what do we tend to do? We do just the opposite. We look away or avoid eye contact which is called **gaze aversion**. We may pretend not to see someone to avoid interaction like when an old love interest walks toward us in the mall. In addition to its role in flirtation, eye contact is a great way to intimidate. My mother had this down to a science. When I was acting up in church, she let me have it with her eyes. Even when I looked away from her, I could feel her piercing glare! **Staring**, as an eye behavior, is generally perceived as rude and invasive. It occurs when we look at a person intensely for a prolonged period of time, especially when the other person is not reciprocating. We may "stare someone down" to intimidate, establish our authority, communicate disapproval, or show defiance.

Oculesics is the study of eye behavior. Communication researchers have found that cultures similar to America value eye contact. Generally speaking, people in these cultures perceive a speaker's gaze aversion negatively. It may signal a lack of confidence, truthfulness, attentiveness, and politeness. On the flip side, some cultures in Africa and the pacific islands see eye contact between young people and elders as highly disrespectful. A Peace Corps member serving as a teacher discovered this quickly when the elders of an African tribe complained that the children were coming home and looking them in the eye. The teacher unknowingly violated the social customs of the tribe in her classroom by requiring the children to look her in the eyes when speaking.[49]

Avoiding eye contact while speaking to an elder or a person of high status is also customary in several Asian cultures.[50]

> Two thirds of the estimated three million sensory fibers in the human body are connected to the eyes.[51]

Paralanguage and Silence

Ever get in an argument with someone and the key antagonizer was not what you said but how you said it? As a child, were you ever admonished with "Don't use that tone of voice with me young man or young lady?" **Paralanguage** is how we use our voice or modulate our vocal sounds. **Paralanguage includes the pitch, rate, volume, and quality of your voice.** Pitch is the intonation or inflection in your voice. Rate is the speed with which you speak. Volume is your vocal loudness. Quality includes your enunciation and pronunciation. **Enunciation** is saying a word clearly. **Pronunciation** is saying the word correctly based on dictionary rules. A lot of meaning is derived from how we say a word. Try the word "fine." Can you think of different ways you could say the word to express different meanings? How about the expression "oh?" I can say it a lot of different ways to convey a different meaning. I may go "oh!" as if I'm surprised. To express excitement, I may say "Oh! Oh! Oh! Oh!" repeatedly, real fast like Joe Pesci's character, Leo Getz, in the *Lethal Weapon* series. I may exclaim, "*uh ohhh*!" to let you know you're in trouble. I may even let out a "Ohhhhh. Ohhhhhhh!" like the Herbal Essence commercial of a woman in the throes of organic pleasure with her shampoo. The meaning of a word may change depending on how we say it. I can say "That shirt looks good on you," but by changing my inflection and placing a strategic pause right after the word "good," I can change the meaning: "That shirts looks good . . . (pause) . . . ***on you***!" Paralanguage is our primary means to communicate sarcasm, distrust, humor, and a host of other emotions.[52]

Research on paralanguage suggests voice plays a significant role in communicating meaning. Dr. Albert Mehrabian, Professor Emeritus of Psychology at UCLA, theorizes that 39% of meaning is derived from a person's paralanguage.[53] How we use our voice when speaking is important not only in terms of the meaning which is conveyed but in how listeners perceive the speaker. An article in the *Journal of Nonverbal Behavior* by researchers Miron Zuckerman and Kunitate Miyake details the results of a study which found that people perceive a monotone voice as unattractive and hard to listen to.[54] People who vary their voices versus using a monotone or flat pitch are perceived as more dynamic and interesting. An attractive voice in American culture is lower for males and a little higher for females. It is also less shrill, regionally accented, and nasal.[55]

Research also suggests people retain what others say more when they are spoken to in a lively, animated manner. Speaking with a higher volume (but not real loud) is socially desirable in American culture. People generally don't like to have to ask a quiet talker to repeat him or herself or speak up.[56] We can vary our pitch, add pauses, or talk slower or faster to communicate enthusiasm and/or drive home a point. A pause or hesitation can communicate a message. Consider what happens between Lucy Van Pelt and Charlie Brown in *A Charlie Brown Christmas* (1965):

Lucy: "You do think I'm beautiful, don't you Charlie Brown?"

Charlie: (pauses)

Lucy: "You didn't answer right away. You had to think about it first, didn't you? If you really thought I was beautiful, you would've spoke right up. I know when I've been insulted."

Charlie: "Good grief!"

Territoriality and Space

Ever notice how students tend to sit in the same seats in class? As a guest for dinner, were you ever told where not to sit at the dinner table? You may notice at a place of worship, certain families occupy the same pews every service. While they do not own this space, they have claimed it. If we occupy another person's "space," we may unintentionally communicate a message of disrespect. Some people are particular about what cup they use, where they park their car, or which side of the bed they sleep on. I even heard one colleague complain once that a person was putting his lunch on a shelf space that he used in the staff lounge refrigerator! This territoriality can include ownership of certain communication rights. At some table settings, particular individuals are the ones who say a dinner prayer. A colleague at work may be the designated or self-appointed "entertainer" or "story teller" for the group. It's advantageous for us as communicators to heighten our awareness of the territorial nature of human beings. People tend to take ownership of space, objects, and certain communication roles within a given context.

In addition to territoriality, let's discuss space a little more. **Proxemics** is the scientific study of how people use space. We all have a need for personal space. It is the space around us which we don't like to share with others. The **protection theory** posits that we maintain some space between ourselves and others to put up a "buffer zone" against unwanted touching or a physical attack.[57] The **equilibrium theory** suggests that the closer we feel towards someone, the more we'll allow a person to enter our personal space.[58] Anthropologist Edward Hall's study of people in Western cultures led him to believe that people operate from four spatial zones which he labeled intimate, personal, social, and public. Intimate space ranges from zero to one and one-half feet. Americans, for example, generally are comfortable allowing only those who are romantic partners and in some cases, extremely close friends and family to enter this space. With their other friends and family members, they may feel comfortable standing or sitting 1 ½ to four feet away which is called personal space. Four to twelve feet Hall called social space. Typically, we feel more comfortable with people standing this far away from us who are acquaintances and strangers. Public distance is often established in public speaking or business contexts. This distance is established to identify one person as the primary speaker or the one in charge of facilitating a meeting or discussion.[59]

Hall's **proxemic theory** suggests that an individual's sense of personal space is influenced by culture.[60] In many southern European and Arab cultures, it is common to conduct face-to-face conversations in closer proximity than what is customary for people living in England, Norway, or New Zealand. Middle Eastern culture values a closer intimate distance. This sense of space also varies in terms of the environment or context we are in. If we are at a bar or dance club, our sense of personal space changes if it is crowded. We'll allow people to stand close or brush up to us because the room is packed. People are also generally intoxicated to some extent, and everyone is there to have a good time.

. . . **Catch this!** Check out this unscientific, yet illuminating, study conducted by college students regarding personal space etiquette Go to www.youtube.com. Also, visit Hamish and Andy—Personal Space Invaders on www.youtube.funny.com. What do these videos suggest in terms of a personal space?

Environment and Artifacts

How might we alter the environment of our condo to bump up intimate dialogue with our romantic partner? Put on *ESPN SportsCenter?* I think not. Well? No, I think not. We might dim the lights. Light some candles. Start a fire in the fire place. Pop the cork of a chilled bottle of sparkling grape juice and slip some Kenny G in our c.d. player. Ok. Kenny G may not work for some of us. In this instance, we are altering the environment to enhance the interpersonal interaction. In one interesting study, patients reported feeling five times more comfortable during visits when doctors removed their desks from their office space and replaced them with a more open, inviting seating arrangement.[61]

© Jennie Book, 2010. Used under license from Shutterstock, Inc.

American culture associates bigger with better. The bigger the office, the more prestige and power a person has—and if it's a corner office with windows—"You've made it baby!" A boss or at least a boss with a big ego has a big desk. We have power ties, watches, suits, and lockers. Take a look at the New York Yankee's locker room a while back. The center lockers were designated for the minor league players, not expected to make the roster. Gary Sheffield, like other star players, claimed a corner locker near a large open space. The lockers for the pitchers and catchers were grouped together along one wall. John Flaherty and Jorge Posada, both close friends, occupied a pair of lockers in the corner.[62] The locker one had represented a player's status and which players had close relationships.

Artifacts are the objects within an environment which may communicate messages about an owner. During certain holidays, people differ in terms of how and if they display decorations. This may suggest something about their values, practices, and beliefs. A home in my neighborhood proudly displays a Michigan State and Michigan flag on its front porch, which suggests the couple graduated from rival schools and are proud of that fact. Some people establish a "Wall of Gaylord" like the one in the movie *Meet The Fockers* or an ego wall displaying their awards, certificates, and diplomas. This may communicate the pride a person feels for having accomplished certain things or his or her commitment to certain pursuits. The things we put on our desk at work or the paintings in our living room communicate something about us.

Time

Chronemics is the study of how people use time. Communication scholars Burgoon, Buller, and Woodall state that "Time is seen as a precious resource, a valuable and tangible commodity. We spend time, save it, make it, fill it, and waste it."[63] How we utilize our time may communicate messages to people whether we are aware of it or not. How long we take to return a phone call communicates something. The time we spend at a party may indicate how much we are enjoying it. A parent who spends time with a child playing a game, shooting baskets, working on a school project, volunteering, or reading together communicates a subtle, yet profound message: "You are important to me. I enjoy you." One woman complained that her husband loved his cars more than her. He spent almost all of his time purchasing and restoring vintage automobiles. She lamented that he is a proud owner of 15 cars, 45 motorcycles in addition to snowmobiles, lawnmowers, and go-karts. Rather than take time to talk to her, she feels he'd rather read a *Hot Rod* magazine.[64]

In addition to how much time we devote to someone, arriving early or late, and starting a meeting late or on time may communicate messages to people about how important they or the event is to us. Some cultures place a high priority on promptness and punctuality while others are more laid back. In the United States, people invited to a New York party at 9:00 p.m. generally don't arrive until 9:30 p.m. In Salt Lake City, guests are generally expected to show up on time or a little early.[65]

Actions

Days after admitting he had an affair, NBA star Kobe Bryant purchased a four million dollar eight-carat ring for his wife, Vanessa Bryant, at an exclusive jewelry store in Santa Monica, California. This action may have been an attempt to communicate nonverbally that he felt bad about his behavior and wanted to save his marriage.[66] Our actions communicate messages. For example, following through on the things we say we are going to do communicates that we are reliable.

YES, HERE I AM AGAIN. A GENERIC LITTLE ARRANGEMENT THAT SHOWS HE WAITED UNTIL THE LAST MINUTE, THEN DIALED SOME 800 NUMBER.
BANNERMAN

FLOWERS THAT SAY TOO MUCH.

Dr. Barton Goldsmith, author of *Emotional Fitness for Couples,* suggests that it's the little "nonverbal" actions that often communicate love and strengthens romantic relationships between straight and gay couples. He suggests doing things "out of the blue" like surprising your spouse or partner by sneaking his or her car out to get it washed and fill up the gas tank or putting a picture of the two of you in a new frame and quietly placing it on a counter or coffee table. A wife might buy her husband tickets to a sports event. A husband may hand his wife the remote and let her pick a show she would like to watch and perhaps pop her some popcorn. A life partner may do something her significant other hates or doesn't know how to do like fix a button on her shirt.[67]

Your Turn: Can you think of other ways we can communicate nonverbally?

A first mate noticed that the captain of a cargo ship would always ask for his red shirt anytime a Pirate ship came at them. Curious, the first mate asked him why he did this. Understanding the importance of nonverbal communication, the captain said that his crew might give up the ship if they saw that he was wounded. A red shirt would mask his wounds and his crew would keep fighting valiantly. From out of nowhere a huge pirate ship barreled down on them. It was quickly apparent that his ship would be outrun by the black sails. The captain turned to his first mate and ordered, "Bring me my red shirt, and uh, you might want to bring me my brown pants."

Jeremy Hotts.
Comedy Central Presents

Now that we have explored many of the different ways we communicate nonverbally, let's take a look at how we can enhance our nonverbal communication.

. . . What are the different types of nonverbal communication? How are they significant in terms of their communicative value?

Ways to Improve Our Nonverbal Communication

There are several ways we can improve our nonverbal communication. This section will explore five. First, we can increase our awareness of cultural and gender differences in nonverbal expression. Second, we can enhance the quality of our vocalics or paralanguage. Third, we can clarify the nonverbal messages we receive from others. Fourth, we may become more sensitive to nonverbal aspects of communication. Finally, we can get more expressive.

Be Aware of Cultural and Gender Differences

American culture, generally speaking, is quite **monochronic** in terms of viewing time. We place a lot more emphasis on adhering to timelines, being prompt, and doing things expeditiously. For example, to arrive even a few minutes late may necessitate an explanation in many contexts. If one is ten to fifteen minutes late, an apology is often expected. Later than this and this is construed as rude and insensitive. However, if we are traveling out of the country to or hosting guests from Latin America, Africa or parts of Asia, we may run into trouble if we expect people from these parts of the world to see time like we do. Many cultures are more **polychronic**. They are more relaxed with timelines. People are often casually late and it's not a big deal.

When it comes to nonverbal communication, another noteworthy cultural difference is in the area of touch. Some cultures are very comfortable with lots of touching. In Middle Eastern and southern European cultures, men are more comfortable showing physical affection with each other. It is not uncommon for them to hold hands or walk with their arms over each other's shoulders in public. However, in Japan touching strangers is not generally welcomed so people give each other more personal space.[68, 69] Having an appreciation and awareness of cultural differences helps us to avoid misperceptions and miscommunication. The same applies to gender differences.

Ever notice the way that men and women sit? Generally speaking, men use up more space and spread their legs out more than women. Women tend to keep their legs close together or they cross them. Research suggests there are some subtle differences between men and women in terms of their nonverbal behavior. Women tend to read people's nonverbal communication, specifically people's vocal and facial cues, better than men.[70] Women tend to give more frequent eye contact during conversations then men do, this is especially true when they are speaking to other women.[71] Women smile more than men, generally speaking, but their smiles are a little harder to interpret.[72] Men are more likely to feel uncomfortable when someone invades their personal space compared to women.

The most significant difference between the sexes in terms of nonverbal behavior is in the area of gestures. These differences are such that in American culture, they are often tied to what is considered masculine and feminine behavior. Women keep their arms and hands closer to their bodies when talking than men do.[73, 74]

While a person's culture and gender do play a role in influencing nonverbal behavior, it is important to note that these differences are generalizations. There are exceptions or individual differences of course. It may be best for us to look at these as explanations for why people may communicate differently in the way they do. It helps us to avoid erroneous perceptions about a person's communication behavior. We may want to ask ourselves if a person's gender or culture is influencing the dynamics of an interaction.

Improve Our Paralanguage

As communicators we can also improve the quality of our paralanguage by avoiding vocal utterances. **Vocal utterances** are silence fillers we use between sentences like, "um, uh, and uh, er, ya know." People who use a lot of vocal utterances are perceived as less interesting, articulate, confident, intelligent and honest.[75] To improve your paralanguage, practice some of the methods highlighted on the right side of this page.

Clarify Nonverbal Communication

When we are uncertain about a person's nonverbal behavior or find it confusing, we can ask a question for clarification, or do a perception check using "I language."

- I notice you are looking away from me a lot as we are speaking. Is there a reason for this?
- I can't help but notice that you are biting your lip? Are you holding back something you need to say? Is everything o.k.?

We want to make sure we don't make quick assumptions about a person's nonverbal behavior. A person's nonverbal behavior

To reduce vocal utterances:
• After you have recorded a message on someone else's voicemail, before sending it, listen to it. If you hear a vocal utterance, delete the message and rerecord it until your message is "V.U." free! Try this twice a day for three weeks.
• On occasion, when you are in a conversation with someone, ask him or her to alert you to any vocal utterances you commit.
To improve enunciation:
• Practice tongue twisters ten to fifteen minutes per day. As you say each word, really extend your mouth muscles and use your tongue to attack each word. Say each word clearly. Pick up your rate or speed each time. For example: Six sick slick slim sycamore saplings. A box of biscuits, a batch of mixed biscuits. A skunk sat on a stump and thunk the stump. Red lorry, yellow lorry, red lorry, yellow lorry.
• For more examples, look up tongue twisters online.
To avoid a flat, monotone voice :
• Read out loud daily. Really exaggerate your expressions. Modulate your voice. Change your voice for each character. Alter your pitch, rate, and volume.
• Do this when you leave messages on other people's voicemail. Listen to your outgoing message before sending it. If your voice is monotone, too slow, or your enunciation is not clear, delete and rerecord the message.
• Read out loud and tape record your voice. Painful? Yes. But a great way to heighten your awareness of how you are using your voice.

can mean several things, or it may not mean much at all. Test your perceptions with a question and/or a perception check.

Pay Attention to Nonverbal Behaviors

We may also pay more attention to people's nonverbal behavior. We can do this by noting how long they take to answer a question, and where their eyes go when we ask them a question. We can observe the subtle nuances of each person's facial expressions and vocal tones, and make a mental note of how he or she is utilizing his or her time.

Get Expressive!

Generally speaking, people enjoy being around others who are expressive, animated, and charismatic. People who are expressive tend to be more interesting to listen to. Actors and comedians have a natural talent in this area. If you think this is an area in your nonverbal communication you'd like to improve a little, try this. Have some imaginary conversations with people while standing in front of the mirror in your bathroom. It may be best to do this when you are home alone! Observe how you gesture, your facial expressions, and what you do with your mouth and eyes. Next, practice adding more expressiveness to your delivery. Not only can you change the rate, pitch, and volume of your voice, try getting more animated with your face, body, and hands. Pretend you are telling a friend something that actually happened to you the other day, and as you do, exaggerate some of your body movements. Raise your eyebrows. Make your eyes dance. Speak a little more with your body and punctuate your points with your hands. Doing this in front of the mirror gives us great feedback. The more we practice being expressive, chances are, we'll feel less inhibited and self-conscious during our interactions with others.

. . . How can we improve aspects of our nonverbal communication?

Research this! For an more in-depth look at nonverbal communication, read *The Nonverbal Communication Reader Classic and Contemporary Readings*, Third Edition by Laura K. Guerrero and Michael L. Hecht.

Unit Summary

A lot of meaning is derived from nonverbal messages. Nonverbal communication complements, contradicts, accents, regulates, and substitutes for our words There are various types of nonverbal communication such as physical appearance, body language, facial expressions, eye behavior, touch, smell, paralanguage, silence, territoriality, space, environment, artifacts, time, and actions. There are several ways to improve our nonverbal communication such as increasing our awareness of cultural and gender differences, improving our paralanguage, clarifying nonverbal messages, and getting more expressive.

Key Questions

1. What is nonverbal communication?
2. Why is it important to improve our nonverbal communication?
3. Why is nonverbal communication important in relation to interpersonal communication?
4. What does Unit 9 say about each of the following types of nonverbal communication:
   - Physical Attractiveness
   - Body Language
   - Facial Expressions
   - Eye Behavior
   - Touch
   - Smell
   - Paralanguage and Silence
   - Territoriality and Space
   - Environment and Artifacts
   - Time
   - Actions
5. What are some of the ways we can improve our nonverbal communication?

Vocabulary Playback

Nonverbal Communication
Leakage
Microexpressions
Turn-taking Behaviors
Kinesics
Posture
Gesticulations
Haptics
Olfactics
Olfactic Association
Facial Management Techniques
Oculesics
Paralanguage
Enunciation
Pronunciation
Proxemics
Artifacts
Chronemics
Monochronic
Polychronic
Vocal Utterances

Theoretically Speaking

- Protection Theory
- Equilibrium Theory
- Proxemic Theory

Focus Group/Discussion Questions

- Individually or as a team, take a word and decide on the different ways you can express (alter your paralanguage) the word to communicate different meanings. Practice and be prepared to present this to your class.
- Visual representations are often powerful nonverbal channels to convey a host of feelings. One high school art teacher, Michael Bricker, gave a unique assignment to his students at Central Dauphin High School in Pennsylvania. He had them draw or photograph something which represented their greatest fear or an issue they faced in their personal life. What he didn't expect was how revealing his students' artwork would be. One student took a picture of her body. It was hard for her to do it, but it forced her to acknowledge her struggle with anorexia. Another student created a beautiful portrait of his brother, who committed suicide after five years as a victim of bullying. Seventeen-year-old Alina Bhatti, a Muslim, addressed the issue of discrimination and how she encountered mean stares and hurtful comments after the September 11, 2001 terrorist attack in New York and Washington D.C.. Her close up picture shows her with a name tag which reads, "Hello, my name is terrorist." Brina McCarthy, drew a backdrop for a picture she took of herself to symbolize how alone she felt after losing her mom to cancer. Visual representations are often powerful channels to convey a host of feelings.

  Many students found the assignment helpful as it encouraged them to talk openly about things they otherwise might have kept private. Some students received emotional support and encouragement from other students.[76] If you were to draw or take a photo of something which represented your greatest fear or personal struggle, what would it be? What do you see as the pros and cons of an assignment like this?
- There is an interesting concept in interpersonal communication called the "Pygmalion gift." Someone who gives a "Pygmalion gift" does so hoping the gift will influence the receiver to do something in particular. The gift also sends a nonverbal message about what the gift giver would like to see the recipient do with his or her life.[77] For example, a friend may give another friend a gift card to a certain clothing store in hopes that it will prompt her friend to change up her wardrobe. Grandparents may buy their very athletic, "tom boyish" granddaughter a necklace and perfume, hoping she may start being more "feminine." A father may buy a football and give it as a gift to his son to encourage him to try out for the team. What gifts have you given and received in the past? Where there any messages implied?
- Do tattoos and body piercings hurt or help our public image? What about in a professional or work setting?
- A school in Vienna, Virginia has a new rule which bans all physical contact between students. This includes holding hands, hugging and even giving each other high fives. The intent of the rule is to reduce fighting and inappropriate touching.[78] Other school districts are adopting similar policies. Do you agree with this policy? Why or why not?
- In all but two states in the U.S., New York and Florida, defense teams in sexual assault cases are still allowed to present evidence pertaining to the dress of the victim at the time of the attack. They can argue the victim's clothing or lack thereof, communicated a message that sexual intimacy was desired or that the defendant was confused by the way the victim was dressed or behaving. What do you think of this argument?[79]
- In some states, citizens can be charged with assault if it appears that they are about to strike a person. Raising a hand, clenching a fist, of holding an object in a manner which suggest one is going to strike another is grounds for arrest on criminal charges. Acting as if you are going to be violent is considered assault. Coming in actual contact is battery. Do you agree with this law? Why or why not.[80] Do you feel there is a double standard in our society that allows athletes in professional sports such as hockey to physically assault each other, without facing legal or criminal consequences?
- Find and be prepared to share a helpful tip, interesting fact, or thought provoking theory relating to one of the following fields of study:

  Haptics: The study of touch.

  Olfactics: The study of smell.

  Chronemics: The study of time.

  Proxemics: The study of space.

Unit 9 Vocabulary Review

___ Nonverbal Communication
___ Leakage
___ Microexpressions
___ Turn-taking Behaviors
___ Kinesics
___ Posture
___ Chronemics
___ Proxemics
___ Olfactics_____
___ Olfactic Association
___ Facial Management Techniques
___ Paralanguage
___ Enunciation
___ Pronunciation
___ Oculesics
___ Vocal Utterances
___ Polychronic
___ Monochronic
___ Artifacts
___ Gesticulations
___ Haptics

A. The inclination of a person or culture to manage time more casually, with a more relaxed view of timelines.

B. The use of one's arms and hands to communicate.

C. The study of smell.

D. The silence fillers we use between sentences like, "um, uh, and uh, er, ya know."

E. Our unconscious, automatic nonverbal expressions.

F. Sudden, spontaneous facial expressions which often reveal what we are thinking or feeling at a given moment.

G. The inclination of a person or culture to strictly adhere to timelines and do things expeditiously.

H. The study of how people communicate messages through body movement.

I. Saying a word correctly based on dictionary rules.

J. How we stand or sit.

K. The study of touch and how it communicates messages.

L. Any aspect of a message which does not involve spoken or written language.

M. When we make an association between a scent and a memory.

N. The facial expressions we make for a desired effect.

O. The study of eye behavior.

P. How we use our voice or modulate our vocal sounds.

Q. Saying a word clearly and succinctly.

R. The objects within an environment which may communicate messages about an owner.

S. The study of how people use time.

T. The scientific study of how people use space.

U. The behaviors applied in our conversations to let each other know when we are going to take turns speaking and listening.

Exercise

Find a spot at the mall where you can comfortably observe people. Take at least thirty minutes and watch people's nonverbal behaviors. You can also do this at an event where there are a lot of people (festival, concert, or park). Notice the different types of nonverbal expression: how people walk, their clothing and artifacts, posture, gestures, eye contact, and facial expressions. What are some of the perceptions you formed based on what you observed? How might they be incorrect? Did you notice any differences in people's nonverbal behavior based on age, race, culture, or gender? How about between children and parents? What was it about people's behavior which made you think that two people were romantically involved or just friends? What other information can you gather about people simply by looking at their nonverbal expression?

Emotions

10

Emotions Unit 10

Emotions such as love, anger, joy, and frustration are influenced by and affect our interpersonal communication. Unit 10 provides suggestions for how to best identify, manage, and express our emotions.

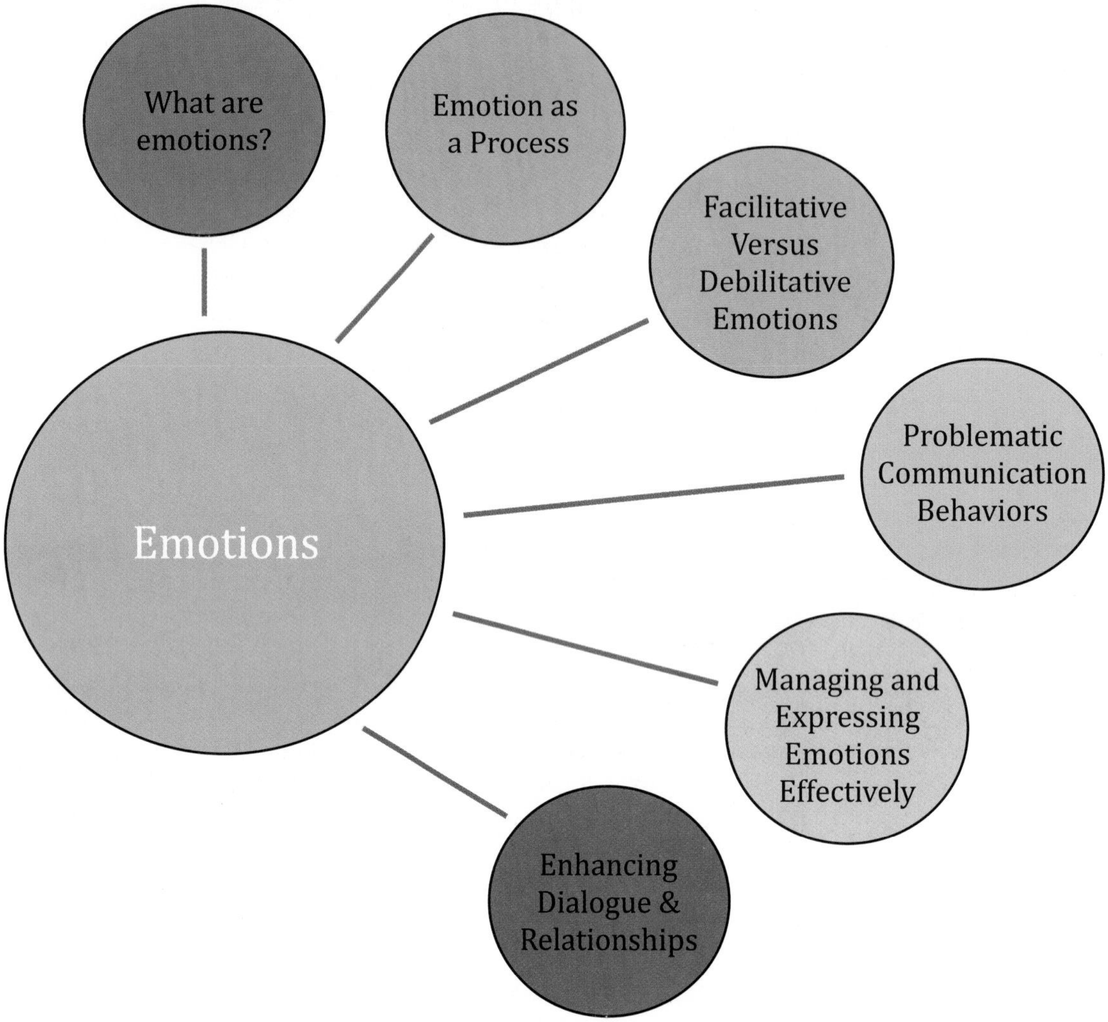

Unit 10 Learning Objectives

As a result of reading and studying Unit 10, you will be able to:

1. Define emotion and know the difference between emotions and moods.
2. Describe the process of human emotion.
3. Explain the facilitative and debilitative aspects of emotions.
4. Identify various communication behaviors which tend to evoke negative emotions and cause problems in relationships.
5. Understand how to manage and express emotions effectively.
6. Identify communication practices which enhance dialogue and relationships.

After a heated argument, a husband and wife refused to talk to each other. They continued giving each other the "silent treatment" for over a week. Just before going to bed one night, the husband realized he needed his wife to help him wake up at 5:00 a.m. the next morning. He had a tendency to sleep through his alarm clock, and he didn't want to miss an early bird flight for an extremely important business meeting, one he hoped would land him a big sales contract. He did not want to break his silence and lose, so he wrote on a note, "Please wake me up at 5:00 a.m.—very important." He left it on her pillow where she would find it. The next morning he woke up and was shocked to see it was 9:00 a.m.! He had missed his flight. Next to his head was a note which read, "It's 5:00 a.m. Wake up."

Elizabeth Kenny once said, "He who angers you conquers you." **A lot of what we say and do is driven by our emotions.** We see this truth dramatized daily at work, at home, and in the media. Emotions are a potential source of external and internal noise. Noise is anything that interferes with our ability to effectively send and receive messages. Research suggests that people generally communicate less effectively when they are experiencing negative emotions. People say things they otherwise would not say when they are angry, sad, enraged, resentful, annoyed, frustrated, or stressed.[1, 2] On the flip side, even positive emotions like extreme happiness, excitement, or love may interfere with our ability to communicate clearly, listen effectively, and respond patiently.[3, 4] A single communication act can spark negative emotions and trigger what is called a conflict spiral.[5]

A **conflict spiral** is an argument which escalates or worsens as it continues. Each subsequent communication act gets progressively more antagonistic and accusatory. A conflict spiral is often sparked and fed by communication "games" people play. In the anecdote at the beginning of the unit, a husband and wife were ignoring each other or withholding interaction. People often rely on certain communication behaviors to express their anger, resentment, or frustration. They also use their communication to "punish" a wrongdoer for something he or she did or didn't do.[6, 7]

Disagreements are expected in relationships. Mahatma Gandhi said, "Honest disagreement is often a good sign of progress." Conflict is a sign that people care about something or about the relationship. While conflict is normal and in some ways necessary, what we want to avoid is conflict which turns ugly. Conflict becomes dysfunctional when there are threats, physical and emotional abuse, mean spiritedness, uncooperativeness, and/or a win–lose or lose–lose outcome. This unit will explore how to express our emotions in ways which are healthy and enhance relationships. Let's begin by defining emotions and understanding emotions as a process.

What Are Emotions?

Affective communication is communication about and involving our emotions. There are numerous definitions for and theories explaining human emotion. We often use the words emotions and feelings interchangeably. An **emotion** is a biochemical, physiological, and psychological response to an event. For example, memories or the mental associations we make elicit emotions. While driving down the highway, we may find ourselves feeling a sudden sense of sadness as soon as a certain song comes on the radio. We may associate the song or its lyrics to a lost love. We may start to smile or chuckle to ourselves as we remember something funny from the past. The memory triggers a sudden burst of happiness or amusement.

Our emotions are reactions to what is going on in our environment. For example, our emotions are influenced by the emotions of others. **Emotional contagion** occurs when people transfer feelings to one another.[8] Like a virus, we spread our emotions to others. We see this at a funeral or a wedding. The sadness or happiness expressed at these events permeates the atmosphere. Feelings spread and are shared by everyone in attendance. If we are out to lunch with a friend, and she is bubbly, enthusiastic, and upbeat, chances are we will begin to experience similar feelings. Have you ever gotten into a laughing frenzy, where you and a friend couldn't stop laughing about something? This is emotional contagion.

We also experience certain emotional states or moods for a variety of reasons. A **mood** is a feeling, which has no identifiable cause and typically lasts for a while.[9] For example, we may feel something which may have little or nothing to do with what is happening around us. We may feel like we are in a funk, but don't really know why. Our "funk" may last for a couple hours, a day, a week or longer. The body's production of certain hormones and brain chemicals are definitely linked to emotions. Now that we know what emotions are and the difference between emotions and moods, let's examine emotion as a process.

"You know, your mood swings are kinda giving me whiplash."
Isabella Swan from *Twilight* (2008)

. . . What is human emotion? What is the difference between emotions and moods?

Emotion as a Process

Harvard professor and psychologist William James and physiologist Carl Lange proposed the James-Lange theory back in the late 1800s, which has served as the foundation for explaining the process of human emotion. Their theory suggested that events cause emotions. The James-Lange theory is represented in the visual below. Other psychologists and physiologists such as Walter Cannon, Phillip Bard, James Papez, and Paul MacLean studied and refined the James-Lange theory throughout the early 1900s.[10, 11]

Activating event = emotional response.

Some psychologists theorize that an event doesn't trigger an emotion. Instead, they argue it is what a person thinks about an event that influences the duration and intensity of an emotion.[12] Albert Ellis, who developed **rational–emotive theory**, believed that a person's interpretation of an event ultimately had more significance than anything a person could encounter. Ellis' theory can be simplified using the following model:

Activating Event >>>>> Cognitive Interpretation of Event = Emotional Response

For example, let's say we interview for a job that we really want. We go through three interviews and make it to the final round. We receive a rejection letter. The event is the news that we

Interpretation #1	Emotional Response
"This was the job of my dreams. I'll never find anything like this again. I must not be hirable. What did I do wrong? I'm going to be stuck with some meaningless job for the rest of my life."	Anguish and Hopelessness
Interpretation #2	**Emotional Response**
"Well, I was qualified. There are other jobs out there that I can go for. This is just a minor setback. I am very disappointed, but I know I will snag a good job, if not a better one, soon. It's their loss."	Disappointment and Determination

Do you agree that our emotional response is likely going to be different depending on how we chose to interpret the event? Why or why not?

did not get the job. The meaning we attach to the news will influence our emotional reaction. Assume we choose one of the following two interpretations. Notice how the emotional response to each interpretation is different.

Many contemporary psychologists and physiologists believe that a more accurate model to describe our emotional reaction to events would show that **our cognitive interpretation and emotional response to an event occur simultaneously**.[13] The model they use to explain emotion as a response mechanism would look like this:

Activating Event >>>> Perceptual Awareness of event = Cognitive Interpretation and Physiological Response

Let's use a communication scenario to demonstrate this model. We are at work, and we overhear a coworker talking about us in an uncomplimentary way. The coworker's opinion is the activating event. Our perceptual awareness of the comments comes from what we hear. Just as we cognitively interpret (decode) the words as an affront to our reputation and an unjustified character assassination, we are also experiencing an increase in body temperature, heart rate, and muscle tension. Our nervous system triggers the release of hormones such as cortisol and norepinephrine. This cognitive interpretation and physiological response is anger.[14]

The many theories explaining emotion have their merit and warrant thoughtful consideration. Most researchers believe that we all experience certain basic emotions such as anger, joy, fear, and sadness.[15] Beyond that, there are other emotions that researchers believe we experience, but there is not a lot of agreement as to what they all are. Robert Plutchik created an emotion wheel to describe what he considers the eight primary emotions: expectancy, joy, acceptance, fear, surprise, sadness, disgust, and anger.

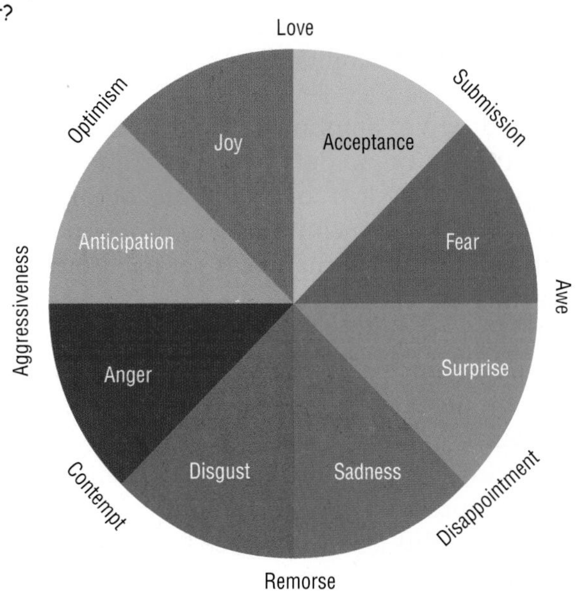

Plutchik's Emotion Wheel

When we experience more than one primary emotion at the same time, we call this **mixed emotions**. According to Plutchik's wheel, if we feel a blend of disgust and sadness, this is called *remorse*. A mix of sadness and surprise is *disappointment*.[16]

Cultures have created their own vocabulary to identify various types of emotions.[17] Cultures also vary in terms of how males and females are socialized to display emotions. In other words, most of us are raised to adhere to certain **gender display rules**, which are normative ways to express our emotions according to cultural expectations.[18] In American culture, what are some of our gender display rules?

Some emotions serve a valuable purpose. Others may hinder our ability to communicate and function effectively.

. . . How would you explain emotion as a process?

Facilitative Versus Debilitative Emotions

Emotions have facilitative and debilitative potential. **Facilitative emotions** assist us or motivate us to perform important tasks; whereas, **debilitative emotions** interfere with effective functioning. Emotions can vary in duration and intensity. The duration and intensity of an emotion often determines whether it is facilitative or debilitative.

Facilitative emotions might include the nervousness or anxiety we feel right before competition. A low or moderate amount of nervousness causes our body to function at its peak level of performance. It serves a facilitative purpose because our heartbeat has quickened. Our body has increased its blood sugar and adrenaline secretions. Extreme nervousness or anxiety, however, can impede performance, making it debilitative. It can affect such things as our coordination, concentration, thought processes, and breathing.[19] A great example of this is when we see a person hyperventilating. He or she appears immobilized and incoherent.

Facilitative emotions such as eager anticipation can motivate us to work harder for something we desire. Even a feeling such as irritation or anger may serve as a catalyst for positive action. Debilitative feelings such as intense anger are major causes of road rage, violence, and property destruction. An emotional state that lasts too long, such as depression, is very debilitative if it causes us to lose our will to live or leaves us unmotivated to carry out daily tasks. Research conducted by Dr. Barbara Fredrickson, Distinguished Professor of Psychology at the University of North Carolina at Chapel Hill, strongly suggests that people who experience and express more positive emotions live longer compared to those who don't.[20, 21]

Not expressing our feelings or expressing them ineffectively can exacerbate stress, anxiety, and depression. If our emotions go unchecked, it also impedes our ability to think and communicate rationally and problem solve. How many times have we said something in the heat of anger and later regretted it? What happens when we bottle up negative feelings for prolonged periods of time? Often, they get unleashed on an innocent, unsuspecting victim who was at the wrong place at the wrong time. We call this **displacement**.

Misdirected aggression, unsatisfying relationships, and social isolation are often the result of poor affective management and expression.[22] When people function in teams at work, certain behaviors such as fault finding, hostile questioning, excessive joking, demands, or threats often surface when conflict is not resolved or negative emotions are allowed to linger. It is important to note that when it comes to our emotions and our communication, what we say or do will affect others. Being able to identify, express, and manage our feelings is directly tied to communication competency and emotional maturity.[23] In the 2007 comedy *Blades of Glory*, rival Olympic ice skaters Jimmy MacElroy (Jon Heder) and Chazz Michaels (Will Ferrell) are stripped of their gold medals for Tonya Harding-like unsportsmanlike conduct and permanently banned from men's single competition. They find a loophole to still compete as the first-ever male pair team. They are forced to quickly adjust to their new working relationship and overcome their differences. This is not without a lot of confrontation, as the following dialogue illustrates:

Jimmy: "You ruined my dreams!" (blaming)

Chazz: "Dreams? What do you know about dreams?" (indirect put down)

Jimmy: "Zip it, Chazz, just zip it, or I'll punch you in your crap-lousy face!" (threat and a verbal attack)

Chazz: "Hey, this ends tonight!" (threat)

Jimmy: "It's daytime, you douche!" (verbal attack)

The communication exchange between Chazz and Jimmy demonstrates a conflict spiral. For example, Jimmy's threat, "I'll punch you in your crap-lousy face," triggers a defensive response from Chazz, who retaliates with: "Hey, this ends tonight!" Each subsequent threat begets another. Reciprocity kicks in. **Reciprocity** as a theory suggests that people tend to return what is dished to out to them during communication. Reciprocity was explored back in 1973 by social psychologist Irwin Altman as it pertained to self-disclosure and a perspective developed with Dalmas Taylor called the Social Penetration Theory. He found that people tend to open up and share personal information in response to someone else's self-disclosure, especially if both parties perceive its intent and outcome positively.[24]

Communication behaviors such as blaming, threatening, or personal attacks are often defense mechanisms used to save face or protect our ego when we feel personally attacked. When we receive messages which challenge the image we have of ourselves or want to project to others (public face), we feel compelled to deflect the message with face-preserving responses. Often, our responses mimic the type of message we are receiving. We also see blaming and personal attacks between Chazz and Jimmy: "You ruined my dreams," and ". . . you douche." To blame someone is to make someone else at fault. Verbal attacks involve evaluative words or labels whose meanings are derogatory or belittling.

Since the purpose of this book is to improve our communication with others, our focus is on how emotion affects, and is affected by, our ability to communicate. For the remainder of this unit, we'll look at communication behaviors which tend to cause relational problems and inflame negative emotions in others. Next, we'll explore communication behaviors and approaches supported by research as effective in curbing unnecessary discord and improving positive affective exchanges.

Your Turn: Describe a time when you experienced an emotion which served a facilitative and debilitative purpose. . . . What is the difference between a facilitative and debilitative emotion? How would you explain the difference using an example?

Problematic Communication Behaviors

Certain communication behaviors can really get under people's skin. They tend to provoke and prolong conflict. When we are guilty of these behaviors, we may also cause others to develop negative perceptions of us. Most communication and relationship experts agree that the behaviors described in this next section test people's nerves in some way.

After reading about each behavior, do some self-monitoring. You may recall from previous units that self-monitoring is a mental process of analyzing our communication with others. A scale is provided for you. The numbers represent the frequency by which we are guilty of committing this behavior, with the number 1 representing "rarely" and 10 "a lot." Identify how often you do the behavior. Be honest with yourself. You may also ask a few people who know you well to rate you. Is there a difference between your perception and theirs?

Blaming

O.A. Battista once said, "Placing the blame is a bad habit, but taking the blame is a sure builder of character." What is blaming? Blaming assigns fault to someone else or an outside force for one's failure, malice, or negligence. Blaming places responsibility for an outcome on someone or something other than ourselves. People vary in terms of how often they pass or accept blame. Here are two examples to distinguish between the two.

Passing blame

"The professor made the exam impossible. He expects way too much."

Accepting blame

"It is my own fault that I wasn't prepared for the exam. I could have studied more."

A person who accepts blame versus passes blame takes ownership of and responsibility for his or her actions, thoughts, and emotions. He or she is more likely to operate from what is called an internal locus of control. The concept was originated by psychologist Julian Rotter in the 1950s. A person with an **internal locus of control** makes herself accountable for her decisions and their outcomes.

Do you perceive that your destiny is greatly influenced by you as opposed to external forces such as the economy, luck, God, or other people? Do you believe you are the master of your fate? If you respond in the affirmative, you conceptualize the world with an internal locus of control. A person with an **external locus of control** perceives that outside factors will determine the outcome of an event more so than one's own actions.[25, 26] He or she tends to look outside him or herself for answers to explain personal failure or inertia. A person with an external locus of control is more inclined to "pass the buck," make excuses, or feign helplessness.

I do this:

Rarely Often A lot

1 2 3 4 5 6 7 8 9 10

Do you perceive people who accept versus pass blame differently? How?

Past Digging

Past digging occurs when we drudge up something from the past in an effort to "win" an argument or drive home a point. We bring up past hurts, misdeeds, fights, or conversations to make our case. An example of this is evident in the exchange between Jeremy Grey (Vince Vaughn) and John Beckwith (Owen Wilson) in *Wedding Crashers* (2005):

Jeremy: "Oh, that's terrific! Why don't you just feed me to the lions? Step on my head when I am drowning."

John: "What?"

Jeremy: "What do you mean 'what'? What a great friend, John. This is completely against the rules. You have a wedding and a reception to seal the deal. Period. There's no overtime."

John: "No overtime. Yeah, well what about the Chang wedding three years ago? 2 a.m.! You drag me fifty miles to watch you and some chick play Mah-Jongg with her grandmother in a retirement home."

Past digging often results in a tit-for-tat exchange where one person slams the other by bringing up something from the past. **We often past dig to prove that: "You've done more wrong than I have."** It can also feed bitterness because one may perceive the other as unwilling to forgive and forget: "Why can't you let this go?" "Here you go again!" "Do you always have to bring that up?" "I thought we've been through all this!"

A form of past digging which can be damaging to a relationship is called **below-the-belt punching**. An example of this is when we share something very personal about ourselves to someone we trust. This person later takes advantage of this vulnerable self-disclosure to attack us in some way. This behavior was coined belt lining by researcher and clinical psychologist George Bach and author Peter Wyden in their 1968 book *The Intimate Enemy.*[27] Here is another example. A guy shares with his girlfriend something he did in a previous relationship that he is not proud of. Later on, he gets in an argument with his girlfriend and in a fit of anger she says: "Well I'm not Sarah. I'm not going to let you do to me what you did to her." Ouch! That's below the belt.

I do this:

Rarely				Often					A lot
1	2	3	4	5	6	7	8	9	10

Verbal Attacking

Verbal attacks include calling a person names or using evaluative language which is demeaning or degrading. We may label a person's behavior or attributes with words which carry a very negative connotation in an attempt to bruise his or her ego or self-concept. **People resort to name calling to win an argument, save face, and exert power by inflicting psychological pain.** Take the words from Dr. Cox of *Scrubs* (2001), played by John C. McGinley and Donald Trump of *The Apprentice:*

Dr. Cox: "Yes, hello? Could we please get my *hormonal, extremely annoying* ex-wife's amnio underway?"

Trump: "Nick, I don't know why you think you're such a great salesman. Your performance was *terrible*."

A close cousin to verbal attacking is **criticizing**. A person who criticizes a lot points out a person's shortcomings. He or she is quick to note out loud a person's flaws. She or he is often perceived by others as very opinionated and negative. Criticizing is evident in the dialogue between Mike Myer's character, Dr. Evil and his son Scott in the movie *Austin Powers (1997:)*

Scott: "Why did you run out on me?"

Dr. Evil: "Because you are not quite evil enough . . . Well, it's true! You're semi-evil. You're quasi-evil. You're the margarine of evil. You're the Diet Coke of evil. Just one calorie, not enough evil."

I do this:

Rarely				Often					A lot
1	2	3	4	5	6	7	8	9	10

Placating

Placating is agreeing or going along with others despite how one may really feel. Family therapist and author Virginia Satir (1972) describes this behavior in her book *Peoplemaking*. Often placating is done to appease or pacify the other person. A placater is overly accommodating: "Go ahead," "I'm fine with it." "Whatever you want is okay." This is done to avoid confrontation or unpleasantness. A person may placate because she or he lacks the ability to express disagreement or needs assertively.[28]

I do this:

Rarely				Often					A lot
1	2	3	4	5	6	7	8	9	10

Interrupting

In unit 5, we discussed this behavior. Interrupting is cutting in on a person who is talking before he or she has a chance to finish a sentence or thought. Interrupting also involves talking over a person until someone backs down.

I do this:

Rarely				Often					A lot
1	2	3	4	5	6	7	8	9	10

Stage-hogging

A behavior associated with interrupting is stage-hogging. Stage-hogging occurs when we attempt to dominate a conversation or shift the focus of a conversation on ourselves. It smacks of: "It's all about me." **The stage-hogger loves the spotlight and is often long winded.** In the following exchange between Sarah and Farrah, Farrah shifts the focus of the conversation toward what she is interested in talking about before Sarah finishes her thought.

Sarah: "We had the most delightful vacation on this quaint little tropical gem."

Farrah: "Where did you go?"

Sarah: "You may not have heard of it. It's called Fantasy Island. We arrived early . . . "

Farrah: (interrupting) "No way! We were there just three months ago. We were greeted by this little man in a white suit who kept saying, 'The plane! The plane! The plane!' He was so cute. This older gentlemen, very distinguished with impeccable style, spoke in this very unique accent. He said we could make a wish and live out our lives on the island in any manner our hearts desired . . ."(blah, blah, blah).

I do this:

Rarely				Often					A lot
1	2	3	4	5	6	7	8	9	10

Bragging

"I don't know how to put this, but, I'm kind of a big deal." This statement was an attempt by Ron Burgundy (Will Ferrell) to impress his new love interest, Veronica Corningstone (Christina Applegate) in *Anchorman* (2004). It, based on Corningstone's reaction, didn't appear to work.

Bragging is boastful, arrogant talk. Sydney J. Harris once said, "It's a curious psychological fact that the man who seems 'egotistical' is not suffering from too much ego, but from too little." Whether that is true or not, bragging is a behavior that is best kept at a minimum. We all like to toot our horns once in awhile. There is nothing wrong with letting people know how proud we feel about our accomplishments and sharing our successes with them from time to time. We need to feel respected, appreciated, and valued. When a person strokes our ego with a compliment, it feels good.

> **"You can make more friends in two months by becoming interested in other people than you can in two years trying to get other people interested in you."**
> **—Dale Carnegie**

People who brag too much are perceived as bigheaded. A research team found that subjects who made boastful statements during their interaction were perceived by both men and women as less socially savvy and sensitive.[29] People may also take a braggart less seriously. Bragging may result in someone calling us out on our claim with the challenge: "Oh, yeah, prove it," or "Put your money where your mouth is." We may not be ready for this, thus proving the saying "his brag is worse than his fight."

Excessive boasting may also breed competition and jealousy. We can avoid this by curbing our self-aggrandizement and showing interest in other people's goals and successes.

I do this:

Rarely				Often					A lot
1	2	3	4	5	6	7	8	9	10

Gunny-sacking

Gunny-sacking is a communication behavior which involves keeping one's negative thoughts and feelings to oneself for prolonged periods of time. Instead of letting people know how we feel about their communication or behavior, we hold it inside or pack it away in this metaphorical gunnysack we strap across our shoulders and carry with us. The more we keep this up, the heavier the sack gets until a major or minor wrongdoing occurs. The contents of the bag spill out, and the recipient is treated to a plethora of past misdeeds and accusations. Each wrongdoing is lumped with a scorecard of past offenses. Often the recipient is completely oblivious to many of them. Sometimes, the gunny sacker may unload on a person who doesn't deserve the heat.

I do this:

Rarely				Often					A lot
1	2	3	4	5	6	7	8	9	10

Negating

Negating involves taking the opposite position. Someone who habitually negates disagrees even when it is not necessary. Some people like to disagree just for the sake of disagreeing. They like to argue the contrary. Take this scene from the novel *The Accidental Tourist* by Anne Tyler. Note how Muriel negates everything Macon says without making an attempt to understand or validate him.

Macon: "I don't think Alexander is getting a good education."

Muriel: "Oh, he is o.k." (negates)

Macon: "I asked him to figure what change they'd give back when we bought the milk today, and he didn't have the faintest idea. He didn't even know he'd have to subtract."

Muriel: "Well, he's only in second grade." (negates)

Macon: "I think he ought to switch to a private school."

Muriel: "Private schools cost money." (negates)

In this interaction, Muriel could validate Macon by saying: "I can see this has you concerned. You want the best for Alexander. I appreciate you sharing this with me. I'm also very impressed that you're willing to pay for private school. Do you think we should talk to his teacher to see what our less expensive options are first before putting him in private school?" Instead, Muriel downplays Macon's concerns and counters with opposing statements.

I do this:

Rarely				Often					A lot
1	2	3	4	5	6	7	8	9	10

Avoiding

Avoiding is staying away from or not acknowledging or addressing something or someone. We avoid interactions that are emotionally unpleasant, take up too much time, or tax our patience. **When we rely on avoidance, certain topics and levels of intimacy are dodged.** This strategy involves dancing around things in our conversations.

We may attempt to change the subject, pretend we're sleeping, or act really busy. We may hide in our office with our door closed to avoid a coworker, act like everything is fine with our romantic partner at home, or not answer a person's phone call. We also use avoidance as a strategy when we experience what is called cognitive dissonance. The **cognitive dissonance theory** originates from the field of psychology. Social psychologist Leon Festinger first described this in his 1957 book *When Prophecy*

Fails. It suggests that people get psychologically uncomfortable when they experience opposing thoughts, needs, or behaviors at the same time.

Cognitive dissonance occurs when our beliefs clash with new information, other needs, or behavior.[30, 31] For example, we may believe that a certain behavior is bad, yet find ourselves doing the very same behavior. We may want to be honest, but feel compelled to lie. We may think that abortion for any reason is morally wrong. We may experience cognitive dissonance when we begin to question those beliefs upon learning that we face an unplanned pregnancy. The expression, "I'd like to have a relationship with you, but I'm not ready" typifies cognitive dissonance. When we experience cognitive dissonance, we sometimes resort to avoiding the things or people who are the source of our internal conflict.

Ronald Adler and Neil Towns' authoritative text, *Looking Out/Looking In* highlights certain strategies we rely on to avoid things such as repression, feigned apathy, regression, and sarcasm.

Repression
We mentally block out what we don't want to hear or deal with.

Feigned apathy
We appear to not care to avoid acknowledging unpleasant truths.

Regression
We play helpless. We fabricate an inability to do something.

Withdrawing
We shut down or become non-communicative. This may occur because we don't know how to express our thoughts, or are fearful of saying what is on our minds.

Relentless Joking
Someone who engages in relentless joking uses humor to sidestep an uncomfortable topic or skirt an issue. By joking around, bellying it up, or acting like Jim Carey, he or she successfully evades discussing things directly.[32]

Unfortunately, avoiding conversations doesn't make problems go away. Problems that are not addressed may worsen and fester. New problems may surface, and like cancer, spread to other areas.

I do this:

Rarely				Often					A lot
1	2	3	4	5	6	7	8	9	10

Withholding

Withholding involves keeping something from another person as a form of punishment. It is also an act to exert power. Ever get the "silent treatment?" This is when we are ignored or get the cold shoulder. **A person withholds love, affection, interaction, or attention to make a point.** He or she may not give us an answer, return our phone call, or include us in a social event. School children may exercise withholding by booting a classmate from their clique or by not allowing someone to sit with them at lunch.

Don McCabe, author of *To Teach a Dyslexic,* writes of how he would withhold something as simple as eye contact as a way to vent his frustrations with teachers he considered unsympathetic to his learning disability. He writes:

> *"I enjoyed baiting teachers. My favorite stunt was to look out the window while the teacher was talking and act like I was not paying attention. Of course I was listening intently. Inevitably, the teacher would try to make an example out of me. The teacher would call on me, fully expecting me to say 'What?' And then she could tell me to pay attention. Only it never worked that way. I would answer the question without bothering to turn my head! More than once the teacher was so furious that I could look out the window and still answer the question that I was sent down to Mr. Mehring's office."*[33]

I do this:

Rarely				Often					A lot
1	2	3	4	5	6	7	8	9	10

Sugar Coating

People who sugar coat hate to clash or allow negative feelings to linger. They feel a strong need to be overly positive about things when problems surface. They are extra nice after a heated exchange and try to get things back on track in a flash by being overtly sweet and pleasant. They may downplay the conflict, make light of it, or act as if everything is o.k. **They may rely on fake flattery, gift giving, or go out of their way to help someone with something, even though there is still hostility or unresolved conflict.**

I do this:

Rarely				Often					A lot
1	2	3	4	5	6	7	8	9	10

Deprecating Humor

Deprecating humor is subtle mean-spirited humor designed to wound. The deprecating humorist uses sarcasm and usually pretends to be "just kidding." The word *sarcasm* originates from the Greek language, meaning "to bite the lips in rage; sneer." For example, a person at work cuts a doughnut in half and says, "I'm going to be good and only eat half." A coworker replies, "Just take the whole thing. You know you're going to come back later when no one is around for the other half." We see this kind of humor exchanged between Jake Perry (Josh Lucas) and his estranged wife Melanie Carmichael (Reese Witherspoon) after she surprises him one day at his house with divorce papers for him to sign after a long separation in the 2002 romantic comedy *Sweet Home Alabama* and in the television comedy *Scrubs* (2001) *starring* Judy Reyes as nurse Carla and Zach Braff as Dr. J.D.:

Jake: "You show up here, after seven years, without so much as a 'Hey there, Jake, remember me . . . your wife?!' Or a, 'Hi honey, lookin' good. How's the family?' "

Melanie: "You expect me to tell you that you look good? What, did they run out of soap at the Piggly Wiggly since I left?"

Carla: [about a male intern] "You're right; he definitely has a cute little butt."

Elliot: "It's almost like it's been sculpted."

J.D.: "Who cares? Everyone has a cute butt; I have a cute butt."

Carla: "You should bring it in someday."

© NBC/Photofest

A deprecating humorist will often say the opposite of what he or she really means. He or she will make a sly remark, which on the surface seems innocent, yet really delivers a putdown. The following comment made by Eric Weiss (Greg Grunberg) to Michael Vaughn (Michael Vartan) in the television series *Alias* (2002) illustrates this:

Eric: "Mike, I'm not going to trivialize your relationship with her by calling it a crush . . ."

Here, Eric underplays the relationship by suggesting what he already thinks about Mike's relationship with a young woman.

I do this:

Rarely				Often					A lot
1	2	3	4	5	6	7	8	9	10

We Speaking

We speaking occurs when someone appoints him or herself as a spokesperson for the group—often to forward his or her own agenda. "We are not liking this idea," or "we all know this isn't going to work" are examples. As he or she is speaking on our behalf, we're thinking "Wait a minute! There's no 'me' in 'we.'"

I do this:

Rarely				Often					A lot
1	2	3	4	5	6	7	8	9	10

Bulldozing

Also called "steamrolling," bulldozing is a tough one to deal with. **Bulldozing** involves making a decision and not budging or refusing to consider another person's point of view or idea. **The bulldozer won't compromise or negotiate**. He or she makes demands. "It's my way or the highway," or "This is how it's going to be—period! He or she refuses to factor in new information or allow for further discussion—"I don't want to hear it, " or "That's not going to work for me, it's either yes or no." This leaves people feeling forced to go along with something with little or no input or power.

I do this:

Rarely				Often					A lot
1	2	3	4	5	6	7	8	9	10

© Arman Zhenikeyev, 2010. Used under license from Shutterstock, Inc.

Threatening

A threat is a statement that implies that there will be some sort of punishment or negative consequence if something does or doesn't happen. Threats involve issuing ultimatums. The words "If you don't, then . . . .," "Fine, I'll just . . .," or "consider yourself uninvited." "You will or else" usually precedes the threat. It is hard to sit through a single television episode and not hear at least several threats in the dialogue. The following are examples of threats made by characters from a variety of television shows:

Cadpig: "Rolly, gluttony is one of the seven deadly sins, and if you do that to me again, I'm going to violate the other six on you!" *101 Dalmations* (1997)

Officer Tom: "Fine. I see I'm going to have to put this into terms you can understand. That's my stepbrother, Douglas. He's kinda lame, but it's not his fault. You kick his tail, he tells my stepdad. My stepdad kicks my tail. Then I'm going to have to come back here and kick your tail." 21 *Jump Street* (1987)

Bridget: "I'm going to have a long-distance, monogamous relationship with my virgin boyfriend just to spite you." *8 Simple Rules . . . for Dating My Teenage Daughter* (2002)

I do this:

Rarely				Often					A lot
1	2	3	4	5	6	7	8	9	10

Guilt Tripping

Guilt-tripping is a behavior which implies in an indirect way that if we don't do what a person wants, we must not care about or love the person the way we should. It also suggests that we have warped priorities or are not doing the right thing. The following dialogue was used successfully by my mom to get my sister and me to do something:

Bev: "If you don't want to pick blueberries with me today, I understand. I'll just do it all by myself in the heat without anyone to talk to. I wouldn't want you to feel inconvenienced with something I look forward to doing as a family just once a year."

(This is where we get the sad looks and drawn out, despondent sighs)

Bruce & Cheryl: "Ok. Ok. Mom. We'll do it."

I do this:

Rarely				Often					A lot
1	2	3	4	5	6	7	8	9	10

Bossing

Bossing involves issuing demands or commands when one doesn't have the implicit authority to do so. People who rely a lot on bossing have a high need for control and often lack the skills to encourage dialogue, collaboration, or compromising. Examples include: "I want that report immediately," "You'd better deal with this," and "Take that back right now."

To appear less bossy in our interpersonal interactions, we may replace a command with a request. In American business environments, people who are in leadership roles with established power often will ask a subordinate to do something versus telling him or her to do it. A CEO may ask his administrative secretary, "Would you please bring me the Initech account file?" versus "Go get me the Initech account file." Why? She poses her directive as a request. Clearly, the secretary is going to say "yes." This polite, less authoritative approach gives the administrative secretary a sense that he is respected as a professional and creates a perception that the two are a team with different, but equally important, roles.[34]

I boss people around:

Rarely				Often					A lot
1	2	3	4	5	6	7	8	9	10

Relentless Debating

Relentless debating involves not taking "no" for an answer. A person will try to convince, persuade, arm twist, and cajole us until we are worn down and submit. She will ask you what you think or want, and if we don't give her the answer she's looking for, she'll launch into a series of questions to try to get us to give in such as "How about . . . ?" "What if . . . ?" "Why not . . . ?" and "We could . . . ?" He may come back us later and say, "I have an idea . . ." in order to try to package the information in a more appealing way.

© hightowernrw, 2010. Used under license from Shutterstock, Inc.

I do this:

Rarely				Often					A lot
1	2	3	4	5	6	7	8	9	10

Passive-Aggressiveness

People who resort to **passive–aggressive** behavior appear to support or agree with something when they actually don't. They may also harbor unspoken resentment about something. Rather than speak to us directly about their feelings, they covertly attempt to sabotage our efforts by doing such things as hiding things we need, taking longer to return our phone calls, "forgetting" to do something, feigning ignorance, "accidentally" messing up, or "unknowingly" misinforming people. He or she may allow and indirectly encourage rumors or dissention in our absence.

I do this:

Rarely				Often					A lot
1	2	3	4	5	6	7	8	9	10

Drama Seeking

Drama seeking involves communication behaviors which thrive on and promote conflict and controversy. A drama seeker reacts to problems. He or she is a crises tickler and will say or do things to stir up trouble and problems. A person may accomplish this by leaking information to certain parties to get people worked up, setting up alliances, exaggerating problems, asking questions that put people on the spot, gossiping, getting worked up about an issue, and other passive–aggressive behaviors. He or she gets stuck in a problem and doesn't, despite clear cut solutions, work to resolve it. A person may thrive on chaos because he or she has lived in the midst of it for long periods of time, and it is normal way to exist. Some people are pot stirrers because they want to create a problem where they are asked to come to the rescue. It is a way to get attention and inflate their sense of importance.

I do this:

Rarely Often A lot

1 2 3 4 5 6 7 8 9 10

Complaining

To complain is to focus on what isn't. A complaint draws attention to what is lacking or wrong versus what is abundant or right about a person or situation. The complainer "awfulizes" things and rarely offers up solutions or takes the action necessary to change his or her circumstances. One operates from the mindset that he or she has been shortchanged somehow. Here is a great example of complaining, compliments of Homer Simpson:

Homer: "Can't we go home yet? My feet hurt. All this fresh air is making my hair move. And I don't know how much longer I can complain." The Simpsons (1989).

I do this:

Rarely Often A lot

1 2 3 4 5 6 7 8 9 10

Question? What effect does a complainer have on a team?

Looking to Complain

A distraught woman called the police to complain about her neighbor who she said was guilty of indecent exposure. A police officer arrives and the woman says, "You're just in time. You can catch him in the act right now." She takes the officer up to the second floor bathroom and points out the window, "See, see what I'm talking about? How disgusting!" The officer looks out the window and says, "Because of the closed curtain at the bottom of the window, I can't tell if he is completely naked or not. With frustration, the woman says, "What are you talking about? Sure you can. Here, step up on this stool."

Source: Funneyjokes.com.

Doom-saying

"There's no way I can get this done." "That simply won't work." "Things are only going to get worse." "They'll laugh at my idea." Chances are, you've heard these statements before. **Doom-saying is anticipating an impending calamity or predicting the worst**. The assumption is made, often without hard evidence, that what one fears will happen. Doom-saying often leads to a negative self-fulfilling prophecy. A self-fulfilling prophecy is the result of what is expected. Our expectations often influence the outcome. If we expect the worst, the end result often matches what we are convinced will happen. An example is, "I can't ask him out. He doesn't give me the time of day. If I do, he'll laugh and make some lame excuse and his friends will laugh, and I can't handle that." This expectation influences the person's decision to not ask him out, resulting in a self-fulfilling prophecy.

I do this:

Rarely Often A lot

1 2 3 4 5 6 7 8 9 10

Trapping

Trapping is asking a person to make greater attempts at a certain behavior, but then criticizing or punishing the person when he or she does the very thing asked. For example, Rob says to Rick, "I want you to be honest with me about this." When Rick gives Rob an honest answer, Rob overreacts or punishes Rick. Rob may pull a below-the-belt verbal punch, employ guilt tripping, and/or use withholding methods to chastise Rick. Recall that withholding as a communication behavior may involve denying a person love, affection, time, or attention to communicate a message of disapproval or hurt. We may say, "I really want you to make a decision here." The person does just what we ask. We then criticize, complain about, or otherwise assuage the person to do what we want instead. This is trapping. It will likely cause the person to feel "set up." He or she may be less willing to do what you want in the future.

I do this:

Rarely | Often | A lot

1 2 3 4 5 6 7 8 9 10

Negative Comparison

With a negative comparison, the person compares you to someone else who possesses a characteristic or quality which you appear to lack, or equates you with someone known for a certain undesirable attribute. This is an ego-busting communication act.

Here are some examples:

- "If your father were alive today to see what you're doing with this company, he would be very disappointed."
- "Why can't you be more responsible for your studies like your sister?"
- "Why can't our relationship be like Denise and Michelle's?"
- "You are so like your mother."

I do this:

Rarely | Often | A lot

1 2 3 4 5 6 7 8 9 10

Other Problematic Communication Behaviors

Other communication behaviors which often inflame negative emotions and are potential conflict magnets include the following:

Deception

This occurs when a person discovers we have withheld information or when we get caught telling a lie.

Impervious Admission

When a person refuses to acknowledge responsibility, apologize, or admit wrong.

Kitchen Sinking

All the dirty dishes (issues or problems) are brought into the argument to the point that the original or real issue is lost.

Wheel spinning

The same problem or issue comes up over and over. Both parties talk about it in a cyclical pattern with no resolution. Here we go again!

Insincerity

The person says things which we perceive are not authentic or heartfelt.

Competent communicators consciously strive to eliminate the aforementioned behaviors. Self-monitoring can help us. Each day, we can take some time to analyze some of the significant conversations we've had to determine if we were guilty of any of these behaviors. We can also make a conscious effort to remind ourselves not to repeat these behaviors in the future. In this next section, we explore how communicators can effectively identify and express their emotions before, during, and after communication.

. . . What are some of the problematic communicating behaviors associated with negative emotions? Which three are you most guilty of? Least?

Managing Emotions Effectively

Many things may trigger an emotional response within us. Often people will deliberately say and do things to get a certain reaction from us. When we do react in less effective fashion, we often give control over to this person. For example, people say things which immediately put us on the defensive. We then feel compelled to justify or explain ourselves. They also say things to catch us off guard, causing us to lose sight of the real issue. For example, a person may say, "If you really cared about me, you'd loan me the cash," or "Do you call this customer service? You've got to be kidding me," or "I bet if I wasn't" (ethnic minority group), you wouldn't have pulled me over."

As was mentioned earlier in this unit, research suggests that when emotions run high, our ability to reason and think rationally decreases. Let's look at strategies which help us to improve our affective communication.

Owning Our Emotions

This seems elementary; however, many people struggle with identifying and attaching words to their emotions. Effective communicators recognize their emotions and pinpoint the emotion's activating event. They figure out why they are feeling a certain way even when the cause is not apparent. In a study conducted by a research team led by Dr. Lisa Barrett, professor of psychology at Boston College, it was found that college students who could accurately pinpoint the unpleasant emotions they felt also identified a greater number of effective strategies for dealing with those emotions.[35]

A sign of emotional maturity is when we can acknowledge that an unpleasant emotion originates within us, and not from some other person or thing. [36] In other words, we recognize that the feeling we have toward a person or event is a manifestation or a misguided projection of something within ourselves such as insecurity, jealousy, laziness, pride, lust, gluttony, or greed. The effort to honestly identify the feeling and its root cause is apparent in the following statements:

- "I am angry at myself for not trying hard enough to get the promotion. I'm also jealous of Ben because he made the right moves to land the Xerox account."
- "I am tense that I have chosen not to get to the gym in three days. I'm being lazy. I just have to do it."
- I say I'm frustrated that I don't have time for myself because of the kids, my job, my yard etc., but then I can make time."
- "I am frustrated with myself for letting her talk to me this way. I need to be more assertive."

Effective communicators take ownership of, and accept responsibility for their feelings with their words and actions. Instead of saying, "You make me angry," it is more accurate to say, "I feel angry because . . .". Using the pronoun "I" shows that we are taking ownership of our thoughts, feelings, and perceptions. It is important to realize that no one makes us feel a certain way. We choose to feel a certain way. A person may say something that is critical. We can take offense to it. We can also brush it off. Someone we love may not follow through on something. We can be hurt by it. We can also decide it is not worth a second thought.

People with a strong internal locus of control don't dwell on things they have little control over. They don't allow things from the recent or distant past to dictate how they will live now. The past is the past. Instead, they see that now is the only time they own. They look at what they can do right now to make them feel better. They may choose to get productive with a project, clean out a drawer, exercise, eat something really healthy, meditate, volunteer, go for a nature walk, help a neighbor, or do something that they have been procrastinating.

Effective communicators choose the most accurate words to reflect how they feel. Words have power. Words are the channels we use to express our inner world. We can improve our ability to clearly communicate our feelings by **(1) expanding our affective vocabulary, (2) avoiding powerless language when direct and assertive communication is needed, (3) avoid trigger words, (4) use "I feel . . . when you . . . " statements, employ "I language" which focuses on the behavior we want, (5) follow the five second rule, (6) stay in the present, and (7) focus our conversations on potential solutions.**

Expand Our Affective Vocabulary

Many people have a very limited arsenal of words to accurately convey what is going on affectively. Imagine describing the colors of the world when the only words we know are brown, blue, and green. How would we describe a rose? This description would leave a lot to be desired. We can add the words on the following page to our vocabulary by looking the definitions up and memorizing them. We can also learn a couple words a day by reading a dictionary or thesaurus. Start using these words in your speaking and writing:

Aggravated	Ecstatic	Smug
Thrilled	Apathetic	Intrigued
Wacky	Pensive	Bewildered
Passionate	Free	Interested
Fortunate	Tenacious	Hyper
Peeved	Liberated	Snoopy

Content	Alarmed	Optimistic
Confused	Hopeful	Genial
Jubilant	Distressed	Repulsed
Saucy	Woeful	Overjoyed
Love struck	Woebegone	Absorbed
Miffed	Sentimental	Virulent
Inquisitive	Perplexed	Weary
Petrified	Paralyzed	Delighted
Questioning	Gallant	Indecisive
Crushed	Rapturous	Desirous
Serene	Aching	Hoodwinked
Somber	Frisky	Alienated
Frustrated	Infuriated	Thrilled
Dejected	Mellow	Suspicious
Sympathetic	Glum	Resolute
Timid		

Be More Direct

According to communication research, some of our verbal messages are not clear and direct. They may lead a person to dismiss or underrate what we are saying. For example, speakers who use a lot of hedges appear less confident, competent, and certain about what they are saying.[37, 38] **Hedges** are words such as "kinda," "sort of," "maybe," "a little," "I suppose," and "I guess." **Vocal utterances** such as "uhm," "uh," and "ah, er," and hesitations such as "well," "let's see," "perhaps," "you know," and long pauses suggest uncertainty and discomfort with the topic. Disclaimers generally are received in the same way as hedges. Disclaimers are found in the following statements:

- "I probably have no right to say this, but . . ."
- "I'm not really sure but . . ."
- "I probably shouldn't feel this way," or
- "I know I tend to be overly sensitive, but . . . ,"

Avoid Trigger Words

Along with making our messages more clear, direct, and assertive, we can choose our words carefully. **Certain words are likely to arouse a defensive reaction from a receiver.** Words like "never," "always," and "whatever," are generally not well received. For example, when you say, "You always say that," or "You never apologize," a person is not likely to accept that he "always" or "never" does was we're suggesting, and will feel compelled to prove us wrong.

Compare the statements labeled "A" with the statements labeled "B", which researchers refer to as powerless language. Which statements are more clear and direct, allowing us to fully and accurately express our emotions?[39]

A. "I'm kinda disappointed."

B. "I am disappointed."

A. "I'm a little upset."

B. "I am upset."

A. "Maybe we should try later."

B. "I want to tackle this job tomorrow."

A. "Sure, I guess."

B. "Yes. I want to go."

A. "I'm sort of confused."

B. "I am not clear what you're saying."

A. "Uh, I' know that these are uhm your kids, and not mine but . . ."

B. "I feel uncomfortable that the children have not received their immunizations."

Use "I feel . . ." Statements

When we need to confront a person about an undesirable behavior, we want to avoid evaluative language that attacks the person and his or her identify. For example, we'll want to stay clear of words or labels such as "idiot," "ridiculous," "shallow," "stubborn," or "backward." We will likely receive a better response if we stick with describing the behavior we are seeing and the behavior we want. Compare the negatively charged "you" statements labeled "A", with the more neutral "I feel" statements labeled "B." Which statements are less confrontational?

A. "You can't be counted on."

B. **"I feel** disappointed **when** you don't show up on time **because** I plan my busy day around your free time. **I need** you to stick with our plans."

A. "You don't have the cahunas to stand up to your father. Be a man!"

B. "**I feel** disrespected **when** you let your father speak to me like that. **I need** you to say something next time."

A. "That's a big fat lie."

B. "**I feel** torn **when** you say that **because** I want to believe you, yet I sense you are not being honest. **I want** you to tell me what really happened."

Your Turn: Think of a situation where you would use an "I feel" statement. Then write an "I feel" statement appropriate for the situation. Include the key words "**I feel . . . when you . . . because . . . I need** (want, like)" in your statement.

Focus On the Desired Behavior or Outcome

One way we can communicate our needs in a nonthreatening way is to **focus on what we would like to see versus what we are not getting from a person.** "I language" is less accusatory and shifts the focus of the dialogue on the outcome we want. Usually we start an "I statement" with the words, "I like . . . I appreciate . . . I need . . . I value . . . I enjoy . . . I hope . . . I want . . . ".

Tammy is feeling that Mike tends to ignore her at social events. Contrast the "you language" statement she makes with the "I statement." Which one would you rather hear if you were Mike?

Tammy: "Why do we even go out together? Every time we hang out with your friends you have to be the life of the party. I may as well not even be there because you are either in the middle of a drinking game getting drunk, or you have your nose in a hand of cards. You pay more attention to Greg's girlfriend than me."

Tammy: "I really like it when you put your arm around me at parties and talk to me. I feel like when you do, it lets people know we're together. I'd also really like it if you invited me to play cards with you next time."

Mature communication involves communicating honestly and clearly what our needs or wants are without making a person feel bad. Tammy does this in the second statement. She states exactly what behavior she wants from Mike without guilt tripping, or implying that he is a total jerk or excessive partier. Now, if she has concerns about his excessive drinking, she may state:

Tammy: "I would really like to see us both limit our drinking to four beers an evening. What do you think?"

She is communicating clearly her needs and inviting Mike to dialogue about it. If Mike asks her for her reasons she may state her observations of Mike's behavior without using evaluative language:

Tammy: "I notice you tend to get loud, make comments about me or other women which make me feel uncomfortable, and get flirtatious with Sarah."

Notice the distinction between the following messages:

A. "You forgot this again."

B. "I need you to remember to call the bank."

A. "You never plan ahead."

B. "I would really like to plan out our weekend."

A. "You're the one who never calls."

B. "I enjoy hearing from you more often."

Your Turn: Think of three situations where an "I statement" that focuses on the behavior desired would be appropriate. Write an "I statement" for each.

Example: "I really like it when you greet me with a hug when I come home from work."

Follow the Five-Second Rule

We often say things we don't want to in the heat of the moment. Before responding back to something a person says, it may be prudent to take a deep breath and wait five seconds . . . or ten, twenty, or fifty before responding. It may be necessary to postpone the conversation until much later. Be sure to include the four steps discussed in unit five on listening and feedback:

1. **State the reason why you need to postpone**.

   "I am feeling very angry."

2. **Recognize the other person's need to talk**.

   "I know that what you are saying needs to be discussed. It is important, and we will do so."

3. **Make a date** (involve the other person in establishing when to reconvene).

   "I need to think this over for a couple hours and cool off. Does later this evening work out for you? How about right after dinner?"

4. **Follow through.**

   "I've had some time to think about what you said. Are you ready to discuss it?"

A great way to postpone is to do so with an agreed-upon assignment. The assignment may involve thinking about the other person's point of view, brainstorming some solutions, or listing priorities. For example, Jayne may say to Scott, "How about we take a break from this discussion and in the meantime each of us think about how we want to spend this money and why?" Or as a twist, Jayne may say, "So that we are being other centered, how about we list the reasons why the other person's ideas are better than ours, and areas where we can agree to compromise?" This gives the "cooling off" period a productive purpose.

A great communication technique is to establish some communication rules with the person to whom we need to have a serious conversation. One rule might be to listen completely to what the other person is saying. When each person finishes his or her thought, the other person paraphrases or restates what the person said, and why he or she is thinking or feeling a certain way.

Here is an example of how we could initiate this approach:

> *"I can see we are getting really upset right now. Let's take a fifteen minute break and think about what each other is saying. We'll come back, and I will tell you what I heard you say and what you need. You do the same. What do you think?"*

Stay in the Present

The goal here is to avoid talking about the past. Bringing up things that were done five days or five years ago will likely escalate the argument. Instead, focus on how we want things to be and stick to the issue at hand. We often think that when we argue or have conflict, that someone has to win. It is not a competition, unless we want there to be a winner and a loser. A disagreement is an opportunity to understand each other, to learn, and to problem solve.

Be Solution Focused

Often, our discussions with people focus on the problem or what isn't working. Clarifying and understanding the ramifications of a problem is important. We want to avoid getting stuck there though. The following are examples of things to say to encourage solution-based communication.

- "Let's take a few minutes to talk about what we can do to solve . . ."
- "I am willing to do the following . . ."
- "What are our options? What can we do about this?"
- "How can we prevent this from reoccurring?"
- "What would you like to see happen?"

While these approaches can help us identify and manage our emotions better, there are other communication behaviors which are very facilitative in nature. They enhance not only the dialogue between people but the relationship people have with each other, including preventing unnecessary miscommunication and conflict.

. . . Which one of the suggestions on managing emotions effectively do you see yourself working on the most to improve your interpersonal communication? Why?

- Owning emotions
- Taking responsibility and action
- Expanding my emotion related vocabulary
- Speaking with less powerless language
- Avoiding trigger words
- Using "I language"
- Applying the five second rule
- Staying in the present
- Being more solution focused

Enhancing Dialogue and Relationships

Stephen Covey, author of *The Seven Habits of Highly Effective People* advocates that we "Seek first to understand before being understood." We can't understand a person if we insist on talking first. If we want others to listen and really make a strong attempt to understand us, we need to first model the "seek first to understand," principle.

Making a conscientious effort to first understand what a person is saying is a critical initial step in communicating effectively. We all want to be listened to. We all have a need to feel that what we are saying is important and that our thoughts and opinions are valued. If we initiate this in our communication with others, we are moving the dialogue in a positive direction. To listen and understand, we need to let the person complete his or her thoughts. We can engage in active listening by **(1) Hearing the person out completely, (2) asking questions for clarification, (3) paraphrasing and (4) validating.**

Hear the Person Out

This is accomplished by not interrupting. Interrupting is one of the most common ways we get sidetracked in our conversations. It is a leading cause of conflict spirals. When tempted to interrupt, we need to mentally "take a sip of water." If we start to interrupt, stop. Apologize and allow the speaker to continue his or her thought. We can encourage the person to finish his or her thoughts by listening patiently and allowing pauses to occur. Here, we fight the urge to finish the sender's sentences and interject comments while the speaker is talking or during moments of silence. We can invite the person to explain his or her thoughts fully by saying things such as, "I understand . . . keep going," "This is good for me to know," "Tell me more about this," and "Give me more details."

Ask Questions for Clarification

Questions can help us decode the speaker's message accurately. Questions, if asked the right way, can encourage a person to open up and steer a conversation toward a solution-oriented, positive direction. For a reluctant or non-communicative person, we can guess at the specifics: "Is it this?" "What else?" If a person is beating around the bush, we can ask questions such "What are you thinking right now?" "What do you want to say next?" and "How are you feeling?"

We can ask two types of questions: **open-ended** and **closed-ended**. Open-ended questions require more than a single word answer like "yes," "no," "good," or "fine." Open-ended questions tend to provide us with more information. For the following questions, indicate whether you think it is open-ended by placing an "O" in the space provided. If it is closed-ended, place a "C" on the line.

__________ "What are your thoughts about the argument we just had?"
__________ "How was your day?"
__________ "Are you mad at me?"
__________ "How would you like me to handle this next time?"

The following questions show that we are willing to take responsibility for improveing communication and future interactions:

- "What would you like to see happen?"
- "How would you like to see me handle this? What do you want me to do?"
- "How did my actions affect you?"
- "What could I have done differently?"
- "How do you see me helping you with this?"

Keep in mind that words alone don't communicate a message. How we say something, our paralanguage, also communicates a message. If we sound sincere, patient, and open, these questions will come across much different than if we sound defensive, accusatory, sarcastic, or angry.

Paraphrase the Message

Paraphrasing involves restating what the person said in our own words. It is a brief sentence that summarizes the essence of what the person has said. We can also reflect back how the person appears emotionally. Paraphrasing is a great "seek first to understand, before being understood," approach. If we approach all of our conversations this way, it gives us more time to process the sender's message and encode the best response. A paraphrase lets the sender know we are engaged and interested. It also allows us to reduce the likelihood of miscommunication, a major cause of interpersonal conflict. The following are examples of paraphrasing.

Tom: "There is damage to the ulnar nerve. I wish I had gone in sooner because he could have repaired some of the damage. He doesn't see any benefit to doing anything else now."

Jean: "Sounds like you found out what you needed to know. I sense that you feel disappointed about the outcome."

Roxane: "All that is going to do is create more confusion."

Tiffany: "So you're concerned that the contractors won't understand the drawing."

Greg: "You're shooting 70% inside the key and 52% outside the arch, yet you're taking more long jumpers."

Torrey: "So based on the numbers, I should shoot more from inside."

Use Validation

Next to being listened to and understood, another very important communication behavior we need from others is validation. **Validation** is recognizing another person's stated or unstated thoughts, feelings, and needs. It is a confirming kind communication which shows that we see where the other person is coming from. **The purpose of validation is to communicate back what we know the other person needs to hear**. This is not intended as a manipulative technique, but as sincere, authentic way to acknowledge something that the other person needs us to affirm. Validation can create greater immediacy (emotional connectedness), promote better under- standing, and reduce the frequency and duration of arguments. Validation lets the person know we care about him or her and the relationship. Examples of statements that validate include:

- "I know you are disappointed with me right now." (validating the person's feelings)
- "You're right, I didn't respond to your question with patience." (validating the person's thoughts)
- "I appreciate your offer to help. I know you care. I need to do this on my own." (validating the person's need to want to help)

Let's look at some additional examples of validation:

Timba: "I don't mind if you borrow money from my wallet, but I need to know when you do, or I'd like you to ask."

Stan: "I can appreciate that. It was probably embarrassing when you went to pay for it in line at the cashiers and the money is not there. I will ask you next time." (validating Timba's thoughts and needs)

Avery: "I am so excited about the art show next Saturday."

Kaitlin: "I know. I'm so happy for you. Your work will be seen by a lot of people. You've worked hard for this." (validating Avery's feelings)

Rob: "Man, I've been open the last five times. You're not banking your shots so share it."

Rick: "You're right. I'm off tonight, and you've been open. Sorry, man. I will look for you." (validates by agreeing with the facts, apologizing, and offering a solution)

Rob: "I know there are some recruiters in the stands, and you must feel a lot of pressure. Relax. Show them how you can move the ball around." (validates what he thinks Rick is thinking and feeling)

Validation reduces defensiveness and increases the person's receptivity to what you have to say. For example, take Kent and Kimberly. They had dinner the other night with Kimberly's mother. During dinner, Kimberly did something that Kent didn't like, and he has decided to tell her. Notice how Kimberly validates him.

Kent: "At dinner, I didn't feel like you gave me much of a chance to talk with your mom and sister. You interrupted me a lot or finished my sentences."

Kimberly: "I'm sorry. I do remember interrupting you several times. I bet that was frustrating for you. Thanks for telling me. I will work hard not to do that again in the future."

Kimberly validated Kent by apologizing without making excuses. She agreed with the facts and acknowledged how she may have made Kent feel. She also thanked him for the feedback and offered up a solution, which was a promise to work on the behavior. Thus, the following are ways to validate someone (AAASI):

- **A**pologize without making excuses—no "yeah, buts."
- **A**gree with the facts or at least with the person's perceptions.
- **A**cknowledge what the person must have thought or felt or how the person is thinking or feeling.
- **S**how appreciation for the feedback you're getting from the other person.
- **I**dentify a solution.

Let's take a look at an example that shows a lack of validation followed by one that does and includes the AAASI approach.

Jacob makes plans for the weekend without including Emily in the decision. Emily does not like it and has communicated in the past that she'd like him to not do this. She shares with him that she is disappointed.

Emily: "I felt disappointed and angry that you didn't talk with me about the plans you made for the weekend. I kept my weekend schedule open because in the past you have expressed feeling hurt when I have made plans without including you."

Jacob: "We didn't have any time to talk about our plans. Lately, you've been doing a lot of studying, and I don't want to wait around for you to decide. Besides, you made plans without me two weeks ago, and those plans didn't include me."

In this response, Jacob does not validate Emily's thoughts or feelings. He makes excuses and digs up the past. Where is this conversation headed? It will undoubtedly escalate into a conflict spiral. Let's see how he might validate her using the AAASI approach:

Emily: "I felt disappointed and angry that you didn't talk with me about the plans you made for the weekend. I kept my weekend schedule open because in the past you have expressed feeling hurt when I have made plans without including you."

Jacob: "You're right. I did do that. I'm sorry. I can see that you are frustrated and disappointed because we've talked about this before and the weekends are our only time to spend together. Thanks for bringing this up. Let's talk about how we can plan our weekends better so that we avoid this situation."

Jacob validates Emily by agreeing with the facts ("You're right. I did do that.") Jacob apologizes without making excuses ("I'm sorry.") He acknowledges why this would bother Emily ("I can see that you are frustrated and disappointed because we've talked about this before and the weekends are our only time to spend together.") He communicates appreciation to Emily for bring this up to him ("Thanks for bringing this up."), and steers the conversation in a solution-focused direction ("Let's talk about how we can plan our weekends better so that we avoid this situation."). Finally, another approach we may use to enhance our dialogue and relationships is to promote positive emotions.

Your Turn: Create a two-person dialogue similar to Jacob's second response to Emily. Try to incorporate the AAASI approach in your dialogue.

Promote Positive Emotions

To promote positive emotions, it helps when we praise and compliment people authentically. One marriage therapist gives this assignment to his clients. She has the couple say three nice things to each other every day. Positive, rapport-building communication may include two people reminiscing about funny, happy, and meaningful events from the past or talking about something that they are looking forward to doing together.

. . . How would you describe the different ways we can enhance dialogue with our communication?

- Ask questions for clarification
- Paraphrase the message
- Validation
- Promote positive feelings

Unit Summary

Affective communication is communication about and involving our emotions. Emotions play an important factor in our interpersonal communication. An emotion is a biochemical, physiological, and psychological process which occurs in response to an event. Moods are feelings which have no identifiable cause and typically last for a while. Emotions are a significant source of internal and external noise at times. Emotions serve a facilitative and debilitative purpose. There are a variety of behaviors such as gunny sacking, threatening, guilt-tripping, and negating which are known to evoke negative feelings and increase interpersonal conflict. Effective communicators are aware of these behaviors and strive to avoid them as much as possible. Ways to improve how we manage our emotions while communicating include recognizing and taking ownership of our feelings, avoiding trigger words, using "I language," and staying in the present. To enhance the dialogue we have with others and our relationships, we are encouraged to incorporate the techniques of paraphrasing, solution-based communication, and validation.

Key Questions

1. What is human emotion? What is the difference between emotions and moods?
2. How would you explain emotion as a process?
3. What is the difference between a facilitative and debilitative emotion? How would you explain the difference using an example?
4. What are some of the problematic communicating behaviors associated with negative emotions? Which three are you most guilty of? Least?
5. What do the following mean in terms of managing and expressing emotions effectively?
   - Owning emotions
   - Taking responsibility and action
   - Expanding my emotion related vocabulary
   - Speaking with less powerless language
   - Avoiding trigger words
   - Using "I language"
   - Applying the five second rule
   - Staying in the present
   - Being more solution focused
6. How would you describe the different ways we can enhance dialogue and relationships with our communication?
   - Hear the person out completely
   - Ask questions for clarification
   - Paraphrase the message
   - Validation
   - Promote positive feelings

Vocabulary Playback

Conflict Spiral
Affective Communication
Emotions
Emotional Contagion
Moods
Mixed Emotions
Gender Display Rules
Facilitative Emotions
Debilitative Emotions
Displacement
Internal Locus of Control
External Locus of Control
Open-ended Questions
Closed-ended Questions
Validation

Theoretically Speaking

- Rational-Emotive Theory
- Reciprocity Theory
- Cognitive Dissonance Theory

Focus Group/Class Discussion

- Which three of the problematic behaviors described in this unit do you think is most common in people's communication? Why?
- Which three are you most guilty of? Least? Why?
- Do you agree or disagree with the cognitive dissonance theory? Why or why not?
- In one study, it was found that people generally communicate with more positive conflict management strategies when communicating face-to-face compared to computer mediated communication such as e-mail or on-line chat. Why do you think this is the case? Do you agree or disagree with the study's findings?[40]
- In one interesting study, men and women were asked to watch a movie with scenes which were very moving and emotional. A "confederate" (played by both males and females) was placed in the group who purposely showed different emotions during the film's showing. Results showed that the male confederates who teared up during the movie were viewed favorably or "liked" more and women were "liked" more when they did not cry? How would you explain these results?[41]
- Employees, according to another study, tend to express more positive feelings and rate the leadership qualities of their managers higher when the managers frequently ask them their opinions—even if the managers don't always go along with their ideas.[42] How can we use these findings to improve our relationships with people at work and outside of work?
- Researchers have found that women's brains generally have a larger inferior parietal lobule, which brain researchers have identified as headquarters for our emotions. Some speculate that this is a major reason why women tend to talk more about and express (smile and cry more) their feelings compared to men.[43] What do you think? Are differences between the sexes the result of socialization, physiological differences, or both?
- How does the following quote relate to what you've read in Unit 10: "Swallowing your pride now will save your eardrums later." —William Tomicki

Unit 10 Vocabulary Review

___ Conflict Spiral
___ Affective Communication
___ Emotions
___ Moods
___ Emotional Contagion
___ Mixed Emotions
___ Gender Display Rules
___ Facilitative Emotions
___ Debilitative Emotions
___ Displacement
___ Internal locus of control
___ External locus of control
___ Open-ended Questions
___ Close-ended Questions
___ Validation

A. When people transfer feelings to one another.

B. The mindset that one has control of a situation or can exert a lot of influence on the outcome.

C. Experiencing two or more emotions at the same time.

D. Communication about and involving our emotions.

E. Emotions which assist us in performing tasks and functioning successfully.

F. A biochemical, physiological, and psychological response to an event.

G. An emotional state which has no identifiable cause and typically lasts for a while.

H. Questions which elicit more than a single word response such as yes or no.

I. Directing our negative feelings towards a person who does not deserve it.

J. Emotions that hinder our ability to function effectively.

K. Questions which often results in a single word response like "fine," or "yes."

L. Recognizing or acknowledging another person's stated or unstated needs, feelings, or wants.

M. An argument which escalates and gets progressively worse with each communication act.

N. The mindset that one has little control over a situation and that outside forces (other people, the economy, tradition) will ultimately determine the outcome.

O. These are the normative ways males and females express their emotions according to cultural expectations and pressures.

Creative Exercise

Blaming
Interrupting
Gunny-sacking
Deprecating Humor
We Speaking
Relentless Debating
Criticizing
Insincerity

Past Digging
Stage-hogging
Avoiding
Relentless Joking
Bulldozing
Passive/Aggressive
Doom-saying
Deception

Verbal Attacks
Bragging
Withdrawing
Guilt Tripping
Threatening
Drama Seeking
Trapping
Wheel Spinning

Placating
Negating
Withholding
Below Belt
Bossing
Complaining
Kitchen Sinking
Impervious Admission

1. Create a scene complete with a cast of characters and compelling plot. Each character is assigned to one of the above communication behaviors. He or she will incorporate the behavior in his or her dialogue. The class will attempt to guess which problematic behaviors the team is performing

Skill Builder: Validation

John: "I really don't like you to go running in the park when it gets dark. I don't think it's safe."

Sarah: "I can see why you would think this. I'm alone and it's dark. I usually run where I see other runners, but still you are worried. There was a mugging a couple weeks ago. (agrees with facts, acknowledges an understanding of where John is coming from)."

Create a skit between two characters like John and Sarah. Have one character validate the other. Try to make sure that the validation includes at least three of the following ways we can validate (AAASI):

- Agree with the facts or at least with the person's perceptions.
- Apologize without making excuses.
- Acknowledge what the person must have thought or felt or how the person is thinking or feeling
- Show appreciation for the feedback
- Identify a solution

Situation:

____

____

____

____

Character A

____

____

____

Character B Validates by saying:

____

____

____

11 Frame of Reference

Frame of Reference Unit 11

This unit focuses on how frame of reference influences our interpersonal communication and relationships.

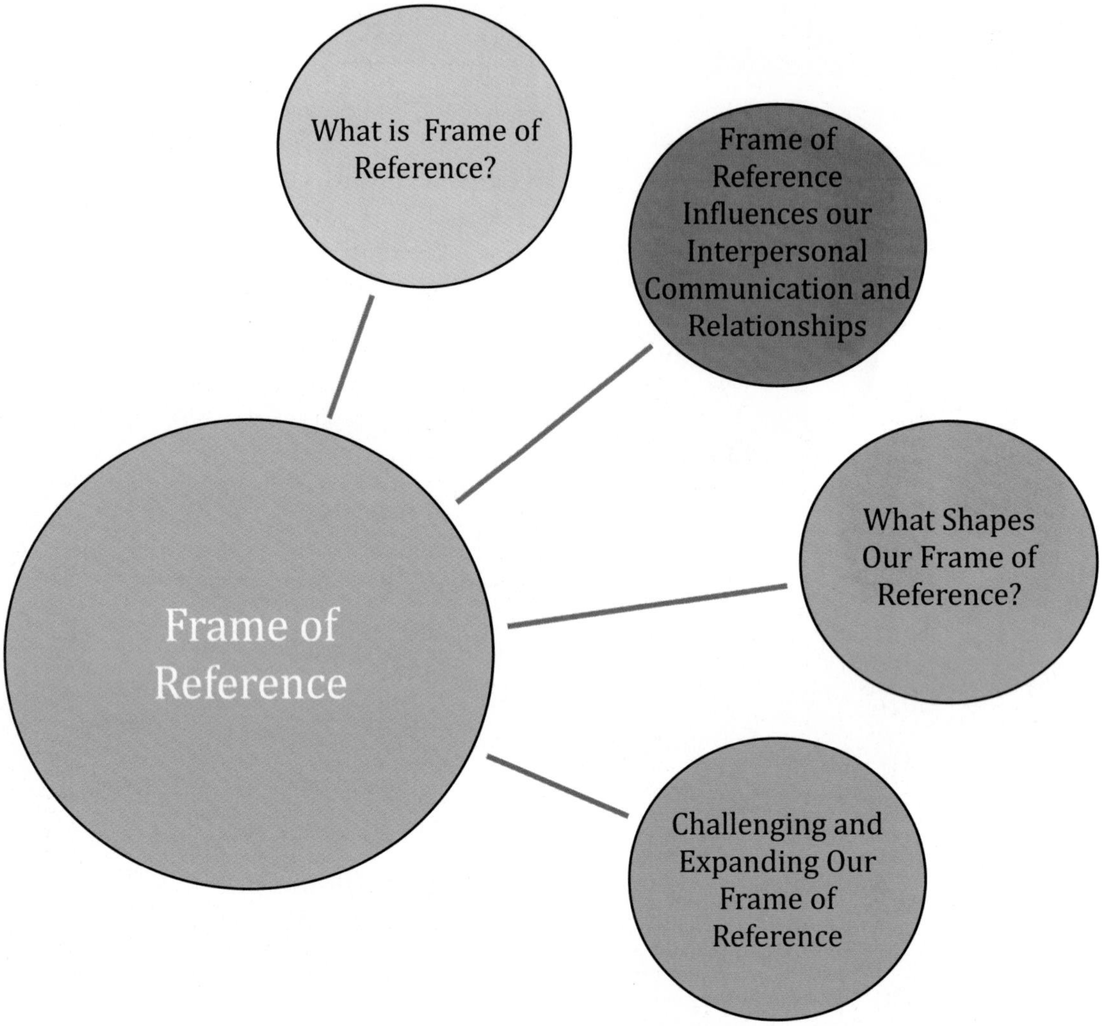

Unit 11 Learning Objectives

As a result of reading and studying Unit 11, you will be able to:

1. Describe frame of reference.
2. Identify the many ways in which frame of reference influences our interpersonal communication and relationships.
3. Appreciate how past experiences, age, gender, and culture shape our frame of reference.
4. Understand the various ways we can challenge and expand our frame of reference.

What happens when a British comedian assumes the persona of a foreign reporter sent by his homeland's Ministry of Information to learn about "the greatest country in the world, the U.S. of A?" You have a movie like *Borat* (2006), a comedic mockumentary that licked the political correctness envelope and poked fun at numerous groups in America. The movie, a hybrid of *Candid Camera* meets *National Lampoon's Vacation*, weaves a fictitious plot with unscripted vignettes of Borat, played by Sacha Baron Cohen, interviewing Americans who believe he is an actual foreign reporter naive to American culture.

During his documentary effort, Borat gets sidetracked after watching Pamela Anderson on *Baywatch*. He then decides to search her out and make her his bride. In the process, he fears for his life and escapes from a bed and breakfast owned by Jews, feigns ignorance of his sexist remarks in an interview with a group of feminists, "accidentally" knocks over confederate antiques at a Southern store, sings his own version of the National Anthem at a rodeo, and "accepts" Christ at a charismatic Pentecostal church service. The movie was rebuked by Russia and banned by every Arab country except Lebanon. The producers of the film, including Cohen, faced numerous lawsuits from groups and individuals depicted in the film. Ironically, it was a box office smash, earning both a 2007 Golden Globe and Best Motion Picture nod by the Academy of Motion Picture Arts and Sciences.[1] What made so many viewers consider his humor sidesplitting while others walked out of theaters condemning the movie? People's reactions and opinions were mixed and perhaps representative of a concept called frame of reference.

What Is Frame of Reference?

As senders and receivers of messages, our communication with others is influenced by our frame of reference. **Frame of reference** is our collective experience, or everything that has ever happened to us up to this moment. This can include our socioeconomic status, upbringing, life events, educational and cultural experiences, and religious background. People often misunderstand each other because of differences in frame of reference.

Numerous reality television shows spotlight the rich diversity found throughout the world. Mike Rowe is Discovery Channel's host of the very unsavory, but insightful show *Dirty Jobs*. Rowe profiles Americans who, as the show's website states, "overcome fear, danger and sometimes stench . . . to accomplish their daily tasks." In each episode, Rowe assumes the responsibilities of the people whose jobs he is featuring. His extensive resume boasts rattlesnake catching, fish processing, hot tar roofing, bee removing, septic-tank cleaning, alligator egg collecting, water vessel fire fighting, stallion sperm collecting, body odor testing, and road kill extracting. Rowe doesn't appear terribly bothered by the dirt, smells, grime, and danger. Perhaps his numerous experiences have dulled his senses. Put me in many of those situations, and I would hurl or run, especially when it comes to smelly jobs. My olfactory perception is skewed due to my acute sense of smell and hypersensitivity to even minor odors.

Viewers are treated to the unique perspective these people have on life and their atypical vocation. A frequent query of Rowe is: "How did you land this job? " The answers vary considerably. They are unique based on each person's path of discovery and life events leading up to his or her career choice, a difference in terms of frame of reference.[2]

Another eye opening show which showers viewers with culture and diverse people is *Going Tribal.* Like *Dirty Jobs,* it challenges the frame of reference of viewers regarding their perceptions of primitive people. Retired Royal Marine Bruce Parry brings cameras to some of the most remote ancient tribes of the Himalayas, Ethiopia, West Papua, Gabon, and Mongolia.

The lengths that Parry will go to gain the tribe's acceptance and trust are amazing. From the Discovery Channel's official *Going Tribal* Web site, we learn what Parry accomplishes as a guest of the Amazon's Jaguar Tribe during season three:

> *"He learns to be a Matis hunter . . . He's whipped with sticks, has excruciatingly painful tree sap dropped into his eyes to improve his vision, learns to hunt monkeys with a 12-foot blow-pipe and finally takes a powerful frog toxin to purge his system. This, inevitably, is a brutal process. Bruce is burnt with smoldering arrows on his upper arms and the blistered skin is smeared with frog toxin. Bruce is then free to join the men on a real hunt, rampaging through the forest in search of wild pigs. . . ."*[3]

Perry spends a month immersed in each society. Parry sheds his clothes, hunts with warriors, worships, dances, cooks, and eats in the sacred traditions and practices that those of us living outside of these cultures may consider backward or bizarre. In order to communicate, Parry is guided by a translator and gets a crash course on the basics of the tribe's language. Parry unveils, sometimes in very graphic detail, how the rituals and mystic ways of the society serve many purposes and are sensible.

In addition to *Dirty Jobs* and *Going Tribal*, another show highlights a way of life that most of us are oblivious to. Imagine being a 15-year-old teenager who has to go to the young children's aisles to buy jeans and shirts. For Zack Roloff, it is one of a number of daily challenges he faces as a dwarf or little person. The hit reality show on The Learning Channel (TLC), *Little People Big World*, chronicles the life of Zach's family, whose world is not height friendly. His parents are Matt and Amy Roloff, two married dwarfs who are four feet tall. He has a twin brother, Jeremy; a younger brother, Jacob; and an older sister; Molly—and all three are of normal height. Zach's father is a former computer software salesman and successful entrepreneur of a company that creates products for little people. Zach's mother runs the Roloff household, which is located on a unique 34-acre theme park farm on the outskirts of Portland, Oregon.

Their everyday triumphs and tribulations are shown from their perspective, like a wholesome adaptation of MTV's *The Osbournes*. Not being able to reach the buttons on an ATM machine, being stared at in public, or trying to get noticed behind the counter at the bank are just a few of the difficulties captured during seven months of filming.[4]

In one of the episodes, Matt tries to decide what Mother's Day gift to give Amy, who is a busy housewife, preschool teacher, and soccer coach. He thinks Amy would love to have the assistance of a domestic consultant to help her manage the home more efficiently, but starts to second-guess himself because he is not sure how she will interpret his gesture. His frame of reference may lead him to perceive that this act demonstrates that "I love my wife and want to help her." Based on her past interactions with Matt, her frame of reference might preclude her to think that "I'm not doing a good enough job, or he's trying to meddle with my system of doing things." The scene depicts, in a "big" way, how frame of reference influences each family member's interactions.[5]

Our frame of reference influences how we look at the world and what we value. Some people throughout the world see America's quest for happiness and shake their heads. They see us as consummate consumers who feed our self-aggrandizement by obtaining, acquiring, and replacing "things." When we have something, we want more: a bigger house, a better car, a faster boat, and the newest electronic gadget. The perception people throughout the world have of Americans is fairly accurate for the most part. Many Americans live seeking to create a life of luxury, like the people featured on MTV's *Cribs* or *Lifestyles of the Rich and Famous*. Interestingly, those who enjoy that life often complain that a life of luxury is a life of heavy maintenance. Things that are owned wear out, break down, and need scheduled maintenance. This costs money. The more we have, the more money we need to keep what we have. Some people who own a lot realize that, as someone once said, "What we own can end up owning us."

Our devotion to the almighty dollar, our penchant for what is "new" or "chic" and our lust for brand names and labels are indicative of our culture's projection of success and happiness. Perhaps, due in large part to our exposure to a multibillion-dollar advertising and media industry, Americans see themselves as lacking, yet compared to the world, many of us live like kings and queens. The United States comprises 5% of the planet's population but consumes approximately 70% of the world's resources![6]

Others, based on their culture and social upbringing, view living life with limited "stuff" as more ideal. They are of the opinion that focusing on relationships and helping others is the key to success, happiness, and purpose. For them, volunteering to help the homeless, mentoring children, spending time with the elderly, and assisting those who are illiterate to read is a greater priority. The same may be said about participating in causes we see as important such as fighting for civil rights, protecting the environment, or raising money for third world community development projects. What we value and believe in influences what we devote our time to, our communication behavior, and how we relate to people. Next, let's take a look at the pervasive influence our frame of reference has on our behavior.

Your Turn: In what ways has your frame of reference shaped your values, beliefs, and goals?

. . . What is frame of reference? What makes up our frame of reference?

Frame of Reference Influences Our Interpersonal Communication

A college student dismisses what an instructor says and questions his expertise because he is young-looking. How might the student's frame of reference factor in here? Perhaps all of the student's professors, up until now, have been old or "chronologically gifted." Maybe she has had a younger professor before who "didn't know what he was talking about." So, the student assumes that this next "grad student" is similar. The student may have been told repeatedly throughout her life that wisdom comes from age. Whatever the reason, the student's frame of reference affects her communication and interaction with the instructor.

A secretary misinterprets a supervisor's instructions because his phone distracted him. Read the previous sentence again out loud. When you read that just now, did you assume that I was talking about the supervisor when I referred to "him" and not the secretary? If you did, why? Your experience (from your past interactions with secretaries and perhaps exposure to media depictions of secretaries) is that a secretary is usually a female. This is your frame of reference in action.

One Family's Frame of Reference

"When some of my friends who are from a different racial background hang with me at my house, they are introduced to what my family often eats. Initially, they are a little shocked. For example, on New Year's Day we have a ritual of eating black-eyed peas with corn bread. For many African American families, black-eyed peas are believed to bring good luck for the coming year. This is often accompanied by something like pigs feet, cow tongue, hog jowls, and/or chicken livers. Our traditional diet dates back to our early African American ancestry. African slaves were given only the scraps or undesirable cuts of meat from their masters, such as beef tongue, ham hocks, chitterlings (hog intestines), and pig ears. Because slaves were forced to work the fields for long hours in the hot sun, they had to be extremely frugal with what food they did have.

Everything was eaten to avoid starvation or malnutrition. Since they could not cook in kitchens, slaves prepared their food in the outdoors using large cast-iron skillets over open fires. They relied on deep frying their meats in order to prevent spoilage, which resulted in fried fish and chicken. The broth from cooking greens was reused for gravy or consumed as a drink. Overripe bananas were whipped into puddings, leftover fish became croquettes, and stale bread found its way into pudding or fried as hushpuppies. In some cases, my early African American ancestors were given a small space to plant their own vegetables. They planted okra, collard greens, watermelon, and yams. Corn was cheap and readily available, so it was a major source of bread and breading for other foods. To enliven a limited diet, they added a lot of salt and various spices. The early life experiences of African Americans contributed significantly to the creation of Creole and Cajun cuisine.

My friends really like some of my mom's traditional soul food and most of the time they really like it! They usually don't want to know where the meat came from, though!"

—*Torrey Thomas*

Our frame of reference shapes our views and reactions. I read about an older gentleman who was standing near a gorilla exhibit at the zoo. The gorillas suddenly charged the glass partition separating them from the crowd. Their sudden display of hostility sent the crowds running, except for this man, who just stood there and didn't even flinch. Someone who was amazed at his courage inquired, "How did you maintain such composure?" The man sighed and said, "I drove a school bus for a living." He had nerves of steel. His response, albeit a humorous one, suggests a history of dealing with the unexpected. This makes up his frame of reference.

The influence our frame of reference has on who we decide to form relationships with is significant. Within every communication context, the people involved have some sort of relationship. If we are speaking to someone dyadically or in a small group, we have a relationship of some sort. It may range from no relationship (complete stranger) to an extremely close, intimate relationship such as with a best friend, spouse, life partner, or sibling. The degree of immediacy or closeness people have with one another in any given context will influence the communication. Do you recall how you acted in elementary school on the days you had a substitute teacher? Did the students act differently towards the substitute teacher compared to the full-time teacher? What was the one thing the substitute teacher would say, "I want to write your teacher a note that says you were an awesome class." Because you most likely valued the relationship you had with your teacher, his or her opinion of you mattered. We act differently with those whom we have a close relationship with compared to those we don't. Each interaction is influenced by how people know each other, how long, what they know about each other, and the shared experiences they've had. This makes up a person's relational history and is a part of his or her frame of reference.

With every relationship, we consider the question "What do I get out of this?" We consider this on a conscious and unconscious level. In every relationship we seek **relational rewards**, which are the things we get from a relationship that we like and value. Relational rewards may include a good time, a great deal on a car, free stuff, a good grade, romance, affirmation, attention, emotional support, a free meal, help with our taxes, membership to a group, or access to people we want to associate with. When we don't see the potential for any rewards, we don't pursue a relationship, or we keep the interaction on an impersonal level.

Who we choose to get to know and establish relationships with is based on a number of factors including similarities, differences, attraction, proximity, and disclosure:

Similarities

We are drawn to people who are similar to us or who share our beliefs, values, and interests.

Differences

What makes us different can be appealing from a relational standpoint.

Attraction

We like people we find attractive in terms of personality, looks, ambitions, lifestyle, and accomplishments; unless competitiveness and jealousy become a problem. We also are drawn to those who like us, and when there is a mutual attraction.

Proximity

We form relationships faster when it is both convenient to connect, and we encounter people frequently. This explains why we more often form friendships with coworkers we interact with more often and the neighbors we live the closest to.

Disclosure

As we share things about ourselves, people tend to reciprocate. Disclosure leads to connectedness and closeness. One of my students wrote:

> *"I developed a friendship with a lady at work (proximity) who was going through a divorce at the same time I was. My wife cheated on me and her husband cheated on her. We had a lot in common (similarities) because of our situations. We were able to share (disclose) what was going on. We helped each other get through those tough "divorce times."*

We may also determine if we want to maintain and develop a relationship based on what we get from the relationship relative to what it costs us to maintain it. There is an interesting theory called the **social exchange theory**.[7] It suggests that we opt to stay in or get out of relationships based on the costs versus the benefits. We may not always consciously consider this, however, on an unconscious level, many psychologists and interpersonal scholars believe we do. We weigh how much a relationship is "worth it" compared to "not worth it." If we can't opt out of a relationship where the costs exceed the benefits, what do we do? We tend to distance ourselves from people emotionally. We may also strive to limit our interaction as much as possible Costs may include a loss of trust, a person's possessiveness, living with someone who is messy, putting up with a person's quirks, a lackluster relationship, or dealing with a spouse's in-laws.

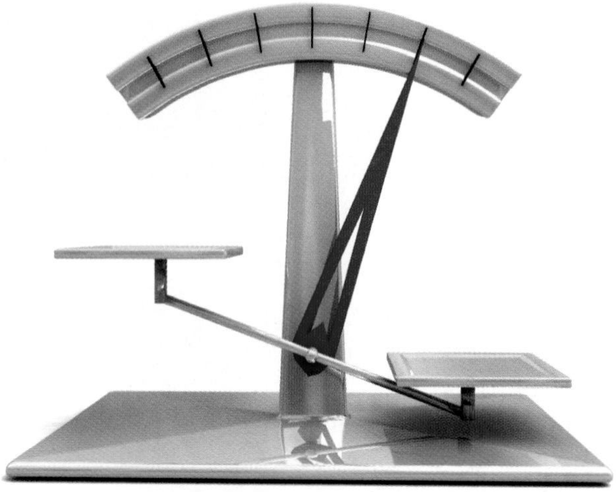

Social Exchange Theory
Rewards − Costs = Outcome.

In the first season of the highly acclaimed television series, *Six Feet Under*, one of the lead characters, Brenda Chenowith has an incredibly strong bond and love for her brother Billy. However when Billy, a diagnosed manic depressive with schizophrenic tendencies, attempts to physically remove a tattoo from her back with his pocket knife because her tattoo is cursed, Brenda decides she's not down with that. She feels heavily burdened by the emotional costs of constantly rescuing her brother and now fears for her safety. She asks him for the keys to her apartment. He tells her "It won't stop me from getting in." Her parents implore her to sign papers to have him committed. She balks because of the tremendous rift in her relationship with them, both psychiatrists who volunteered their children to participate in highly controversial psychological experiments. She can't completely cut off her relationship with them, but she has distanced herself greatly. She laments the decision, but finally signs on the dotted line to have Billy institutionalized. Like her relationship with her parents, the costs of maintaining her relationship with her brother surpassed the benefits, and she takes measures to separate physically and emotionally.

The social exchange theory is applicable in explaining why people divorce. What causes people to get a divorce? One or both individuals conclude that the costs outweigh the benefits, or one or both decide to pursue a relationship with someone else who has more to offer. When we see that the relationship brings us more costs than rewards, our communication behaviors shift to avoidance, a lack of affection, and deception. Instead of being at ease and feeling relaxed with sharing our honest thoughts and feelings, we are guarded. What is happening in a relationship is a part of each person's frame of reference. At any point in time, people who are in a close relationship are in a certain relational stage and may experience different dialectical tensions.

Do you agree or disagree with the social exchange theory? Why or why not?

Your Turn: Think of a person you have a close relationship with. What are some of the costs and benefits associated with this relationship for you? What do you think this person would see as the costs and benefits associated with having a relationship with you?

The **relational development theory** suggests that relationships "evolve through stages defined by participants' expectations, perceptions, and meanings."[8] Communication experts Mark Knapp and Anita Vangelsti created what they call the **relational stages model** which is used to represent where a relationship may be at starting with early interactions and ending in termination.[9] Their model relates to all relationships, platonic and romantic.

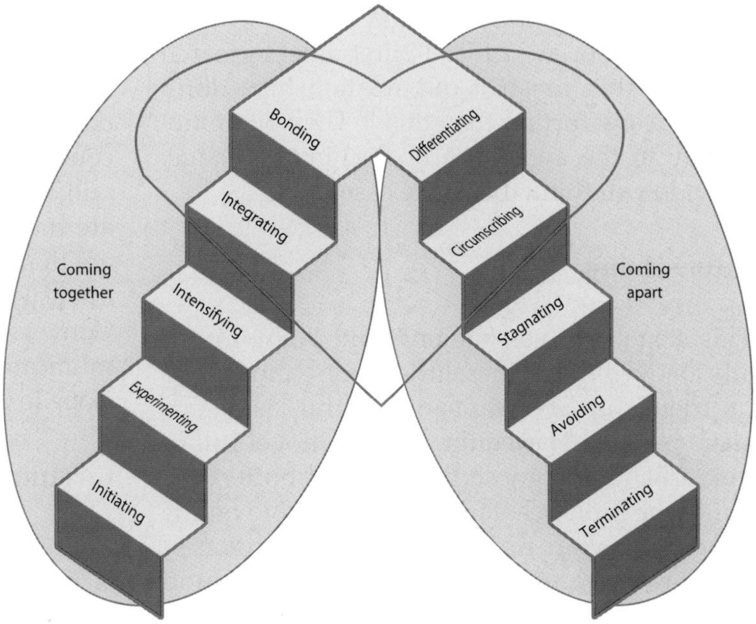

Observe the diagram and read a brief description of each stage.

Initiating

Brief interactions and exchanges characterize this stage.

Experimenting

Small talk and a few substantive conversations mark the start of the experimenting stage. There are more questions and self-disclosure to reduce uncertainty. (**Uncertainty reduction**). Individuals discover their commonalities. From a

A lesbian couple enjoying a concert

romantic standpoint, there may be a few "unofficial dates" or an "official" first date. Research suggests that most of our relationships don't advance any further than this.[10] They go immediately to the avoidance or termination stage. Why do you think this is the case?

Intensifying

This stage involves hanging out, doing mutually enjoyable activities, little favors, and tokens of friendship. For romance enthusiasts, this stage is like a Harlequin romance novel full of moon lit walks, goose bumps, and butterflies, not of the Monarch variety. It's the Fabio on the gondola or your first read of a new edition of *Hot Rod Magazine*, everything is exciting and new and . . . temporary.

Integrating

Rituals, routine outings, and a mixing of family and friends are occurring at the integrating stage. A shared relational history is forming. For romantic relationships, more things are done as a couple. "I" is replaced with "we."

Bonding

Commitment and comfortability exists at the bonding stage. People are no longer out to impress. There is a well established history with memories of events and times, along with a sense that this person is going to be there for the long haul. Individuals know each other and accept one another, the good and the bad. People usually formalize their relationships at this stage with business partnerships, marriages, engagements, and commitment ceremonies. People may refer to this person as my "best friend" or "one of my closest friends."

Differentiating

At the differentiating stage, people in relationships are changing and their needs differ. Conflict rears its head more. For example, parents may clash with their teenage son or daughter as he or she exerts more independence or doesn't accept all of their values or beliefs. A couple may realize that they are each spending less time together as each is pursuing his or her own interests. People begin to note more how the other person is different. This stage requires adjusting, accommodation, and a willingness to find new ways to connect. The kind of communication we have will influence what stage we go to next. If we are successful with our communication, chances are that the relationship will bounce back to the intensifying, integrating and/or bonding stage. Conversely, if we have a lack of effective communication, the relationship is sent on a slippery slope to one of the next three stages.

Circumscribing

In a relationship that is circumscribing, a plateau is reached. The quantity and quality of communication wanes. We see withdrawal, resentment, avoidance, and reduced self-disclosure.

Stagnating

At this stage we experience no growth. Activities are carried out without feeling or excitement. Predictability is the rule.

Avoiding

At this point, there is a lack of effort to improve or change things. Issues and topics are not addressed or ignored. Less and less time spent together. In marriages, we may see people separate before divorce.

Terminating

There is no "I'll be back." The relationship strolled its last catwalk. People disassociate and go their separate ways.[11]

> **"Those you love the most are the ones who, sadly, also hurt you the most."**
>
> **Author unknown**

Mark Knapp and Anita Vangelsti believe that in real life, relationships move back and forth between stages. They may skip a stage. Some relationship researchers believe it is possible for a relationship to be in more than one stage at the same time. In the case of a friendship, people may make choices whether to stay at one stage, move it forward or back, or end the relationship. For example, have you ever been in a fight with a friend when you were in the bonding stage and the rift was so deep you were convinced you would never speak to her or him again? For a while the relationship was in the termination stage. After not communicating for some time, something may have brought the two of you back together. Your "reunion" may send the relationship back to the intensifying or integrating stage.

Your Turn: Consider one of the close relationships you are in right now. What stage are you in with this person? Why? Where would you like it to be?

Humorist Dave Barry talks about the potential boredom that couples face. "After a decade or so of marriage, you know everything about your spouse, every habit and opinion and twitch and tic and minor skin growth. You could write a seventeen-pound book solely about the way your spouse eats." He quips that knowing this could come in handy in a dating game type show where you have to identify your spouse from a group of others all in a separate room based on the sounds he or she makes from chewing.[12]

In addition to being in certain stages, all relationships experience dialectical tensions. **Dialectical tensions** are the inevitable extremes we gravitate to in relationships in terms of needs. It is possible for two people in a close relationship such as a husband/wife, parent/child, or neighbor/neighbor to want opposing things at the same time. **The tensions are: connection versus autonomy, predictability versus novelty, and openness versus privacy.**[13]

Connection versus Autonomy

Is it possible to be "over-loved?" There is a saying, "How can I miss you if you never go away." The connection versus autonomy tension involves working out the need to be together versus the need to have time apart. Desmond Morris, author of the book *Intimate Behavior* refers to this as "Hold me tight," and "Let me be." One of my students writes,

> *"My junior year I had a friend, Lindsey. We hung out a lot. I had every class with her. We drove to school together. We were in the same clubs. She even joined the cheerleading squad I was on. I was spending about 10 hours a day, six days a week with her. I started getting really annoyed with her and didn't really know why because she wasn't doing anything to bother me."*

Predictability versus Novelty

This tension occurs when two people want the opposite of stability and change. In other words, repetition and consistency goes twelve rounds with novelty and spontaneity. Sometimes doing the same things, at the same times, in the same way is nice. Many people enjoy some level of consistency and like routines. A couple, Chris and Logan, may enjoy a weekly ritual where they share a quiet dinner at their favorite restaurant followed by a movie on Friday nights. It is something they look forward to doing after a long week. However, Chris may need to change things up a bit. He may want to travel to some place new, go out with different people, or take off on an unplanned weekend excursion. Chris and Logan will need to work these opposing needs out. There is a saying that "If you always do what you've always done, you'll always get what you've always got."

Openness versus Privacy

This dialectical tension relates to the need to share things with others versus keeping them private. We have times when we want to share things about our personal life, and when we don't. In a family context, certain individuals may feel more comfortable keeping less than ideal family information a family secret, whereas others may see the need to talk openly with others about it. A couple may differ with each other in terms of whether it is acceptable to open each other's mail or if personal information should stay private between the two of them. At times, we'll have people who want to know more about us than we are willing to share.[14]

These stages and tensions are present in every relationship at some point. **Our frame of**

reference influences these stages and tensions because where we are at in a relationship at any given moment is affected by all of our past conversations, interactions, and events. For example, if we are feeling a real need to spend some time away from our parents, it has a lot to do with our frame of reference. Perhaps, we've spent a lot of time with them lately and need a break. Our parents may feel just the opposite because for them, having us home from college during our spring break is a welcomed change. Perhaps our parents need a break from each other (autonomy versus connectedness dialectical tension) and they are excited that we are now home so they can focus their attention on someone else for a change. They're wanting to spend every free minute with us, and we're needing some space. The key to working through these stages and tensions is open, honest, and direct communication where we recognize these needs and express them to one another in a positive, loving way. We can also work together to identify solutions and make decisions which allow both parties to get their needs met. Now that we recognize how pervasive frame of reference is in our interpersonal communication and relationships, let's identify some of the major factors which shape our frame of reference.

Your Take: Describe a time where a dialectical tension affected one of your relationships. How did you handle it? What are some other possible dialectical tensions we can experience in a relationship?

. . . In what ways does our frame of reference influence where we are at in a relationship and why we experience dialectical tensions?

What Shapes Our Frame of Reference?

There are several factors which make up an individual's frame of reference. These include, but are not limited to, a person's prior associations, gender, age, and culture.

Prior Associations

We often attribute our reactions to prior associations and past experiences. After returning a 100-yard touchdown from the opposing team's kickoff, University of Virginia's senior tailback Marquis Weeks described it as "Just instinct. Kind of like running from the cops."[15] His humorous remark suggests a prior association. Some people love the smell of a cigar, lilacs, or gasoline. Others find these smells repulsive. Take a cigar, for example. We may love the smell of a cigar because we have fond memories as children sitting on our grandfather's lap while he smoked his cigar and read us stories. We may enjoy being around the smell because of the positive memories we associate with it. Recently, I had dinner with a friend who soaked his slab of beef ribs with Anchor Bar's Suicidal Buffalo Wing Sauce and took a huge bite without flinching. The waiters raced to bring me pitchers of ice cold water after I sampled the concoction. People's senses vary. My friend grew up accustomed to eating hot and spicy foods throughout his childhood. My palate is accustomed to more bland foods. These are differences in terms of our frame of reference.

Gender

Research suggests men and women differ from one another physiologically. For example, men and women produce different levels of certain hormones. From a sociological perspective, boys and girls are raised differently, generally speaking. Society often perpetuates certain biases and norms when it comes to what it means to be a male or female. This can influence communication behavior. Do males and females communicate differently? Communication research suggests the differences in how men and women communicate are subtly divergent. Some popular authors or pop psychologists, such as John Gray, suggest that men and women are from different worlds, that "men are from Mars and women from Venus." In reality, men and women experience the world in more ways common than uncommon. There are always exceptions to the generalizations people make about men and women because every individual is unique. It is also important to note that research findings regarding gender differences are sometimes conflicting. Research does suggest that, generally speaking:

- Women tend to engage in more eye contact during a conversation than men, but men stare or lock eyes longer.
- Men like more space around them when standing or sitting. Women stand closer to each other when speaking.
- Women smile more than men during conversations.
- Women are more expressive with their faces.
- Men and women cross their legs differently when sitting.
- When women listen, they are more expressive and interject more listening cues such as head nodding, smiling, and vocal encouragers such as, "oh really?" "Yeah?" and "uh-huh."
- Men tend to interrupt more.
- Women are more adept at detecting and remembering events and details tied to heightened emotions and are more likely to overtly express emotions verbally and nonverbally.
- Women disclose more personal information to each other and to men, and men tend to disclose more to women than they do to other men.
- Results from a 1995 study by scholars Nancy Briton and Judith Hall suggest that women are able to encode and decode other people's nonverbal messages more skillfully than men.
- In social situations, women tend to casually touch others more often than men.[16, 17, 18, 19, 20, 21, 22, 23, 24, 25]

Why these differences exist is largely a matter of speculation. Certainly they are influenced to some extent by the physiological and biochemical differences between men and women. Also, males and females are raised differently to some extent so socialization plays a factor. Finally, our exposure to stereotypical depictions of men and women via media outlets such as advertising, television, and movies may influence communication behavior to some extent.

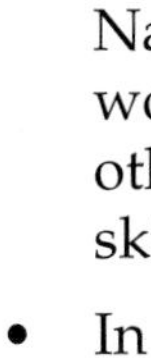

Do you agree or disagree with any of these generalizations? Why or why not?

Age

Do you look at the world differently than your parents or grandparents? Has someone ever told you (to your chagrin), "When I was your age . . . ?" There are generational differences when it comes to likes/dislikes, values, and experiences. These variations lead us to perceive things that, at times, are poles a part. My parents grew up during the Great Depression. My father witnessed my grandfather struggle valiantly to counter an impending economic threat to his business. Like so many other businesses, my grandfather's company collapsed. There was nothing to fall back on and poverty loomed. My grandfather struggled with alcoholism for a time. My father and his siblings were separated and sent to live with different relatives. My father's frame of reference influences his views and practices as it relates to money, spending, and financial planning. I am more comfortable taking financial risks and accumulating debt compared to my parents. In fact, we both avoid talking about money matters because our views are divergent and generally lead to uncomfortable conversations, mainly for my father. How much time we've been on the planet and what we've experienced during this time, comprise our frame of reference.

Culture

Grace Tsao, whose first published work, *Growing Up as an Asian American with a Disability*, illustrates how culture influences a person's frame of reference:

"I can remember distinct times when I was younger when my parents did not allow me to attend certain functions where a lot of first-generation Chinese, other than family, were in attendance. They told me that the traditional Chinese would gawk at me and gossip about the fact that I use a wheelchair . . . My mother would often tell me that the perceptions these people held about disabilities came from superstitions in Asian culture that bad things could only happen to people who have done wrong. They would look down on our family because only a family who has done wrong would deserve such a fate and shame. I didn't believe my parents at first. In fact, I accused them of being ashamed of who I am. They kept assuring me that they loved me no matter what, and that this sheltering was for my own good."[26]

Tsao's account portrays one person's reality in terms of cultural pressures. The same can be said about people's reactions to certain behaviors based on norms established by a society. **Norms** are rules or standards for what is considered appropriate or customary behavior. When President George W. Bush welcomed Saudi Arabia's Crown Prince Abdullah at his Texas ranch, the two leaders greeted reporters holding hands. This surprised a lot of American viewers who were not used to seeing men holding hands while standing side by side. In Arab culture, men hold hands as a sign of kinship and solidarity. They are much more physically expressive with each other with hugs, hand-holding, and kisses than American men.

Cultures have their own brand of masculinity or femininity. The culture one grows up and lives in can greatly influence one's identity. **Culture** is defined as the lifestyle and social identity of a group of people. A person's culture can include one's ethnic identity, art, laws, religion, practices, values, and ways of communicating. Culture is passed down from generation to generation via communication. This process is referred to as **enculturation.** When we learn, adapt to, and assimilate another group's culture this is called **acculturation.**[27] **Intercultural communication** is the study

of how people from different cultures communicate with each other.

Cultures differ from one another. Generally speaking, some cultures value their seniors or elders more. Some cultures attach more importance to the group than the individual. Cultures differ in how they establish social order and status as it relates to class, regionalism, gender, and sexual orientation. There are school and work-related cultures. Cultures are tied to music, politics, and hobbies. **Cultures vary in how they establish normative ways to express emotions, communicate nonverbally, and handle conflict**. Cultures are distinct in their inclusion of religion in public life. Communication scholars have noted some generalized differences between cultures with regard to the following characteristics.

Mobile versus Rigid

Some cultures allow for mobility in terms of class status, political participation, and economic opportunity. The average person in a mobile culture has a greater chance to advance from one socioeconomic level to another by means of education or ambition. Greater educational opportunities exist for the masses in mobile cultures. Political power is less concentrated. Equality is emphasized more between the sexes. Countries that are mobile include New Zealand, Denmark, Sweden, and the United States. In rigid cultures, political power is delegated to a few. People are encouraged not to challenge or question those in authority. People are born into a certain social class and are expected to stay there. People are socialized to "know your place" and date only individuals from the "same side of the tracks." Countries such as Mexico, India, Philippines, China, and Brazil are considered rigid.[28, 29]

Individualistic versus Collectivistic

Cultures that are predominately individualistic place heavy emphasis on self-determination and personal success. Freedom and autonomy is highly valued. Teams look to individuals to lead and move an organization forward. Corporate and education cultures reward individual achievement and initiative versus team performance. Families steer children toward independence early in life. The elderly strive to maintain their independence late into life to avoid being a burden to their children. The United States, Great Britain, Australia, Canada, Ireland, and France are predominantly individualistic. Collectivistic cultures emphasize what a work or family unit can accomplish. No single person stands out. These cultures focus more on interdependence between individuals. There is a long-standing tradition of doing what is best for one's employer or family, regardless of the personal costs. These cultures discourage individual competition and encourage relational harmony. Guatemala, Ecuador, Panama, Indonesia, South Korea, Pakistan, and much of Asia are considered collectivistic.[30, 31]

Low Context versus High Context

Most communication scholars agree that certain cultures are characterized as being primarily low or high context. In low context cultures (German, Norwegian, Swedish, and American), people are socialized to communicate assertively and directly. Conflict is addressed in a more "in-your-face" manner. These cultures are also more task oriented and value short-term time tables and tangible results. Cultures that are high context (Japanese, Native American, Korean, Mexican, and Arabic) emphasize group harmony and relationship building. In business transactions, a lot of time is spent getting to know each other before deals are sealed. People from low-context cultures may view this as time consuming and unnecessary. High-context cultures place more emphasis on compromise and negotiations, even when the end results are less than ideal. When deals are reached, they are done more often with a handshake and an unwritten verbal agreement versus formal, explicitly written contracts as are common in low-context cultures. High-context cultures discourage overt conflict and disagreements. While this is great for intergroup harmony, it may result in members providing less genuine feedback and harboring unspoken resentment.[32, 33]

Polychronic versus Monochronic

Anthropologist Edward T. Hall has noted that cultures differ in terms of how they view and manage time. European and North American cultures promote a fast-track life. People juggle multiple commitments and strive hard to get things done. The pace of life for people living in India, Kenya, and Argentina is generally slower. There is an emphasis on being "in the moment" with less concern for schedules, tasks, and deadlines. Hall also notes that cultures vary, not only in terms of their pace, but how they allocate time. He labels cultures that emphasize promptness, strict adherence to plans, and doing things one at a time before starting new projects as monochronic. Cultures that are more flexible and laid-back with time constraints and deadlines are polychronic. In polychronic cultures, appointments are not made as often. Being early or right on time is not common. People get together at a roundabout time frame. Plans are often changed and interruptions are tolerated, especially if the interruption involves a social or relationship building opportunity.[34, 35]

Monochronic Cultures
German
Austrian
Swiss
American

Polychronic Cultures
Latin American
Caribbean
Middle Eastern
African

Masculine versus Feminine Cultures

Sociologists and communication scholars note that, generally speaking, cultures differ in terms of masculine or feminine social propensities. In masculine cultures, gender roles are more distinct. Men are encouraged to be strong and assertive. They are expected to strive for material and career success. Children are raised to see the male as having more status and power. Men are the breadwinners and heads of the household. Women are encouraged to be modest, tender, and focused on improving the quality of life via traditional feminine roles: childrearing, cooking, and other domestic duties. In masculine cultures, ambition and competition are valued and promoted by men and to some extent women.

In feminine cultures, both men and women are raised to practice modesty, cooperativeness, and compromise for the sake of maintaining harmony and close relationships. The gender roles are less distinct. Men and women often share a similar status. The political, social, and economic rights and opportunities for both sexes are more egalitarian. According to one study, the United States was ranked fifteenth compared to all other countries in masculine propensity.[36, 37]

Masculine Cultures
Japan
Austria
Venezuela
Italy
Switzerland
Mexico
Ireland
Jamaica

Feminine Cultures
Sweden
Norway

Denmark
Costa Rica
Finland
Chile
Portugal

Think about your family, school, and work environment. What type of culture orientation does each have?

Your Take: If you could move right now to any part of the world, which cultural orientations would you feel more comfortable living in? For example, would you prefer living in a collectivist versus individualistic culture? How about a polychronic versus monochronic? Why?

Research on Interpersonal Communication and Culture

Does research suggest that there are cultural differences in terms of people's communication behaviors? Generalizations can be made; however, they do not apply to all individuals. Research does suggest that, generally speaking:

- Native American culture tends to value succinctness and getting right to the point. Native Americans tend to value silence more when in an uncertain social situations.[38, 39]
- The Arabic language tends to be more emotive and expressive than the English language. Strong assertions and exaggerations are made more often in everyday conversation among Arabs. If we were in an Arab home eating a meal as a guest, when asked if we wanted something more to eat and drink, a simple "no" may not suffice. We might need to assert this several times, "no, no, no. Thank you, I'm full."[40]
- People in Asian cultures tend to express emotions less publicly compared to other cultures. In one study, Japanese and American students were videotaped as they watched graphic surgical scenes from a documentary. American students' revulsion to the scenes were more pronounced as determined by their facial reactions.
- People in Asian, Native American, Latin, and some African cultures tend to limit direct eye contact with someone in authority as a sign of respect.
- In American culture, we tend to call someone we wish to date about three to four days in advance. In traditional Asian cultures, it is not uncommon for one to call not the potential date directly, but *the parents* to set something up weeks or even months ahead of time.
- Colors mean different things depending on one's culture. In Iran, the color blue has negative associations. For the Cherokee it stands for defeat. To the people living in Ghana and Egypt, it represents joy and virtue.[41, 42, 43]

Communication researchers have also found that certain nonverbal behaviors are considered taboo or impolite in different cultures. Blinking one's eyes is seen as rude in Taiwan. Placing one's foot on a table or chair is disrespectful in several Middle Eastern countries. Folding your arms over your chest is disapproved in Fiji. Placing your hands in your pockets is construed as ill-mannered in Malaysia. In America, we commonly point at things or people with our index finger. In parts of China, Indonesia, and the Middle East, that gesture is considered discourteous. The same can be said about waving the hand. In America, we do this as a nonverbal way to say "hi." It is offensive to do so in Nigeria and Greece. In parts of the world, posture is considered very important. It wouldn't look good to slouch at a meeting with Chinese businessmen.[44, 45, 46] International communication expert and author Roger Axtell provides cross-cultural travel and business guidelines in his book *Do's and Taboos Around the World.* He states that in some parts of the world, certain topics are best avoided. For example, if Americans are visiting Mexico, they are advised to not discuss anything related to illegal aliens or the Mexican–American war. If you're in Columbia, he suggests that you keep your critical comments about bullfighting to yourself. In Japan, World War II is a sensitive topic for older Japanese.[47, 48, 49]

It is important to note that cultural differences in terms of communication are becoming more difficult to delineate. Today, workplaces and schools are more culturally diverse. The broad use of the internet, increased intercontinental travel, migration, and exposure to the world media has had a homogenizing effect. Still, for those of us interested in international business, travel abroad, intercultural dating, or gaining a broader appreciation of different ways of life, learning about other cultures is advantageous: culture influences our frame of reference. Let's look next at how we can challenge and expand our awareness when it comes to our frame of reference.

. . . How does the following potentially impact our interpersonal communication?

- Prior associations/past experiences
- Age
- Gender
- Culture

Challenging and Expanding Our Frame of Reference

NBC's winner of nine Primetime Emmys, the *West Wing*, gave viewers an inside look into the White House and a fictional president's administration. In one dramatic scene, President Jed Bartlet, played by Martin Sheen, is about to address a group of radio talk show hosts assembled at a White House reception. In the middle of his speech, he gets distracted by a female talk show host, Dr. Jen Jacobs, who has been critical of his policies in support of gay rights. He abruptly stops his speech to challenge her public statements:

Bartlet: "I like your show. I like how you call homosexuality an abomination."

Jacobs: "I don't, Mr. President . . . the Bible does."

Bartlet: "Yes it does, Leviticus."

Jacobs: "18:22"

Bartlet: "Chapter and verse. . . . I'm interested in selling my youngest daughter into slavery as sanctioned in Exodus 21:7 . . . what would a good price for her be? . . . My Chief of Staff . . . insists on working on the Sabbath. Exodus 35:2 clearly says he should be put to death. Now am I morally obligated to do that myself. . .?

Touching the skin of a dead pig makes one unclean. Leviticus 11:7. If they promise to wear gloves can the Washington Redskins still play football? Can Notre Dame? West Point? Does the whole town really have to be together to stone my brother John for planting different crops side by side? Can I burn my mother in a small family gathering for wearing garments made from two different threads? Think about those questions, won't you?"

The president's retort is intended to question the talk show host's literal interpretation of the Bible. He suggests that her interpretation, influenced by her own religious indoctrination, was not based on undisputed authority. He cited scripture that religious people don't adhere to today and implied that she should base her frame of reference on a more modern interpretation, or at least not use her religious views as justification for depriving a certain group of people equal rights.

A foreign exchange student shared with me that, in the Netherlands, it is customary to invite someone over to your house after you have developed a strong relationship with that person. In American culture, we tend to invite people over to develop a relationship. Men in the United States tend to greet each other with handshakes, whereas men in European countries such as Italy and France are more likely to hug and kiss each other on the cheeks. In some cultures, men walk arm in arm down the streets. In America, we would assume the men who do this are bisexual or gay. Some people outside of American culture think it is strange that male athletes often pat each other on the behind during games. These differences are cultural and reflect a person's frame of reference.

Differences do not have to be good or bad, just different. We should avoid assuming that how we do things is right, and what other groups or cultures do is inferior. A person is considered **ethnocentric** if he or she believes his or her culture's or group's values and customs are "right" or "natural" and others are "wrong" or "unnatural."

In 2006, 56% of American adults were Caucasian. By 2050, it is expected that they will become a minority. There will be no majority race. Today, fifty percent of all people living in California are nonwhite.[50, 51]

Ethnocentric beliefs are often grounded in what is called dichotomous thinking. A **dichotomous thinker** perceives things as strictly black or white. She or he has a difficult time looking at the intricacies of an issue or situation beyond an either/or or an all right/all wrong mindset. Many issues or situations are more complex and warrant thoughtful consideration beyond what is immediately apparent. For example, many people expect and appreciate receiving gifts on their birthdays. Jehovah Witnesses abstain from this custom and do not celebrate birthdays.[52] Those of us who are not Jehovah Witnesses may immediately criticize this. However, with open-minded curiosity and a little research, we can appreciate and understand the religious and practical reasons why Jehovah Witnesses do not celebrate birthdays. One of the basic tenants Jehovah Witnesses strive to adhere to is humility. They see some customs such as holidays and birthdays as very self-serving and materialistic.

© Ramzi Hachicho, 2010. Used under license from Shutterstock, Inc.

There is also a practical side to their custom, too. How many times have we been hurt or disappointed when our birthday was not recognized by someone important to us or in a way that we wished? Jehovah Witnesses do not have to deal with this common problem, nor do they bother with awkward party situations, obligatory attendance at other people's birthdays or holiday get-togethers, stressful trips to multiple stores to buy a present, or long waits at the customer service desk to return an unwanted gift. Dichotomous thinking often results in and reinforces ethnocentrism.

In addition, other beliefs are a byproduct of our frame of reference. **Stereotypes** are broad, sweeping generalizations or distorted views about a group of people. Even though it may be hard to do so, write down the first thing that comes to mind for the following:

Blondes are ______________________.
Women are ______________________.
Jews are ______________________.
If you are Dutch you are ______________.
Asians are ______________________.
Rich people are ___________________.
If you are homeless you are ____________.
Arabs are ______________________.
Effeminate men are ________________.
African American women are ___________.
Gothic teens are ___________________.
Tomboys are ______________________.

Your Turn: Have you ever found yourself believing in these or any other stereotypes? Why? How might this stereotype affect your interpersonal communication?

If we have had little or no experience interacting with people who are different from us as far as race, ethnicity, religious affiliation, disability, gender, or sexual orientation, we are more prone to harbor stereotypical views. An able-bodied person may not want to do a project with someone who is physically challenged because he assumes he will have to do most of the work. This is an assumption based on a stereotype. The same can be said about not hiring a woman because it is believed she is incapable of doing a job or task traditionally done by a man. Stereotypes are reinforced by the media. Many people criticized the producers of the hit HBO series *The Sopranos,* especially Italian-American anti-defamation groups for what they saw as a stereotypical portrayal of an Italian family. Organizations such as The Commission for Social Justice have applied pressure on movie producers to stop their heavy characterization of Italians as unintelligent, poor, or mobsters.

"My family is super religious. Two years ago, I met my boyfriend (the sweetest, nicest guy in the world who just so happened to be an atheist). I started reading several books such as *The God Delusion* by Richard Dawkins, Professor of Public Understanding of Science at Oxford University, which offered a different view about religion and the Bible. I started reading the Bible from an analytical and critical view. I found that religion and a belief in a spiritual being is not necessary to create a sense of purpose and appreciation for life or develop a moral code. I learned it was ok to question my previous unchallenged religious beliefs. I now consider myself an atheist. 'Atheist' is a taboo word in my family. I have encountered hostility and aggressive conversion attempts by concerned friends and family. Someone I work with runs a Freethinkers meeting locally and invited me to go. I do, and it is so nice to have a place to wear my 'Recovering Christian' shirt, and not feel like the biggest outcast."

—*Chandah*

If our ethnocentric or stereotypical views lead us to have a negative attitude or feeling toward a group of people, we are considered *prejudiced*. **Prejudice** is possessing negative beliefs about a person who is representative of a certain group or classification of people. This can include feelings of disdain or distrust toward a certain group. "There is no way I'm voting for a female president" or "He is way too old" are prejudicial statements. Prejudice may cause us to feel uncomfortable approaching and getting to know people who are different from us. At the same time, we may be robbing ourselves of potential friendships, new insights, and meaningful interaction. If the negative view is towards a person of a certain race, this is called **racism**. If we harbor negative views about or are not sensitive to the concerns of gay and or bisexual people, this is called **heterosexism**. **Sexism** is viewing people critically based on their sex. Shortly after the September 11, 2001 terrorist attack in New York and Washington D.C., it came as a shock to many Americans when news outlets reported how women were treated under the Taliban, a ruling religious sect in Afghanistan. Females could not go to school. They were forbidden to step out in public without a male relative. They were required to cover their entire bodies with a tent-like article of clothing called a burqa. A November 17, 2001 report released by the U.S. Department of State's Bureau of Democracy, Human Rights, and Labor details what happened to one unnamed mother:

> *"The day was much like any other. For the young Afghan mother, the only difference was that her child was feverish and had been for some time and needed to see a doctor. The mother was alone and the doctor was across town. She had no male relative to escort her. To ask another man to do so would be to risk severe punishment. To go on her own meant that she would risk flogging. Because she loved her child, she had no choice . . . She set out, cradling her child in her arms . . . She was spotted by a teenage Taliban guard who tried to stop her. Intent on saving her child, the mother ignored him, hoping that he would ignore her. He didn't. Instead he raised his weapon and shot her repeatedly. Both mother and child fell to the ground. They survived because bystanders in the market intervened to save them. The young Taliban guard was unrepentant—fully supported by the regime. The woman should not have been out alone."*[53]

In some parts of Asia, especially Bangladesh, a man who is disgraced by his wife can spray sulfuric acid on her and receive little or no punishment, despite recent laws making the act illegal. The acid will melt the skin all the way through, leaving the bones of its victims exposed, causing grotesque, permanent disfigurement. According to a CNN report, acid spraying is on the rise.[54] In another part of the world, many young African girls undergo forced female genital circumcision. This entails the removal of the clitoris and other genital tissue, often with no anesthetic and with unsterilized knives or razor blades. The practice is now considered a legitimate reason to issue asylum to women who want to escape from having to endure this custom in several countries.[55] For the last 3,000 years, social and politician institutions have been dominated by men and their attitudes and values. Historical and religious writings over the years illustrate the way societies have viewed and treated women:

- *"I permit no women to teach or have authority over men, she is to keep silent."*
  1 Timothy 2:12 New Testament
- *"Women should remain at home, sit still, keep house and bear children."*
  Martin Luther (1483–1546)
- "The souls of women are so small that some believe they have none at all."
  Samuel Butler (1612–1680)

One could argue that the way women are treated in various parts of the world is discriminatory. **If we act out in certain ways based on prejudice, this is called discrimination. Discrimination** is the act of treating a person in a hurtful or unfair manner because of an observable or known characteristic such as race, age, gender, body weight, disability, religious affiliation, or sexual orientation. Discrimination can come in the form of words and actions. In an *ABC 20/20* investigation just a few years ago, concealed cameras captured the interaction between car salesmen and car buyers at different dealerships throughout the country. The buyers were hired by ABC to act like they were looking to purchase a car. Half of the buyers were Caucasian and half were African American. Viewers witnessed how salesmen spent less time with and quoted higher prices to the African American buyers.

> Up until 1967, it was illegal in parts of the U.S. for blacks and whites to marry each other.

Our frame of reference also plays a role in influencing our assumptions. If we know that a coworker earns the same income as we do, we may assume: "I can't afford that expensive of a

"Different from me does not mean less than me."

car, so how can she?" This assumption may not be correct because other factors may contribute to our coworker's ability to purchase the car.

Examples of assumptions people have:

- Once a cheater, always a cheater.
- My parents did the best they knew how to do.
- What goes around, comes around.
- Men are only as faithful as their options.
- A woman can keep a secret until she talks to another woman.
- No one is ever going to fall in love with me.

It may be prudent for us to question some of our assumptions and consider that there are other possibilities to explain what we observe about other people, and different ways to think about something.

Challenging Our Frame of Reference: The Pillow Method

Communication scholars and authors Saundra Hybels and Richard Weaver suggest in their 2007 text *Communicate Effectively* that there are assumptions we have regarding communication and culture that warrant evaluation. They state that we should not assume that there is only one right way to communicate.[56] It also helps to consider why a person is communicating or acting a certain way. A good question to consider is: "What is it about this person's frame of reference that may play a role in how he or she is responding to me?" If we take the time to get into another person's head, connect with his or her past, or consider recent events that may have an influence on the person's psyche, we may approach a person with more patience and sensitivity. In addition, we can employ a technique designed to encourage us to look at another person's perspective called the **pillow method**. Author and poet Paul Reps describes how a group of Japanese school children created it to encourage people to look at all sides of an issue. It is now taught in business schools throughout the world! I have modified the method. Imagine a couch with two pillows. A pillow has two sides. Each side represents a position we can take when we are in disagreement with someone. Here are the four sides:

1. **I am right, you are wrong.**
2. **I am wrong, you are right.**
3. **There is truth in both our views**.
4. **This issue is not as big as I am making it.**[57]

The one side we are most accustomed to is "I'm right, you are wrong." We usually approach our conversations with those we are not in agreement with from this position. It usually leads to more disagreement and a stalemate. If we flip the pillow, the other position is "You are right, I am wrong." Here, we jot down or consider all of the reasons why the other person may be right. We attempt to think about the other person's frame of reference, and consider the other person's feelings and needs. We may answer the questions: "What is she or he is saying that is justified?" "How are her or his perceptions and opinions understandable and legitimate?" "If I was him or her, what would I want or need and why?" Let's grab the other pillow. In position three, we identify where there is common ground. There is merit in all views. Both sides have valid points. Are there areas were the two of you agree? What are they? Finally, the last position encourages us to consider how important the issue is compared to everything else we could be concerned about.

We may find that the issue or disagreement is not as important as we are making it. Here, we may ask ourselves the question: "Is this what I really want to focus my time and attention on?"

The skill builder at the end of this unit will give us a chance to practice this. After we have considered each of these positions carefully, we can rehearse or prepare what we are going to say. The person may be more inclined to listen to us, compromise, and cooperate, once he or she senses that we are considering the issue in ways other than position one—"I'm right, you are wrong."

> **"You will find many of the truths we cling to depend greatly on our own point of view."**
>
> **—Yoda**

In addition, we can challenge our frame of reference by avoiding the tendency to base our perceptions about other groups or cultures strictly from popular media images alone. It takes a willingness to read about, interact with, and visit people from other cultures or backgrounds.

Those of us who are gay or bisexual still conditioned in a powerful way to be secretive, paranoid, and fear-laden about our sexual feelings. Comedians tell jokes about us and fail to see us sitting in the audience. Classmates ridicule us in the locker rooms and fail to see us wince in pain. Family members lob hurtful slurs at us and fail to see us in their own family. Mystery and fear feeds prejudice and cruelty. The very friends and family that we can turn to for support are may be the very ones who insult us and ridicule us. Because it is a very essential need as a human being to fit in, to belong, and feel accepted, those of us who are bisexual or gay take this part of us that is natural and innate and we repress, deny, and disown our sexual feelings. We hide and mask this part of ourselves. We try to conform—which is to our detriment."

—*Davin*

Ways we can do this include:

- Listen to or watch a radio or television station from another country or culture.
- Go out of our way to work with, recruit, select, train, and promote people from outside our group.
- Read a religious book other than the one we base our faith on.
- If we are religious, read a published work by someone who is agnostic or atheistic to understand and appreciate why someone may doubt or deny the existence of a God or gods.
- Attend lectures on topics with which you are not familiar.
- Visit museums and art shows featuring exhibits from other countries.
- Learn about the dos and don'ts of intercultural communication by reading such popular books as *Multicultural Manners: Essential Rules of Etiquette For The 21st Century* by Norine Dresser, *Dos and Taboos Around the World* by Roger Axtell, and *Communicating with Asia: People and Customs* by Harry Irwin.

- Take classes and attend conferences on intercultural communication and world studies.

As communicators, we also can be authentic in our communication. When we are in a communication situation, we can admit our need to learn more and invite people who are different from us to teach us about their practices, beliefs, and values. Dialogue that reflects this may include:

- "This is new to me. What is the customary way to handle this?"
- "I would like to be more knowledgeable about your culture. I'm wondering if you would feel comfortable sharing with me why you . . ."
- "I would appreciate learning about your faith. Would you mind sharing with me the significance of . . . ?"
- "Some of your artwork (jewelry, clothes, music) is unique and unfamiliar to me. I want to compliment you on it. Does it mean something?"

Being sincere in our desire to learn from others and expressing appreciation for the information we receive will go a long way to increase dialogue between diverse people. A statement showing appreciation may include:

> *"That is great to know. Thank you for sharing some of your heritage with me."*

The key here is to learn and appreciate. We may not always agree with, or fully understand, what a person is saying. To encourage people to open up to us, they need to perceive that our motives are to learn more and appreciate them, not criticize or judge.

. . . In what ways can we challenge and expand our frame of reference to improve our intercultural communication? How would you incorporate ethnocentrism, dichotomous thinking, stereotypes, prejudice, discrimination, and the pillow method in your answer?

Unit Summary

Frame of reference is our collective experience or everything that has happened to us up to this moment. It includes such things as our family upbringing, gender, social/economic status, educational experiences, and culture. Our frame of reference influences our perception of and interactions with others. It has a pervasive influence on our life choices, attitudes, assumptions, and values. Significant aspects of our frame of reference explored in this unit include our prior associations, age, gender, and culture. Cultures vary in terms of their norms and practices. It behooves us as communicators to guard against ethnocentrism and challenge stereotypes and prejudices which can lead to discrimination. Ways to understand other people's points of view and life experience is the pillow method, asking questions for clarification, and learning about people from other cultures or groups.

Key Questions

1. What is frame of reference? What makes up our frame of reference? How does it impact our interpersonal communication?
2. In what ways does our frame of reference influence who we chose to have relationships with, why our relationships move from various relational stages, and when we experience dialectical tensions?
3. How does the following potentially impact our interpersonal communication:
   - Prior associations/past experiences
   - Age
   - Gender
   - Culture?
4. In what ways can we challenge and expand our frame of reference to improve our intercultural communication? How would you incorporate ethnocentrism, dichotomous thinking, stereotypes, prejudice, discrimination, and the pillow method in your answer?

Vocabulary Playback

Frame of Reference
Relational Rewards
Relational Stages Model
Dialectical Tensions
Norms
Culture
Enculturation
Acculturation
Intercultural Communication
Ethnocentrism
Dichotomous Thinking
Stereotypes
Prejudice
Racism
Heterosexism
Sexism
Discrimination
Pillow Method

Theoretically Speaking

- Social Exchange Theory
- Relational Development Theory
- Spiral of Silence Theory

Focus Group/Class Discussion

- Identify a time when your frame of reference (such as your past experiences, age, gender, and culture) influenced how you communicated with someone. Describe it.
- Do you agree or disagree with the social exchange theory? Why?
- Chief Wahoo is the Cleveland Indians mascot. Some argue that it is culturally insensitive to use Native American tribes as sports team mascots? Do you agree or disagree?
- Why might it be perceived as acceptable for two black men to call each other "nigger?" or for two gay men to call to each other "queens" or "bitches?" Why do some black men and gay men consider this offensive even between black and gay men respectively?
- In terms of our interactions and communication, how do opposite gender friendships differ from same gender friendships? How are romantic relationships between people of the same gender similar or different from opposite gender romantic relationships? To what extent does frame of reference influence these differences?
- Do you think that cross-cultural couples experience greater difficulties than same cultural couples in terms of societal acceptance and relational conflict? Why or why not?
- Many cultures practice arranged marriages, where the parents select their child's husband or wife. Those of us who are socialized to view courtship from a contemporary Western or European perspective may immediately criticize this practice. Having one's family choose your life partner clashes with our notions of romantic, independent selection. Using the pillow method, especially step 2, consider how arranged marriages may be ideal or work for a lot of people. You may want to do some on-line research. Be prepared to share your responses with the class.

Unit 11 Vocabulary Review

___ Frame of Reference
___ Norms
___ Acculturation
___ Intercultural communication
___ Ethnocentrism
___ Dichotomous thinking
___ Stereotypes
___ Prejudice
___ Racism
___ Discrimination
___ Enculturation
___ Relational Rewards
___ Relational Stages Model
___ Dialectical Tensions
___ Culture
___ Heterosexism
___ Pillow Method
___ Sexism

A. The things we get from a relationship that we like and value.

B. Having negative beliefs and feelings toward people based on their gender.

C. A technique designed to encourage us to look at another person's perspective or different sides of an issue.

D. Possessing negative beliefs and feelings about a person who is representative of a certain group or classification of people.

E. The belief that the values and customs of one's own group or culture are superior to others.

F. Rules or standards for what is considered appropriate or customary behavior.

G. This is a term which refers to the negative views and feelings people have towards people who are gay or bisexual.

H. The study of communication between people of different cultures.

I. Having negative beliefs and feelings towards a person based on his or her race.

J. The process of passing culture from generation to generation via communication.

K. The kind of thinking that leads a person to perceive things as entirely either/or or good/bad.

L. The process of learning, adapting to, and assimilating another group's culture.

M. Treating a person in a hurtful or unfair manner because of an observable or known characteristic such as race, age, gender, body weight, disability, religious affiliation, or sexual orientation.

N. This is our collective experience, or everything that has ever happened to us up to this moment.

O. A model used to represent where a relationship may be at starting with early interactions and ending in termination.

P. These are the inevitable extremes we gravitate to in relationships in terms of needs.

Q. The lifestyle and social identity of a group of people.

R. Broad sweeping generalizations or distorted views about a group of people.

Exercise

Elisabeth Noelle-Neumann is a German political scientist who proposed the Spiral of Silence Theory. The theory suggests that people are less likely to express their opinion if they think that they are in the minority or that their position is unpopular. She theorizes that it is because we fear social isolation or rejection. In one of her studies, subjects who were smokers were invited to respond with their opinions to a statement made by someone in the study group who was set up as a confederate. In research terms, a confederate is an actor who performs a role during a study. The confederate says or does something and researchers observe the reactions of the other people in the study to the confederate's actions.

While the participants in the study were doing an activity, the confederate stated emphatically, "It seems to me that smokers are terribly inconsiderate. They force others to inhale their health-endangering smoke." When the smokers knew that nonsmokers were present in the room, they were more guarded in what they said and were less adamant in their opinions regarding smokers' rights.[58, 59]

Your professor may have you complete any one or combination of the following:

1. As a group, decide if you agree or disagree with Noelle-Neumann's theory? Why or why not?
2. Have you ever participated in a small group where all the other members seemed to think a certain way which was contrary to your way of thinking? How did you handle it? What were the results?
3. As a group, answer the question, "If we know that a person's communication behavior is influenced by his or her frame of reference, which is often a reflection of the dominate culture, what are the implications for people who are in the minority?"
4. Brainstorm as a group different scenarios where it would be difficult, like the smokers in Noelle-Neumann's study, for someone to share his or her true opinions and feelings.
5. Create and act out a scene in which characters demonstrate the spiral of silence theory via a real life scenario.
6. What are some strategies we could use to encourage people with unpopular opinions to speak freely and candidly?

Skill Builder: The Pillow Method

Anytime we disagree with someone or feel an argument brewing. We can take some time to think about and focus on the last three positions of the pillow method by posing them as questions to ourselves. We can consider these positions while we rehearse what we are going to say before saying it. This will help us to determine where there are areas for compromise and understanding. A powerful technique is to communicate to the person we are having a disagreement with how we understand where he or she is coming from based on position 2 of the pillow method.

1. How might I be wrong and the other person right? (position #2)
2. How are we both right (justified) regarding this? (Also ask yourself: What can we agree on?) (position #3)
3. In what other ways can I look at this so that the issue is not blown out of proportion? (position #4)

For practice, think of a conflict or disagreement that you are having or have had with someone. Using the last three positions as prompts, identify the reasons, facts, or examples that support each position.

I am wrong, you are right

____

____

____

There is truth in both our views.

____

____

____

How is this issue not as big as I am making it?

___

___

___

References

Unit 1 References

1. Humorous anecdotes from Ahajokes. Retrieved from http://ahajokes.com
2. Collins, R. (2008, July 02). Miscommunication blamed for Massachusetts gaffe. *Fire House News Web site*. Retrieved from http://cms.firehouse.com
3. Associated Press, (2008, September 26). Lawyer says penis amputation was authorized. MSNBC.MSN. Retrieved from http://www.msnbc.msn.com/id/26903756
4. Araiza, K. & Lattanzio, V. (2009, March 11). Airline delivers dead body to pet store. NBC /Philedelphia News. Retrieved from http://www.nbcphiladelphia.com
5. Lincoln, R. (2009, March 01). Miscommunication dooms Wolverines down the stretch against Wisconsin. Daily Sports Web site. Retrieved from http://www.michigandaily.com/node/47907/talk
6. (2007, June 21). Police: Pacman's cash display sparked Vegas melee. ESPN Sports Web site. Retrieved from http://sports.espn.go.com/espn/print?id=2775250&type=story
7. (2005). Memorable quotes from *Hitch*. The Internet Movie Data Base. Retrieved from http://www.imdb.com/title/tt0386588/quotes
8. Senge, P., Keiner, A., Roberts, C., Ross, R., & Smith, B. (1994). *Fifth discipline fieldbook: Strategies and tools for building a learning organization*. New York: Doubleday. In Stewart, J., Zediker, K., & Witteborn, S. (2005). *Together communicating interpersonally: A social construction approach.* (Vol 6, p. 47). Los Angeles: Roxbury Press.
9. Scott, S. (2002). *Fierce conversations.* Viking Penguin. In Stewart, J. (2006). *Bridges not walls.* (Vol 9, 50–52). Boston: McGraw Hill.
10. (2005). Memorable quotes from *The Office*. The Internet Movie Data Base. Retrieved from http://www.imdb.com/title/tt0386676
11. Soper, P. (1963). *Basic public speaking*. New York: Oxford University Press.
12. Hoehn, D. (2001). *Understanding communication.* (3rd ed.). Dubuque, IA: Kendall Hunt Publishing.
13. Buckley, M. (1992). Focus on research: We listen to a book a day. *Language Arts. 69*, 101–109.
14. Nellermoe, D.A., Weirich, T.R., & Reinstein, A. (1999). Using practitioners' viewpoints to improve accounting students' communications skills. *Business Communication Quarterly, 62*(2), 41–60.
15. Adler, R. & Towne, N. (2003). *Looking out, looking in.* (10th ed.). Belmont, CA: Thomson Wadsworth.
16. The *Pickup Artist*. VH1 Shows Web site. Retrieved from http://www.vh1.com/shows?dyn/the_pick_up_artist/series_about.jhtml
17. Walker, V. & Brokaw, L. (2001). *Becoming aware.* (8th ed.). Dubuque, Iowa: Kendall Hunt Publishing.
18. Swets, P. (1983). *The art of talking so that people will listen: Getting through to family, friends, and business associates.* New York: Fireside, p. 5.
19. A brief history of the academy. West Point Web site. Retrieved from http://www.usma.edu/history.asp
20. Information paper on (honor). West Point Web site. Retrieved from http://www.usma.edu/Commitees/Honor/Info/main.htl

21. Adler, R. & Towne, N. (2003). *Looking out, looking in*. Belmont, CA: Thomson Wadsworth.

22. (1973). An end to silence. *Time Magazine*. Retrieved from http://www.time.com/time/magazine/article/0,9171,910676,00.html

23. Lodge, H. (2007, June 17). Why emotion keeps you well. *Parade Magazine*, p. 12.

24. Jackson, W. (1978, September 7). *Wisconsin State Journal*. UPI.

25. Lodge, H. (2007, June 17). Why emotion keeps you well. *Parade Magazine*, p. 12.

26. Vedentam, S. (2006, June 23). The number of people who say they have no one to confide in has risen. *Washington Post*, p. A03.

27. Putnam, R. (1995). Bowling alone: America's declining social capital. *The Journal of Democracy, 6:1*, 65–78.

28. Putnam, R. (2000). *The collapse and revival of American community*. New York: Simon and Shuster.

29. Galston, W. (1996). Won't you be my neighbor? *The American Prospect, 26*.

30. Borom, E. (2000). Study offers early look at how internet is changing daily life. Stanford Institute for the Quantitative Study of Society Web site: Retrieved from http://www.stanford.edu/group/siqs

31. Gordon, S. (2009). Fourteen surprising signs you'll live longer than you think. *Prevention*. Retrieved from http://www.prevention.com/suprisingsigns/

32. Diener, E. & Seligman, M. (2002). Very happy people. *Psychological Science, 13*, 81–84.

33. Eisenberger, N., Lieberman, M., & Williams, K. (2003). Does rejection hurt? An MRI study of social exclusion. *Science, 302*, 290–292.

34. Epley, N., Akalis, S., Waytz, A., & Cacioppo, J. (2003). Creating social connection through inferential reproduction: Loneliness and perceived agency in gadgets, gods, and greyhounds. *Psychological Science, 19*, 114–120.

35. Twenge, J. (2000). The age of anxiety? Birth cohort change in anxiety and neuroticism. *Journal of Personality and Social Psychology, 79*, 1007–1021.

36. Cohen, S., Doyle, W., Skoner, D., Rabin, B., & Gwaltney, J. (1997). Social ties and susceptibility to the common cold. *Journal of the American Medical Association, 277*, 239–242.

37. Case, R., Moss, A., Case, N., McDermott, S., & Eberly, S. (1992). Living alone after myocardial infarction. *The Journal of the American Medical Association*, 267, p. 515–519.

38. Uchino, B. (2004). *Social support and physical health: Understanding the health consequences of relationships*. New Haven: Yale University Press.

39. Berk, L. & Tan, S. (2006). Bet-endorphin and HGH increase are associated with both the anticipation and experience of mirthful laughter. *FASEB Journal, 20*, A382.

40. Adams, E. & McGuire, F. (1986). Is laughter the best medicine? A study of the effects of humor on perceived pain and affect. *Activities, Adaptation and Aging, 8*(3–4), 157–175.

41. Yovetich, N., Dale, A., & Hudak, M. (1990). Benefits of humor in reduction of threat-induced anxiety. *Psychological Reports, 66*, 51–58.

42. Berk, L., Tan, S., Napier B., & Eby W. (1989). Eustress of mirthful laughter modifies natural killer cell activity. *Clinical Research* (1989), *37*, 115A.

43. Berk, L., Tan, S., Nehlsen-Cannarella, S., Napier, B., Lewis, J., Lee, J., et al. (1988). Humor associated laughter decreases cortisol and increases spontaneous lymphocyte blastogenesis. *Clinical Research, 36*, 435A.

44. Buchowski, M., Majchrzak, K., Blomquist, K., Chen, Y., Byrne, D., & Bachorowski, J. (2006). *International Journal of Obesity, 31*, 131–137.

45. Fleshner, M. & Laudenslager, M. (2004). Psychoneuroimmunology: Then and now. *Behavioral & Cognitive Neuroscience Reviews, 3*, 114–130.

46. Segerstrom, S. & Miller, G. (2004). Psychological stress and the human immune system: A meta-analytic study of 30 years of inquiry. *Psychological Bulletin, 130*, 601–630.

47. Meyer, R. & Haggerty, R. (1962). Streptococcal infections in families: Factors

alterating individual susceptibility. *Pediatrics, 29,* 536–549.

48. Narem, R. (1980). Try A Little TLC. *Science,* 80, 15.

49. Legarde, E., Chastang, J., Gueguen, A., Coeuret-Pellicer, M., Chiron, M., & Lafont, S. (2004). Emotional stress and traffic accidents: The impact of separation and divorce. *Epidemiology, 15,* 762–766.

50. Augustyn, M. & Simons-Morton, B. (1995). Adolescent drinking and driving: Etiology and interpretation. *Journal of Drug Education, 25,* 41–59.

51. Flewelling, R. & Bauman, K. (1990). Family structure as a predictor of initial substance abuse and sexual intercourse in early adolescence. *Journal of Marriage and The Family, 52,* 171–181.

52. Jackson, R. (2006, February). Maria Bello's aha moment. *Oprah Magazine.* p. 6.

53. Scott, S. (2002). *Fierce conversations.* Viking Penguin. In Stewart, J. (2006). *Bridges not walls.* (Vol 9, 50–52). Boston: McGraw Hill.

54. (1999). How Americans communicate. *National Communication Association.* Retrieved from http://www.natcom.org/research/Roper/how_Americans_communicate.htm

55. Kirchler, E. (1988). Marital happiness and interaction in everyday surroundings: A time-sample diary approach for couples. *Journal of Social and Personal Relationships, 5,* 375–382.

56. Nutting, R. (2007, February 23) Majority of Americans dislike their jobs. *MarketWatch.Com.* Retrieved from http://www.marketwatch.com/news/story/majority-americans-dislike-their-jobs/story.aspx?guid=%7B7841B7C5-1536-46EE-D74BC674582C%7D

57. West, K. (2007, November 19). The top five reasons employees hate their jobs. *National Business Research Institute Blog.* Retrieved from http://www.nbrii.com/blog/TheTop5ReasonsEmployeesHateTheirJobs

58. Peoples, D. (1992). *Presentations Plus.* (2nd ed.). New York: John Wiley & Sons.

59. Morreale, S. (2001). Communication and career promotion. *Spectra, 8.*

60. Morreale, S., Osborn, M., & Pearson, J. (1998). Why communication is important: A rationale for the centrality of the study of communication. *Journal of The Association For Communication Administration 29,* 1–25.

61. (2005). Job outlook. National Association of Colleges and Employers Web site. Retrieved from http://www.jobweb.com/joboutllok/2005outlook/1a.htm

62. Peoples, D. (1992). *Presentations Plus.* (2nd ed.). New York: John Wiley & Sons.

63. Hoehn, D. (2001). *Understanding Communication.* Dubuque, Iowa: Kendall Hunt Publishing.

64. Winsor, J., Curtis, D., & Stephens, R. (1997). National preferences in business and communication education: An update. *Journal of the Association for Communication Administration, 3,* 170–179.

65. Peoples, D. (1992). *Presentations Plus.* (2nd ed.). New York: John Wiley & Sons.

66. How to improve your people smartness. *Society for the Advancement of Education.* Retrieved from http://www.findarticles.com/p/articles/mi_m1272/is_267

67. Strachan, H. (2004). Communication. *Research and Theory for Nursing Practice: An International Journal, 18,* 7–10.

68. Winokoor, C. (2007, February 09). Joe Biden, our next talk show host. Taunton Gazzette Web site. Retrieved from http://www.tauntongazzett.com

69. Schacter, S. (1959). *The Psychology of Affiliation.* Stanford: Stanford University Press.

Unit 2 References

1. Free, C. (2007, February). Divine intervention. *Readers Digest*, 10.
2. Associated Press. (2007, April 09). Imus, Sharpton spar over racial comments. MSNBC. Retrieved from http://www.msnbc.msn.com/id/17999196/fromRS.4/
3. Shannon, C. & Weaver, W. (1949). *The mathematical theory of communication*. Urbana: University of Illinois Press.
4. Wilmot, W.W. (1987). *Dyadic communication*. (3rd ed.). New York: Random House.
5. Watzlawick, P., Beavin, J.H., & Jackson, D.D. (1967). *Pragmatics of human communication: A study of interactional patterns, pathologies, and paradoxes.* New York: Norton.
6. Miller, G.R. & Steinberg, M. (1975). *Between people: A new analysis of interpersonal communication.* Chicago: Science Research Associates.
7. Streek, J. (1980). Speech acts in interaction: A critique of Searle. *Discourse Processes, 3*, 133–154.
8. Rademacher, T. (2006, March 04). Retiring Zeeland teacher takes the (cup) cake. *The Grand Rapids Press*, A24.
9. Warren, S.F. & Yoder, P.J. (1998). Facilitating the transition from preintentional to intentional communication. In A.M. Wetherby, S.F. Warren, & J. Reichle (Eds.) *Transitions in prelinguistic communication* (pp. 365–385). Baltimore, MD: Paul H. Brookes.
10. Watzlawick, P., Beavin, J.H., & Jackson, D.D. (1967). *Pragmatics of human communication: A study of interactional patterns, pathologies, and paradoxes.* New York: Norton.
11. Rademacher, T. (2006, October 15). Coaches move shows 'incredible class'. *The Grand Rapids Press*, B1.
12. Blumer, H. (1969). *Symbolic interactionism: Perspective and method*. Berkeley: University of California Press.
13. Marshall, G. (1998). Symbolic interactionism. *A Dictionary of Sociology*. Encylopedia.com. Retrieved from http://www.encyclopedia.com/doc/1O88-symbolicinteractionism.html
14. Leeds-Hurwitz, W. (1995). *Social approaches to communication*. New York: Guilford Press.
15. Memorable quotes from *The Matrix* (1999). Internet Movie Database. Retrieved from http://www.imdb.com/title/tt0133093/quotes
16. Ekman, P., Friesen, W.V., & Baer, J. (1984, May 18). The International language of gestures. *Psychology Today*, 64–69.
17. Adler, R. & Towne, N. (2003). *Looking out, looking in*. (10th ed.). Belmont: Thomson Wadsworth.
18. AOL News Staff. (2007, February 12). Kate Winslet threatens to sue over diet claims. *AOL Entertainment News*. Retrieved from http://news.aol.com/entertainment
19. Max, A. (2006, November 17). More than 60 years later, details of Holocaust keep unfolding. *International Herald Tribune*, A20.
20. NBA. (2005, October, 20). National basketball association dress code. Retrieved from http://www.nba.com/news/player_dress_code_051017.html
21. ABC News Staff. (2006, June 12). MySpace teen demonstrates larger problem. ABC News Internet. Retrieved from http://abcnews.o.com/GMA/Story?id=2065543&pae=1
22. Fletcher, D. (2010, February 15). Facebook gifts get real. *Time Magazine*, p. 54.
23. Australian family learns of tragedy on Facebook. (2010, February 8). Yahoo! News. Retrieved from http://news.yahoo.com/x/afp/20100208/wl_austrailiaitfacebookaccident.
24. Dominick, J. (2006). *The dynamics of mass communication.* (8th ed.) New York: McGraw Hill.
25. McLuhan, M. & Fiore, Q. (1996). The medium is the message: An inventory of effects. San Francisco: HardWired.
26. McLuhan, M. & McLuhan, E. (1988). Laws of media: Then new science. Toronto: University of Toronto Press.

27. Raine, L. & Horrigan, J. (2005, January 25). A decade of adoption: How the internet has woven itself into American life. Pew Internet and American Life Project. Retrieved from http://www.pewinternet.org/ppf/r/148/report_display.asp31

28. Breed, A. (2006, October 22). "Texting can be used for good or evil." *The Grand Rapids Press,* A13.

29. Brunker, M. (2009, January 15). Sexting surprise: Teens face child porn charges. MSNBC. Retrieved from http://www.msnbc.msn.com

30. USA Today News Staff. (2008, June 25). More states say cell phones and driving don't mix. USA Today.com. Retrieved from: http://news.yahoo.com/s/usatoday/morestatessaycellphonesanddrivingdontmix&printer=1

31. Jordon, M. & Vancil, M. (2005). *Driven from within.* New York: Simon & Schuster.

32. Gray, J. (2006, December 02). Reflect before talking to cold husband. *The Grand Rapids Press,* C4.

33. Skinner, M. (2002, June). In search of feedback. *Executive Excellence,* 18.

34. Fried, S. (2006, April). Confessions of a naked man. *Ladies Home Journal,* 78–80.

35. Samovar, L.A. & Porter, R.E. (2000). Understanding intercultural communication: An introduction and overview. In L.A. Samovar and R.E. Porter (Eds.). *Intercultural communication: A reader,* (9th ed.), pp. 375–387. Belmont, CA: Wadsworth.

36. Verderber, K., Verderber, R.F., & Berryman-Fink, C. (2007). *Interact.* (11th ed.). New York: Oxford University Press.

37. Burgoon, J.K., Le Poire, B.A., Beutler, L.E., Bergan, J., & Engle, D. (1992). Nonverbal behaviors as indices of arousal: Extension to the psychotherapy context. *Journal of Nonverbal Behavior, 16,* 159–178.

38. Burgoon, J.K. (1978). A communication model of personal space violation: Explication and an initial test. *Human Communication Research, 4,* 129–142.

39. Burgoon, J.K. & Hale, J.L. (1988). Nonverbal Expectancy Violations: Model Elaboration and Application to Immediacy Behaviors. *Communication Monographs, 55,* 58–79.

40. Burgoon, J.K., Buller, D.B., & Woodall, W.G. (1996). Nonverbal communication: The unspoken dialogue. (2nd Ed.). New York: McGraw Hill.

41. Kanner, B. (1989, April 03). Color schemes. *New York Magazine,* 22–23.

42. Walker, M. (2002). *The power of color.* New Delhi: B. Jain Publishers.

43. Holt, S. (2007, September 18). Lauren Upton, Miss Teen South Carolina answers her pageant question. Associated Content. Retrieved from http://www.associatedcontent.com/pop_print/shtml?content

44. Reuters Press. (2008, January 23). Pet girl kicked off bus for wearing leash. Yahoo News. Retrieved from http://realnews.yahoo.com/s/nm/20080123/od_nm/girl_leash1_dc;_ylt=AuXSBvbsMx>

45. Celebrity Vibe. (2008, September 05). Robin Thicke: Vibe Responds To Race Comments. TheCelebrityTruth http://www.thecelebritytruth.com/robin-thicke-vibe-responds-race-comments/004407

46. CNN. (2007, November 26). Reports: Sudan arrests UK teacher for teddy bear blasphemy. CNN.com. Retrieved from http://www.cnn.com/2007/WORLD/africa/11/26/sudan.bear/index.html

47. Colbert, K. (1993). The effects of debate participation on argumentativeness and verbal aggression. *Communication Education, 42,* 206–214.

48. Argyle, M.F., Alkema, F., & Gilmour, R. (1971). The Communication of friendly and hostile attitudes: Verbal and nonverbal signals. *European Journal of Social Psychology, 1,* 385–402.

49. Hale, J. & Stiff, J.B. (1990). Nonverbal primacy in veracity judgments. *Communication Reports, 3,* 75–83.

50. Burgoon, J.K., Birk, T., & Pfau, M. (1990). Nonverbal behaviors, persuasion, and credibility. *Human Communication Research, 17,* 140–169.

51. Kubany, E.S., Richard, C., Bauer, G.B., & Muraoka, M.Y. (1992). Impact of assertive and accusatory communication of distress and anger: a verbal component analysis. *Aggressive Behavior, 19,* 337–347.

52. Proctor II, R.F., & Wilcox, J.R. (1993). An exploratory analysis of responses to owned messages in interpersonal communication. *Et Cetera: A Review of General Semantics, 50,* 201–220.

53. Proctor, II, R.F. (1989). Responsibility or egocentrism?: The paradox of owned messages. *Speech Association of Minnesota Journal, 16,* 59–60.

54. Counseling Center. (2007, May 7) Help with roommate troubles. Ball State University Counseling Center. Retrieved from http://www.bsu.edu?students/cpsc/article/o,1384,22917-3997-26811,00html

55. Devito, J. (2007). The interpersonal communication book. (11th ed.). Boston: Pearson Education.

56. Jones, Q., Ravid, G., & Rafaeli, S. (2004). Information overload and the message dynamics of online interaction spaces: A theoretical model and empirical exploration. *Information Systems Research, 15* (June), 194–210.

57. Kruger, J. & Epley, N. (2005). Egocentrism over e-mail: Can we communicate as well as we think? *Journal of Personality and Social Psychology, 89,* No. 5, 925–936.

58. Microsoft, Inc. (2006). The first smiley :-). Retrieved from http://research.microsoft.com/smiley

59. Morris, M.W., Nadler, J., Kurtzberg, T.R., & Thompson, L. (2002). Schmooze or lose: Social friction and lubrication in e-mail negotiations. *Group Dynamics: Theory, Research, and Practice, 6*(1), 89–100.

60. Drolet, A.L., & Morris, M.W. (2000). Rapport in conflict resolution: Accounting for how nonverbal exchange fosters cooperation on mutually beneficial settlements to mixed-motive conflicts. *Journal of Experimental Social Psychology, 36,* 26–50.

61. White, C., Vanc, A., & Stafford, G. (2010, January). Internal communication, information satisfaction, and sense of community: The effect of personal influence. *Journal of Public Relations Research, 22,* p. 65.

62. Rainey, V.P. (2000, December). The potential for miscommunication using email as a source of communication. *Transactions of the Society for Design and Process Science, 4,* 21–43.

63. Baird, A. (2010). *Think Psychology*. Upper Saddle, NJ: Prentice Hall.

64. Ahmed, S. (2008, July 14). World's Oldest Blogger Dies at 108. CNN News. Retrieved from http://www.cnn.com/2008/WORLD/Europe/07/14/oldest.blogger/index.html?iref=newssearch

65. Phillips, J. (2006, December 11). Hubby longing for a kiss. *Kalamazoo Gazette,* C4.

66. News Channel Three. (2008, January, 29). Woman May Have Tried Multiple Methods To Kill Lover's Wife. WWMT Channel 3. Retrieved from www.wwmt.com/news/linscott_1346573_article.html/kill_november.html

Unit 3 References

1. Associated Press. (2004, July 5). Tsunami ingests 53-1/2 hot dogs at contest. *ESPN*. Retrieved from http://sports.espn.go.com/espn/news/story?id=1834236
2. Dresang, J. (2006, July 12). Are you ready for some gluttony? ESPN is. *Milwaukee Journal Sentinel*. Retrieved from http://www.jsonline.com/story/index.aspx?id=465159
3. Kim, K., Conger, R., Lorenz, F., & Elder, G. (2001). Parent-adolescent reciprocity in negative affect and its relation to early adult social development. *Developmental Psychology*, 37, 775–790.
4. Hudson, J. & Rapee, R. (2000). The origins of social phobia. *Behavior Modification, 24*(1), 102–129.
5. Arruaga, X. & Foshee, V. (2004). Adolescent dating violence: Do adolescents follow in their friends', or parents' footsteps? *Journal of Interpersonal Violence, 19*, 162–184.
6. Spitzburg, B. (2000). What is good communication? *Journal of the Association for Communication Administration, 29*, 103–113.
7. Beatty, M., Marshall, L., & Rudd, J. (2001). A twins study of communicative adaptability: Heritability of individual differences. *Quarterly Journal of Speech, 87*, 366–377.
8. Zuckerman, M. (1991). *Psychobiology of personality*. Boston: Cambridge University Press.
9. Bouchard, T., Lykken, D., McGue, M., & Segal, N. (1990). Sources of human psychological differences: The Minnesota study of twins reared apart. *Science*, (October, 12), 223–228.
10. Stewart, J. (2009). *Bridges not walls: A book about interpersonal communication*. Boston: McGraw Hill, p. 22.
11. Wackman, D., Miller S., & Nunnally, E. (1976). *Student workbook: Increasing awareness and communication skills*. Minneapolis: Interpersonal Communication Programs, p. 6.
12. Langer, E. (1989). *Mindfulness*. Reading, MA: Addison-Wesley.
13. Langer, E. (1998). *The power of mindful learning*. New York: Perseus Books Group.
14. Schraw, G. (1999). Promoting general metacognitive awareness. *Instructional Science, 26*, 113–125.
15. Sypher, B. & Sypher, H. (1983). Perceptions of communication ability: self-monitoring in an organizational setting. *Personality and Social Psychology Bulletin, 9*, 297–304.
16. Goleman, D. (2006). *Social intelligence: The new science of human relationships*. New York: Bantam Books.
17. Kolbe, J. (1998). The relationship between self-monitoring and leadership in student project groups. *Journal of Business Communication, 35*, 264–282.
18. Sypher, B. & Sypher, H. (1983). Perceptions of communication ability: self-monitoring in an organizational setting. *Personality and Social Psychology Bulletin, 9*, 297–304.
19. Ohair, D., Frierich, G., Wiemann, J., & Wiemann, M. (1997). *Competent communication*. Boston: Bedford/St. Martins.
20. Whitchurch, G.G. & Constantine, L.L. (1993). Systems theory. In *Sourcebook of family theories and methods: A contextual approach*. (pp. 325–352). Boss, P.G., Doherty, W.J., LaRossa, R., Schumm, W.R., & Steinmet, S.K. (Eds.), New York: Plenum.
21. Samovar, L.A. & Porter, E. (2003). Understanding intercultural communication: An introduction and overview. In *Intercultural communication: A reader* (10th ed.). (pp. 6–17). Samovar, L.A., & Porter, R.E. (Eds.). Belmont: Wadsworth.
22. Verderber, R. & Verderber, K. (2005). *Communicate!* (11th ed.). Belmont, CA: Thompson, p. 256.
23. Shimanoff, S. (1980). *Communication rules: Theory and research*. Beverly Hills, CA: Sage.
24. Buller, D. & Aune, R. (1992). The effects of speech rate similarity on compliance: Application of communication accommodation theory. *Western Journal of Communication*, 56, 37–53.
25. Jordan-Jackson, F. & Davis, K. (2005, March 22). Men talk: an exploratory study of communication patterns and communication. *The Journal of Men's Studies, 13*(3).

26. Giles, H. (1973). Communication effectiveness as a function of accented speech. *Speech, 40*, 330–331.

27. Sharkey, W., Hee, S., & Kimm, R. (2004). Intentional self-embarrassment. *Communication Studies, 55*, 379–399.

28. Rubin, R., Graham, E., & Mignerey, J. (1990). A longitudinal study of college students' communication competence. *Communication Education, 39*, 1–14.

29. Dwyer, K. (2000). The multidimensional model: Teaching students to self-manage high communication apprehension by self-selecting treatments. *Communication Education, 49*, 2–81.

30. deTurck, M. & Miller, G. (1990). Training observers to detect deception: Effects of self-monitoring and rehearsal. *Human Communication Research, 16*, 603–620.

31. Honeycutt, J. (2003). *Imagined interactions: Daydreaming about Communication.* Cresskill, N.J: Hampton Press.

32. Abbott, J. (2004). Imagined interactions: Daydreaming about Communication. *Canadian Journal of Communication, 29* (3).

33. Bargh, J., Bargh, J.A., Chen, M., & Burrows, L. (1996). Automaticity of social behavior: Direct effects of trait construct and stereotype priming on action. *Journal of Personality and Social Psychology, 71*, 230–244.

34. Burch, M. (2005). *Interpersonal communication: Building your foundations for success.* Dubuque, IA: Kendall Hunt.

35. (2007, November 15). Austin Powers: International man of mystery. Internet Movie Data Base. Retreived from http://www.imdb.com/title/tt0118655/

36. Golan, S. (1990). A factor analysis of barriers to effective listening. *Journal of Business Communication, 27*, 25–36.

37. Brownell, J. (1990). Perceptions of effective listeners: A management study. *Journal of Business Communication, 27*, 401–415.

38. Witcher, S. (1999, August 09). Chief executives in Asia find listening difficult. *Asian Wall Street Journal Weekly, 21*, 11.

39. Listening factoid. *International Listening Association*. Retrieved from http://www.listen.org/pages/factoids.html

40. Kolker, K. (2007, December 15). "Dispatch delayed 3 minutes in apartment blaze." *Grand Rapids Press.* Retrieved from http://www.mlive.com/news/grpress/indes.ssf?/base/news33/116619173318030.xml&c

41. Johnson, S. & Belcher, C. (1988). Examing the relationship between listening effectiveness and leadership emergence: Perceptions, behaviors, and recall. *Small Group Research, 29*, 452–471.

42. Levine, D. (2000). Virtual attraction: "What rocks your boat." *CyberPsychology and Behavior, 3*, 565–573.

43. Kramer, R. (1997). Leading by listening: An empirical test of Carl Roger's theory of human relationship using interpersonal assessments of leaders by followers. *Dissertation Abstracts, International Section A. Humanities and Social Sciences, 58*, 514.

44. Wingert, P. (2007, February 23). The baby who's not supposed to be alive: Amillia's doctor didn't realize just how premature she was. *Newsweek*. Retrieved from http://www.msnbc.msn.com/id/17304274/1098/

45. Wiio, O. (1978). *Wiio's Laws—and Some Others*. Espoo, Dinland: Welin-Goos.

46. Ruben, B. (1989). The study of cross-cultural competence: Traditions and contemporary issues. *International Journal of Intercultural Relationships, 13*, 229–240.

47. Chen, G. & Starosta, W. (2000). The development and validation of the intercultural sensitivity scale. *Human Communication, 3*, 1–14.

48. Cloven, D., & Roloff, M. (1991). Sense-making activities and interpersonal conflict: Communicative cures for the mulling blues. *Western Journal of Speech Communication, 55*, 134–158.

49. McCroskey, J. & Wheeless, L. (1976). *Introduction to human communication*. Boston: Allyn & Bacon.

50. Piaget, J. (1930). *The child's conception of physical causality*. London: Routledge & Kegal.

51. Retreived from http://www.comedycentral.com/jokes/index.jhtml

52. (2007, February 27). Eddie Murphy not a sore loser. *People Magazine*. Retrieved from http://www.people.com/people/package/redcarpet/2007/EddieMurphy

53. (2006, August). Confessions: Will you marry me . . . nah. *Cosmopolitan*, 60.

54. Freud, S. (2005). *The psycopathology of everyday life.* Stilwell, KS: Digireads.com

55. Anderson, K. (2009). What are you telling the world? Say it better: Communicate, persuade, collaborate, sell to live a richer life. Retrieved from http://sayitbetter.typepad.com/say_it_better/2009/01/without-words-what -are-you-telling-the-world.html

56. Loban, W. (1963). *The Language of elementary children*. Champaign. IL: NCTE.

57. Gleason, J.B. & Tanter, N.B. (2009). *Development of Language.* Boston: Allyn & Bacon.

58. Associated Press. (2007, February, 27). Mother coached children to fake retardation. associatedpress/site/Newweek/print/1 displaymode.

59. Johannesen, R.L. (2002). *Ethics in Human Communication*. (5th ed.). Prospect Heights, Ill: Waveland Press.

60. Verderber, K., Verderber, R., & Berryman-Fink, C. (2007). *Interact*. (11th ed.). New York: Oxford University Press.

61. (2007, January 24). Man, 81, visited by secret service over letter to editor. *Kalamazoo Gazette.* p. 4.

62. Larson, A. (2003, November 11). Defamation, libel, and slander law. *Expert Law.* Retrieved from http://www.expertlaw.com/library/personal_injury/defamation.html>

63. Roberts, B., & Mann R. (2000, December 05). Sexual harassment in the workplace: A primer. *University of Akron*. Retrieved from www.3uakron.edu/lawrev/robert1.html

64. (2009, March 11). Sexual Harassment. *U.S. Equal Employment Opportunity Commission.* Retrieved from http://www.eeoc.gov/types/sexual_harassment.html

65. Beebe, S.A., Beebe, S.J., & Redmond, M.V. (2008). *Interpersonal Communication: Relating to Others.* (5th ed.). Beverly Hills, CA: Sage.

Unit 4 References

1. *Office Space*. (1999). Retrieved from The Internet Movie Data Base Web site: http://www.imdb.com/title/tt0151804/plotsummary
2. Rubin, R.B., Perse, E., & Barbato, C. (1988). Conceptualization and measurement of interpersonal communication motives. *Human Communication Research, 14*, 602–628.
3. McCafferty, M (2007, January). I tracked down the man who broke my heart. *Glamour*, 153–154.
4. Maslow, A.H. (1954). *Motivation and personality*. New York: Harper and Row.
5. Maslow, A.H. (1968). *Toward a psychology of being*. New York: Van Nostrand Reinhold.
6. Biederman, I. & Vessel, E. (2006). Perceptual pleasure and the brain. *American Scientist, 94*, 247–253.
7. Marziali, C. (2006, June 23). Grasping the pleasure principle. Retrieved from USC News Web site: http://www.usc.edu/uscnews/stories/12543.html
8. Maslow, A.H. (1943). A theory of human motivation. *Psychological Review, 59*, 370–396.
9. Encyclopedia of world biography on Candy Lightner. *BookRags*. Retrieved from http://www.bookrags.com/biography/candy-lightner2
10. Associated Press. (2007, January 19). How did a runaway child get on two flights?. *MSNBC.com*. Retrieved from http://www.msnbc.msn.com/id/16713920/
11. (2007, April). Astronaut granted bond on attempted murder charge. *CNN.com*. Retrieved from http://www.cnn.com/2007/US/02/06/astronaut.arrested/index.html
12. Associated Press, (2009, March 12). Novel DUI defense: I'm my own country. *DUI.com*. Retrieved from http://www.dui.com/dui-library/pennsylvania/news/man-claims-novel-pennsylvania-dui-defense
13. Brenner, C. (2008). Aspects of psychoanalytic theory: drives, defense, and the pleasure-unpleasure principle. *Psychoanalysis Quarterly, 77*(3), 707–717.
14. Dsilva, M.U. & Whyte, L.O. (1998). Cultural differences in conflict styles: Vietnamese refugees and established residents. *Howard Journal of Communications, 9*, 57–68.
15. Oetzel, J.G. & Ting-Toomey, S. (2003). Face concerns in interpersonal conflict: A cross-cultural empirical test of the face negotiation theory, *Communication Research, 30*, 599–625.
16. *Dumb and Dumber*. (1994). Retrieved from the Internet Movie Data Base Web site: http://www.imdb.com/title/tt0109686/
17. Berger, C.R. & Calabrese, R.J. (1975). Some explorations in initial interaction and beyond: Toward a developmental theory of interpersonal communication. *Human Communication Research, 1*, 99–112.
18. Neuliep, J.W. & Grohskopf, E.L. (2000). Uncertainty reduction and communication satisfaction during initial interaction: An initial test and replication of a new axiom. *Communication Reports*, 13 (summer), 67–77.
19. Derlega, V.J. & Chaikin, A.L. (1975). *Sharing intimacy: What we reveal to others and why.* Englewood, N.J.: Prentice-Hall.
20. Altman, I. & Taylor, D. (1973). *Social penetration: The development of interpersonal relationships.* New York: Holt, Rinehart, & Winston.
21. Sunnafrank, M. (1986). Predicted outcome value during initial interactions: A reformulation of uncertainty reduction theory. *Human Communication Research, 13*, 3–33.
22. Sunnafrank, M. (1988). Predicted outcome value in initial conversations. *Communication Research Reports, 5*, 169–172.
23. Kellermann, K, & Cole, T. (1994). Classifying compliance-gaining messages: Taxonomic disorder and strategic confusion. *Communication Theory, 4*, 3–60.
24. Gass, R.H. & Seiter, J.S. (1999). *Persuasion, social influence, and compliance gaining.* Boston: Allyn & Bacon.
25. Goss, B. & O'Hair, D. (1988). *Communicating in interpersonal relationships.* New York: Macmillan.
26. Christopher, F.S. & Frandsen, M. M. (1990). Strategies of influence in sex and dating. *Journal of Social and Personal Relationships, 7*, 89–105.
27. Tracy, K. (1984). The discourse of requests: Assessment of a compliance-gaining approach. *Human Communication Research, 10*, 513–538.

28. Dillard, J.P. (1990). *Seeking compliance: The production of interpersonal influence messages.* Scottsdale, AZ: Gorsuch Scarisbrick.

29. (2006). Mother's day reflections. *O Magazine.* Retrieved from http://www.oprah.com/presents/2006/mothersday/reflect_lessons_101.jhtml

30. Quick thinking saves woman from assault. (2007, February 2). *Kalamazoo Gazette*, p. A2.

31. Baumeister, R. & Leary M. (1995). The need to belong: Desire for interpersonal attachments as a fundamental human motivation. *Psychological Bulletin, 117*, 497–529.

32. Donahue, W. & Kolt, R. (1992). *Managing interpersonal conflict*. Newbury Park, CA: Sage.

33. Schultz, W. (1996). *The interpersonal underworld.* Palo Alto, CA: Science and Behavior Books.

34. Frost, D. & Stahelski, A. (2006). The systematic measurement of French and Raven's bases of social power in work groups . *Journal of Applied Social Psychology, 18*, 375–389.

35. Nansel, T.R., Overpeck, M., Pilla, R.S., Ruan, W.J., Simons-Morton, B., & Scheidt, P. (2001). Bullying behaviors among US youth: Prevalence and association with psychosocial adjustment. *Journal of the American Medical Association*, 285(16), 2094–2100.

36. Forward, S. (1997). *Emotional blackmail: When the people in your life use, fear, obligation, and guilt to manipulate you.* New York: HarperCollins Publishers.

37. Steiner, C. (1981). *The other side of power.* New York: Grove.

38. Forward, S. (1997). *Emotional blackmail: When the people in your life use, fear, obligation, and guilt to manipulate you.* New York: HarperCollins Publishers.

39. (2007, April 1). Alicia Keys. Hollywood.com. Retrieved from http://hollywood.com/celebs/alicia_keys1htm

40. Kelly, A.E. (1999). Revealing personal secrets. *Current Directions in Psychological Science, 8*(4), 105–108.

41. Pennebaker, J. (2004). *Opening up: The healing power of emotions.* Oakland, CA: New Harbinger, 2004.

42. Slater, L. (2006, February). Love: the chemical reaction. *National Geographic*, 32–49.

43. Marazziti, D., Akiskal, H.S., Rossi, A., & Cassano, G.B. (1999). Alteration of the platelet serotonin transporter in romantic love. *Psychological Medicine*, 29: 741–745

44. Krupa, D (2005, May). Love really is 'all in your head,' though intense romantic love looks more like the brass ring then the bouquet of flowers. *The American Physiological Society*. Retrieved from http://www.the-aps.org/press/journal/05/9.htm

45. Aron, A., Fisher, H.E., Mashek, D.J, Strong, G., Li, H.F., Paris, M., Slater, L., & Brown, L. (2005). Reward, motivation, and emotion systems associated with early-stage intense romantic love: An MRI study. *Journal of Neuropsychology, 94*, 327–357.

46. Slater, L. (2006, February). Love: the chemical reaction. *National Geographic*, 32–49.

47. (2007, February 3). Chewbecca arrested for head-butting. *MSNBC*. Retrieved from http://news.msnbc.msn.com/id/12370520/print/1/displaymode/1098

48. (2007, March 6). Naomi Campbell sentenced to mop New York floors. *Reuters* News Service, from http://www.reuters.com/article/peopleNews/idUSN0642174020070308

49. Mayne, T.J. (1999). Negative affect and health: The importance of being earnest. *Cognition and Emotion, 13*, 601–635.

50. Grewal, D. & Salovey, P. (2005). Feeling smart: The science of emotional intelligence. *American Scientist, 93*, 330–339.

51. (2006, July 28). Gibson's DUI. Showbiz CNN. Retrieved from http://www.cnn.com/2006/Showbiz/movies/07/28/gibson.dui

52. Lim, T.S. & Bowers, J.W. (1991). Facework: Solidarity, approbation, and tact. *Human Communication Research, 17*, 415–449.

53. Ting-Toomey, S., Oetzel, J.G., & Yee-Jung, K. (2001). Self-construal types and conflict management styles. *Communication Reports, 14*, 87–104.

Unit 5 References

1. How do we hear? (2009). *Mayo clinic*. Retrieved from http://www.mayoclinic.org/hearing-disorders
2. Macrae, C.N. & Bodenhausen, G.V. (2001). Social cognition: Categorical person perception. *British Journal of Psychology, 92*, 239–255.
3. Duncan, S. & Fiske, D.W. (1977). *Face-to-face interaction: Research, methods, and theory*. New York: Wiley.
4. Lewis, M.H. & Reinsch, Jr., T.R. (1988). Listening in organizational environments. *Journal of Business Communication, 25*, 49–67.
5. Nichols, R.G. (1948). Factors in listening comprehension. *Speech Monographs, 15*, 154–163.
6. Thomas, L.T. & Levine, T.R. (1994). Disentangling listening and verbal recall: Related but separate constructs? *Human Communication Research, 21*, 103–127.
7. Myron, W. & Kester, L. (2006). *Intercultural competence: Interpersonal communication across cultures*. (5th ed.). New York: Pearson, Allyn, & Bacon.
8. Dindia, K. & Kennedy, B.L. (2004, November). Communication in everyday life: A descriptive study using mobile electronic data collection. Paper presented at the annual conference of the National Communication Association, Chicago, IL.
9. Wolvin, A. & Coakley, C.G. (1996). *Listening*. Madison, WI: Brown and Benchmark.
10. Barker, L., Edwards, R., Gaines, C., Gladney, K., & Holley, F. (1980). An investigation of proportional time spent in various communicating activities by college students. *Journal of Applied Communication Research, 8*, 101–109.
11. Johnson, S.D. & Belcher, C. (1998). Examining the relationship between listening effectiveness and leadership emergence: Perceptions, behaviors, and recall. *Small Group Research, 29*, 452–471.
12. Castleberry, S.B. & Shepard, C.D. (1993). Effective interpersonal listening and personal selling. *Journal of Personal Selling and Sales Management, 13*, 35–49.
13. Windsor, J.L., Curtis, D.B., & Stephens, R.D. (1997). National preferences in business and communication education: A survey update. *Journal of the Association for Communication Administration, 3*, 170–179.
14. McCornack S. (2010). *Reflect and Relate*. (2nd ed). Boston: Bedford/St. Martins.
15. Prager, K.J. & Buhrmester, D. (1998). Intimacy and need fulfillment in couple relationships. *Journal of Social and Personal Relationships, 15*, 435–469.
16. Vangelisti, A.L. (1994). Couples communication problems: The counselor's perspective. *Journal of Applied Communication Research, 22*, 106–126.
17. Chesebro, J.L. (1999). The relationship between listening styles and conversational sensitivity. *Communication Research Reports, 16*, 233–238.
18. Payne, M.J. & Sabourin, T.C. (1990). Argumentative skill deficiency and its relationship to quality of marriage. *Communication Research Reports, 7*, 121–124.
19. Infante, D.A., Chandlelr, T.A., & Rudd, J.E. (1989). Test of an argumentative skill deficiency model of inter-spousal violence. *Communication Monographs, 56*, 163–177.
20. Brownell, J. (1990). Perceptions of effect-tive listeners: A management study. *Journal of Business Communication, 27*, 401–415.
21. Spinks, N. & Wells, B. (1991). Improving listening power: The payoff. *Bulletin of the Association for Business Communication, 54*, 75–77.
22. Benoit, S. & Lee, J.L. (1986). Listening: It can be taught. *Journal of Education for Business, 63*, 229–232.
23. Versfeld, N.J. & Dreschler, W.A. (2002). The relationship between the intelligibility of time-compressed speech and speech-in-noise in youth and elderly listeners. *Journal of the Acoustical Society of America, 111*, 401–408.
24. Fiske, S.T. & Taylor, S.E. (1991). *Social cognition*. (2nd ed.). New York: McGraw Hill.
25. Goffman, E. (1979). Footing. *Semiotica, 25*, 319–345.

26. Golen, S. (1990). A factor analysis of barriers to effective listening. *Journal of Business Communication, 27*, 25–36.

27. McComb, K.B. & Jablin, F.M. (1984). Verbal correlates of interviewer empathic listening and employment interview outcomes. *Communication Monographs, 51*, 367.

28. Wolvin, A.D. (1987). Culture as a listening variable. Paper presented at the summer conference of the International Listening Association, Toronto Canada.

29. Wolvin, A. & Coakley, C.G. (1996). *Listening.* Madison WI: Brown and Benchmark.

30. Redeker, G. & Maes, A. (1996). Gender differences in interruptions. In Slobin, D., Gerhardt, J., Kyratzis, A., & Guo, J. (Eds.). *Social interaction, social context, and language,* (pp. 579–612). Mahwah, NJ: Lawrence Erlbaum Associates.

31. Vangelisti, A.L., Knapp, M.L., & Daly, J.A. (1990). Conversational narcissism. *Communication Monographs, 57*, 251–274.

32. Foul-mouthed pilot grounds flight. (2007, April 07). MSNBC. Retrieved from http://www.msnbc.com

33. *The Hurt Locker.* (2008). Internet Movie Data Base. Retrieved from http://www.imdb.com/title/tt088791

34. Britt, R.R. (2006, January 04). Sound science: Pete Townsend blames headphones for hearing loss. Live Science, retrieved from http://www.livescience.com/health/060104_earbuds.html

35. 5.2 million Americans have hearing problems. (2001, July 04). *New York Times,* A11.

36. Wood, J. (2007). *Communication in our lives.* (3rd ed., p. 32). Belmont, CA: Wadsworth.

37. Holtgraves, T. (2002). Language as social action: Social psychology and language use. Mahwah, NJ: Erlbaum.

38. Quotes from *"How to lose a guy in 10 days".* (2003). The Internet Movie Database. Retrieved from www.imdb.com/title/tt0251127

39. Scott, S., Warren, J., Sauter, D.A., Eisner, F., Wiland, J., Dresner, A.M., Wise, R.J., & Rosen, S. (2006, December). Positive emotions preferentially engage an auditory motor "mirror" system. *Journal of Neuroscience, 26*(50) 13067–13075.

40. Hayes, J. (2002). Interpersonal skills at work. (2nd ed.). New York: Routledge.

41. Notarius, C.J. & Herrick, L.R. (1988). Listener response strategies to a distressed other. *Journal of Social and Personal Relationships, 5*, 97–108.

42. Burleson, B.R. (2003). Emotional support skills. In J.O. Green & B.R. Burleson (Eds.). *Handbook of communication and social interaction skills.* (pp. 551–594). Mahwah, NJ: Erlbaum.

43. Burleson, B.R. & Goldsmith, D.J. (1998). How the comforting process works: alleviating emotional distress through conversationally induced reappraisals. In P.A. Anderson & L.K. Guerrero (Eds.). *Handbook of communication and emotion: Research, theory, applications, and contexts.* (pp. 248–280). San Diego, CA: Academic Press.

44. Goldsmith, D.J. & Fitch, K. (1997). The normative context of advice as social support. *Human Communication Research, 23*, 454–476.

45. Worthen, J.B., Garcia-Rivas, G., Green, C.R., & Vidos, R.A. (2000). Tests of cognitive-resource-allocation account of the bizarreness effect. *Journal of General Psychology, 127*, 117–144.

Unit 6 References

1. Jordon, M. & Vancil, M. (2005). *Driven from within.* New York: Simon & Schuster.
2. Andersen, P.A. (1992*). Nonverbal communication: Forms and functions*. Palo Alto, CA: Mayfield.
3. Macrae, C.N. & Bodenhausen, G.V. (2001). Social cognition: Categorical person perception. *British Journal of Psychology, 92,* 239–256.
4. Michener, H.A. & DeLamater, J.D. (1999). *Social Psychology.* (4th ed.). Orlando, FL: Harcourt Brace.
5. Weingarten, G. (2007, April 08). Pearls before breakfast: Can one of the nation's great musicians cut through the fog of a D.C. rush hour? Let's find out. *The Washington Post.* Retrieved from http://www.washingtonpost.com/wp-dyn/content/article/2007/04/04/AR2007040401721.html
6. Floyd, K., Ramirez, A., & Burgoon, J.K. (2008). Expectancy violations theory. In L.K. Guerrero, J.A. Devito, & M.L. Hecht (Eds). The Nonverbal communication reader: Classic and contemporary readings (3rd ed., pp. 503–510). Prospect Heights, IL: Waveland.
7. Zajonc, R.B. (2001). Mere exposure: A gateway to the subliminal. *Current Directions in Psychological Science, 10,* 224–228.
8. Goldstein, E.B. (2007). *Sensation and perception.* (7th ed.). Pacific Grove, CA: Wadsworth.
9. Weiner, B. (2000). Intrapersonal and interpersonal theories of motivation from an attributional perspective. *Educational Psychology Review, 12,* 1–14.
10. Pascarella, E.T., Edison, M., Hagedorn, L.S., Nora, A., & Terenzini, P.T. (1996). Influences on students' internal locus of attribution for academic success in the first year of college. *Research in Higher Education, 37,* 731–756.
11. Weiner, B. (1986). An *attributional theory of motivation and emotion*. New York: Springer-Verlag.
12. Heider, F. (1958). *The Psychology of Interpersonal Relations.* New York: Wiley.
13. Radar, D. (2007, February 04). You can find a way to heal. *Parade*, pp. 4–6.
14. Baron, R.A. & Bryne, D. (2000). *Social psychology.* (9th ed.). Boston: Allyn & Bacon.
15. Mruk, C. (1999). *Self-esteem: Research, theory, and practice.* (2nd ed.). New York: Springer.
16. Demo, D.H. (1987). Family relations and the self-esteem of adolesents and their parents. *Journal of Marriage and the Family, 49,* 705–715.
17. Rayner, S.G. (2001). Aspects of the self as learner: Perception, concept, and esteem. In R.J. Riding & S.G. Rayner (Eds.), Self-perception: International perspectives on individual differences (Vol 2). Westport, CN: Ablex.
18. Grant, M. (2002, November). At home with the best looking dad in Hollywood. *Reader's Digest*, p. 129.
19. DeGeneres, E. (1995*). My point . . . and I do have one.* New York: Bantam Books.
20. Alberts, J.K., Nakayama, T.K., & Martin, J.N. (2007). *Human communication in society.* (1st ed.).Upper Saddle River, NJ: Pearson Education Inc.
21. Weiten, W. (1998). *Psychology: Themes and variations.* (4th ed.). Pacific Grove, CA: Brooks/Cole.
22. Felix, A. (2002). *Condi: The Condoleezza Rice story.* New York: Newmarket Press.
23. Crain, W. (2000). *Theories of development: Concepts and applications*. (4th ed.). Upper saddle River, NJ: Prentice Hall.
24. Festinger, L. (1954). A theory of social comparison processes. *Human Relations, 7,* pp. 117–140.
25. Hergovitch, A., Sirsch,U., & Felinger, U.M. (2002). Self-appraisals, actual appraisals and reflected appraisals of preadolescent children. *Social Behavior and Personality, 30,* 603–612.
26. Cooley, C.H. (1912). *Human nature and social order.* New York: Scribner.
27. Mruk, C. (1999). *Self-Esteem: Research, theory, and practice.* (2nd ed.). New York: Springer.
28. Leary, M.R. (2002). When selves collide: The nature of the self and the dynamics of interpersonaL relationships. In A. Tesser, D.A.

Stapel, & J.V. Wood (Eds.). Self and motivation: Emerging psychological perspectives (pp. 119–145). Washington DC: American Psychological Association.

29. Hamachek, D. (1982). *Encounters with the self.* (2nd ed.). New York: Rinehart and Winston.

30. Hamachek, D.E. (1982). *Encounters with others: Interpersonal relationships and you.* New York: Holt, Rinehart & Winston.

31. Adler, R.B., Rosenfeld, L.B., & Proctor, R.F. (2007). *Interplay.* (10th ed.). New York: Oxford University Press.

32. Tafarodi, R.W. & Vu, C. (1997). Two-dimensional self-esteem and reactions to success and failure. *Personality and Social Psychology Bulletin, 23,* 626–635.

33. Buhrmester, D., Furman, W., Wittenberg, M.T., & Reis, H.T. (1988). Five domains of interpersonal competence in peer relations. *Journal of Personality and Social Psychology, 55,* 991–1008.

34. Rosenfeld, R. & L. Jacobson. (1968). *Pygmalion in the classroom.* New York: Holt, Rinehart, & Winston.

35. Adler, R.B., Rosenfeld, L.B., & Proctor, R.F. (2007). *Interplay.* (10th ed.). New York: Oxford University Press.

36. Alberts, J.K., Nakayama, T.K., & Martin, J.N. (2007). *Human Communication In Society.* (1st ed.). Upper Saddle River, NJ: Pearson Education Inc.

37. Judge, T.A., Erez, A., Bono, J.E., & Thoresen, C.J. (2002). Are measures of self-esteem, neuroticism, locus of control, and generalized self-efficacy indicators of a common core construct? *Journal of Personality and Social Psychology, 83,* 693–710.

38. McCroskey, J. & Wheeless, L. (1976). *Introduction to human communication.* (8th ed.). Boston: Allyn & Bacon.

39. McCroskey, J.C., Booth-Butterfield, S., & Payne, S. (1989).The impact of communication apprehension on college student retention and success. *Communication Quarterly, 37,* 100–107.

40. Ayres, J. & Hopf, T. (1995). An assessment of the role of communication apprehension in communicating with the terminally ill. *Communication Research Reports, 12,* 227–234.

41. Beatty, M.J. (1988). Situational and predisposition correlates of public speaking anxiety. *Communcation Education, 37,* 28–39.

42. Richmond, V.P. & McCroskey, J.C (1988). *Communication apprehension, avoidance, and effectiveness.* (5th ed.). Boston: Allyn and Bacon.

43. Motley, M.T. (1997). *Overcoming your fear of public speaking: A proven method.* Boston: Houghton Mifflin.

44. Desberg, P. (2007). *Speaking scared, sounding good.* Garden City Park, New York: Square One Publishers.

45. Simmons, A. (2007, October). So sue me! The $67 million pants, and other crazy lawsuits. *Reader's Digest,* p. 33.

46. Henry, M. (2007). With a little help, Oden is prepped for media game. *Brandenton Herald.* Retrieved from <www.brandenton.com/mike_hery/story/87074.html>

47. Benjamin, J. (2007). 7 Things you must know about other couple's love. *Cosmopolitan,* pp. 135–137.

48. Allen Iverson news conference transcript. (2002, May, 10). *Sports Illustrated.* Retrieved from http://sportsillustrated.cn.con/basketball/news/2002/05/09iverson_transcript

49. Open Water. (2003). Memorable Quotes. The Internet Movie Data Base. Retrieved from http://www.imdb.com/title/tt0374102/

50. Sypher, B. & Sypher, H.E. (1984). Seeing ourselves as others see us. *Communication Research, 11,* 97–115.

51. Harger, J. (2007, April 22). Are legislators as green as they think? *The Grand Rapids Press,* p1.

52. UPI. (1986, July 14). Most men would marry wife again. *The Bryan Times.* Retrieved from http://news.google.com/newspapers?nid=799&dat=19860714&id=fgoLAAAAIBAJ&sjid=n1EDAAAAIBAJ&pg=4533,1094422

53. Baron, P. (1974). Self-esteem, ingratiation, and evaluation of unknown others. *Journal of Personality and Social Psychology, 30,* 104–109.

54. Hamacheck, D.E. (1982). *Encounters with others: Interpersonal relationships and you.* New York: Holt, Rinehart, and Winston.

55. Giles, H., Coupland, N., & Wiemann, J.M. (1992). Talk is cheap, but 'my word is my bond': Beliefs about talk, in K. Bolton, H. Kwok (Eds.). Socialinguistics Today: International Perspectives. London: Routledge & Kegan Paul.

56. Gottman, J. (2007, December 22). Initial impressions of couples long term relational potential. *The Gottman Institute.* Retrieved from http://www.gottman.com/inthenews/media/

57. Tetlock, P.E. (1983). Accountability and the perseverance of first impressions. *Social Psychology Quarterly, 46,* 285–292.

58. Bremer, J. (2007). The power of first impressions. *Bremer Communications*. Retrieved from http://www.bremercommunications.com/First_Impressions.html

59. Ybarra, O. (2001). When first impressions don't last: The role of isolation and adaptation processes in the revision of evaluative impressions. *Social Cognition, 19,* 491–520.

60. Lupfer, M.B., Weeks, M., & Dupuis, S. (2000). How pervasive is the negativity bias in judgments based on character appraisal? *Personality and Social Psychology Bulletin, 2,* 1353–1366.

61. Cummins, R.A. & Nistico, H. (2002). Maintaining life satisfaction: The role of positive cognitive bias. *Journal of Happiness Studies, 3,* 37–69.

62. Adler, T. (1992, June). Enter romance, exit objectivity. *American Psychological Association Monitor*, 18.

63. Adler, R.B. & Proctor, R.F. (2007). *Looking out, looking in*. (12th ed.). Belmont, CA: Thompson and Wadsworth.

64. Kelly, C.M. (1996). Adult egocentrism: Subjective experience versus analytic bases for judgment. *Journal of Memory and Language, 35,* 157–175.

65. Hattie, J. (1992). *Self-concept*. Hillsdale, NJ: Erlbaum

Unit 7 References

1. Norment, L. (2006, November). Kirk and Tammy Franklin: Speak out on love, family, and overcoming his addiction to pornography. *Ebony,* pp. 185–190.
2. Health Section. (2005, December). *Men's Health,* p. 128.
3. Mann, D. Out of the blue: Brooke Shield's struggle with postpartum depression. *WebMD the Magazine*. Retrieved from www.webmd.com/depression/guide/brooke-shields-depression-struggle? page=1>
4. Matt Foley Quotes. *Wikipedia: The Free Encyclopedia.* Retrieved from http://en.wikipedia.org/wiki/Matt_Foley#Quotes
5. Mr. T speaks: I pity these fools. (2006, November). *US Magazine,* p. 79.
6. Lindsey, J. (2006, December.). A cyclist's stunning confession. *Men's Journal,* pp. 93–100.
7. Reiss, S. (2006, December). The United States of Schwarzennegger. *Men's Journal,* p. 103.
8. Janas, M. (2001). Getting a clear view. *Journal of Staff Development, 22,* pp. 32–34.
9. Adler, R.B., Rosenfeld, L.B., & Proctor, R.F. (2007). *Interplay: The process of interpersonal communication.* (10th ed.). New York: Oxford University Press.
10. Welcome to Scientology. (2008, February). *What is Scientology?* Church of Scientology. Retrieved from http://www.scientoloy.org/en_US/l-ron-hubbard/index.html
11. Lehmkuhl, R. (2006). *Here's what we'll say.* New York: Avalon.
12. Tualo, E. & Rosengren., J. (2006). *Alone in the trenches.* Naperville, IL: Sourcebooks.
13. Amaechi, J. & Bull, C. (2006). *Man in the middle.* New York: ESPN Books.
14. Bartolomeo, J. (2006, November). Bitter splits. *US Magazine,* pp. 66–68.
15. Forward, S. (2001). *Emotional blackmail: Why the people in your life use fear, obligation, and guilt to manipulate you.* New York: HarperCollins.
16. O'leary, K. (2006, November. 06), Grey's Anatomy drama on set. *US Magazine,* p. 32.
17. Collins, N.L. & Miller, L.C. (1994). Self-disclosure and liking: A meta-analytic review. *Psychological Bulletin, 116,* 457–475.
18. Wheeless, L.R. & Grotz, J. (2001). The Measurement of trust and its relationship to self-disclosure. *Human Communication Research, 3,* 250–257.
19. Berg, J.H. & Archer, R.L. (1983). The disclosure-liking relationship. *Human Communication Research, 10,* 269–281.
20. Won-Doornink, M. (1985). Self-disclosure and reciprocity in conversation: A cross-national study. *Social Psychology Quarterly, 48,* 97–107.
21. Schmidt, T.O. &. Cornelus, R.R. (1987). Self-disclosure in everyday life. *Journal of Social and Personal Relationships, 4,* 365–373.
22. Fincham, F.D. & Bradbury, T.N. (1989). The impact of attributions in marriage: An individual difference analysis. *Journal of Social Personal Relationships, 6,* 69–85.
23. Downs, V.G. (1988). Grandparents and grandchildren: The relationship between self-disclosure and solidarity in an intergenerational relationship. *Communication Research Reports, 5,* 173–179.
24. (2003, April 28). Snow job: How did David Hempleman-Adams get away with his latest trip? *People Magazine,* p. 103.
25. Lutz, W. (1989). *Doublespeak: From revenue enhancement to terminal living.* New York: HarperCollins.
26. Sobol, B. (2006, October). Girls Uncensored: How sneaky women get their way with men. *Cosmopolitan Magazine,* p. 54.
27. Reynolds, D. & Sowry, M. (2007, April). An alibi for all occasions: Web-based company will sell you a way out of a sticky situation. *ABC News Nightline.* Retrieved from http://abcnews.go.com/Nightline/print?id=3034259
28. Rosellini, L. (2007, March). Cybersleuth mom. *Readers Digest,* pp. 39–42.
29. Carter, K. (2006, June/July). Internet terror: These teens busted a suspected MySpace predator. *Teen People,* pp. 122–123.

30. Lieberman, D.J. (1998). *Never be lied to again.* New York: St. Martins Press.

31. Lieberman, D.J. (1998). *Never be lied to again.* New York: St. Martins Press, p. 104.

32. Humes, J.C. (1983). *More podium humor.* New York: Harper Perennial.

33. Many men and women lie in their online dating profiles. (2007, February 08). *Online Dating Magazine*. Retrieved from http://www.onlinedatingmagazine.com/news2007/profi lelies.html>.

34. Murphy, M. (2007, December). The lies dudes tell to avoid relationship drama. *Cosmopolitan Magazine,* pp. 165–167.

Unit 8 References

1. Rock and Roll/Pop: Lynyrd Skynyrd. (2010, August). Ticketmaster.com. Retrieved from http://www.ticketmaster.com/Lynyrd-Skynyrd-tickets/artist/735560
2. White. D. (2010). Lynyrd Skynyrd. About.com. Retreived from http://classicrock.about.com/od/artistpr ofilesko/p/lyn_skyn.htm
3. What P Diddy got his 16-year-old son for his birthday: a £304k supercar and a chauffeur to drive it. (2010, January 26). Scottish Daily Record. Retreived from http://www.dailyrecord.co.uk/showbiz/celebritynews/2010/01/26/what-p-diddy-bought-his-16-year-old-son-for-his-birthday-a-304k-supercar-86908-21995748/
4. Diddy. (2010). MTV Networks. Retrieved from http://www.mtv.com/music/artist/puff_daddy/artist.jhtml#biographyEnd
5. Smith, G.W. (1998). The political impact of name sounds. *Communication Monographs, 65*, 154-172.
6. Foss, S.K., Foss, K.A., & Trapp, R. (1991). *Contemporary perspectives in rhetoric.* (2nd ed.). Prospect Heights, IL: Waveland press.
7. McWhorter, J.H. (2001). *The power of Babel: A natural history of language.* New York: Times Books/Henry Holt.
8. Wade, N. (2006). *Before the dawn: Recovering the lost history of our ancestors.* New York: Penguin Group.
9. Finch, G. (2003). *Word of mouth: A new introduction to language and communication.* New York: Palgrave.
10. Wang, W.S.Y. (1982). *Human communication: Language and its psychological basis.* San Francisco: Freeman.
11. Gleason, L.B. (1989). *The development of language.* Columbus, OH: Merrill.
12. Chen, G.M. & Starosta, W.J. (1989). *Foundation of intercultural communication.* Boston: Allyn and Bacon.
13. O'Grady, W., Archibald, J., Aronoff, M., & Rees-Miller, J. (2010). *Contemporary linguistics.* (6th ed.). Boston: Bedford/St. Martin's.
14. Engleberg, I.N. & Wynn, D.R. (2008). *The challenge of communicating: Guiding principles and practices.* Boston: Allyn & Bacon.
15. Delia, J.G. (1972). Dialects and the effects of stereotypes on interpersonal attraction and cognitive processes in impression formation. *Quarterly Journal of Speech, 58*, 285–297.
16. O'Grady, W., Archibald, J., Aronoff, M., & Rees-Miller, J. (2010). *Contemporary linguistics.* (6th ed). Boston: Bedford/St. Martin's.
17. Gumperz, J.J. & Levinson, S.C. (Eds.). (1996). *Rethinking linguistic relativity.* New York: Cambridge University Press.
18. Finch, G. (2003). Word of mouth: A new introduction to language and communication. New York: Palgrave.
19. Schiebel, D. (1995). Making waves with Burke: Surf Nazi culture and the rhetoric of localism. *Western Journal of Communication, 59*, (4), 253–269.
20. Koerner, F.F.K. (2000). Towards a "full pedigree of the Sapir-Whorf hypothesis," In Putz, M., and Verspoor, M.H. (Eds.), Explorations in linguistic relativity. Amsterdam: John Benjamins.
21. Nincompoop is Britain's favorite word. (2007, November 24). Fox News.Com. Retrieved from http://www.foxnews.com/story/0,2933,312725,00.html
22. Thiederman, S. (2003). *Making diversity work: seven steps for defeating bias in the workplace.* Chicago: Dearborn Trade Publishing.
23. McCornack, S. (2010). Reflect and relate. Boston: Bedford/St. Martin's.
24. Malkin, M. (2009, December 10). Jersey Shore's The Situation Loves Attention from Women, Men, Wateva. E!online. Retreived from http://www.eonline.com/uberblog/marcmalkin/b157421_jersey_shores_situation loves_attention.html
25. Jersey Shore: Meet the Cast. (2010). MTV Networks. Retrieved from http://www.mtv.com/shows/jersey_shore/cast.jhtml
26. Adler, R.B. & Rodman, G. (2009). *Understanding human communication.* New York: Oxford.

27. Floyd, K. (2009). *Interpersonal Communication: The whole story*. New York: McGrawHill.

28. Nelson, M.C. (2004, March 15). On the path: Business's unfinished journey to diversity. *Vital Speeches of The Day, LXX(11)*, 337.

29. Hybels, S. & Weaver, R. (2007). *Communicate effectively*. (8th ed.). New York: McGraw Hill.

30. Philipsen, G. (1995). The coordinated management of meaning theory of Pearce, Cronen, and associates. In D.P. Cushman & B. Kovacic (Eds.). *Watershed Research Traditions in Human Communication Theory.* (pp. 13–43). Albany: State University of New York Press.

31. Ramirez-Esparza, N., Gosling, S.D., Benet-Martinez, V., Pottter, J.D., & Pennebaker, J.W. (2006). Do bilinguals have two personalities? A special case of cultural frame switching. *Journal of Language and Social Psychology, 22*, 210–233.

32. Swaminathan, N. (2007, October 10). Use it or lose it: Why language changes over time. *Scientific American.* Retrieved from http://www.scientificamerican.com/article.cfm?id=use-it-or-lose-it-why-lang

33. Trudgill, P. Myth 1: The meaning of words should not be allowed to vary or change, in Language Myths, ed. Bauer, L., & Trudgill, P. (London: Penguin, 1998), p. 2.

34. Ogden, C.K. & Richards, I.A. (1923). *The meaning of meaning.* London: Kegan, Paul Trench, Trubner.

35. Wallstein, T. (1986). Measuring the vague meanings of probability terms. *Journal of Experimental Psychology: General, 115*, 348–365.

36. Bryson, B. (1990). *The mother tongue: English and how it got that way*. New York: William Morrow.

37. Hayakawa, S.I. & Hayakawa, A.R. (1991). *Language in thought and action.* San Diego, CA: Harcourt.

38. Paul, J. & Strbiak, C.A. (1997). The ethics of strategic ambiguity. *The Journal of Business Communication, 34*, 149–159.

39. Bavelas, J.B., Black, A., Bryson, L., & Mullett, J. (1988). Political equivocation: A situational explanation. *Journal of Language and Social Psychology, 7*, 137–145.

40. Keillor, G. (2005). *A prairie home companion pretty good joke book.* MN: Highbridge Company.

41. Lutz, W. (1987). *Doublespeak. How government, business, and advertisers use language to deceive you.* New York: Harper and Row.

42. Bandura, A. (1999). Moral disengagement in the perpetuation of inhumanities. *Personality and Social Psychology Review, 3*, 193–209.

43. Hamilton, M.A. & Mineo, P.J. (1998). A framework for understanding equivocation. *Journal of Language and Social Psychology, 17*, 3–35.

44. Motley, M.T. & Reeder, H. M. (1995). Unwanted escalation of sexual intimacy: Male and female perceptions of connotations and relational consequences of resistance messages, *Communication Monographs, 62*, 356–382.

45. Pidd, H. (2009, March 29). All-white England kit could highlight stains of defeat. Guardian.co.uk. Retrieved from http://www.guardian.co.uk/football/2009/mar/29/new-england-kit-white

46. Lee, W.S. (1994). On not missing the boat: A processual method of intercultural understanding of idioms and life world. *Journal of Applied Communication Research, 22*, 141–161.

47. Nordquist. R. (2010). Jargon. About.com. Retrieved from: http://grammar.about.com/od/il/g/jargonterm.htm

48. Urban Camping. (2009). Jargon Database.com. Retrieved from http://www.jargondatabase.com/Jargon.aspx?id=686

49. What does G.S.W. stand for? (2010). The Free Dictionary.com. Retrieved from http://encyclopedia.thefreedictionary.com/Gun+Rock

50. Labov, T. (1992). Social and language boundaries among adolescents. *American Speech, 4*, 339–366.

51. Hosman, L.A. (1989). The evaluative consequences of hedges, hesitations, and intensifiers: Powerful and powerless speech styles, *Human Communication Research, 15*, 383–406.

52. Bradac, J. & Mulac, A. (1984). Attributional consequences of powerful and powerless speech styles in a crises intervention context. *Journal of Language and Social Psychology, 3*, 1–19.

53. Johnson, C.E. (1987, April). An introduction to powerful talk and powerless talk in the classroom. *Communication Education, 36*, 167–172.

54. Haleta, L.L. (1996, January). Student perceptions of teachers' use of language: The effects of powerful and powerless language

on impression formation and uncertainty. *Communication Education, 45*, 20–27.

55. Kalbfleisch, P.J. & Herold, A.L. (2006). Sex, power, and communication. In Dindia, K. & Canary, D. (Eds.). Sex differences and similarities in communication. (2nd ed., pp. 299–313). Mahwah, NJ: Lawrence Erlbaum Associates.

56. Bradac, J.J. (1983). The language of lovers, flovers, and friends: Communicating in social and personal relationships. *Journal of Language and Social Psychology, 2*, 141–162.

57. Samovar, L.A. & Porter, R.E. (1998). *Communication between cultures*. (3rd ed.). Belmont: Wadsworth.

58. Barge, J.K. (2004). Articulating CMM as a practical theory. *Human Systems: The Journal of Systemic Consultation and Management, 15*, 193–204.

59. Cassell, J. & Tversky, D. (2005).The language of online intercultural community formation. *Journal of Computer-Mediated Communication, 10*, Article 2.

60. Dreyer, A.S., Dreyer, C.A., & Davis, J.E. (1987). Individuality and mutuality in the language of families of field-dependent and field-independent children. *Journal of Genetic Psychology, 148*, 105–117.

61. Memorable quotes from *The Mexican* (2001). Internet Movie Database. I.M.D.B.com. Retrieved from http://us.imdb.com/title/tt0236493

62. Streisand, B. (1992). Crystal Award speech delivered at the Crystal Awards, Women in Film Luncheon, 1992.

63. Kubany, E.S., Bauer, G.B., Muraoka, M.Y., Richard, D.C., & Read, P. (1995). Impact of labeled anger and blame in intimate relationships. *Journal of Social and Clinical Psychology, 14*, 53–60.

64. Huston, T.L., Caughlin, J.P., Houts, R.M., Smith, S.E., & George, L.J. (2001). The connubial crucible: Newlywed years as predictors of marital delight, distress, and divorce. *Journal of Personality and Social Psychology, 80*, 237–252.

65. Kubany, E.S., Richard, D.C., Bauer, G.B., & Muraoka, M.Y. (1992). Impact of assertive and accusatory communication of distress and anger: A verbal component analysis. *Aggressive Behavior, 18*, 337–347.

66. Floyd, K., Mikkelson, A.C., Tafoya, M.A., Farinelli, L., LaValley, A.G., Judd, J., Haynes, M.T., Davis, K.L., & Wilson, J. (2007). Human affection exchange: XIII. Affectionate communication accelerates neuroendocrine stress recovery. *Health Communication, 22*, 123–132.

67. Jones, T.S., Remland, M.S., & Sanford, R. (2007). *Interpersonal communication through the life span*. (1st ed.). Boston: Houghton Mifflin Company.

68. Pennebaker, J.W. (1995). Emotion, disclosure, and health. Washington D.C., American Psychological Association.

69. ESPN News Services. (2008, January 17). Golf Channel anchor apologizes for 'lynch' remark about Tiger. *ESPN.COM*. Retrieved from http://sports.espn.go.com/golf/news/story?id=3186158

Unit 9 References

1. Richards, B. (2009). *Heart of a champion: Inspiring true stories of challenge and triumph.* Grand Rapids, MI: Revell.
2. Bridges, A. (2006, June 10). Survey suggests 24% of adults between 18 and 50 are tattooed. *ABC News*. Retrieved from http://abcnews.go.com/US/wireStory?id=2062343
3. Yen, H. (2010, March 07). Democrats' youth support waning amid gridlock. *Grand Rapids Press*, p. A5.
4. Adler, R. & Towne, N. (2003). *Looking out, looking in*. (10th ed.). Belmont, CA: Thomson Wadsworth.
5. Fitzpatrick, T. (2004, October. 11). The eyes have it: Candidates' eyes could be revealing. *Washington University in St. Louis Newsroom*. Retrieved from http://news.wustl.edu/news/Pages/4018.aspx
6. Boyce, N. (2001, January 15). Truth and consequences: Scientists are scanning the brain for traces of guilty knowledge. *U.S. News & World Report*, p. 42.
7. Burgoon, J.K. & Bacue, A. (2003). Nonverbal communication skills. *Handbook of Communication and Social Interaction Skills.* Mahwah, NJ: Lawrence Erlbaum.
8. Burgoon, J.K. & Hoobler, G.D. (2002). Nonverbal signals. In Knapp M.L. & Daly J.A. (Eds.). Handbook of interpersonal communication. (3rd ed.). Thousand Oaks, CA: Sage.
9. Carton, J.S., Kessler, E.A., & Pape, C.L. (1999). Nonverbal decoding skills and relationship well-being in adults. *Journal of Nonverbal Behavior, 23*, 91–100.
10. Hodgins, H.S. & Belch, C. (2000). Interpersonal violence and nonverbal abilities. *Journal of Nonverbal Behavior, 24*, 3–24.
11. Lapakko, D. (1997). Three cheers for language: A closer examination of a widely cited study of nonverbal communication. *Communication Education, 46*, 63–67.
12. Hickson, M. III, Stacks, D.W., & Moore, N. (2004). *Nonverbal communication: studies and applications.* (4th ed.). Los Angeles, CA: Roxbury Publishing.
13. Mehrabian, A. & Wiener, M. (1967). Decoding of inconsistent communications. *Journal of Personality and Social Psychology, 6*, 109–114.
14. Richmond. V.P. & McCroskey. (2004). *Nonverbal behavior in interpersonal relations.* (5th ed.). Boston: Allyn & Bacon.
15. Knapp, M. & Hall, J. (2002). *Nonverbal communication in human interaction.* (5th ed). Belmont: Wadsworth.
16. Guerrero, L.K., DeVito, J.A., & Hecht, M.L. (1999). *The nonverbal communication reader: Classic and contemporary readings.* (2nd ed.). Prospect Heights, IL: Waveland Press.
17. Liberty, J. (2006, November 09). Grills: those pearly . . . white golds. *Kalamazoo Gazette*, p. 6.
18. Expressions of Love. (2004, October). *Self-Magazine*, p. 106.
19. Extreme Makeover. (2007). TV.com. Retrieved from http://www.tv.com/extreme-makeover/show/18722/summary.html
20. Walter, E.H., Aronson, E., Abrahams, D. & Rohmann, L. (1966). Importance of physical attractiveness in dating behavior. *Journal of Personality and Social Psychology, 4*, 508–516.
21. Efran, M.G. (1974). The effect of physical appearance on the judgment of guilt, interpersonal attraction, and severity of recommended punishment in a simulated jury task. *Journal of Research in Personality, 8*, 45–54.
22. Hatfield, E.E. & Sprecher, S. (1986). *Mirror, mirror . . . the importance of looks in everyday life.* Albany: State University of New York.
23. Dion, K.K., Berscheid, E., & Walster, E. (1972). What is beautiful is good. *Journal of Personality and Social Psychology, 24*, 285–290.
24. Glenn, W. & Nias, D. (1999). Beauty can't be beat. In *The Nonverbal Communication reader: Classic and Contemporary Readings.* (2nd ed.). Guerrero, L.K., DeVito, J.A., & Hecht, M.L. (Eds.). Prospect Heights, IL: Waveland Press, p. 102.

25. Eagley, A.E., Ashmore, R.D., Makhijani, M.G., & Longo, L.C. (1991). What is beautiful is good, but . . . : A Meta-analytic review of research on the physical attractiveness stereotype. *Psychological Bulletin, 110,* 109–139.

26. Molloy, J.T. (1983). *Molloy's live for success.* New York: Bantam Books.

27. Adler, P. & Proctor, R. (2003). *Looking out, looking in.* (10th ed.). Belmont, CA: Thomson Wadsworth.

28. Sybers, R. & Roach, M.E. (1962). Clothing and human behavior. *Journal of Home Economics, 54,* 184–187.

29. Richmond, V.P., McCroskey, J.C., & Payne, S.K. (1991*). Nonverbal behavior in interpersonal relations.* Englewood Cliffs, NJ: Prentice-Hall.

30. Davidson, J.P. (1988). Shaping an image that boosts your career. *Marketing Communication, 13,* 55–56.

31. Burgoon, J.K., Buller, D.B., & Woodall, W.G. (1996). *Nonverbal communication: The unspoken dialogue.* (2nd ed.). New York: McGraw Hill.

32. Prehistoric lovers found locked in eternal embrace. (2007, February 7). CNN.com. Retrieved from http://cnn.com/2007/TECH/science/02/07prehistoric.love.ap/index.html

33. Associated Press. (2006, November 17). Washington's trading card for the 'birds'. *ESPN NFL.* Retrieved from http://sports.espn.go.com/nfl/news/story?id=266266

34. Streek, J. (1993). Gesture as communication: Its coordination with gaze and speech. *Communication Monographs, 60,* 275–299.

35. Ekman, P. & Friesen, W.V. (1969). The repertoire of nonverbal behavior: Categories, origins, usage, and coding. *Semiotica, 1,* 49–68.

36. Rosenfeld, H.M. (1987). Conversational control functions of nonverbal behavior. In Siegman A.W. & Feldstein S. (Eds.). Nonverbal behavior and communication. (2nd ed., pp. 563–602). Hillsdale, NJ: Erlbaum.

37. Goss, B. & O'hair, D. (1988). *Communicating in interpersonal relationships.* New York: Macmillan.

38. Scientists Train Soldiers in Non-Verbal Communication. (2006, February 20). Fox News.com. Retrieved from http://www.foxnews.com/printer_friendly_story?0,3566,185405,00.html

39. Crusco, A.H. & Wetzel, C.G. (1984). Midas touch: The effects of interpersonal touch on restaurant tipping. *Personality and Social Psychology Bulletin, 10,* 512–517.

40. Adler, T. (1993, February). Congressional staffers witness miracle of touch. *APA Monitor,* 12–13.

41. Smeltzer, L.R. & Waltman, J.L. (1991). *Managerial communication: A strategic approach.* Needham, MA: Ginn Press.

42. Floyd, K. (2009). *Interpersonal communication: The whole story.* Boston: McGraw Hill.

43. Mosher, D. (2007, September 16). Man's scent depends on woman's perception. *Yahoo News.com.* Retrieved from http:www.news.yahoo.com/s/live science/20070916/sc_livscinece/mansscetdependsonwoman

44. Richmond, V.P., McCroskey, J.C., & Payne, S.K. (1991). *Nonverbal behavior in interpersonal relations.* Englewood Cliffs, NJ: Prentice-Hall.

45. Ekman, P., Friesen, W., & Ellsworth, R. (1972). *Emotion in the human face: Guidelines for research and an integration of findings.* New York: Pergamon.

46. Knapp M.L. & Hall, J.A. (2002). *Nonverbal communication in human interaction.* (5th ed.). Belmont, CA: Wadsworth Thomson Learning.

47. Adler, P. & Proctor, R. (2007). *Looking out, looking in.* (12th ed.). Belmont, CA: Thomson Wadsworth.

48. Pease, A. & Pease, B. (2004). *The definitive book of body language.* New York: Bantam Dell.

49. Matsumoto, D. (2006). Culture and nonverbal behavior. In Manusov, V. & Patterson, M.L. (Eds.). The Sage handbook of nonverbal communication. (pp. 219–236). Thousand Oaks, CA: Sage.

50. Andersen, P.A. (1999). *Nonverbal communication: Forms and functions.* Mountain View, CA: Mayfield.

51. Grumet, G.W. (1983). Eye contact: The core of interpersonal relatedness. *Psychiatry, 48,* 172–180.

52. Planalp, S., DeFranciso, V.L., & Rutherford, D. (1996). Varieties of cues to emotion occurring in naturally occurring situations. *Cognition and Emotion, 10,* 137–153.

53. Mehrabian, A. (1981). *Silent messages: Implicit communication of emotions and attitudes.* (2nd Ed). Belmont: Wadsworth.

54. Zuckerman, M. & Miyake, K. (1993). The attractive voice: What makes it so? *Journal of Nonverbal Behavior, 17,* 119–135.

55. Zuckerman, M. Hodgins, H. S., & Miyake, K. (1993). Precursors of interpersonal expec tations: The vocal and physical attrac tiveness stereotypes. In Blanck, P. D. (Eds.). *Interpersonal Expectations: Theory, Research, and Applications.* Cambridge: Cambridge University Press, pp. 194–217.

56. Zuckerman, M. & Miyake, K. (1993). The attractive voice: What makes it so? *Journal of Nonverbal Behavior, 17,* 119–135.

57. Dosey, M. & Meisels, M. (1976). Personal space and self protection. *Journal of Personality and Social Psychology, 38,* 959–965.

58. Bailenson, J.N., Blascovich, J., Beall, A.C., & Loomis, J.M. (2001, December). Equilibrium theory revisited: Mutual gaze and personal space in virtual environments. *Presence: Teleoperators and Virtual Environments, 10,* 583–595.

59. Hall, E.T. (1959). *The silent language.* Garden City, NY: Doubleday.

60. Hall, E.T. (1963). System for the notation of proxemic behavior. *American Anthropologist, 65,* 1003–1026.

61. Sommer, R. (1969). *Personal space: The behavioral basis of design.* Englewood Cliffs, NJ: Prentice-Hall.

62. Burgoon, J.K., Buller, D.B., & Woodall, W.G. (1996). *Nonverbal communication: the unspoken dialogue.* (2nd ed.). New York: McGraw-Hill.

63. Burgoon, J.K., Buller, D.B., & Woodall, W.G. (1996). *Nonverbal communication: the unspoken dialogue.* (2nd ed.). New York: McGraw-Hill.

64. Brown, M. (2006, September). He loves his cars more than he loves me. *Redbook,* p. 104.

65. Adler, R. & Proctor, R. (2003). *Looking out, looking in.* (10th ed.). Belmont: Thomson Wadsworth.

66. Kobe gives wife ring shortly after admitting adultery. (2003, July 24). ESPN.com News Services. Retrieved from http://espn.go.com/nba/news/2003/0724/1585001.htm

67. Goldsmith, B. (2005). *Emotional fitness for couples: 10 minutes a day to a better relationship.* Oakland, CA: New Harbinger Publications.

68. Gudykunst, W.B. & Kim, Y.Y. (1997). *Communicating with strangers: An approach to intercultural communication.* (3rd ed.). Boston: Allyn & Bacon.

69. Anderson, P.A. (1977). Cues of culture: The basis of intercultural differences in nonverbal communication. In Samovar L.A. & Porter R.E. (Eds.). *Intercultural communication: A reader.* (8th ed., pp. 244–255). Belmont, CA: Wadsworth.

70. Knapp, M.L. & Hall, J.A. (2002). *Nonverbal communication in human interaction.* (5th ed.). Belmont, CA: Wadsworth Thomson Learning.

71. Cegala, D.J. & Sillars, A.L. (1989). Further examination of nonverbal manifestations of interaction involvement. *Communication Reports, 2,* 45.

72. Hall, J.A. (1998). How big are nonverbal sex differences? The case of smiling and sensitivity to nonverbal cues. In Canary, D.J. & Dindia, K. (Eds.). *Sex differences and similarities in communication: Critical essays and empirical investigations of sex and gender in interaction.* (pp. 155–178). Mahwah, NJ: Erlbaum.

73. Pearson, J.C., West, R.L., & Turner, L.H. (1995). *Gender and communication.* (3rd ed.). Dubuque, IA: Brown & Benchmark.

74. Hall, J.A., Carter, J.D., & Horgan, T.G. (2000). Gender differences in nonverbal communication of emotion. In Fischer, A.H. (Ed.). *Gender and emotion: Social psychological perspectives.* (pp. 97–117). Cambridge, England: Cambridge University Press.

75. Burgoon, J.K., Birk, T., & Pfau, M. (1990). Nonverbal behaviors, persuasion, and credibility. *Human Communication Research, 17*, 140–169.

76. Fishlock, D. (2008, January 21). Photo project sheds light on students' deepest fears. *Kalamazoo Gazzette*, p. C3.

77. Devito, J.A. (2007). *The interpersonal communication book.* Boston: Pearson Education.

78. School Enforces Strict No-Touching Rule. (2007, June 18). MSNBC.Com. Retrieved from http://wwww.msnbc.com/id/19293872/print/1/displaymode/10

79. Devito, J.A. (2007). *The interpersonal communication book.* Boston: Pearson Education.

80. Floyd, K. (2009). *Interpersonal communication: The whole story.* Boston: McGraw Hill.

Unit 10 References

1. Roseman, I.J., Wiest, C., & Swartz, T.S. (1994). Phenomenology, behaviors, and goals differentiate discrete emotions. *Journal of Personality and Social Psychology, 67*, 206–221.
2. Izard, C.E. (1991). *The psychology of emotions.* New York: Plenum.
3. Lazarus, R.S. (1991). *Emotion and adaptation.* New York: Oxford University Press.
4. Canary, D. (2003). Managing interpersonal conflict: A model of events related to strategic choices. In Greene, J.O. & Burleson, B.R. (Eds.). *Handbook of communication and social interaction skills.* (515–549). Mahwah, NJ: Erlbaum.
5. Canary, D.J. & Messman, S.J. (2000). Relationship conflict. In Hendrick, C. & Hendrick, S.S. (Eds.). *Close relationships: A sourcebook.* (pp. 261–270). Thousand Oaks, CA: Sage.
6. Barrett, L.F., Gross, J., Christensen, T., & Benvenuto, M. (2001). Knowing what you're feeling and knowing what to do about it: Mapping the relationship between emotion differentiation and emotion regulation. *Cognition and Emotion, 15*, 713–724.
7. Goleman, D. (1995). *Emotional intelligence: Why it can matter more than I.Q.* New York: Bantam.
8. Sullins, E.S. (1991). Emotional contagion revisited: Effects of social comparison and expressive style on mood convergence. *Personality and Social Psychology Bulletin 17*, 166–174.
9. Morris, W.N. (1992). A functional analysis of the role of mood in affective systems. In Clark, M.S. (Ed.). *Emotion.* (pp. 256–293). Newbury Park, CA: Sage.
10. On This Day August 27 1910 William James Dies; Great Psychologist. *New York Times On the Web.* Retrieved from http://www.nytimes.com/learning/general/onthisday/bday/0111.html
11. James, W. (1884). What is an emotion? *Mind, 9*, pp. 188–205.
12. REBT: Rational Emotive Behavior Therapy: How it works. (2008, May 6). *Albert Ellis Institute.* Retrieved from http://www.albertellisinstitute.org/aei/rebt_how_it_work_main.html>
13. Rolls, E. (2005). *Emotions explained.* New York: Oxford University Press.
14. Maglione-Garves, C.A., Kravitz, L., & Schneider, S. (2005). Cortisol connection: Tips on managing stress and weight. *ACSM's Health and Fitness Journal, 9*(5), pp. 20–23.
15. Scherer, K. R. & Ekman, P. (1984). *Approaches to emotion.* Hillsdale, NJ: Erlbaum.
16. Plutchik, R. (2001). The nature of emotions. *American Scientist, 89*, p. 344.
17. Plutchik, R. (1991). *The emotions. Revised.* New York: The Free Press.
18. Oatley, K. & Duncan E. (1994). The experience of emotions in everyday life. *Cognition and Emotion, 8*, pp. 369–381.
19. Bourhis, J. & Allen, M. (1992). Meta-analysis of the relationship between communication apprehension and cognitive performance. *Communication Education, 41*, pp. 68–76.
20. Fredrickson, B.L. (2001). The role of positive emotions in positive psychology: The broaden-and-build theory of positive emotions. *American Psychologist, 56*, pp. 218–226.
21. Fredrickson, B.L. (1998). What good are positive emotions? *Review of General Psychology, 2*, pp. 300–319.
22. Gottmann, J.M. & Silver, N. (1999). *The seven principles for making marriages work.* New York: Three Rivers Press.
23. Bedford,V.H. (1996). Relationshps between adult siblngs. In Auhaen, A.E. & von Salisch, M. (eds.). *The diversity of human relationships.* (pp. 120–140). New York: Cambridge University Press.
24. Altman, I. (1973). Reciprocity of interpersonal exchange. *Journal for the Theory of Social Behavior, 3*(2), pp. 249–261.
25. Rotter, J. (1966). Generalized expectancies for internal versus external control of reinforcements. *Psychological Monographs, 80*, p. 609.
26. Mamlin, N., Harris, K.R., & Case, L.P. (2001, Winter). A methodological analysis of research on locus of control and learning disabilities: Rethinking a common assumption. *Journal of Special Education.*

27. Bach, G.R. & Wyden, P. (1968). *The intimate enemy*. New York: Avon.

28. Satir, V. (1972). Peoplemaking. Palo Alto, CA: Science and Behavior Books.

29. Miller, J.C., Cooke, LL., Tsang, J., & Morgan, F. (1992). Should I brag? Nature and impact of positive and boastful disclosures for women and men. *Human Communication Research, 18(3)*, pp. 364–399.

30. Festinger, L. (1957). *A theory of cognitive dissonance*. Stanford, CA: Stanford University Press.

31. Aronson, E. (1969). The theory of cognitive dissonance: A current perspective. In Berkowitz, L. (Ed.). *Advances in Experimental Social Psychology*. (Vol 4, pp. 1–34). New York: Academic Press.

32. Adler, R.B & Towne, N. (2003). *Looking out, looking in*. (10th ed.). Belmont, CA: Wadsworth.

33. McCabe, D. (2002). *How to teach a dyslexic*. Dyslexa Research Foundation.

34. Geddes, D. (1992). Sex roles in management: The impact of varying power of speech style on union members' perception of satisfaction and effectiveness. *Journal of Psychology, 126*, 337–347.

35. Barrett, L.F., Gross, J., Christensen, T., & Benveuto, M. (2001). Knowing what you're feeling and knowing what to do about it: Mapping the relation between emotional differentiation and emotion regulation. *Cognition and Emotion, 15*, pp. 713–724.

36. Grewal, D. & Salovey, P. (2005). Feeling smart: The science of emotional intelligence. *American Scientist, 93*, pp. 330–339.

37. Hosman, L.A. (1989). The evaluative consequences of hedges, hesitations, and intensifiers: Powerful and powerless speech styles. *Human Communication Research, 15*, pp. 383–406.

38. Bradac, J. &. Mulac, A. (1984). Attributional consequences of powerful and powerless speech styles in a crises intervention context. *Journal of Language and Social Psychology, 3*, pp. 1–19.

39. Bradac, J.J. (1983). The language of lovers, *flovers*, and friends: Communicating in social and personal relationships. *Journal of Language and Social Psychology, 2*, 141–162.

40. Zamoza, A., Ripoll, P., & Peiro, J.M. (2002). Conflict management in groups that work in different communication contexts: Face-to-face and computer mediated communication. *Small Group Research*, 481–508.

41. Labbott, S.M., Martin, R.B., Eason, P.S., & Berkey, E.Y. (1991). Social interactions to the expression of emotion. *Cognition and Emotion, 5*, pp. 397–417.

42. Allen, M.W. (1995). Communication concepts related to perceived organizational support. *Western Journal of Communication, 59*, pp. 326–346.

43. Brody, L.R. (1985). Gender differences in emotional development: A review: of theories and research. *Journal of Personality, 53*, 102–149.

Unit 11 References

1. Borat. Cultural learnings of America for make benefit glorious nation of Kazakhstan. (2006). Internet Movie Database. Retrieved from http://www.imdb.com/title/tt0443453
2. Dirty Jobs: About The Show. (2010). Dis covery channel. Retrieved from http://dsc.discovery.com/fansites,dirtyjobs/about/about/html
3. Going Tribal. Discovery channel. (2010). Retrieved from http://dsc.discovery.com/fansites/goingtribal/about/about.html
4. Seplow, S. (2006, October 07). Review: Little people big world. AllYouTV.Com. Retrieved from http:://www.allyourtv.com/0607season/littlepeoplebigworld.html
5. Lee, F. (2006, March, 02). Little people, big world: Documenting a family that comes in 2 sizes. Independent Living U.S.A. Retrieved from http://www.ilusa.com/News/little_people_big-world.html
6. Rogers, J. & McWilliams, P. (1993). *We Give To Love*. New York: Prelude Press.
7. Roloff, M.E. (1981). *Interpersonal communication: The social exchange approach*. Beverly Hills: Sage.
8. Wood, J. (2007). *Communication in our lives.* (3rd ed.). Belmont, CA: Wadsworth.
9. Knapp, M.L. & Vangelsti, A.L. (2000). *Communication and human relationships.* (4th ed.). Boston: Allyn and Bacon.
10. Gouran, D., Wiethoff, W.E., & Doelger, J.A. (1994). *Mastering communication*. (2nd ed.). Boston: Allyn and Bacon.
11. Knapp, M.L. (1984). *Interpersonal communication and human relationships*. Boston, MA: Allyn & Bacon.
12. Barry, D. (1990). *Dave Barry turns 40*. New York: Fawcett.
13. Baxter, L.A. (1990). Dialectical contradictions in relationship development. *Journal of Social and Personal Relationships*, 7, pp. 69–88.
14. Baxter, L.A. (1988). A Dialectical perspective on communication strategies in relationship development. In *Handbook of Personal Relationships: Theory, Research and Interventions*. Duck, S. (Ed.). New York: John Wiley & Sons.
15. Sports mirrors real life. Netfunny.com. Retrieved from http://www.netfunny.com/rhf/jokes/04/Sept/Virginia.html
16. Cegala, D.J. & Sillars, A.L. (1989). Examination of nonverbal manifestations of interaction involvement. *Communication Reports, 2,* p. 45.
17. Ivy, D.K. & Backlund, P. (1994). *Exploring genderspeak*. New York: McGraw Hill.
18. Burgoon, J.K., Buller, D.B., &. Woodall, W.G. (1996). *Nonverbal communication: The unspoken dialogue.* (2nd ed.). New York: McGraw Hill.
19. Hanna, M.S. & Wilson, G.L. (1988). *Communicating in business and professional settings* New York: McGraw Hill.
20. Gamble, T.K. & Gamble, M.W. (2003). *The gender communication connection*. Boston: Houghton Mifflin.
21. Briton, N.J. & Hall, J.A. (1995). Beliefs about female and male nonverbal communication. *Sex Roles, 32,* pp. 79–80.
22. Tannen, D. (1990). You just don't understand: Women and men in conversation. New York: Morrow.
23. Salminen, S. & Glad, T. (1992). The role of gender in helping behavior. *Journal of Social Psychology, 132,* pp. 131–133.
24. West, C. & Zimmerman, D.H. (1977). Women's place in everyday talk: Reflections on parent-child interaction. *Social Problems, 24,* pp. 521–529.
25. Pearson, J.C., West, R.I., & Turner, L.H. (1995). Gender and communication. (3rd ed.). Dubuque Iowa: Wm. C. Brown.
26. Tsao, G. (2000). Growing up Asian with a disability. *The International Journal of Multicultural Studies.* (10th ed.). Retrieved from www.colorado.edu/journals/standards/V7N1/FIRSTPERSON/tsao.html
27. Chun, K.M., Balls, O.P., & Marn, G. (2003). *Acculturation: Advances in theory, measurement, and applied research.* Washington D.C.: American Psychological Association, 2003.
28. Hofstede, G. (1983). National culture revisited. *Behavior Science Research, 18,* pp. 285–305.

29. Gudykunst, W.B. (1991). *Bridging differences: effective intergroup communication.* Newbury Park, CA: Sage.

30. Kapoor, S., Wolfe, A. & Blue, J. (1995). Universal values structure and individualism-collectivism: a U.S. test. *Communication Research Reports, 12,* pp. 112–123.

31. Jandt, F.E. (2001). *Intercultural communication: An introduction.* (3rd ed.). Thousand Oaks, CA: Sage.

32. Gudykunst, W.B., Ting-Toomey, S., & Chua, E. (1988). Culture and interpersonal communication. Thousand Oaks, CA: Sage.

33. Victor, D. (1992). *International business communication.* New York: HarperCollins.

34. Hall, E.T. & Hall, M.R. (1990). *Understanding Cultural Differences: Germans, French, and Americans.* Yarmouth, ME: Intercultural Press.

35. Foster, D.A. (1992). *Bargaining across borders.* New York: McGrawHill.

36. Hofstede, G. (1997). *Cultures and organizations: Software of the mind.* New York: McGraw Hill.

37. Hofstede, G. (1998). Masculinity and femininity: The taboo dimension of national cultures. Thousand Oaks, CA: Sage.

38. Basso, K. (1970). To give up on words: Silence in Western Apache culture. *Southern Journal of Anthropology, 26,* pp. 213–230.

39. Hett, A.M. (1993). Language of silence: An ethnographic case study of the expressive language skills of preschool Native American girls. *Dissertation Abstracts International, 53,* p. 3062.

40. Almaney, A. & Alwan, A. (1982*). Communicating with the Arabs.* Prospect Heights, IL: Waveland.

41. Orbe, M.P. & Harris, T.M. (2001). *Interracial communication theory into practice.* (1st ed.). New York: Wadsworth.

42. Devito, J. (2008). *Interpersonal messages.* New York: Pearson Education.

43. Floyd, K. (2009). Interpersonal communication: the whole story. New York: McGraw Hill.

44. Dresser, N. (1996). *Multicultural manners: New rules of etiquette for a changing society.* New York: Wiley.

45. Axtell, R.E. (1990). *Do's and taboos of hosting international visitors.* New York: Wiley.

46. Axtell, R.E. (1993). *Do's and taboos around the world.* (3rd ed.). New York: Wiley.

47. Axtell, R.E. (1993). *Do's and taboos around the world.* (3rd ed.). New York: Wiley.

48. Sabath, A.M. (1999). *International business etiquette.* New York: Career Press.

49. Sabath, A.M. (1999*). International business etiquette in Europe: What you need to know to conduct business abroad with charm and savvy.* New York: Career Press.

50. The 300 millionth footprint on U.S. soil. (2006, October 08). *The New York Times,* p. WK2.

51. U.S. Census Bureau, www.census.gov/population

52. Devito, J. (2007). *The interpersonal communication book.* New York: Pearson Education Group.

53. Report on the Taliban's War Against Women. (2001, November). Bureau of Democracy, Human Rights, and Labor. U.S. Department of State. Retrieved from http://www.state.gov/g/drl/rls/6185.htm

54. Associated Press (2000, November). Bangledesh combats an acid onslaught against women. CNN.Com. Retrieved from http://archives.cnn.com/2000/ASIANOW/south/11/11/bangladesh

55. Female genital mutilation. (1998, December 23). BBC News World Edition. Retrieved from http://news.bbc.co.uk/2/hi/health/medical_notes/241221

56. Adler, R.B. & Towne, N. (2003). *Looking out, looking in.* (10th ed.). Belmont, CA: Thomson Wadsworth.

57. Adler, R.B. & Towne, N. (2003). *Looking out, looking in.* (10th ed.). Belmont, CA: Thomson Wadsworth.

58. Noelle-Neumann, E. (1974). The spiral of silence: The theory of public opinion. *Journal of Communication, 24,* 43–51.

59. Noelle-Neumann, E. (1977). Turbulences in the climate of opinion: Methodological applications of the spiral of silence theory. *Public Opinion Quarterly, 41,* pp. 143–158.

Index